AN
EXAMINED
FAITH

James Luther Adams

An Examined Faith

SOCIAL CONTEXT AND RELIGIOUS COMMITMENT

Edited and with an Introduction by George K. Beach

BEACON PRESS · BOSTON

Beacon Press
25 Beacon Street
Boston, Massachusetts 02108

Beacon Press books
are published under the auspices of
the Unitarian Universalist Association of Congregations.

98 97 96 95 94 93 92 91   8 7 6 5 4 3 2 1

Text design by Dennis Anderson

Library of Congress Cataloging-in-Publication Data

Adams, James Luther, 1901–
An examined faith : social context and religious commitment /
James Luther Adams ; edited and with an introduction
by George K. Beach.
p.   cm.
Includes bibliographical references and index.
ISBN 0–8070–1611–X
1. Theology. 2. Religion and sociology. 3. Liberalism (Religion)
4. Adams, James Luther, 1901– . I. Beach, George K.   II. Title.
BR85.A293   1991
230'.9132—dc20   90-21240
CIP

To Rudolf Otto

Affectional mentor, yet hard taskmaster,
who combined religious apprehension of the Holy,
engendered by grace
in the intimacy of the small, committed group,
with a seeking of universality of expression
in political responsibility and action.

John answered,
"Master, we saw a man casting out demons in your name,
and we forbade him,
because he does not follow with us."
But Jesus said to him,
"Do not forbid him;
for he that is not against you is for you."

Luke 9:49–50

You will know them by their fruits.
Are grapes gathered from thorns,
or figs from thistles?

Matthew 7:16

Contents

Acknowledgments

Jim Adams likes the biblical image of fishing with nets. It suggests many things—the cooperative endeavor of several sets of hands in a great labor, the network of human associations that both lightens and enlightens the effort, the riskiness of the outcome, and the often surprising abundance of the catch. The image recalls to me my own feelings of manyfold reward for having worked with Dr. Adams toward the publication of this book. His assistance, encouragement, and friendship have been constant. First, and with great affection, my thanks to him.

Others have had a hand in this work, as well, and I wish to acknowledge my gratitude to them: to Eugene Pickett, Chairperson, and the other members of the Unitarian Universalist Denominational Grants Panel, for providing financial assistance for editorial and publishing expenses; to Joan Helde for undertaking the exacting task of preparing the index; to Barbara Gilligan for her ever-cheerful clerical assistance; to Wendy Strothman, Director of Beacon Press, for her editorial assistance and her interest in carrying the work through to publication; to the members of the Unitarian Church of Arlington, Virginia, for affording me the opportunity during my sabbatical leave to complete work on the manuscript. Last and with love, I want to thank my wife and helpmate, Barbara, for her creative, critical, and caring support in this work.

G.K.B.

Introduction

GEORGE K. BEACH

"An unexamined faith is not worth having," James Luther Adams asserts, turning Socrates' famous dictum, "An unexamined life is not worth living," to his own, well-honed purposes. Having *some* faith, Adams holds, is a human inevitability. At the root of our existence we necessarily seek sources of confidence, resources of meaning and courage, something on which we rely. An authentic faith, then, will be experiential and self-reflective.

Throughout his life Adams has examined his faith, the sources and resources of his own ultimate reliance. Some of these occasions—like the choosing and shaping of his vocation as a young man—have been predominantly personal; others—like the cultural and moral crisis induced by the rise of Nazism in Germany—have been predominantly public and historical. He has asked himself: What, in the light of such occasions, do I believe in, and what will I stand for? What—in his own characteristic phrase—is "the response of responsibility"? By questioning the personal and social import of his own religious commitment, Adams invites us to do the same.

"A faith worth having is a faith worth discussing and testing," Adams continues. "It is something intelligible and verifiable."[1] A healthy skepticism not only toward received pieties but also toward one's own biases opens the way to a more authentic faith. But a searching self-examination can scarcely be sustained by the individual in isolation; it needs the presence of others in a community dedicated to the process. An authentic religious community is one that constantly encourages and, indeed, challenges its members to examine their faith. This conception sharply contrasts with the idea that the church gathers people around a fully defined, received faith. It also contrasts with the view that religion is a purely individual matter, or the cultivation of an inward spirituality. In Adams's words, "It is the community in which women and men are called to recognize and abandon their ever-recurrent reliance on the unreliable" and to deliberate and decide "what is rightly of concern to persons of free faith."

Adams is by profession a theological social ethicist. For him, moral concern lies at the heart of theology, and religious commitment at the

I

theology—
faith seeking understanding in the realm of moral action

heart of social ethics. He adopts the ancient definition of theology as "faith seeking understanding." He recognizes also the converse—the ways in which "understanding," wrought through action and reflection, re-shapes and enlarges faith. Accordingly, he defines ethics as "faith seeking understanding in the realm of moral action,"[2] that is, examining the meaning of our ultimate reliance in terms of the social context and the consequences of our actions.

Adams's conception of "a faith worth having" is variously reflected in this volume. Throughout, he is centrally interested in the uses and abuses of human freedom, or, more pointedly, in the social consequences of faith. He recalls a sentence from Ernst Troeltsch: "The highest act of freedom is faith." Freedom so conceived is a creative freedom, a shaping of human existence with full awareness of what we value and choose to live for. In short, freedom requires a reasoned examination of one's faith. Authentic faith is ultimate reliance, and it is anything but blind.

I

With his assistance and encouragement, several editors have undertaken to collect and publish Adams's writings. It is a daunting task because his works range broadly and do not easily fall into categories. They reflect his interests in theology, social and intellectual history, contemporary culture, and sociology. Like its earlier companion volume, *The Prophethood of All Believers* (1986), the present volume includes works touching upon the whole range of his thought. Also in 1986, J. Ronald Engel published a set of Adams's essays under the title *Voluntary Associations: Socio-critical Analyses and Theological Interpretation.* Engel's volume incorporates works on the historical, practical, and religious significance of voluntary associations in a free society. A decade earlier Max L. Stackhouse edited and published *On Being Human Religiously,* a collection of Adams's essays on the meaning of liberalism in religion and in social and political life, and on several thinkers who have figured significantly in his intellectual career.[3]

In each case Adams gave the editors a free hand in shaping the collection for publication. For the present volume he provided numerous suggestions, but final responsibility for the selection and editing of the texts belongs to the editor. Adams has created an important and a distinctive intellectual legacy that deserves to be read, studied, and discussed.[4] The primary aim of this book is to make a significant portion of his work, created during an astonishingly productive six decades and scattered in unpublished manuscripts and in various journals, available to a wider audience. A second aim is to further the reader's recognition of the unifying ideas among his various works.

That Adams has not himself sought to collect and organize his writings thematically is characteristic, I believe, of the style of his life and thought. His interest is regularly drawn to matters of "seasonal relevance." Even looking back, as in a retrospective essay, becomes for him another way of moving forward. William Johnson Everett comments, "The essay form speaks his own theology—timely, intentional address to specific audiences in particular times and places. . . . Theology emerges, for Adams, not as mental architecture, but as a way of addressing action."[5]

The term "action" here may seem to draw the matter too narrowly. While Adams has often addressed current social-ethical issues, his central interest has been the democratic and organizational processes through which they are addressed. Thus he enters into and draws others into a continuing dialogue on the important issues of the day, rather than generating arguments for "correct positions" or supposed "solutions." His approach is pragmatic in the sense of practical, timely, and improvisational.[6] In theoretical terms, he has been more concerned with ethical consequences than with "pure" principles. In practical terms, he has been constantly busy with the next scholarly project or request—for a book introduction; for bibliographical references and guidance on research; for an essay, an ordination sermon, or an encyclopedia assignment. The requests come with great frequency, and he seems to respond as frequently, all the while maintaining a lively correspondence with a vast network of friends, acquaintances, and former students.

Although Adams has not created a system, a consistent conceptual repertoire marks his theological and social-ethical positions, which is visible in virtually all of his writings. Dialectical method characterizes his thought, reflecting his intellectual kinship with Paul Tillich; thus ideas are often set forth in polarities, and the resulting tensions between them point to something new. He often analyzes social-ethical issues by describing their roots in historical conflict; the resulting social and moral cleavages are resolved through a new cultural synthesis. Still, each cultural synthesis remains provisional; history moves on and today's moment of historical transcendence ("theonomy," in Tillich's term) becomes tomorrow's external, oppressive rule ("heteronomy"), which eventually breaks down under new demands for "autonomy."[7]

But Adams is wary of theorizing in abstraction from the concrete, historical situation. He succinctly defines the religious compass by which he has set his course: "The liberal Christian outlook is directed to a Power that is living, that is active in a love seeking concrete manifestation, and that finds decisive response in the living posture and gesture of Jesus of Nazareth. In a world that has with some conscientiousness turned against this kind of witness and its vocabulary, the effect of this witness will in a special way depend upon the quality of its costingness in concrete action and upon its relevance to the history that is in the making."[8]

II

James Luther Adams was born in Ritzville, Washington, in 1901, the son of an itinerant Baptist preacher and farmer. When his father, James Carey Adams, went on his Sunday preaching circuit, young Luther often went along, taking his violin so he could accompany the hymns. At age sixteen, when his father fell seriously ill, he went to work for the Northern Pacific Railroad, acquired speed shorthand, and soon rose to the position of secretary to the regional superintendent. To his boss's astonishment, however, he turned down the offer of a permanent position in order to further his education (his "deprovincialization," as he has come to call it). The superintendent then helped young James Adams find a suitable university on the rail line so that he could continue to work while pursuing his studies.

Adams entered the University of Minnesota in 1920. After graduating in 1924, he entered Harvard Divinity School with the intention of becoming a Unitarian minister. In an autobiographical essay of 1939, he recounts his transitions from the "premillenarian fundamentalism" of his youth, to "scientific humanism" (as expounded by the Reverend John Dietrich in Minneapolis), to liberal Christianity. A sharp sense of rejecting his prior faith came with each of these "conversions," but with the passing years, he says, he has become increasingly aware that important elements of his childhood faith were retained in new form.[9]

In 1927 Adams was ordained and installed as minister of the Second Church (Unitarian) of Salem, Massachusetts. In the same year he and Margaret Ann Young, an accomplished pianist and a graduate of the New England Conservatory of music, were married. In their more than fifty years together—Margaret died in 1978—they raised three daughters and shared musical and many other interests. During his pastorates in Salem and, subsequently, in Wellesley Hills, Adams pursued graduate studies in comparative literature at Harvard. He also taught English at Boston University. At least once, in a mood of disillusion, he considered abandoning the ministry for a teaching career in the university. In the end he combined these competing commitments by teaching in theological schools. Jim and Margaret opened their home for late-evening conversations to generations of students; she became as well-known and beloved a figure as he. "Margaret was more radical than I," he enjoys telling. "Thus she always insisted that her bathroom towel go to the *left* of mine."

Among the professors who influenced him at Harvard, Adams speaks especially of Irving Babbitt, Alfred North Whitehead, and George Lyman Kittredge. He recalls Professor Kittredge's comment, made in the course of introducing him when he was to present a paper in a Shakespeare seminar: "In my youth it was not understandable that a Unitarian minister would not be a poet. They wrote the great hymns of the nineteenth-century." [10] Adams's broad knowledge of literature and his attention to the literary quality of his own rhetoric are apparent in his writings.

From his Salem pulpit Adams championed the cause of striking textile workers at the Pequot Mills. The ensuing controversy, in which he gained local notoriety, became for him a paradigm for the role of the church in social issues and public policy. It became a lifelong interest. Today he relishes his role as a counselor to the new clerical workers' union at Harvard University. In the course of several trips to Europe in 1927 and in the late 1930s, he sought out church leaders and theologians. Among them he was especially influenced by Rudolf Otto, a Marburg University professor and a publicly avowed anti-Nazi, and by Peter Brunner, a Lutheran pastor and theological teacher. Brunner, who some years before had become a close friend of Adams's at Harvard, was at this time a leader in the anti-Nazi Confessing Church movement. Adams's personal encounters with Nazism, including being detained for questioning by the Gestapo, deepened his sense of global political crisis, a crisis that demanded the response of social-ethical engagement.

Adams credits Rudolf Otto with insights into the origins and meaning of Jesus' announcement of the kingdom of God, insights which gave fresh relevance to eschatology. Jesus proclaimed the kingdom of God not as a future event (hence, it is not a failed prediction) but, paradoxically, as both already present and yet to come. As a religious symbol drawn from the political realm, the kingdom of God signifies "the pull of the future" toward fulfillment, an image of hope in dark times. The present, then, becomes a time of courageous and hopeful decision, a creative thrust to-

Kingdom of God — pull of the future toward fulfillment — image of hope in dark times.

ward meaning in history. Otto, in turn, was deeply interested in Adams's idea that personal identity and social-ethical purpose are significantly formed by voluntary associations. In his experience with small groups Adams finds both "intimacy" and "ultimacy," the twin qualities that have always attracted him. He felt them also in his friendship with Otto. He recalls walks with Otto during visits to Marburg in the 1930s, and long conversations while sitting with feet propped up in the bay of the ancient Hohenstaufen castle. From this favorite place, with its commanding view of the countryside, Otto later suffered a fatal fall. As recounted by Adams, the tragic event seems a portent of the descending night of Nazism.

In 1937 Adams joined the faculty of Meadville Theological School, a Unitarian seminary in Chicago, as professor of religious social ethics. From 1943 he was also a member of the Federated Theological Faculty of the University of Chicago. In 1956 Adams returned to Cambridge, to become the Edward Malinckrodt, Jr., Professor of Christian Ethics at Harvard Divinity School. In addition to his regular teaching duties, he conducted an extracurricular seminar on religion and law with Professor Harold Berman at Harvard Law School and a seminar on religion and business decisions with Professor Arch Dooley and others at Harvard Business School. In 1968 he retired from Harvard, where he holds the title Professor Emeritus, and accepted temporary appointments at Andover-Newton Theological School and at Meadville/Lombard Theological School. In 1976 he and Margaret again returned to their Cambridge home on Francis Avenue, within the precincts of the former Shady Hill estate. At the celebration of the 350th anniversary of Harvard in 1986, he was awarded a medal for distinguished service to the University.

Adams has been a major transmitter and translator of the work of the German theologians and historians Ernst Troeltsch, Karl Holl, and Paul Tillich. In 1948 the University of Chicago Press published his translation of early essays by Paul Tillich under the title, *The Protestant Era*. His doctoral dissertation at Chicago became the basis of his major work on Paul Tillich, *Paul Tillich's Philosophy of Culture, Science, and Religion*. Tillich, who became his colleague at Harvard during the last phase of his career, once said (without exaggeration) that Adams knew more about his work than he did himself.[11]

Adams is perhaps best known for his writings on the role of voluntary associations in society. And he has practiced what he preached. Adams has founded groups for study and devotional discipline (Greenfield Group, Brothers of the Way), participated in a therapeutic community (Gould

Farm), and been active in denominational programs for renewal and for social action (as a founder of the original Unitarian Commission of Appraisal, a member of the Advisory Committee to the Unitarian Universalist Association Department of Social Responsibility). He has been a leader in professional societies (past president of the Society of Christian Ethics, past president of the American Theological Society, a founder and president of the Society for the Scientific Study of Religion, and president of ARC, the Society for the Arts, Religion and Contemporary Culture). Adams also served for various periods during the 1930s and 1940s as editor of *The Christian Register* and *The Journal of Liberal Religion,* and as associate editor of *The Protestant.*

When he speaks of "the disciplines of social responsibility," he has in mind primarily issue-oriented social action groups. His personal engagements have been with groups of a decidedly liberal bent. In the American Civil Liberties Union he served for fifteen years as Chairman of the Committee on Church and State in the Massachusetts branch. He helped found FREE, the Fellowship for Racial and Economic Equality, which continues today as the Southeastern Institute. But he seems to have enjoyed most his participation in grass roots political groups, such as the Independent Voters of Illinois, of which he was a founder and leader. Adams relishes telling how, at a meeting in Washington, Harold Ickes, Secretary of the Interior under President Franklin D. Roosevelt, once told him that the I.V.I. was producing "the best damn political literature in America today."

A list of the voluntary associations that have engaged Adams's energies over the decades hardly conveys the intensity of his activities in the struggles against racism, poverty, and the violation of civil liberties and rights. He tells, for example, of an all-night vigil in a new federal housing project in Chicago from which whites were excluding blacks: "A brick thrown at the police paddy wagon in which I was riding demolished the windshield." He tells of representing race-relations organizations before officials of the Red Cross, in Washington, to demand an end to the racial segregation of blood for soldiers in World War II. He tells of being ejected from a ministers' meeting in South Chicago, in the midst of racial hostilities, on grounds that he was an "outsider" from the University of Chicago. He tells of working with Homer Jack of the Mayor's Commission on Race and with Wallace Robbins for the desegregation of the Billings Hospital of the University of Chicago. Of the latter effort he writes, "As a consequence of our all-night conflict with the hospital authorities we were able to bring the whole issue before the University Senate, of which we were members," resulting in an official desegregation ruling. He tells of carrying on a project of "aggressive love" to bring blacks into the First Unitarian Church of Chicago—"and to insist that they be given responsibilities other than that of ushering on Sunday morning." He tells how Margaret served for years on the YWCA Chicago Committee on Domestic Aid, demanding equal pay for blacks. "On one occasion the wife of the head of the Board of Trustees of the University of Chicago said at a meeting that she was constrained to resign, for her husband insisted on it. He said that these radical women would end in encouraging domestics to form a union—'absolutely unthinkable!'"

Each experience has its story, lending drama to the message within Adams's message: in the struggle for social justice the prize will be won (in John Milton's phrase) "not without dust and heat."

III

What is the unity within the diversity of James Luther Adams? Pondering this question, James Gustafson wrote:

> To those who believe that great and important scholarship has to be rigorously systematic, JLA looks eclectic. My impression is that JLA, whose insomnia is legendary, does not lose sleep over this issue, thanks be to God. I do not have a settled answer to what holds the work together. I think I am correct to say that it is not a *system* of ideas, though many ideas and interests persist across his decades of publication. I think the center of gravity is more personal; it combines his moral and intellectual passions, his native brilliance, his insatiable curiosity, his learning, and his powers of articulation. I have pondered this issue . . . and have come up with a hypothesis. "Free women and men put their faith in a creative reality that is re-creative." [12]

Approaching this book, readers are likely to move about from essay to essay and to discover that one essay sparks their interest in others. Finding a recurrent set of ideas in remarkably diverse contexts, and, like Gustafson, being intrigued by the question of his "personal center of gravity," they may also want some interpretive key to his thought. The selection and arrangement of the works—independently written over a period of several decades—can be rationalized only to a limited extent. Yet they are unified by the author's personal angle of vision—his examination of every human reliance in the light of a perception of what is ultimately reliable. This perception is variously formulated, in Adams's works, depending on the subject at hand; yet it is not arbitrarily chosen, nor personally idiosyncratic, but a broadly and deeply informed decision. A good decision about what to rely on in a given situation, like a good tree, will bear fruit; there is no other test. Yet we need not choose blindly, as Adams suggests in his two variations on Jesus' saying: "By their *groups* shall ye know them" (human "groups" being our primary means of reliable commitment), and "by their *roots* shall ye know them" (historical "roots" being our primary source of reliable meaning).

The essays and addresses in this volume are arranged in five parts, each of which begins with a brief introduction. Further comment on the volume as a whole is in order at this point. In Part One, "Reflections of a Lifetime," Adams recounts important moments in his religious and intellectual development, and in the formation of his sense of personal and professional vocation. The second chapter, "A Time to Speak: Conversations at Collegium," calls attention to numerous themes—many of them developed at length in later sections—that have been central to his life and work. Here he formulates in his own words his "personal center of gravity."

Adams cites Martin Luther's words, making them his own: "Everyone must do his [or her] own dying, and everyone must do his [or her] own believing." Nevertheless, examining one's faith is not a solitary exercise. Throughout his life Adams has engaged in wide-ranging conversations with his teachers and students, his colleagues and friends. He has an inclusive habit of mind—as his student I was often struck by his appreciations, frequently and enthusiastically announced: "Now isn't that a remarkable idea!" Part Two, "Great Companions," reflects some of his appreciations (and critiques) of others, and the contributions they have made to the development of his thought. In sum, he says, "fellowship is life."

The winds of doctrine, secular and religious, have swept across the twentieth century. In Part Three, "History and Theology," Adams considers contemporary theology in the context of the political and cultural "storms of our times." Thus he speaks of God as "the inescapable, commanding reality that sustains and transforms all meaningful existence," a reality that operates by the lure of attractive power; Whitehead called it "the divine persuasion." "It is transforming," Adams says, "because it breaks through any given achievement, it invades any mind or heart open to it, luring it on to richer or more relevant achievement. . . . [It] finds its richest focus in meaningful human history, in free, cooperative effort for the common good."[13] This is the heart of the matter, God-in-history, the "creative reality that is re-creative."

Theology, then, is intimately related to social ethics. Religious conceptions legitimate, or sometimes delegitimate, a society and the institutions that sustain it. Conversely, the groups to which we belong and give our commitment tend to shape the moral and spiritual qualities of our lives. The essays in Part Four, "Religion and Society," examine religious movements and ideas in terms of their institutional and historical consequences, to the end that persons and groups may make more responsible decisions.

In the final section—Part Five, "Liberal Christianity"—Adams critically examines the nature and destiny of his own religious stance and institutional loyalties. He celebrates the virtues of his adoptive Unitarian Universalist denomination; he also criticizes it and seeks to deepen its theological self-understanding. In a 1987 sermon Adams recounted a story that he had heard Jane Addams tell in her 1931 Ware Lecture at the "May Meetings" of the American Unitarian Association:

> She recalled that Horace Greeley, the famous Universalist, when challenged as to the tenets of his church, said, "Yes, it is true that the Unitarians consider themselves too good ever to be sent to hell, whereas the Universalists think God is too good to send anybody there." Miss Addams saw this Universalist view in sharp contrast to that of the pioneer women and men living in the great stretches of the country. Their state of mind, she said, was not unlike that of the vagrant who envied his faithful dog, not only that he grew his own canine clothing and was fashioned to forage easily for his own food, but that his luck was that when he died he would be dead. Here he was unlike his disconsolate master who said, "*He had to go to hell yet.*"[14]

Ever since Origen of Alexandria (c. 185–c. 254), theological universalists have affirmed, paradoxically, both free will and the sovereign power of divine love. In his sermon Adams went on to acknowledge the tension between divine sovereignty and human freedom and to seek their common ground. "Authentic autonomy must be seen as a relational, an interrelational, concept. It gains concrete reality and ethical significance only through interdependence, and only through our commitments, religious and ethical. The source and object of fundamental commitment, as [the Universalist minister] Quillen Shinn has suggested, is 'the almighty force of love.' Autonomy finds fulfillment not in self-enclosure but rather in response to the creative, sustaining, commanding, community-forming power of God."

free will vs. sovereign power of divine love.

In the end, the response to God will be multiple. Finally, in Adams's work as a whole, a multiplicity of appreciations, interpretations, values, visions overwhelms the urge toward unity. Just this makes him a theological liberal. Still, the attempt to look at the whole may help us understand why Adams has cast his net so broadly and has come up with a great draught of fishes.

IV

Unreflective theists and reactive atheists alike tend to assume that the meaning of God "goes without saying"—the dictionary or popular imagination suffices to define it. The only question, they think, is whether such a God exists. To Adams, this is to invite an unexamined faith, a faith not worth having. An authentic faith seeks God in what is ultimately reliable in our personal and social existence. Thus Adams speaks of God as "the community-forming power"; the God he seeks is "the creative reality that re-creates." Such definitions invite us to ask, Where have we experienced these processes? How do we take part in them? How does this source of power become available to us? This approach does not yield precision or proof, which in any event is unavailable. It invites reflective questioning, to the end of defining a reliable faith.

For James Luther Adams, awakening to the historical drama of human life sets the stage for a faith worth having. "I believe time itself to be of the essence of God and human being." [15] His theology is a way of coming to terms with the human necessity of "taking time seriously." We live forward in time, to ends beyond our complete and confident knowing. Being creatures of what he calls "eschatological orientation"—living toward ends both chosen and unchosen—we bind and loosen, promise and forgive, attest and protest, consent and dissent, covenant and atone. In time our covenants harden into contracts, or lapse through careless disregard, or break under the force of betrayals; we renew them by loosing, forgiving, protesting, dissenting, atoning. We renew them, also, in hope—in the expectation of a more inclusive covenant yet to be. There are many thoughtless, deceptive, or spurious promises; an examined faith seeks the ground of their correction and renewal, for this alone promises authentic fulfillment. Hence, we must take seriously the imperatives of our social and institutional life—of history in the making.

In consequence we also become more keenly aware of our human vocation, the calling and tasks that humanize us. Making Milton's phrase his own, Adams says we live "under the Great Taskmaster's eye." The

context of such a calling goes far beyond the workplace or the home; it is
world-historical. Our lives are located in time and history: the human
condition is informed by past realities and future possibilities; in the present we are called to address our immediate situation, speaking the truth
prophetically and concretely. Prophetic speech is both critical and creative: it interprets the signs of the times; it judges and decides among
possibilities; it participates in "the community-forming power." Wishful,
arbitrary, self-serving, or willful speech is inauthentic. Only by devotion
to truth will our words serve God's Word—the symbol of transcendent
meaning in time and history. So too, authentic self-understanding enables
us to act with creative freedom, to act with transforming intent, to make
a new beginning. "Come, my friends, 'tis not too late to seek a newer
world."

Still, every temporal transformation is provisional; the dialectic of freedom and necessity, of change and stability, of history and nature, continues. There are no utopias, and no achievement is above criticism and
change. If there is progress, there is also decline. Voices of prophetic
dissent, even warnings of "doom," will be heard again and again. "The
time is out of joint."

It remains that, for prophets as much as for poets, cultural continuities
are as important as discontinuities; in fact, the recognition of a historical
caesura stimulates the quest for deeper lines of connection. Thus, as
Adams notes, our ability to recognize a prophet (a notoriously difficult
achievement, especially in "his own hometown") depends on a living tradition of prophetic figures—a historical continuity. So too, questions of
"legitimation" and "institutionalization" are prominent in Adams's
thought. Thus a democratic society legitimates prophetic dissent by establishing the rights of free speech and association; voluntary associations
institutionalize it.

Adams also recognizes the necessity of involuntary associations; we do
not freely choose our families of origin, and the state properly exercises
coercion under limits imposed by the law. He is not, for example, a pacifist. But voluntary associations—created by free will, nourishing diversity, expressing personal and corporate eros—remain, for Adams, the primary agents of creativity in history. His devotion, finally, is not to a
utopian ideal of harmony, but to a dynamic and prophetic vision of history: the promise of a rich cultural unity and a just society—an inclusive
covenant.

James Luther Adams is a liberal Christian who looks for the renewal of
liberalism in religion, in politics, and in culture. All the forms of liber-

alism share a common historical fate, he believes; they hold in common the tasks of self-criticism and of renewing the covenants of civilization. We make agreements; we can also improve our agreements.

He has enacted this calling and commitment in several vocational roles. He is a scholar of theological social ethics who understands human existence as essentially social, historical, and institutional. He is a teacher—one who "has not taught without parable"—who seeks to further our understanding of the relation between religious meaning and ethical practice. He is a lifelong social activist, "a man for committees" that do both the daring and the humdrum work of a democracy. As this volume attests, each of the protean forms of his vocation makes its contribution to our own deep need for an examined faith, for a faith worth having.

Notes

1. James Luther Adams, *The Prophethood of All Believers,* ed. George K. Beach (Boston: Beacon Press, 1986), pp. 48, 53.

2. James Luther Adams, "Ethics," *A Handbook of Christian Theology,* ed. Marvin Halverson and Arthur A. Cohen (New York: Meridian Books, 1958), p. 111.

3. Two other smaller collections of Adams's essays have been published: *Taking Time Seriously* (Glencoe, Ill.: Free Press, 1957) and a special issue of *The Unitarian Universalist Christian* 32, nos. 1–2 (Spring/Summer 1977), ed. Herbert F. Vetter, Jr. Several of the essays in these two collections have been reprinted in subsequent publications, including *On Being Human Religiously,* ed. Max L. Stackhouse (Boston: Beacon Press, 1976); *Voluntary Associations: Socio-cultural Analyses and Theological Interpretations,* ed. J. Ronald Engel (Chicago: Exploration Press, 1986); *The Prophethood of All Believers.*

4. For studies of Adams's thought see John R. Wilcox, *Taking Time Seriously* (Washington, D.C.: University Press of America, 1978); George K. Beach, "Awakening to History: The Prophecy of James Luther Adams," *American Journal of Theology and Philosophy* 7, no. 2 (May 1986):59–74. For biographical and interpretive essays on Adams see "James Luther Adams, A Biographical and Intellectual Sketch," by Max L. Stackhouse, and "Voluntary Associations as a Key to History," by James D. Hunt, in *Voluntary Associations: A Study of Groups in a Free Society, Essays in Honor of James Luther Adams,* ed. D. B. Robertson (Richmond, Va.: John Knox Press, 1966). See also the introductions to the volumes of Adams's essays edited by Vetter, Stackhouse, and Beach (note 3) and the essay reviews by Everett and Gustafson (notes 5 and 12).

5. William Johnson Everett, "On James Luther Adams," *Theology Today* 45, no. 1 (April 1988):82.

6. Adams appeals to C. S. Peirce's pragmatic theory of meaning—"the meaning of a symbol is to be observed in its effect on action, on habits [of action]"—to express the close relation between theory and practice, or between theology and ethics. See "The Use of Symbols," originally presented in 1969 as his presidential address to the Society for Christian Ethics as "The Pragmatic Theory of Meaning," in *Voluntary Associations,* ed. J. Ronald Engel, pp. 120–37.

7. For his discussion of the triad, autonomy, heteronomy, and theonomy, see James Luther Adams, *Paul Tillich's Philosophy of Culture, Science and Religion* (New York: Harper and Row, 1965; Washington, D.C.: University Press of America, 1982), pp. 52–56.

8. Quoted from "Neither Mere Morality nor Mere God," Chapter 32 in this volume.

9. On his "conversions," see my introduction and Adams's "Taking Time Seriously," in *The Prophethood of All Believers,* pp. 14–17, 25, 33–42.

10. See *An American Reformation: A Documentary History of Unitarian Christianity,* ed. Sydney E. Ahlstrom and Jonathan S. Carey (Middletown, Conn.: Wesleyan University Press, 1985), pp. 311–19.

11. For references to Adams's works on Tillich, Troeltsch, and Holl, see *The Prophethood of All Believers,* n. 37, p. 29. For extensive bibliographies of Adams's works generally, see John R. Wilcox, *Taking Time Seriously,* pp. 163–206; and *Voluntary Associations: A Study of Groups in Free Societies,* ed. D. B. Robertson, pp. 375–95.

12. Gustafson continues: "I gloss this a bit. They do not put their confidence in any given system of ideas or in any institution that judges how one ought to think or what one ought to think about, based on external authority or social expectations. Their confidence is in a creative reality that is re-creative; the object of their confidence contains a dynamism and a kind of indeterminacy. To have confidence in such a reality is surely personally freeing, and is a ground for creativity and responsiveness of the human spirit to a wide range of persons, ideas and movements." James M. Gustafson, "Review of *The Prophethood of All Believers,* by James Luther Adams," *The Unitarian Universalist Christian* 43, no. 1 (Spring 1988):53.

13. *The Prophethood of All Believers,* pp. 49–50.

14. From an unpublished sermon, "The Almighty Force of Love," for the installation of the Rev. Marta Flanagan at the First Universalist Church, Salem, Massachusetts, on November 15, 1987.

15. *The Prophethood of All Believers,* p. 34.

Part One

Reflections of a Lifetime

F RIENDS AND FAMILY MEMBERS, COLLEAGUES AND FORMER STUDENTS had gathered at Boston's Arlington Street Church for a singular event—the celebration of the eighty-fifth birthday of James Luther Adams. The program noted that, following a series of addresses honoring the man, he would himself give "The Last Word." When his turn finally came, Adams abruptly registered a "correction." "What is meant," he said with a wry smile, "is the *latest*."

Now in his ninetieth year, Adams continues to give us his latest word. Despite a debilitating back condition (pain medications make him drowsy, he complains, so he takes them only reluctantly), he pursues research and writing projects, maintains a voluminous correspondence, and entertains a constant stream of visitors. On one recent occasion a group of laypersons announced that they had come because they "had heard of the legendary JLA" and wanted to meet him. Launching into stories from his teenage years on the Northern Pacific Railroad, Adams told of the time he refused the offer of a lucrative position on the railroad in favor of entering college. The gruff, profane district superintendent, a man not accustomed to being turned down, was incredulous. He asked, "How can you do that?" "Because," Adams answered, adopting a tone of youthful mock meekness, "I've heard the name of Shakespeare and wanted to know who he is."

The autobiographical mood comes readily to Adams. He enjoys the riveting effect his stories have on an audience, and his auditors respond warmly to him. In Part One Adams reflects on his life and thought, accenting the formative events of his vocation as minister, scholar, teacher, and social activist.

15

The opening essay, "A Come-Outer," is multidimensional. In brief compass Adams relates his shift from fundamentalism in his youth to Unitarianism; the timely counsel of an insightful and caring undergraduate teacher; the beginnings of his lifelong drive for learning; the later recovery of vitalities from his earlier, once-forsaken faith; the joining of religious commitment and ethical concern in the "existential" moment. Each of his recollections reflects also a basic theme of his life and thought—each marks some moment in his quest for an examined faith.

The second piece, "A Time to Speak: Conversations at Collegium," records his two evening-long conversations with the Collegium Association for Liberal Religious Studies. It is, I believe, his best self-introduction. Adams moves from topic to topic, relating event to idea, then returning to his underlying theme—the dynamic tension and unity between two basic orientations to life, "the intimate" and "the ultimate." We become aware of them in associations that offer personal relationships and orient our lives to ends that transcend us. Belonging to small, face-to-face groups is essential to the formation of personal identity and intimate, caring relationships. But if such groups are only focused on themselves, they are only self-serving. To be personally and socially transforming, they must also be oriented to ends that transcend themselves, to "the ultimate."

In "The Vocation of Ministry and *The Praying Hands*," several of Adams's characteristic themes—the concept of vocation, ministry among the professions, forms of social organization (especially the voluntary association) in church and in society, the symbolic power of art—are illustrated by his own experiences of ministry. A reproduction of Albrecht Dürer's drawing *The Praying Hands* hangs over his desk.

The section concludes with "The Latest Word," spoken at his eighty-fifth birthday celebration. Adams alludes to his sometime career as a professor of English and goes on to develop a "clinching metaphor" of his theme—a crowded, racing passenger train. It is an image of the intimate and ultimate pilgrimage in which we find ourselves, thrown together with humanity in all its diversity. To what destination is such a restless life drawn? The story ends on a sardonic note—"Omaha, I hope"—but some celebrants thought they heard him speak poignantly—"Home, I hope." Augustine's prayer, "And restless is our heart until it comes to rest in Thee," is apt for such a life and message.

G.K.B.

I · A Come-Outer

Having been reared in the family of a fundamentalist minister in the Pacific Northwest, I at the University of Minnesota not only abandoned the fundamentalism, I also began to declaim against it in season and out. With other students I edited a "radical" campus sheet with the self-adoring name *The Angels' Revolt*, adapted from the title of a novel by Anatole France. Whenever my turn came in a public-speaking class I usually gave a speech against religion. The professor gave me a hard time as a critic of my noisy rhetoric. Yet, he seemed to enjoy my antireligious pugnacity, and I enjoyed shocking the pious students in the class—attacking Bibliolatry, creationism, self-righteousness, hostility to modern culture.

One day in my senior year at the end of the class period I said to the teacher, Professor Frank M. Rarig, that I had started in college with the intention of studying law (previously I had been secretary to a prosecuting attorney) but had decided against it, that now I did not know what I was going to do; at the end of the semester I was to receive a bachelor's degree and to be forced out into the world, knowing not whither. What with some of the students overhearing the professor, he embarrassed me in front of them by saying, "You don't know what you are going to do? I have known that for some time." I realized that he was aware of my enthusiasm for philosophy courses and for economics and constitutional law. I immediately asked, "What do you have in mind? Could you give me an inkling of it here?" He replied with unconcealed teasing, "Yes, you are going to be a pr–eacher"—he pronounced the word with my habitually scornful accent. "Come and see me if you wish to discuss this."

By appointment I went to his office on a Saturday morning, and we talked for three and a half hours. He told me that I was provincial and naive, that I apparently had never encountered a self-critical religion, and that this was the reason for my blanket hostility. He went on, however, to say that obviously my most passionate interest was religion. He turned out to be a Unitarian. By the end of the morning he, as it were, had convinced me that my "shots" at religion were from an obsolete blunderbuss, in short that I should consider entering Harvard Divinity School to

This essay was written in 1982; previously unpublished.

study for the Unitarian ministry. (To be sure, I had heard of Unitarianism; I had attended some lectures at the Unitarian church in Minneapolis.) After that conversation I called on the Rev. Frederick M. Eliot in St. Paul and on the Rev. John H. Dietrich in Minneapolis. Not being a "born Unitarian," I was becoming a "come-outer Unitarian," a member of the group that was to become the predominant constituency in our Unitarian Universalist churches.

To my surprise and that of my fellow students, I adopted Professor Rarig's proposal and migrated to Cambridge. I remained there for six years, the while singing lustily in the Harvard Glee Club and studying languages and comparative literature. Meanwhile, I had graduated from Harvard Divinity School and had become assistant minister in the Second Church in Salem, a term punctuated by a summer at Heidelberg University. There I first encountered Nazi students—I one day in Nuremberg was almost beaten up by Nazi "heroes."

Looking back on all of this, I would say two or three things without assessing my intermittent doubts about the wisdom of remaining in the ministry (doubts shared by others).

Whether or not the Minnesota professor should have given me better and different counsel, his action shows the crucial role that a professor possessing concern and insight can have. What a mentor he was! (A generation later a handsome, new building at the university was to be named in his honor.) He of course knew that he was taking a risk. Twenty years later I delivered a sermon in the church in Minneapolis, and he sent me a rather strongly critical letter regarding my "style" (one of his favorite words).

His action revealed another thing, that sometimes the religion from which one is alienated may nevertheless have at its core something profoundly vital, something prodding us to ask fundamental questions even if the answers are unacceptable. If we can recognize this, we can begin improving our questions and our commitments.

In a special way I was forced to do just this a decade after my professor sent me off to Harvard Divinity. I found myself in Nazi Germany in association with a German Harvard classmate who had just served time in the concentration camp in Dachau. Immediately on release from Dachau he had boldly resumed his leadership in the dangerous anti-Nazi underground movement of the resisting churches. There I came to appreciate at first hand the vocation, the calling, of prophetic religion in its perennial and creative struggle against the false gods of idolatry—racism, classism and sexism. I learned anew and "existentially" the meaning of the Commandment, "Thou shalt have no other gods before me." I learned that as soon as the universal God is forgotten, false gods rush in to fill the vacuum.

2 · A Time to Speak: Conversations at Collegium

Some of you will remember the story I've told about Erich Fromm. One night I was talking to him until three o'clock in the morning, and I finally said, "I don't know how I'd answer this question. . . ." "Go ahead," he said. So I asked, "Erich, what makes you tick?" "Well," he said, "I think I know what makes me tick. I learned from the Old Testament prophets that the meaning of human existence is the struggle for justice." That's a very interesting notion—the idea that we get a basic drive toward meaning from the prophets' demand for justice.

THE INTIMATE AND THE ULTIMATE

Trying to answer for myself the question I put to Erich Fromm, I experience some difficulty. G. K. Chesterton once said that he had toyed with the idea of writing a novel in which a group would undertake an expedition of exploration. They would sail for many months, the voyagers seeking hitherto unknown territory to be declared a colony for Great Britain. Finally land would be sighted, and they would head for the shore and would plant the Union Jack and the flag of St. George, doing all the things necessary to claim the land. Previously they had noticed some barbarous buildings and appurtenances. But now as they advanced they would discover that they had landed on the southern coast of England at the bathing resort of Brighton!

This text has been edited from the transcription of dialogues of James Luther Adams with George K. Beach and J. Ronald Engel, at the annual meeting of Collegium, at Craigville, Massachusetts, on October 11 and 12, 1986. Questions and comments have been omitted. Bracketed words are the editor's.

I take it that Chesterton's intention was to remind us of the variety of things, amazing things, that we fall into the habit of taking for granted. The novel would show how difficult it was and what a great thing it would be to discover England—or even to discover oneself! So that is the kind of excursion we are embarked on this evening.

I would start off by using a phrase that needs slight expansion: the principal things that concern me are *intimacy* and *ultimacy*—the intimate and the ultimate. "The intimate" is not an adequate term because I am concerned not only with the interpersonal relations but with meaningful human fellowship, with the human drive for fellowship. Aristotle said that the human being is "an associating being." The quality of one's associations determines the character and the meaning of one's existence.

"The ultimate" is difficult to articulate in our day, for we live in a time when the ancient myths and the ancient vocabularies are anachronistic, or are not properly understood. I could call it the Transcendent, but that is not an absolutely indispensable way of speaking about the ultimate. But I'll tell a story about it.

I was very influenced in my youth by reading the autobiography of George Gordon. He was a miner's son who, without the normal prerequisites, was admitted to Harvard College as a special student. In fact, I believe he is the only person in the history of Harvard who was given a degree by acclamation after two years. He tells the story of studying Greek and coming in with his bluebook for the midterm exam. Professor William Goodwin said, "You're not permitted to take the exam—you're a special student." Gordon then said, "But I'd like to take it." "No, no, you're not getting credit," Dr. Goodwin said, "you don't need to take it." But Gordon protested: "You make me feel like an idiot—I'm not even worth being examined!" Finally Dr. Goodwin relented and let him take the exam. George Gordon concludes the story by saying: the meaning of human existence is to live in a community where there are standards, where there is judgment. If you don't live in a community where there is a shared sense of judgment—and ultimately the judgment of God—then you're not on the way to becoming human.

Theology is faith seeking understanding—understanding of yourself and understanding of reality. One of my favorite aphorisms is from Alfred North Whitehead: "Definition is the soul of actuality." That is the task of theology: to define reality, but also to define that capacity *in the human being*. Reality is not only that which we confront, but also that which is in the human being. There will always be an element of faith—unless you are in complete despair and say that nothing has any meaning. If you don't go that far, you are involved in trying to define, to articulate, to locate meaning. So that is the search of faith for understanding—our understanding of the reality which we confront, and which we are.

This raises the question, where do we begin? Do we begin with a search for meaning? That's one possibility. I would like to suggest, rather, another approach. Some years ago I was asked by the dean of the University of Chicago to give a series of radio talks on theology. I decided, possibly under the influence of Whitehead, to articulate the series in terms of the five moods: the declarative, the imperative, the subjunctive, the interrogative, the exclamatory. That's a good way to suggest that theology begins with the recognition of some kind of fact: *it begins with the declarative mood.* It is fascinating to study the way this comes out in different kinds of religious literature. In the Bible you have the rhetoric of narration—"And it came to pass"—a concrete event. Even the first words in Genesis—"In the beginning God . . ."—is in the declarative mood.

I am saying that faith should take into account the realm of fact, in contrast to the realm of value. Theology is an attempt at a rational understanding of faith; it asks: what does one place one's confidence in? With that kind of definition of faith you can say that there is no one—except a kind of idiot—who does not have some kind of faith. Everyone must have something to place confidence in. In this sense there is no such thing as an irreligious person. Every person is concerned with a basic fact, something in which one has confidence. The central task of theology is to articulate that which is ultimately reliable.

articulate that which is ultimately reliable

THE QUEST FOR CONSENSUS

When I entered the Unitarian ministry I became increasingly distressed—a feeling occasioned not only by Unitarianism but by liberalism in general—by what I called fissiparous individualism, the claim that religious authenticity depends upon your individual freedom. This raised the question: What is the basis for community?

Early in my studies I had worked on the thought of Friedrich Schleiermacher. I was struck by the young Schleiermacher's saying that the function of the church was to bring together people who had a variety of religious experiences and to "exchange" religious experiences. He did not stress the importance of achieving some kind of consensus. I was not alone in this yearning for consensus, and yet I was quite unwilling to view a creedal statement as the common basis. There were many reasons for that, but what was the consensus? How could we state it?

We started the Greenfield Group [a study group for Unitarian ministers] over sixty years ago, in 1927, so it's been through some phases. In the earlier days we were especially concerned about what we called atomistic individualism. We were concerned about the lack of consensus—the idea that when you became a Unitarian "you are free to do your own thing." Then the idea of some kind of cooperation toward the end of a transcending or an enriching meaning gets lost. At the end of each session we naive liberals thought we ought to be able to put down what we had come to agree on. We had long discussions trying to formulate something, but by the next meeting we had to start over again.

In the Greenfield Group, when we thought we had some basis for a consensus, we advertised that we would like to speak in parish groups. But we would never offer a single member of the group—they had to take three of us. This was our way of saying, "You can't slough it off and say, 'Well, this is so-and-so's view, and I happen not to agree.'" We said to them, "We do have some agreement here, and we are trying to present a challenge to you."

The disciplines we adopted were rather severe. Indeed, a little later on I published an article on the use and abuse of discipline. Everybody at the first meeting of the retreat had to indicate precisely what he or she had read or not read of the assigned readings. Also—it sounds like Moscow, doesn't it!—the members had to accept the topic decided upon by the group and their respective assignments. We spent a great deal of time, first, trying to formulate consensus, and second, devising a way for these discussions to have some effect upon the parish.

Therefore we devoted attention to the literature of preaching and to biblical studies. Over a period of two or three years every member was expected to give a series of sermons on the topic we had been dealing with. We also studied liturgy. We were interested also in religion and art and in hymns we wanted to recommend for the forthcoming Unitarian hymnal. At these meetings we sang many chorales, with the result that *Hymns of the Spirit* [Boston, 1937] includes about twenty-five chorales that we recommended.

We also discussed the question of public prayer and had some rough times—some ruckuses!—about that. Maybe I shouldn't name the young minister here. He wanted to be examined by a congregational council before he was ordained. I was minister in Wellesley Hills at that time and

I got three of my board members—all men of high professional skill—to serve. We gathered at this fellow's new parish for the congregational council to be held directly before the ordination service. He had managed to persuade Louis Cornish [President of the American Unitarian Association] to chair the council.

On that Sunday there was a heavy snowstorm, which I knew would limit the attendance. Three of the members from my board who had been selected wanted to stay home. But I said, "No, if you please, we must go." So we plowed through the deep snow and got there but found very few others. And then Dr. Cornish didn't start at the appointed time. I finally said, "We've gathered here for a purpose, to examine this man and see if he's fit for ordination. I think we ought to start questioning him." Dr. Cornish said, "All right. Do you have a question?" I then said to the candidate, "You will be conducting public worship. Would you tell us, what is your conception of prayer, either private or public?"

The candidate responded, "You don't think we get rain from prayer, do you?" I said, "Dr. Cornish, I thought *this* man was answering the questions. If you insist that *I* answer the question, I can tell you unambiguously, *No.*" The laymen there were somewhat shocked by the superficiality of the exercise. The answers didn't give evidence of the candidate's having cerebrated on such matters. But as the time went on, we could hear the organ next door playing the prelude—so we finally voted him in!

Say, how did we get onto that? I would like to raise the question as to whether we could define what we are doing in Collegium [a ministerial and scholarly association] in these terms: we would like to have some consensus, not simply with regard to the answers but with regard to what the right questions are that we should be facing, in our several vocations, in the context of the church. I think that if we had a modicum of agreement about what the right questions are, the differentiation among us would prove stimulating and would promote genuine interchange.

For a long time it has also seemed to me that it is important to have dialogue among the different professions. I have spent a decade in seminars at the Harvard Business School on religion and business decisions, and about a decade at Harvard Law School on questions of religion and law. Then, too, for the last twenty years I've been involved in ARC, the Society for the Arts, Religion, and Contemporary Culture. In all of these enterprises there have been dialogues between religious leaders and artists and art critics and so on. That's a second suggestion I'd like to mention—

to have members of other professions be with us and share the kinds of concerns they have.

INSTITUTIONAL STANDARDS AND FELLOWSHIP

Another thing also became important for me at this time. A sense of frustration took form in my thinking due to my recognition of the importance of institutionalization. In my young ministry I became keenly aware of the privatization of religion. (On the one hand, I also believed we should not have conformism. In my inaugural public lecture at Harvard, "The Uses of Diversity" [see chapter 31], I warned against conformism, saying that *uniformity* leads to *deformity*.) But in face of a liberalism that was emphasizing freedom of thought, I had also become aware of the importance of institutions. This was not to call into question the importance of freedom, but rather to suggest that freedom leads to some kind of fellowship, and fellowship has to find some kind of institutionalization.

Kenneth MacDougall and I started the Commission of Appraisal [in 1934] because we had the feeling that [in the American Unitarian Association] we had feeble leadership. The leadership was primarily bureaucratic. I don't like to fall into cliches, but we felt it was impoverished of anything that was soil for or nourishment for a renewed faith. We went to many places talking passionately in favor of recognition of the role of institutions, as affecting the organization of the church and as producing some kind of continuity in the church. We spoke of emphasizing something other than the "me-me-me" and "what *I* think" and "*my* freedom." Rather, we said, we should emphasize social responsibility and cooperative endeavor, in order to be able to articulate and to transmit values that nourish the community of faith.

I became disenchanted with the ministry in my first parish because I thought—though I don't like to use this word—that there was no discipline, no standard that brings judgment upon us. I thought, you have something different in a university—standards, examinations; people have to pass or fail. But there's no way of flunking as a Unitarian! Since I had completed several years of academic work in comparative literature, I got a job at Boston University (without giving up the parish) teaching the history of English and American literature and English composition. For the latter I used the writings of William James as a model.

I came into close association with the other members of the faculty and within a year's time decided I had made a mistake! They may have discipline in the university, but they don't have fellowship. I began to reevaluate the life of the church in spite of the lack of obvious consensus. I felt that, nevertheless, there was in the community of faith something that gave fellowship. I have spoken about intimacy and ultimacy. We are not merely talking about fellowship, about humans merely as associating beings, but about institutions. I'm saying that that's the problem for liberalism.

The Prophetic Covenant

So institutions had become for me a major theme. I had already seen the importance of this when I got into the underground anti-Nazi movement. I discovered that the conditions in the German universities were not good. They were made up of scholars who had no institutional commitments, except for those directly dealing with education.

I saw that the people in the anti-Nazi movement were willing to go to jail or to a concentration camp. I had the good fortune to have an old friend in Germany, Peter Brunner. He had secured his degree at Harvard in the same year that I received my bachelor's degree at the Divinity School. A few years later he was sent to Dachau concentration camp by reason of his anti-Nazi activity. But the minute he got out of Dachau he began making speeches in various churches (I sometimes accompanied him), every day ruthlessly attacking the Nazis, even though they had just released him. Now that takes starch!

However, the attempt to state the basis for the objection to Nazism was frustrating. I wasn't the only one to make this criticism, but the position of the Confessing Church was formulated in a way that could appeal only to a small segment of the population. They insisted on formulations that only a narrow section of the German Lutheran public could accept, and thus they alienated those who had moved in the direction of liberal theology.

So there you had a highly organized form of frustration. I became acquainted with liberals who didn't like this, but nevertheless they joined. They became card-carrying members of the Confessing Church. I soon learned, however, that the people who were liberals were not given any positions of responsibility. Before long I saw that the people who were "standing for Jesus Christ," against Nazi racism, had themselves narrow, bureaucratic standards of service. So that was somewhat disheartening. In that situation it was extremely difficult for these people to achieve a consensus that was broader than their own particular form of Lutheranism— their "spatialization."

Beginning with my experience in the anti-Nazi movement, I began to see that the Old Testament prophetism was much broader than the prophetism of the anti-Nazi movement of the Confessing Churches. They were mainly interested in preserving the freedom of the church and not in human rights as such. This is now coming out more fully in the literature.

I came to interpret the Old Testament prophets as an illustration of a voluntary association that appealed to a covenant. The covenant involved the total life of the people—not only family existence but political and economic existence. The call to voluntary commitment by the Old Testament prophets is accompanied by a concern for the nature of the whole society and for the violation of the covenant. The idea that there would be prophets who would appear and play this role had to be invented over the centuries. It is interesting to see the contrast between them and the prophets in Babylon. The prophets in Babylon were on expense accounts, but the prophets in Israel were not. They had "no place to lay their head."

I saw in the Old Testament prophets the voluntary principle working in a twofold way. On the one side, they appealed to the broader covenant of Israel; on the other side, they developed the capacity to organize schools of the prophets, and the concept of the role of the prophet. The voluntary effort involves something more than the voluntary organization; it also involves appeal to a broader covenant.

Following recent biblical scholarship, I came to feel that a good deal of Christian talk about "Christian love" as against "Jewish legalism" has been off the track. Actually, the fundamental motive in the covenant and of the granting of the covenant was not obedience. In contemporary rhetoric one hears much about "obedience to Christ" and the like, but the concept of obedience is not entirely appropriate. The fundamental motive of the Old Testament covenant is affection. "It was given to us out of God's love, and our response is a response of love, a response of gratitude." The idea of obedience is inimical to the notion of authentic human fulfillment. The goal of covenant is not merely justice; ultimately it is love, as in Augustine's thought.

AN AMERICAN TRAGEDY

Here I see something so bewildering that I'm tempted to call it tragic. In the twentieth century, in contrast to earlier centuries, American politics and culture have become oriented to foreign affairs. I became agonizingly conscious of this when I arrived back in this country [in the mid-

1930s] and found myself in the midst of widespread isolationism. I went up and down the land attacking this unwillingness to recognize that the United States was part of an international, a global, network called to oppose Nazism.

Now this is the tragic element: I became aware that any party in power in a democratic society must be fearful at every moment of the possibility that the opposing party will say, "You've been soft." I hope it is not a misunderstanding if I say that [President John F.] Kennedy came to power by claiming that there was an ammunition gap; then, after it was all over, there was an increasing consensus among the historians and journalists that the gap hadn't existed. But that was the way to get the votes.

In this kind of situation anyone in political life—and this includes the citizen who has to make choices—has to be aware of the fact that in face of an enormous power, such as the Russian power, there is always the possibility that the party in power may be accused of "the gap." It will be said, "You didn't fight Communism." Anyone can be accused, in the nationalistic picture, of lacking something. It seems to me an almost tragic aspect of democratic existence that one of the ways to get into power is to define the situation in such a way that people who are incumbent are spotted as having been "soft on Communism."

I agree with Jacob Viner of Princeton University, who said, at the time that the United Nations Charter was formed, that it is impossible for the United Nations to be a viable organization when you have two enormous powers opposing each other. It will become simply a matter of these powers achieving satellites. This is a tragic aspect of our kind of global existence.

A democratic society depends on at least a two-party system, and one in which the two parties are not far distant from each other. And if you get into a situation of polarization, where there is great distance between the two sides and no possibility of further discussion, then this is a form of the demonic. It means yielding to the temptation to believe that one has found a pipeline to the infinite, and that one knows the will of God unambiguously. That's a rather dangerous thing. T. V. Smith, at the University of Chicago, used to say, "There's nothing quite so dangerous in Congress as a man of principle. You can't talk to him. You can't get some kind of compromise."

Being a human being means that one has to take the risk of making a decision. But it needs also to be said, one should not claim holiness for one's decision. There is risk in decision, and there will always be serious-minded people who do not agree with your decision. Even on an issue like apartheid in South Africa, where the matter seems so clear, there's no doubt that if one tries to take seriously the opposing points of view, one always finds oneself in a situation in which there are conflicting values.

A lot of the excitement about apartheid is directing the American conscience to "over there." Consider the number of people in this country who are in poverty—the proportion seems not to change very much—and who are under a form of oppression. Consider the great number of people who, according to the polls, think that the administration [of President Ronald Reagan] is doing a great job—the best in history! This is not the way to solve that problem "over there." I would like to see a little more passion directed at the situation in the ghettos of Boston.

There is something frustrating about the way people with good conscience can get excited about apartheid "over there" but aren't ready to work on that problem right here. You might say, "Well, for goodness' sake, do you expect to do everything at once?" I say, "Yes, if we're going to take a very high moral stand for 'over there,' we ought to be willing to pay a cost for correcting our own situation, instead of being comfortable about it." We're comfortable also in the sense that we say, "Well, what will the Democratic Party be able to do, what's their policy going to be?" That's a labor-saving device. Am I communicating?

LIBERALS AND EVANGELICALS

When I started out in the ministry I was an antihumanist. Wherever two or three were gathered together and there was a humanist in the group, I was after him. But I finally decided that that was wrong. Insofar as there was a prophetic element among the humanists—they have had some difficulty, here, since some of the people who joined were shocked to discover the socially prophetic element in the humanist movement—I decided to stop attacking humanists.

I also decided I was going to follow a kind of lifestyle with which they could feel affinity. There is a place in the New Testament where it says, There are those who say they will do my will, and they go away and don't do it; and there are those who say they won't do my will, and they go away and do it [see Matt. 7:21]. So I decided that, in the main, I would try to do the kind of things that the humanists could support, without theological interpretation, and that we could cooperate on that basis.

I am indebted to an essay by George [H.] Williams on the Evangelicals and the divisions among them. There is a progressive wing among them (though we would probably do damage to them if we praised them—the conservative Evangelicals will say, "Ah ha, there you are, the Unitarians like them!") But I could mention names of liberals who have been satisfied to condemn the Evangelicals wholesale. I think this is a moment in history when we should recognize the differences among them. The Gordon-Conwell Seminary [in Beverly, Massachusetts] and *Sojourners* magazine [Washington, D.C.] are examples of prophetic and progressive elements among the Evangelicals.

What do we view as the future possibilities and responsibilities of the liberal church in face of the other denominations and in face of the uncertain future of political liberalism? It seems to me we ought to try to have some substantial discussions of what our actual situation is, informed by sociological and other cultural analyses. I would like then to raise the question whether liberalism itself does not have the obligation and the opportunity to be more creative in the American situation than merely to say, "We're agin' all that." We ought to be able to find some method of cooperating with contrasting groups.

One reason I am saying this comes from a broader consideration. As you know I've been laboring with the work of Ernst Troeltsch for some years. Troeltsch tried to understand the history of Western culture in terms of synthesis, not in the Hegelian, rationalistic sense but in the sense of the interplay of forces. He saw that creativity and novelty come from the interplay of contrasting forces in culture and history. There is something similar to that in Whitehead, who said that even the zest for living depends upon contrast.

So I would suggest that religious liberals ought to try to learn something about what the progressive Evangelicals are doing. We could learn from them the uses of the prophetic elements in the Bible, elements that we have not been unaware of but that they are exploiting to good effect. I would like to hear such perspectives on the radio, or in the Harvard Memorial Church, rather than hearing liberals, including Unitarians, just flatly and uncreatively condemning them. I hide my face when that happens. In view of the divisions among the Evangelicals, we might even see possibilities in liberalism that are not being realized, such as the way the progressive Evangelicals are dealing with the conservatives.

SECULARIZATION AND THE SPIRITUAL VOID

The question of contemporary cultural and religious change is a difficult one for all of us. As early as the 1850s Henry Whitney Bellows wrote a

powerful essay describing secularization as the disappearance of the sense
of the holy, the disappearance of a commitment beyond "doing your own
thing." It is included in the new book, *An American Reformation* [Middle-
town, Conn., 1985], edited by Jonathan Carey and Sidney Ahlstrom, a
collection of Unitarian documents of the nineteenth century. I don't remember any essay by a Unitarian that makes such a cogent statement on
the role of institutions as Bellows does in this essay, "The Suspense of
Faith" [1859]. The idea is presented there that you can't deal with secularization unless you have some kind of institutionalization. That is his
fundamental criticism of liberal religion.

The question remains: How to define secularization? The difficulty is
that some elements in secularization represent a thrust towards autonomy
or freedom, and others represent a thrust towards a kind of relativism,
lacking any sense of standard.

I am impressed by the present excitement among some of the students
in the Harvard Divinity School about a new course on secularization. It
would seem to me highly productive for all of us to deal with that issue
from the perspective of our different vocations and disciplines. We observe
in contemporary writing increasing concern about the nature of secularization at the hands of the nontheological disciplines. At Harvard one of
the most potent writers in this area is Daniel Bell—a layman whose academic background is mainly the trade-union movement. See his essay on
secularization, in *The Contradictions of Capitalism* [New York, 1976], and
his address to the American Academy of Arts and Sciences, "The Loss of
the Sacred."

The theme of secularization is central to an understanding of what is
taking place in Western culture, and, increasingly, in the Orient. Anybody who has been in Japan, for instance, is aware that it presents a great
crisis because the younger generation no longer feels religiously committed. Secularization is a planetary phenomenon.

In this connection the whole question arises of the character of the
youth culture today. Here, I think, we have something to learn from the
German experience. The lack of a sense of a meaningful existence among
German youth, the vacuum there, provided the opportunity for Nazism.
One of Goebbels' works of genius was to manipulate that emptiness and
give it a sense of direction—a sense of new faith and of German destiny.
We need in our thinking and our preaching to find ways of making the
character of secularization evident, especially the sense of a void that can
come with secularization.

Already in the 1920s, Ernst Troeltsch was saying what Paul Tillich was saying in the 1960s: we face an increasing void, a lack of commitment—to use Milton's term—"under the Great Taskmaster's eye." Obviously this is a difficult thing to deal with. It is difficult to get a form of religious conviction that impinges upon the social order and not merely upon individual piety and individual integrity. The lack of such an effective form is precisely the void.

I don't know the situation in contemporary Unitarianism well enough to evaluate this, but others have reported that we are becoming increasingly narcissistic. In both the churches and the fellowship groups we see a flight from the tough problems of national existence, a flight into the privatization of piety. Unitarian students at Harvard Divinity School who are taking a special interest in "spirituality" seem to me to be trying to avoid basic institutional, social, and political questions.

The Prophetic and the Sacramental

Recently I noticed in a German theological magazine an interesting history of the concept of spirituality. The author points out that, in the nineteenth century, *Frommigheit*—"piety" or "religiousness"—was the common coinage. Then, around the turn of the century there began a turn toward "spirit" language. The idea of spirituality that developed in both Protestant and Catholic circles—for instance, in the tradition of Catholic spiritual directors—was conceived in terms of interpersonal authenticity, as distinct from the sense of social responsibility or concern for institutional analysis and change. So the word "spirituality" has flattened out. We see this also in Oriental literature; now they are asking, "What is Buddhist spirituality?" There, too, the same issue arises: is spirituality to be defined in such a way as to avoid the prophetic element? May I give you an excursus on the idea of the prophetic dimension?

What is a prophet? We used to get that question on the final exam at Harvard Divinity School. The student lore had it that one could safely give the answer: "A prophet is one who proclaims doom." But the thing that is noteworthy here is the great amount of time it took for the definition of a prophet to be recognized. A kind of institutionalization of the concept had to take place. You have Amos declaring, "I am not a prophet or the son of a prophet, but. . . ." You see, something is getting defined there. And what is it that is being defined?

One way of looking at that development is to see the origins of what we call "the separation of powers." The prophet stood on the basis of the

def of prophet

covenant but in a sense outside the society, attacking the society—attacking its betrayal, its violation of the covenant. That function of the prophet is a cultural product, one that took half a millennium to develop.

An analogous thing can be said regarding the concept of a mahatma. Isn't that a striking idea! There comes a time in history when a special figure appears, and then somebody says, "Ahhh, a mahatma!" The person fits a form that has been culturally created over centuries. I am saying, then, that when the original spirituality becomes flattened out—when it becomes narcissistic and spatialized, when it becomes interiorized, privatized, or applied only to narrow fellowship—then the prophetic element is lost. That is the character of a good deal of what calls itself "spirituality."

Let me interject a comment here about the sacramental element in religion. In the prophetic outlook the divine gives a call to vocation. In the sacramental dimension the divine is experienced by the worshippers as a "presence." This does not mean that the prophetic element is absent; in fact, the prophetic presupposes the sacramental. But if the sacramental element is weak, the prophetic has little to stand on. In his essay, "The Possibility of a Liberal Christianity," Ernst Troeltsch asserts that the lack of the sacramental element in religious liberalism is a characteristic weakness. To be sure, both sacramentalism and prophetism can become demonic. The prophet appeals to a covenant which is above both the sacramental and the prophetic. The authentically sacramental element, then, contains a prophetic demand. Consequently, the inauthentic attitude appears when one hears someone say gushingly, "I do love the liturgy."

METANOIA AND PROPHETIC PRAYER

I come from a fundamentalist background, the Plymouth Brethren, and I now have a new appreciation for those roots, largely because they imply a radical criticism of "the world." Having those roots, I must confess that I think that something like conversion is essential—although I don't like the term "conversion" because it has been badly used and misused by revivalists. In my Berry Street Conference address ["The Changing Reputation of Human Nature," 1941] I said that the characteristic accent of the Gospels, *metanoia,* is lacking in liberalism and that we are "an uncommitted and therefore a self-frustrating people."

Now these are imponderables. A sense of commitment requires a change of priorities, and a shared commitment involves a change of shared priorities. The concept of *metanoia,* which is falsely translated "repent ye," is properly translated "change of heart, mind, soul." But as Unitarians we tend to assume we are liberated already. It is even said, "You can be a Unitarian without knowing it." Maybe this is a hangover from the Enlightenment, imagining that we are emancipated because we don't accept the inerrant authority of the Bible, or something like that.

Let me put it autobiographically and say that in Nazi Germany I soon came to the question, "What is it in my preaching and my political action that would stop this?" Maybe it was an extreme judgment of myself, but I said, "If you have to describe me, you'd say I'm not really involved, for example, in combating anti-Semitism as it is in the United States." It is a liberal *attitude* to say that we keep ourselves informed and read the best papers on these matters, and perhaps join a voluntary association now and then. But to be involved with other people so that it costs and so that one exposes the evils of society—in Boston we're right across the tracks from poverty—requires something like conversion, something more than an attitude. It requires a sense that there's something wrong and I must be different from the way I have been.

I would make a generalization: *metanoia* should be a continuing process. The function of a vital church would be *metanoia* as a continuing process. There should be an increasing awareness, a raising of consciousness with regard to the evils around us. There should be a specification of evils, including the evils that cause people in our society to become drug-addicted. So there should be moments of commitment, for example, in prayer as a prophetic form of spirituality.

One of my teachers at Marburg University, Friedrich Heiler, drew a distinction between mystical prayer—a sense of communion—and prophetic prayer. Prayer that is prophetic is prayer that aims to share, in a congregation, the sense of responsibility. Prayer, then, is a discipline whereby one offers oneself and the community to the Ultimate for the sake of, for the nourishment of, for the establishment of, authentic community.

Some of these things have to be made more articulate. There are some religious liberals who will accept this, but I have the feeling we don't talk about it quite enough. We don't personalize it. We need to develop an alternative to the privatization of piety—a personalization of piety that gives people the joy of commitment, a "costing" commitment.

THE MAKING OF A VOLUNTARIST

Fairly early, when I was a parish minister, I developed the idea that one could grow in stature primarily through coming to know successively, increasingly, and somewhat thoroughly, the thought of a few people. I think I could outline my autobiography in terms of figures who held the center of focus at different periods of my life.

After I graduated from Harvard Divinity School I became absorbed with the thought of Baron Friedrich von Hügel, the Roman Catholic lay philosopher. I was stimulated in this direction by the Quaker professor at Haverford College, Douglas Steere, who wrote his dissertation at Harvard on von Hügel as a critical realist. Partly through von Hügel and the influence of his spiritual director on him, I became interested in the practice of spiritual direction. When I had the good fortune to live in Paris— I think it was Henry James who said that a good American when he dies may go to Paris—I persuaded one of the major Catholic spiritual directors to "adopt" me. I spent several hours each week with him, an enterprise that involved, among other things, my giving attention to the writings of Saint Francis de Sales.

Even down to my Meadville Theological School days I read a chapter a day of de Sales. He became for me a kind of type-figure, combining the major motifs of the classical tradition and the biblical tradition. Leigh Hunt, the English literary critic, calls de Sales "the gentleman saint," one who combined the cultural ideas of "the saint" and "the gentleman."

I gradually moved on, then, to the study of Henry Nelson Wieman, and then to Paul Tillich. After some years of work on Tillich, translating a goodly number of his writings, I moved on to the study of Ernst Troeltsch. My general theory, as I mentioned, was that if one became sufficiently familiar with one particular thinker, one could become aware of the structure of his thought. One could also develop a structure in one's own thinking, in the various dimensions—epistemological, theological, sociological, and so on.

But the major thing that happened to me was my experience of Nazism in 1927, 1936, and again in 1938. In connection with the church people and with the Evangelical academies in Germany, my major mentor in those years became Rudolf Otto, a retired professor at Marburg University. In his earlier years Otto had been politically active, even having won election to the *Landtag*. This was striking because I had become aware of the apolitical character of both the religious leadership and the academic leadership in Germany. I became convinced that it was much easier for Hitler to take over this culture because of the apolitical character and apolitical behavior of the intellectual leadership. In those years in Germany I spent a good deal of time with the church people, and I finally decided that the lack of social infrastructures had made even the so-called democratic society of the Weimar Republic ineffectual.

The embracing structures of a culture cannot be viable or effective if they are not supported by infrastructures. The infrastructures of a society provide the occasion for the individual's participation, not only to the end of effective political life, but also to the end of a vital lay existence in the church.

In those years I saw T. S. Eliot somewhat regularly in London. He believed in the importance of infrastructures. He said that he had learned from his grandfather, William Greenleaf Eliot—the distinguished Unitarian minister in St. Louis—the importance of civic responsibility and of participation in committees. Eliot said he came to believe that one should be involved, and he was so involved for the rest of his life. An example is his work in England, forming or helping to sustain committees, with a group of Anglo-Catholic laity who met more or less regularly near Westminster to discuss impending legislation. They would try to achieve theological and ethical consensus with respect to the legislation.

I began to study the sources of a religious and an institutional conception of infrastructures through the study of seventeenth-century England and left-wing Puritanism. One finds, there, especially under the aegis of a doctrine of the Holy Spirit, a developing conception of the church in which it is the obligation of the majority to protect and to listen to the minority. One even finds the idea that, if God is going to speak to us, God will speak through the minority! The idea arises that the Holy Spirit is creative in a form of dissent, and that, instead of calling it heresy and expelling it, one is obliged to listen.

In the study of the left-wing Puritans in England, among whom some of the spiritual ancestors of religious liberalism were born, I became aware of the importance of the institutionalization of the basic dimensions of life—those that are necessary to viable human existence. I became excited by the way these Puritans spread their ideas. Some of them would dig down in their jeans, get a fund together, and hire somebody to go on a preaching tour. Then they would keep in touch with the new contacts made in this way. I found that by the end of the first quarter of the eighteenth century the major techniques for influencing public opinion had been devised by the left-wing Puritans and the Quakers. For instance, they were able in only two weeks to assemble twenty-five thousand signatures to present to the royal family or to Parliament!

So I came to the notion that the freedom claimed by the free churches was fought for first in the struggle for freedom of association. The idea of the freedom to form associations was shocking to the establishment. The demand for the freedom to form a voluntary association actually preceded

the demand for the freedom to form a voluntary church—a believers'
church, one that did not depend on government support.

Some of you may remember that I have perpetrated the notion that, in
the voluntary church, the collection plate became a symbol. It said: We
pay for this, not the state, and we're responsible for it—it's our show, and
we pay for it. So the collection plate, the very notion of collecting from
the members and not expecting support from coercive state taxation, became a kind of sacrament for them. It seems that the thrust for freedom
of the churches spilled over, secondarily, into the demand for freedom of
association. So the demand for freedom started under religious impulses
and motives. Only in the next century was freedom politically instituted
in England.

COURAGEOUS DECISION

I got fed up with the Barthian Neo-Reformation movement in theology.
I began saying we needed a neo-left-wing of the Reformation. George
Williams and I worked together on that for several years. Why did I do
that? It began, I suppose, because (as I have said) I had the good luck of
having for my closest friend in Germany a leader in the anti-Nazi movement in the underground Confessing Church, Peter Brunner. He had been
interned in Dachau concentration camp. Immediately after he was released I accompanied him through the Rhineland where he spoke every
day, ruthlessly, courageously attacking the Nazis. Although he was
warned practically every day of the Gestapo's being present in the congregation, he would say, "They certainly know what I'm going to do—I am
going to be obedient to my ordination vows." The association with these
people profoundly affected me.

How could I give you a little bit of the flavor of that? There were so
many incidents! Well, the Gestapo finally caught up with me in a melodramatic fashion. They sent two officers with bloodhounds to the *pension*
where I was staying, and they went through all of my papers. I didn't see
any evidence that they knew what they were looking for; they simply had
instructions to make a general search. At all events I had assembled a lot
of underground papers—which I later turned over to the U.S. War Department—including lists of people who were among the anti-Nazis. I
had cut out stiff cardboard for each of the drawers in my desk and put the
papers underneath, so they didn't discover them. They were even more
stupid than I! They were perhaps looking for these things and didn't find
them.

At the same time I was smuggling money for a Jewish family, so I thought that might be the reason they were after me. Of course that was risky to do, but I needn't go into detail about that. I didn't know why the Gestapo seemed to be after me, but they left the message that I must go immediately to the Gestapo office. I decided to play the role of the *Herr Professor.* I went to a public telephone and said I understood that they wanted to see me. I said, "I am heavily occupied today and I have an engagement—it is not convenient for me to come this afternoon, but I'll be there in the morning." In just a minute the fellow came back and said, "All right. Eight o'clock. Punctual!"

That gave me time to go around town and talk with people, for example, Rudolf Bultmann. He warned me against going alone to the Gestapo headquarters. But where was I to find anyone to go with me? That night I couldn't sleep, and the landlady—a wonderful anti-Nazi— couldn't sleep either. I got up early in the morning and started off about an hour before I was due at the Gestapo office. I passed the house of a pastor who had been in jail, and I thought I'd stop in to see him. I told him what had happened and what everybody had said. He said the same thing, "You can't go there alone. They'll slit your throat. You'll just disappear. You've got to have somebody go with you."

Eventually he telephoned the mayor. They talked in a coded fashion and soon the mayor said, "I'll go to my office immediately to meet him." Then the pastor said to me, "First, I am going to tell you something, and you're not ever to breathe a word of this in Germany. Do you promise solemnly that you'll never tell anyone?" He said, "The major anti-Nazi in this city is the mayor."

When I got to the mayor's office he was pacing the floor, and he said, "You know, you can't go alone." I said, "Well, that's what I've been told." He said, "I'll tell you what I've decided. I'm going to call them and tell them you're in my office, and that I'm sending you to their office." I said, "Thank you very much. But would you tell me what that does for me?" "Certainly," he said. "I have told them that I know you. And if anything happens to you, I'll find out about it."

This gives something of the flavor of the anti-Nazi movement as a voluntary association. It was made up of people who had to risk their lives, their reputations, their salaries, everything—and risk going to jail or to the concentration camp. So the word *decision* became a kind of slogan in these circles: You have to make a decision and not be content with apathy, for that is a decision by default.

THE PRIMACY OF THE WILL

How do I understand myself in the context of American culture and in light of the fact that I was reared a fundamentalist—a Baptist and a Plymouth Brethren fundamentalist? It has been interesting for me to try to assess this because of the radical rejection of culture by the Brethren. The strong eschatological element in this group—"Jesus Christ is coming at any moment," they would say—has had some effect on me. I remember from my earliest years a map of the history of salvation, from the Creation right through to the Last Judgment, on the wall of a Presbyterian church sanctuary. Also I had the *Scofield Reference Bible,* with its copious footnotes and with a whole philosophy of history—a periodization of history.

Years later, when I started reading Troeltsch and found him saying that the problem for the philosophy of history is the periodization of history, I said, "I learned that already from my fundamentalist map of eschatology!"

At Harvard I was taking courses and lectures with Whitehead, Kittredge, Lowes, Robinson, and others. But especially at this time I was a pupil of Irving Babbitt. In *Democracy and Leadership* [Boston and New York, 1924] Babbitt gives an excursus on the idea of "the primacy of the will"—an outline of the history of the concept of the primacy of the will over the intellect, beginning in ancient times. In this history Augustine plays a considerable role. Dealing with the question of the psychology of attention, Augustine asks: What determines what individuals give attention to? He answers: We give attention in accord with our basic will, with our basic desire, our basic orientation or our love. Ultimately our love determines what we give our attention to.

Augustine's psychology is a psychology of love: what one is committed to determines what one gives attention to. This is a good illustration of the primacy of the will, including the affections. Babbitt's history of Western thought, as well as of Oriental thought, was centered around the concept of the will. In fact his whole classical humanism was built around this theory of human nature. T. S. Eliot, who also studied under Babbitt at Harvard, was fundamentally affected by this idea for the rest of his life, even though Babbitt's was an antitheological humanism.

So I came to think of my early, fundamentalist years as oriented to the Pauline conception of the will and the "war in the members" [see Rom. 7:23]. Years before I had talked with my father about this. The concept of "the war within the members," that is, a conflict of wills, can also be understood in the voluntaristic sense of the primacy of the will.

What do we pay attention to

The basic idea is summarized in Babbitt's conception of the conflict between the higher and the lower will. There are various ramifications of this idea, such as "the will to restraint." Babbitt placed emphasis on self-restraint as against the Bergsonian idea of *l'élan vital.* The characteristic feature, the indispensable factor, in human being, he said, is the capacity for restraint, the capacity to say, "No." So over against what Bergson called *l'élan vital* Babbitt put *le frein vital,* that is, vital restraint instead of mere expressiveness. This was his way of dealing also with the nature of the demonic.

In light of all that, I came to the notion that I was brought up on voluntarism, that is, the idea of the decisive nature of the will. The idea of conversion, or *metanoia,* is operative here. Granting its primitive character, I'll tell one story about it.

My father tried his best to "save" me. But I wouldn't respond. And then an itinerant evangelist came to the country church and I was "converted." I walked down the path. I gave my life to Jesus. But I was sorry for it within twelve hours. The next morning—it was a Saturday morning and I wasn't in school—I overheard my father and this itinerant evangelist arguing over Scripture. My father pushed him into the corner. I was proud of him; my father knew the Scripture better than that fellow! But the evangelist finally said, "Carey, you may know the Scripture better than I do, but you weren't able to save your own son—and I did!" I was so sorry, I wished I could have lived over the night before and stuck to my chair and not given my life to Jesus under *his* auspices!

At any rate, I began to see the continuity between this Pauline doctrine of will and Babbitt's conception of the primacy of will. In this light I was now able to understand von Hügel and his critical realism in a new way. And when I came to Tillich and Troeltsch, I saw the same thing. I noticed that Tillich would now and then refer to himself as a voluntarist, so I tried to find out what *that* was. I began collecting a file of everything I could find on "voluntarism." Especially important to me was Harold Höffding, *Outlines of Psychology* [London and New York, 1919].

More recently I have written a number of articles for the new *Encyclopedia of Religion* [New York, 1987], edited by the late Professor Mircea Eliade. To my great pleasure I was asked to prepare an article on Ferdinand Tönnies. Tönnies is best known for his typology, *Gemeinschaft* and *Gesellschaft,* "community" and "society." I found, to my surprise, that Tönnies was the first to use the term "voluntarism" as the name for a philosophy that holds this same conception of the primacy of the will, as distinct from the intellectualist point of view, for example, in Socrates.

This was fascinating to me, because I found that the book I had absorbed when I was a freshman at Harvard Divinity School, Friedrich Paulsen's *Introduction to Philosophy* [New York, 1898], develops Tönnies' conception of the primacy of the will. Then I discovered that William James was excited about Tönnies and still more about Friedrich Paulsen. I was able to trace in a tentative way the concept of the primacy of the will, as understood by Tönnies, down to William James's concept of "the will to believe." It was a delight to be able to follow this idea through and to discover that Tillich, too, was familiar with Tönnies and used the term "voluntarism." In *The Socialist Decision* [New York, 1977] he adopts the corollaries, community and society. My opening chapter for the volume *The Thought of Paul Tillich* [San Francisco, 1985] is an attempt to understand Tillich as a voluntarist.

I came to see that a continuing thread in my existence could be defined as "the primacy of the will." There are some difficult questions to answer about this concept, for instance, what is the role of reason? Alfred North Whitehead is helpful in this respect, especially his volume *The Function of Reason* [Princeton, N.J., 1929]. But Whitehead, too, is a voluntarist in the sense that in his thought the fundamental salvatory reality is creativity. It is something that is given; so we may say that "creativity" is his way of talking about "the will of God" and about grace. Henry Nelson Wieman, too, has the idea that the fundamental reality is creativity, a reality that includes both grace and judgment. For Wieman there is that which is inescapable, and if it is not taken into account there are consequences of the sort that the Old Testament calls "the wrath of God."

VOLUNTARY ASSOCIATIONS

A covenant is something that one can accept or reject. There are nonvoluntary elements in human existence that are indispensable in a continuing society, but a covenant always involves choice. What are the marks of an authentic voluntary association? The major thing is that a voluntary association brings together people of differing perspectives. The sociology of knowledge points to the significance of associations that reflect some kind of common mind, but that also bring together individuals with different social rootages. For several years I worked with Louis Wirth of the University of Chicago on the sociology of knowledge, developed by Karl Mannheim in *Ideology and Utopia* [New York, 1936] and by Robert K. Merton of Columbia University.

The voluntary association, then, is one that brings together people not only of differing perspectives, but further, of perspectives that are understood to be rooted in their own social experience. That was Mannheim's insight. There are various types of voluntary associations, but in the authentic voluntary association the *group* must come to a decision. Now, many of us are greatly indebted to Henry Nelson Wieman; his conception of God as "the inescapable" has deeply affected me. But in Wieman the interplay of perspectives—"creative interchange," an idea he illustrates from history—did not involve the group's coming to a consensus and a decision, then finding a way to act on the decision. A voluntary association that is significantly functioning is not only one that achieves some kind of consensus, through an interplay of perspectives. Through compromise, rough experience, and the like, it also finds some way of making a decision. I learned this in the Independent Voters of Illinois, of which I, together with Charlotte Carr of Hull House, was one of the founders. The I.V.I., founded in 1941, is still going strong.

For me the outstanding, world-shaking voluntary association in Western history was the formation of the Christian church. It transcended not only ethnic and nationalist but also family loyalties.

What are the limits of the voluntary association? Society cannot be viewed merely under the rubric of the voluntary association. You also have the state, with its legal monopoly on the use of coercion. Coercion is not appropriate for a voluntary association. It can expel members from the group, but some things—criminality, for instance—the state has to take seriously into account. Voluntary associations may deal with criminality, seeking to improve or reform the situation, but only the state has coercive power. So there are some problems that cannot be taken care of by voluntary associations. American Federalism recognized that there are some problems that require the consensus, the will, of the entire community, and ultimately, then, resort to some kind of coercion.

This complex of ideas came very much to my consciousness when I was co-chair of the Montgomery Ward strike committee in Chicago. In the development of voluntary associational theory, I worked among the unions. Kermit Eby of the C.I.O. and I taught courses every two or three years on Protestantism and trade unions, or on Protestantism and voluntary associations, or on Protestantism and the theory of politics. Eby was at an earlier time the first executive director of the Independent Voters of Illinois.

The association with Eby was a heartening experience. He was reared in the Church of the Brethren and I in the Plymouth Brethren. It is interesting to observe how the meaning of experiences of one's youth will, at certain moments, become crystallized. On one occasion I went with Eby to participate in the foot-washing ceremony at the Church of the Brethren. What a unique experience! You participate in the Lord's Supper, and then you take turns washing each other's feet and drying them. Then after that the kiss of peace. Eby and I shared this kind of background, so we had strong motives in common, growing out of this earlier tradition of intimacy and ultimacy.

THE POWER OF ORGANIZATION

There is a sense in which, if you make a decision, there will necessarily be an arbitrary element. You have to make a decision before you would like to. You cannot wait to have all the facts in. It's just not possible, whether it is personal, domestic, or business—whatever the context—to make purely rational or empirical decisions. So an authentic voluntary association is one that not only provides an opportunity for the interplay of different lifestyles and perspectives; it provides also the occasion for group decisions.

From my experience I came to the view that voluntary associations oriented to social concerns represent a major ecumenical movement of modern history. In them you have people of various religious perspectives—Protestants, Catholics, atheists, and people who would admit to no religious commitments. In a voluntary association there is some problem which these people of different perspectives want to deal with, and in the process you discover that their differences in religious perspective are not adequately expressed by their labels.

I had some instructive experiences in Chicago with the Roman Catholic labor arbitrator, John Lapp. He and I took turns as head of the Independent Voters of Illinois. Once we decided to bring together the executives of certain major voluntary associations of Chicago. There would be about ten or a dozen of us, and we would spend a whole weekend together, discussing group interrelationships and such questions as, What were we trying to do, anyway? By one o'clock the question would be, Why are we trying to do it? And then someone would ask, "Jim, what does the theologian say?"

The important thing about these experiences was that, despite the different religious labels that would have separated us, including those who had no conscious theological interest, come one or two o'clock in the morning you found an opportunity finally to get underneath the labels. You found that, in some measure, with frustrations due to the inadequacy of the language that we have inherited, and especially the fact that the language of traditional Judaism as well as of Christianity became moldy, this was an opportunity to try to identify—what?—the vitamins, the vital elements in another person's existence.

So a voluntary association is the means of bringing together people with radically different roots, different social roots. The ideal voluntary association is the one in which you have a plurality, including ethnic plurality. In Chicago we fought very hard and with some success to bring blacks and women into associations like the I.V.I.

Eventually a group has to make a decision. For instance, in the I.V.I. we had to endorse candidates for public office. After we had established a reputation as being not merely a self-interest group, we were ourselves astonished at the influence we had. We simply had to pass out sample ballots. Because so many people were convinced that we were not self-serving, our workers would simply stand in front of voting booths and people would come by and ask, "Where's the I.V.I. ballot?" We'd say, "Just take a copy of it here!"

On one occasion we refused to support the handpicked candidate of the mayor of Chicago, a Democrat. Finally he called me in and said, "Do you mean to say you're willing to have the Republican isolationist go to Congress?" I said, "We don't care. It's just as good for an isolationist to go as this fellow." But the next day he called me up and said, "I'll give you twenty-four hours. If you can name a candidate that I can accept, I'll throw my fellow out." We did. And he did throw him out. The reason for that was we controlled two hundred precincts. That's an aspect of power.

ESCHATOLOGICAL AND MYSTICAL RELIGION

One can make the distinction between religions that are eschatological and those that are mystical. Mystical religions tend mainly to emphasize the suprahistorical. Eschatological religions see some end and responsibility in history. The idea that history is going somewhere is characteristic of Old Testament prophetism. The messianic idea, the demand for a society of justice and mercy, is found there. So in an eschatological religion there is a sense that God has a purpose in history: the creation of the society of justice and mercy. An eschatological religion says, you have to find the fundamental meaning of human existence in human community and in human history. Therefore it is also a historical religion. Time is of the essence—and hope.

This is of tremendous significance in contrast, for instance, to Buddhism. Buddhism is not a historical religion; Nirvana represents an attempt to escape from history into authentic existence, a fulfillment of being. There was a rule in the *Sangha,* the Buddhist community: You may not discuss politics. To be sure, it extols self-control and compassion, and there have been changes in time—Buddhism has a long history. But Buddhists have mainly been ahistorical and apolitical. I would not say that an eschatological religion is antimystical but that it tries to find meaning in the struggle for mercy and justice.

Secondly, and of equal importance for me, an eschatological religion is political. In continuity with ancient Mesopotamian religion, Old Testament symbolism is political. If you ask what are the motives and basic concepts of Old Testament prophetism, you can see that the possibilities are fairly limited. There is the symbolism that is drawn from the political order, symbolism drawn from the domestic order (the family), and symbolism drawn from the personal or individual order (for example, *metanoia*). There are a lot of sub-symbols in the Old and New Testament, for instance, "shepherd," or "vine and branches." But the primary symbols in the Old Testament are political symbols—covenant, Messiah, and the Reign of God. "Covenant" is the transformation of a symbol that came out of international politics in the ancient Middle East.

In the prophet Hosea you have a combination of political and domestic symbolism. The relationship between Yahweh and the "faithless bride" he is pursuing suggests the family symbolism. But I think it is wrong to say there is a great contrast between Hosea and Amos, for both prophets hold to the idea of the covenant. I would say that, insofar as the domestic symbolism is brought in, there is an enrichment. You have a mixture also in New Testament symbolism; "the Father" is a domestic symbol, but the Reign of God, "kingdom of God," is a political symbol.

Kingdom! The distinctive feature of the political symbolism of the Old Testament and ancient Mesopotamia is that the political symbolism insists that the meaning of human existence has to take into account the whole of existence—the life of the entire territory, and not merely personal or interpersonal life or individual devotion.

As I have suggested, however, in a democracy there must be a "separation of powers." Whitehead had an insight into this when he said that, when the axiom "Render unto Caesar the things which are Caesar's and unto God the things which are God's" [Matt. 22:21] was propounded, a new principle of social organization came into being.

An eschatological religion is one that attempts to overcome the spatialization of loyalty. A good illustration of demonic loyalty to spaces and the denial of a universal loyalty is seen in the Nazi slogan, *Blut und Boden,* our blood and our soil. In the Old Testament prophets the temporal element brings all spaces under judgment. At the same time, all spaces are supported by the divine, so there is not a radical asceticism but a recognition of divine creativity with respect to space. But in the last analysis time informs and overcomes space.

Idolatry is a form of spatialization, a belief that you can identify particular spaces as ultimate—"my church, my national tradition." "This Bible which I can carry right in my pocket will protect me if a bullet comes . . . I can also pull it out and I can answer any question you like." All of these exaggerated claims represent a form of idolatry, a spatialization of the divine. My colleague at Harvard Divinity School, Professor Frank Cross, has reminded us that Yahweh resided in a tent, not to be confined to a particular space.

One can admit with Plato that you cannot take any one symbol to be adequate. Whitehead used to say in his lectures that the genius of Plato rested in the fact that he was never able to settle for any one perspective. You have to work one through until it won't work any longer, and then try another one. Plato developed a polymorphous conception of truth.

If we survey the history of the eschatological and the mystical views of religion, we find that they are again and again joined. For example, Helen C. White in the introductory section of her *Mysticism of William Blake* [New York, 1927, 1964] gives an account of great mystics who maintained the eschatological outlook. Here she mentions such figures as Isaiah, Joachim of Fiore, the Spiritual Franciscans, and the Quaker leaders George Fox and John Woolman.

The theory of spatialization is spelled out best of all in Friedrich Schelling. Spatialization is the type of religion that says the holy—that which is exempt from criticism—is found in "our tradition," or in "our book," or in "my inner life." The interiorization of piety is also a kind of spatialization, insofar as it represents a neglect of social responsibility in the larger territory.

"A TIME TO KEEP SILENCE" (ECCLESIASTES 3:7)

I'm sorry I did not have the occasion, this evening, to talk to you about Margaret, because when we got into the area of religion and art she would always play a great role. And in the realm of politics, as well. You know the story about Margaret: she insisted that since I was such a conservative in politics, my towel must always be on the right on the towel rack.

So I have spoken about "intimacy and ultimacy" and have tried to show that intimacy is to be understood in the social and not merely individual context, to be authentically personal.

Before we came together this evening I recalled a story that joins these two dimensions of existence. In Germany there was a vigorous anti-Nazi, a professor of the Old Testament at Marburg, Professor Balla. He had acquired national notoriety among the Nazis when he translated a passage from Jeremiah, "My people say, '*Heil, Heil,*' and they know not what they mean" [see Jer. 8:11].

One evening shortly before I went back home some of the faculty at Marburg arranged a farewell party for me. There Professor Balla had a newspaper clipping from London in his hand which he read to me—a report on what the dean of St. Paul's had told about his experience in Nazi Germany. Among other things he said the British were astonished to hear people speak of the Fuhrer as "our redeemer." He said there couldn't be anything more blasphemous than that. And Balla, ashamed of what the Nazis were doing, sarcastically complained about it. He held out the clipping and said, "He accepted hospitality over here, and then he goes home to London, and look what he says about us! Aaah!" A silence fell over the room.

"Well," I said, "I really am stuck. Here's a farewell party for me, and I'm going back now, and the word will come back to you about what I say about Germany. I have accepted hospitality, right here and in plenty of other places. If I go home and—recognizing that I'm indebted to you for your hospitality—say 'The trains are running on time, things seem to be going very well,' you'll look at each other and say, 'I didn't know he was half as stupid as that!' But on the other hand, if I tell what I have seen, then you'll say I have violated my hospitality! So I have to ask you, what should I say?"

Balla was so excited—he had a wineglass in one hand and the newspaper clipping in the other—and he came across the living room to me with his hand shaking. I said again, "I ask you, *what should I say? What should I say, then? I've accepted hospitality here.*"

He shouted at me, "Say *Nichts! Nichts!*"

Belatedly, I recognize that now is the time for me to say "*Nichts.*"

3 · *The Vocation of Ministry and*
The Praying Hands

Was it Harold Laski who projected a vision of a future society in which there would be no more religion—no clergy, no churches, and no theologians? It would be a completely secular society. The antipathy is an old one, based on a hatred of a vaguely defined authoritarianism. Recognizing this antipathy to organized religion, I as a young minister was complimented when anyone told me that I did not look like a minister. I was pleased when William Wallace Fenn, Professor of Systematic Theology and the former Dean of Harvard Divinity School, said in a lecture that Jesus was not a parson. He thought there is an important difference between a parson and an authentic example of the vocation of the ministry.

Religion is often discussed and agonized over because it has to do with the basic meaning of human existence. And that meaning has to do with the relationships between the parts and the whole. For the original meaning of the term *vocation* we must turn to passages in the Bible: Jesus calling his disciples; Isaiah's response to a call, insisting upon his unworthiness—"Woe is me, for I am a man of unclean lips"; Elijah being confronted by a great wind, an earthquake, and a fire, and finding God not in them but in the "still small voice" commanding him to regain his mission as a prophet. In the Old Testament, God's call is directed not only to the individual but also to Israel, a faith community.

In the Gospels we find that ministry is a call to servanthood. "Even the Son of man came not to be ministered unto," says Jesus, "but to minister" [Mark 10:45]. The ministry is a proclamation of good news, the news that there is a sustaining, loving, creative, judging, forgiving, transforming power ushering in a new community. This power is not made with human hands and is not under human control. Again the message is to the individual, urging *metanoia*, "a change of heart, mind, and soul." It is also a call to a newly burgeoning community, transcending nation, race, sex, and class. In the first call to the individual the fundamental change is *intimate;* but in both the first and the second it is *ultimate.*

The Lowell Lectures are broadcast under the auspices of The Cambridge Forum, Herbert F. Vetter, Jr., Director. Adams's lecture, given as part of a series in which the guests discussed their vocations, was broadcast on June 5, 1985. His prayer for the ordination of the Rev. Ann Margaret Schellenberg is appended.

Within the first century the young church adopted a sense of corporate responsibility, such as caring for widows, caring for and educating orphans, and even devising credit unions. Most important, here, is the assertion by this newly formed group of the right to form an independent association—one recognizing an authority higher than that of Caesar. That the Christians had presumed to form an independent association was taken as the legal basis for their persecution. Alfred North Whitehead described this as a new principle of social organization; today we call it the freedom of association and the separation of powers. In this ancient association a person was a member not by reason of birth or some other ascription, but by voluntary choice. Here we see continuity with the Old Testament idea of the voluntary acceptance of a call. Striking is the fact that the dominant biblical symbols, or root metaphors, for this conception of the call are not private symbols, or even merely personal symbols. They are political symbols, such as covenant, king, kingdom of God, messiah. The call, then, is not a call to a merely privatized piety; it points to one's responsibility in the entire community.

An even more embracing and centering symbol is available. I am thinking, here, of Albrecht Dürer's drawing of 1507, from the Albertina Collection in Vienna, *The Praying Hands* [a study for the altarpiece of the Dominican Church in Frankfurt]. The praying hands point to the source of being and meaning beyond all creatures. As Boswell's Dr. Johnson would say, "These hands express more than wonder. They express awe before the divine majesty." Or as Augustine would say: They warn us against giving to any creature the love that belongs alone to the Creator, whether that creature be a liturgical formula, an institution, or a document. Each of these creatures may point to the ultimate ground, but none can exhaust it or define its bounds. It cannot be spatialized.

Vocation, then, is something that comes from a formative and transformative power that is sovereign and is the enemy of idolatry, whether it be a religious, ecclesiastical, cultural, or secular idolatry. The idea of vocation of course has a long history. For fifteen hundred years it was elaborately articulated in monasticism, which came to birth to recover the church from an easy accommodation to the world. Later, after monasticism was rejected in the Reformation, it was said that the Christian should be a monk in the world.

From the Middle Ages came another invention—the idea of a profession, a conception that impinged upon the vocation of the ministry. A professional in the medieval view was one certified to wear an academic gown, that is, one who had had an education in the arts and sciences and thus had become familiar with the characteristic value preferences of the tradition, and with the criticism or legitimation of these preferences. Secondly, a professional person was expected to have a systematic theory of the purpose and function of a given profession, that is, a theory on the basis of which one could critically understand and improve the particular skills of the profession. The primary responsibility of the professional, however, was to provide leadership—a servanthood—in the community. Modern theological education has adapted something of this paradigm, recognizing that the vocation of ministry requires disciplined training.

But the history of the professions in large measure has tended toward increasing specialization. Each of these specializations claims a department in the university. Dean Willard Sperry, of Harvard Divinity School, used to tell the story of his first evening as a graduate student at Yale. In the refectory he spoke to the student sitting next to him, announcing that his specialty was New Testament Greek; the other student said that his field was mathematics, whereupon the conversation ended!

It is in this context that one must define the ministry, if it is to be viewed as a profession. One must, to be sure, recognize the dangers of professionalism: a threat to the wholeness and personalism of a dedicated ministry.

Now I must mention an additional feature of the ministry: the roles of the minister are usually more numerous than in any other profession. I cannot presume to name all of them. The minister is expected to be a religious leader, responsible for religious education; in crucial ways the administrator of a religious institution with a budget; a liturgist; a spiritual director; a skilled person constantly facing problems of the family, including birth and death, and the rites of passage. The minister is expected also to be a skilled preacher, familiar with the lore of the tradition, and a theologian withal, and perhaps even a prophet. The minister also aims to be the curer of souls for the whole person in a community of faith—all of this with praying hands.

This is a staggering list. The minister has some difficulty maintaining self-respect with regard to any particular specialty. I had this experience in my parish in Wellesley [Massachusetts], where I had some of the best physicians, lawyers, and publishers of greater Boston. I felt many times these fellows were looking at me and saying, "What do you know comparable to what I have to do?" But the history of the professions, as I say, has been moving in the direction of specialization, while the roles of the minister remain more numerous than in any other profession. They are not possible to perform except through the assistance not only of other clergy but also and especially of the laity, that is, of the lay apostolate.

One thing more has been implicit in a community of faith such as appears within the church. I recall that when I was a student I once ventured to consult Dr. Samuel M. Crothers, the eminent essayist and minister of the First Parish in Cambridge. I told him that I was considering going into teaching rather than into a parish. Immediately he said that he had a special sympathy for the college or university teacher, who has students passing through his courses. He can become personally acquainted with a few of them, but then they disappear, as a new four-year class appears. In the church, he said, there is a larger measure of continuity. I am now performing, he said, the marriage ceremony for members whom initially I christened and whom I have known all of these years. And here he was of course displaying some of the variety of roles already mentioned.

In the face of this variety of roles, the minister, especially the young minister, attempts to achieve personal identity within the community of faith where challenge and change are always present, and within a wider community, including even the community of humankind. In my first parish I took my turn as visitor at the hospital and as preacher at the jail. In addition to customary parish calling, I regularly visited an elderly woman suffering from an incurable disease. Then there were the talks I made at the public school. On one occasion the Protestant Ministers Association confronted the Roman Catholic local authorities, who had urged the mayor to close the movie theaters on Sunday. These authorities were unwilling to rely upon the attempt to persuade their flocks. They wished to resort to the secular arm, although there was no evident consensus in the community. Here they were following a strategy similar to that of the so-called religious right today, to bring about legislation against abortion and free choice in the face of widespread conscientious disagreement with them in both church and non-church circles. The Ministers Association opposed the closing of the theaters, much to the surprise of the mayor, who thought it was a very good idea. Here, then, I encountered a problem related to civil liberties which constantly appears in the church and in the community.

Later on I was to serve for over a decade as chair of the Committee on Church and State of the Massachusetts Civil Liberties Union. (And let me pause here to express warm appreciation for the lawyers who give their time dealing with these problems in the Civil Liberties Union.) Here is an area in which the local minister must attempt to acquire some competence, or at least to remain informed. With praying hands.

As a fledgling minister, in Salem, I acquired experience very early. The city was in turmoil because of the strike of thousands of mill workers, some of the mill executives being in my congregation and in adjoining Protestant parishes. On inquiry the Ministers Association was told by the mill executives that they had the situation under control. But this was an overstatement. After several weeks, violence in the streets erupted, and increased. I began to attend union meetings, and I learned something about the people across the tracks. It turned out that the "right thinking" people were, through the newspapers, receiving a lopsided account of the issues. I discovered that mill executives in other companies in other cities were outraged by the claims being made in the press by the local executives. In a way, that was a relatively easy situation to deal with, namely to preach and to claim publicly that we were entitled to increasing violence unless we possessed informed public opinion.

In this situation I enjoyed a certain advantage. After graduating from Harvard Divinity School in 1927, I had gone to Heidelberg, Germany for a summer course. Before the summer was over I attended a Nazi rally and parade, got into an argument with Nazi sympathizers, and then almost got beaten up. I was rescued somewhat forcibly by an unemployed anti-Nazi who took sympathy on this innocent abroad. After taking me out of harm's way, he shouted at me, "You fool! Don't you know that in Germany today you keep your mouth shut or you get your head bashed in?" I thought that was the next thing on the agenda.

In this whole scenario I learned by reason of increased palpitation the meaning of the word *existential*. Nine years later I was to learn more by spending almost a year in Germany, in association with the underground anti-Nazi movement of the Confessing Churches, finally myself being taken in by the Gestapo. So I saw here not only the heroism of the dissenters, some of whom were sent to concentration camps, no doubt with praying hands; I noticed also the failure of the majority in the churches who by default collaborated with Hitler.

In this somewhat dangerous situation I felt more and more the need for some kind of interior privacy, for getting to my "center." So I went off to live in the Benedictine monastery at Maria Laach, where I learned a good deal about spiritual direction, prayer, and new conceptions of liturgy. I learned also that the conflicts in church and society in Europe were much similar to those at home. They were in part conflicts over freedom of association—Hitler having succeeded in suppressing all free association, including the churches and the unions.

They were also conflicts about what the sociologists call *ascribed* status, status over which the individual has no control, such as one's race, sex, and class, in contrast to *achieved* status, status depending upon one's own free capacity for performance. The famous German Catholic political scientist, Carl Schmitt, called these conflicts struggles over "powers of origin"—origin of race, sex, and so on—as seen in the Nazi designation of "alien races," especially, of course, the Jews.

The American counterpart is discrimination against blacks, as well as against Jews and other ethnic minorities. The power of origin or ascribed status, here, is the superiority of so-called white pigment—you might say "pigment idolatry." So discrimination against blacks turned out to be the Nazism in us and in our churches. This religion of pigment is still very much alive, although in optimistic moments we like to think otherwise.

But what of the status of women? As you remember, Hitler insisted that women should stay in the church and in the kitchen. This ascribed status for women has been under scrutiny and attack for a long time. In certain respects greater progress has been made in the worlds of business and government than in the church. We should be proud that half of the students at the Divinity School today are women.

Constance Parvey gave a lecture recently on the topic, "Why Do I Stay in the Patriarchal Church?" Her answer was that the transformation of institutional structures is at least in principle possible in the church, particularly since the number of women seeking to enter the ministry is increasing; here we see people seeking to participate in making social decisions, without the restrictions of ascribed status, of being "only a woman."

One of the frustrations in this area, as well as in that of race relations, is that of only attitudes being changed. In the black power movement we heard again and again from the blacks, "We are weary to death of your liberal *attitudes*. We want to see a change in institutional structures, and jobs made available." What is the principle at stake in all of this? It is that a person be permitted and encouraged to be a deliberating, deciding, responsible person. Ascribed status reduces the person to something like a thing, encased in a constructed cage, limiting the ways in which the transforming power of the divine may work in the human realm.

But there is a wide range of problems confronted by the vocation of the ministry and of the church—at the macrocosmic level of the political and the economic orders, for example, in the problems of the nuclear age. I have already hinted at some of these matters. In the church none of these problems may be dealt with adequately from the pulpit alone. They require discussion in small groups from a variety of perspectives, in face of the actualities to be analyzed and with the assistance of leaders and of commissions within the church and the society. The vitality of the church, as we saw also in Nazi Germany, depends upon the small groups of the church, often across denominational boundaries. The vitality of the church depends on what Luther called the *ecclesiola in ecclesia,* the small church in the large. In this involvement of the laity we are ideally led not only to the priesthood but also to the prophethood of all believers, recognizing that God moves in mysterious ways, even through secular agencies and figures and, of course, with the assistance of the other professions.

The process of transformation begins with the individual in the faith community. I recall a meeting of the board of trustees of a local church in which a member had frequently used racial epithets. At this meeting he was challenged: Did he wish his racial views to be proclaimed from the pulpit? Oh, no, he said. Then the question was put to him: What then is the purpose of this church? He said he was no theologian. But then he was reminded that he was a member of the board of trustees. What is the purpose of this church? he was asked again. What do you say is the purpose of this church? Finally, at a late hour in the evening he said, astoundingly, "The purpose of this church—well, the purpose of this church is to get hold of people like me and change them."

Praying hands were appearing. Here, then, is the ultimate and the intimate thrust of the vocation of ministry, of all ministry and every dedicated profession—openness to and reliance upon the judging and transforming power of the divine, praying hands.

AN ORDINATION PRAYER (1988)

Infinite Source of all Being, the Sun beyond the suns, the sap of life in our bones and being, we are grateful that Thou hast called us into a community of faith with its covenant and its vocations. Our covenant is from Thee, with Thee and with each other in a community reaching beyond the boundaries of parish and denomination and nation. Our vocations lay and clerical are rooted in the local community of faith, but in

their service and responsibility they are directed to both the world and
the church, critical of both, yea also of the vaunted spirit of the age.

In the hallowed place of this congregation we acknowledge the gifts of
nature and of grace, the unearned heritage of the freedom to believe and
also the freedom to raise unsettling questions. We acknowledge that war
and exploitation, arrogance and intolerance, apathy and complacency, the
poverty and homelessness around us, are a part of us, that we in our
suburban captivity cannot wash our hands in soothing innocency. We remain aware of our responsibility for the form and import of religious
education, of our responsibility to encourage critical appreciation of our
tradition and of other faiths and traditions. We acknowledge that mere
conformity can lead to deformity, also that thoughtless nonconformity is
itself a deformity.

To beloved Meg Schellenberg, who is now being ordained into the
ministry, shared by the laity, of truth communicated with humility and
compassion, into the ministry of nurturing individual persons and families, of youth and age, may there be granted the spirit that informs and
also bursts through the letter, remembering yet that the letter can give
life and that the spirit can kill. May she remain firm in her conviction of
the divinely derived dignity of every person, ready to bring the grace and
healing of thy divine presence. May she in the freedom of the pulpit strive
ever for a balance between the priesthood and the prophethood of all believers, endeavoring to bring them together, the priest offering the gentle
balm of mercy to those who are discouraged or are ill in body, mind, or
estate, the prophet under the covenant rightly dividing the word of truth
about us and our society. May she be the sharer of our joys and our sorrows, the witness to thy sustaining, judging, and transforming power.
May she continue in her disciplined pursuit of learning, and also in her
already probing curiosity to illumine the brighter and the darker corners
of human being in both its individual and its corporate forms.

And may this hour be for us all one of the common rededication to the
authentic life and joy of the church and its families, leading us to the
fulfillment of freedom in faith. Amen.

4 · *The Latest Word*

I remember reading the literary critic Kenneth Burke years ago. He said there is no happier moment in our lives than the moment when we can give utterance to unambiguous vituperation. I can name a happier moment, the moment when one is the recipient of unambiguous hyperbole. I remember that Christopher Morley years ago said that after he had published a book he was very anxious to read the reviews because he would then find out what he had been doing. And so today, I have been recipient of many a surprise.

But I have been a pastor, and from time to time became aware of the limitations of the endurance of the people in the pews. I can remember when I used to preach occasionally as a visitor in the Danvers Church. There was a clock at the other end of the sanctuary, and around the clock was the legend: Redeem the Time [see Col. 4:5].

I want to make a few additional brief remarks. As a former instructor in English composition at Boston University, where I taught History of English and American Literature in my youth, I want to make a correction. The item here assigned me is entitled: "The Last Word." I would like to correct that. What is meant is, the *latest*.

Now, finally, I want to read to you a favorite set of lines by Carl Sandburg: "I am riding on the limited express, on one of the crack trains of the nation. Hurtling across the prairie in the blue haze of the dark air, go fifteen all-steel coaches holding a thousand people. All the coaches shall be scrap and rust, and all men and women laughing in the diners and sleepers shall pass to ashes. I ask the man in the smoker where he is going, and he answers, 'Omaha, I hope.'"

So here we are, as pilgrims—friends here together today, as a part of our pilgrimage, the pilgrimage in which we have been learning who we are, and, sometimes, whither we are bound. It is that fellowship and that pilgrimage that has provided the strength of our lives, and the sense of our destiny.

Like other people, from time to time, we come to moments of despair. When we look at the suffering around us, and think daily of the enormous

Adams gave this response to tributes to him and his work at a celebration of his eighty-fifth birthday, at the Arlington Street Church (Unitarian Universalist) in Boston, Massachusetts, on November 8, 1986. Reprinted by permission from *Honoring JLA on His 85th Birthday,* ed. Judy Deutsch (James Luther Adams Foundation, 1987).

grief of suffering, when we include also the third world, not to speak of the deprived in our own so-called culture—at those moments, I recall one of the great passages in my judgment in the history of literature, and of religious literature. That passage is in the prophet Hosea. Hosea, apparently considering the emphasis on God's wrath and God's judgment set forth in Amos, decided that if we are all to be understood only in terms of that judgment, we're all lost. And then he presented that remarkable parable—one of the outstanding ideas in the history of thought, especially when you contrast it with the Greek sense of Nemesis, according to which the wrath of the gods continues through the generations. But Hosea says that Yahweh, in the face of the faithless Israel, pursues Israel, and pleads, "I care not what you have done. Know you not that I love you? Come back. Come back for new beginnings."

And so for me, this is a basic element of faith—in the face of despair regarding our own accomplishments or that which is going on around us. We can hear the plea, "Come back. There are always new beginnings."

So today, I express my appreciation to you all for the new beginning—*not* the last word—the new beginning we are experiencing today.

Part Two

Great Companions

"PRACTICE OPPOSITE VIRTUES AND OCCUPY THE DISTANCE BETWEEN them." Adams cites Pascal's maxim to amplify his view that the task of a person's life is "the achievement of unity or harmony while embracing contrast." His own thought embraces strong contrasts, notably his emphases on the institutional and the personal sides of human life. Many of his essays accent the embodiment of historically significant commitments in social institutions; the essays in this section accent the decisive role of individual personalities as agents of creative thought and action.

Throughout his life Adams has developed his thought in dialogue with colleagues and great thinkers of his own and past generations. He locates each of these "great companions" within a major institution—a university, a voluntary association, a church, a profession, a political community; typically, then, he focuses attention on the social-ethical import of the individual's life and thought. The social context of religious commitment is "the distance between" that Adams finally seeks to occupy.

"Roger Baldwin: By Their Groups Shall Ye Know Them" celebrates the life of the founder of the American Civil Liberties Union and, in brief compass, treats the roots of civil liberty and modern democracy among the left-wing Puritans of the seventeenth century. Adams reminds us that individual freedom is itself an institutional achievement, sustained by freedom of association.

In the second essay, "The Classical Humanism of Irving Babbitt," Adams develops a philosophical theme, "the primacy of the will," which recurs at several points in these essays (see Chapters 2, 16, 17). It first emerged for Adams during his studies of comparative literature at Harvard with Professor Babbitt, a teacher in whom he found "a tempered mind, almost abysmal knowledge, and the ability to make imperative the study of perennial and fundamental questions." Adams dissents from the conservative implications of Babbitt's "answers," but he takes the man as a pedagogical and scholarly model. In a personal tribute to Babbitt, he cites Friedrich von Hügel's words about Ernst Troeltsch—another intellectual mentor who figures in these essays—as applying equally to Babbitt: "Surely . . . the most ready, yet also the most costly method of learning deeply, that is, of growing in our very questions and in our whole temper of mind, is to learn in admiration of some other living fellow man, recognized as more gifted, or more trained, or more experienced than ourselves." A central purpose of education, Adams holds, is "to grow in our very questions."

In "Charles Eliot Norton, *Genius loci,* Shady Hill," Adams notes that it was Babbitt who first introduced him to Charles Eliot Norton, the Harvard professor of art history in an earlier generation. The affinity Adams feels for Norton is evident in his portrait of the man as "gentleman scholar" and "genius of the place"—the grounds of the Shady Hill mansion in Cambridge where Jim and Margaret built their home.

Adams has said that he used to assign William James to students of English composition as a model of lucid prose style. Nevertheless, in "William James: 'No Man for Committees,'" he seeks the biographical roots of James's mystical conception of religion and criticizes its individualistic, ahistorical character. The essay, occasioned by Adams's discovery of a letter from Friedrich von Hügel to James, is a notable example of original research in intellectual history.

George Huntston Williams has been Adams's student at Meadville Theological School, his colleague at Harvard Divinity School, and his close friend for many years. The essay on Williams, an erudite and prolific church historian, reviews Williams's broad-ranging scholarly and social concerns and locates him within the history and philosophy of church history.

Students of Adams are familiar with his lament that the history and philosophy of law tend to be bypassed in the now dominant "case-study" method of legal education pioneered at Harvard. The essay, "Ernst Troeltsch and Harold Berman on Natural Law," exhibits Adams's keen interest in the philosophical basis of law. Troeltsch, the German historian, liberal theologian, and philosopher of history, is the figure to whom Adams bears the closest affinity. (Asked if he were closer to Tillich or to

Whitehead, Adams once said, "There is always Troeltsch!") Together with
Harold Berman, Adams for a number of years taught seminars in religion
and law at Harvard Law School.

"John XXIII: The Pope Who Would Go Window-shopping" is an af-
fectionate portrait of the pope who said he wanted to "open the windows"
of his Church, and a commentary on the obstacles to agreement between
Catholics and Protestants. Adams first encountered Angelo Giuseppe
Roncalli, Pope John XXIII, during his appointment as a Protestant observer at the Second Vatican Council.

The final two essays in this section are on Paul Tillich, whose writings
Adams translated in *The Protestant Era* (1948) and interpreted in numerous works. "Reminiscences of Paul Tillich" is a unique record of the development and personality of this vastly influential liberal theologian. "*In
Memoriam:* Words for Paul Johannes Tillich" is a moving, personal tribute.
In closing, Adams celebrates the companionship enjoyed in dialogue with
a great figure of our time, a teacher who enables us to grow in our very
questions.

G.K.B.

5 · Roger Baldwin: By Their Groups Shall Ye Know Them

He has showed you, O man, what is good;
and what does the Lord require of you but to do justice,
and to love kindness,
and to walk humbly with your God?

Micah 6:8

Let me first express my appreciation and satisfaction to join you here in the Unitarian Society of Wellesley Hills, to celebrate the anniversary of the birth of Roger Baldwin, the founder of the American Civil Liberties Union. Fifty years ago, when I was minister in this parish, the Baldwin family had lived on this avenue at the top of the hill. Indeed, Roger was born there.[1]

I early became vividly aware of the significance of the ACLU. Let me explain this briefly. Here, in 1935, I was called to be a professor at Meadville Theological School, the Unitarian seminary in Chicago. Before going to Chicago, however, Mrs. Adams and I went abroad for almost a year. In Germany—Nazi Germany—I became fully aware of the contribution of Roger Baldwin and of the importance of the ACLU in a democratic society. One of the first things Hitler did was to abolish or suppress all associations independent of or critical of the state. With the alleged approval of the majority he negated every claim to democratic rights. Actually, however, authentic democracy is not the rule of the majority. It is a constitutional order limited by a bill of rights, as Roger never tired of reminding us. In Germany I became associated with the anti-Nazi underground of the Confessing Churches. Mrs. Adams prudently removed with the children to Holland, possibly anticipating that I would come under the scrutiny of the Gestapo. Later on, back in this country, I became a member of the ACLU; I served on the Board of Directors for almost a decade, and was also the chairperson of the Committee on Church-State relations.

This address was given at the Unitarian Society of Wellesley Hills, Massachusetts, on January 20, 1984, for a celebration of the hundredth anniversary of the birth of Roger Baldwin.

61

Considering Roger's role as founder of the ACLU, one recalls the words of Ralph Waldo Emerson, "an institution is the lengthened shadow of one man." Roger would not like to have those words applied to him; he was irrevocably modest and would insist that the ACLU was the work of many men and women. Included among them he would mention particularly John Haynes Holmes, Minister of the Community Church in New York, also a Unitarian. For years Dr. Holmes was chairman of the Board of Directors of the ACLU.

Speaking of Unitarianism, I should note that Roger attended and later taught in the Sunday School of this parish. He said he grew up recognizing that Unitarianism is a heresy, "a very respectable heresy." "I got to revere Jesus, not as a divine figure but for what he said." In answer to a question from Peggy Lamson, his biographer, he said,

> Yes, I went to church very regularly. I helped to teach Sunday School, and I even listened to the preacher. In fact, as I look back I would say that social work began in my mind in the Unitarian Church. . . . My grandmother's pastor was Dr. Edward Everett Hale, a Unitarian gentleman who was distinguished in Boston annals. I knew him toward the end of his life. He had started a society called "Lend a Hand" to help people who couldn't help themselves, and a group of us children banded together at our Unitarian Church to join the "Lend a Hand Society" there. I took it all quite seriously.

We need not go further into his family background than to say that his grandfather Baldwin was founder in Boston of the Young Men's Christian Union, and that Roger liked to walk the streets with him and meet his constituents. His uncle for many years occupied the former residence of William Ellery Channing on Mt. Vernon Street. He was president of the Long Island Railroad, but also the Director of the National Child Labor Committee and a trustee of Tuskegee College. "My father," Roger said, "was a business associate and a friend of Jews, my mother an agnostic and something of a feminist."

After his graduation from Harvard College, Roger went to St. Louis to engage in social work. After a time, one of his associates dared him to go to hear a lecture by the anarchist Emma Goldman. He was permanently influenced by her opposition to all coercion. Indeed, he published a small volume of anarchists' writings, though he never called himself one. He thought of it as one approach to the problems of democracy, the decentralization of power.

When the First World War came, his conviction of pacifism was strengthened. A Harvard classmate wrote to him asking him to protest the pacifist stance of Jane Addams of Hull House in Chicago. He responded by writing, "I am thoroughly with Miss Addams and the pacifists, now and all the time. I am unfortunately one of those who takes the Sermon on the Mount seriously, which does not square with the current conception of patriotism." And he went on in this vein. This letter was written in March 1917. In April he left St. Louis to donate his services to the American Union Against Militarism in New York City.

From New York he went on to Washington and started a society to defend people who were prosecuted for their pacifism. In 1920 he founded the American Civil Liberties Union. He tells us that the Union defended around a thousand people, tirelessly working for their pardons, succeeding fully only twelve years later under President Roosevelt. It was only years later that it became possible by law for conscientious objectors to become exempt from military service under certain conditions. Roger remained director of the ACLU from 1920 to 1950.

Whatever you or I think of pacifism, we must say that the ACLU became a major source of appeal to the Bill of Rights, and especially to the First Amendment with its guarantee of the freedoms of speech, assembly, and association, and the separation of state and church. In a fairly short time the ACLU branched out to oppose the deportation of aliens by reason of their opinions. The ACLU promoted self-government for Indians, and also collective bargaining. Formerly, Roger reminds us, the struggle between employers and the unions caused the death of two hundred people a year; a great number also were killed by lynching. Baldwin and the ACLU opposed violence, demanding the settlement of disputes on constitutional principles. So the ACLU promoted the constitutional principle of due process and brought into service hundreds of volunteer lawyers. Thus the ACLU defended the rights of blacks and other minorities. Roger was for years a supporter of the National Urban League. Eventually, the National Labor Relations Board was established.

On one occasion, Roger stood on the steps of a hall with Margaret Sanger when she was refused the freedom to promote the dissemination of information about birth control. He had been an officer of the juvenile court in St. Louis and turned his attention to the problems of criminal justice, holding that a better parole system and the use of work camps were required. He always held that so-called criminal justice was too much motivated by retribution. People as individuals need restitution. In his last years he asserted that the goal should be the eventual abolition of prisons. Widespread publicity came for the ACLU when they secured Clarence Darrow to defend the schoolteacher John Scopes against William Jennings Bryan. I need not fill in the list of Roger's activities in various international organizations, for example, in collaboration with Eleanor Roosevelt. After World War II he was invited to Japan by General MacArthur, who wished him to promote civil-liberty organizations in Japan.

"Civil liberty," said Roger, "is a refined way of life. It must always work against violence or special privilege in some form." And it cannot do this simply by cultivating liberal attitudes. It requires the power of organization, the organization of power.

Civil and religious liberty, we should remember, has a long, long history. In the modern era it began with the left-wing Puritans of the seventeenth century who struggled for the freedom to form a congregation, in contrast to the established church in which the monarch was the head. These spiritual ancestors of ours were working for a differentiated society in which ecclesiastical influence on politics would be reduced and in which political influence in the church would be eliminated. Toward this end they had to struggle for freedom of association, in order to establish a voluntary church. Previously one was a member of the church as well as of the state simply by being born in a territory. The left-wing Puritans were struggling for a free church in which membership would be voluntary, in which every man and woman had the right and the obligation to cooperate in making decisions on policy.

These Puritans found their model in the New Testament church. Here was a group depending only upon disciples and converts, a group independent of the mother church, the synagogue, but equally independent of the emperor. This independence brought them into conflict with the state, for no association was permitted except one licensed by Caesar. From a legal point of view these Christians had formed an illicit, and illegal, association. This was the legal basis for the persecution of the Christians. They had said, "Render unto Caesar that which is Caesar's, and unto God that which is God's." This was viewed as a shocking, indeed an atheistic, view. Alfred North Whitehead has said that this bifurcation of God and Caesar brought into history a new principle of social organization, the separation of powers, the separation of the public from the private sector.

In the seventeenth century the separation of powers meant that only believers should be members of a voluntary church. The voluntary church should not depend upon enforced taxation at the hands of the state. It is *our* enterprise, they said, and we pay the bills. For them the collection plate became a sort of sacrament.

This struggle was accompanied by the struggle against chartered monopolies or monopolies of any sort, including monopoly in religion. The demand for the independence of the voluntary church gave rise to demands for freedom of other associations, especially of dissenting organizations. From this came the invention of political parties. Previously, dissenters had been beheaded, but, with the formation of two or more parties, the dissenters were placed on expense accounts to occupy the opposition benches. Authentic freedom, then, requires freedom to form an association, freedom to leave the church, freedom to criticize church or state, freedom to bring about change or to resist change. This idea became an integral part of "the Protestant ethic."

This aspect of the Protestant ethic was present from the beginning in the American colonies, in the formation of the independent congregation in Scrooby, England, among the founders of the Plymouth Colony. Already in that century Cotton Mather promoted the formation of small groups "essaying to do good." Later on, independent groups were formed to promote the independence of the colonies. Benjamin Franklin, who formed major associations in his time, acknowledged his indebtedness to Cotton Mather. William Ellery Channing two generations later, in his essay entitled "Remarks on Associations," produced the first systematic study of the subject in American literature, also warning against the possibilities of tyranny within the structure of these associations. We also must recognize the freedom of antisocial and antiracial organizations to form.

We see, then, that Roger Baldwin bore witness in his life to a venerable heritage manifest already in the "Lend a Hand Society" in his parish.

Roger knew very well, however, that not all problems can be solved by voluntary associations; many of them should be on the conscience of the entire national community and should be dealt with through government action. Indeed, Roger witnessed changes of position in the Supreme Court as a consequence of ACLU activities.

From Roger's life we learn that through voluntary associations the responsibilities of citizenship are to be met in significant ways.

Our text for the morning from the Prophet Micah reads: "What doth the Lord require of thee but to do justice . . . and to walk humbly with thy God?" But that is a generality. So we may recall an old saying, "We think in generalities, but we live in details." The details need to be worked out through the groups in which we participate. Failure to participate is to transfer responsibility and power to others by default.

To participate, however, is more than a responsibility. It is the way in which the tie that binds, the bond of love, brings us together in a community seeking and engendering justice and mercy for all, including those Jesus called "the least of these."

This responsibility and love are implied in the New Testament saying, "By their fruits shall ye know them" [Matt. 7:20, King James Version]. A lesson to be drawn from Roger Baldwin's experience may be stated in a paraphrase: By their groups shall ye know them. He who says this is imbued with faith and hope.

Roger in his later life was once asked to say in one sentence how he would like to be remembered. In reply he said, "I would like to be described as a man of hope with faith in mankind."

Note

1. For the biographical details recounted here I am indebted to Mrs. Roy (Peggy) Lamson's biography of Roger Baldwin, and to the Cambridge Forum for a videotape of a conversation with Mr. Baldwin, recorded by David P. Allen.

6 · The Classical Humanism of Irving Babbitt

CONFUCIUS: *Tsze-Kung, you think, I suppose, that I am the one who learns many things and keeps them in memory.*
TSZE-KUNG: *Yes, but perhaps it is not so.*
CONFUCIUS: *No. I seek unity, all pervading.*

Theology, the queen of the sciences, is dead, or moribund. Not one of our theologians has had the virility or comprehensiveness of intellect to give unity to the efforts of influential and sensitive minds or to inject new vitality into institutions of religion. That is why many American students have had to turn to Irving Babbitt, a literary critic and a man avowedly outside all religious traditions, theological or institutional, for a philosophy of values.

What we need perhaps is a second Thomas Aquinas, someone who can correlate art, science, sociology, and religion into a hierarchy of values, someone who can suggest standards which may at the same time furnish a stimulus and a corrective. "Stimulus or correction," as Walter Pater said, "one hardly knows which to ask for first." Or, as Aristotle might have put it, we are rightly stimulated only when we are drawn to our true end.

Babbitt, professor of French literature at Harvard University, has not tried to furnish a synthesis of Thomistic dimensions, but he has at least begun with Aristotelian aims. The connecting theme of the essays collected in the volume, *On Being Creative,* is expressed in the Aristotelian dictum which is taken as its epigraph: "The first is not the seed but the perfect," with its implied disapproval of what we would term nowadays the "genetic method" and its implied approval of formative standards.

Babbitt is centrally concerned with the standards of cultural values, but his final appeal is neither to reason nor to the wisdom of the ages. The basis of his humanism is superrational insight. Let us recount the stages by which he has arrived at his new humanism.

We find ourselves today in a world in which the controls of traditional Christianity have to a great extent disappeared. How shall we replace

This essay is abridged from a review of *On Being Creative: And Other Essays* (Boston and New York: Houghton Mifflin, 1932) by Irving Babbitt; it appeared in *Hound and Horn* 6, no. 1 (October–December 1932).

those controls and still remain positive and critical? Naturally we cannot accept a dogmatic and revealed religion, Babbitt holds; he turns to the older humanism:

> The aim of the humanist, and that from the time of the ancient Greeks, has been the avoidance of excess. Anyone who sets out to live temperately and proportionately will find that he will need to impose upon himself a difficult discipline. His attitude towards life will necessarily be dualistic. It will be dualistic in the sense that he recognizes in man a "self" that is capable of exercising control and another "self" that needs controlling. The opposition between the two selves is well put by Cicero, one of the most influential of occidental humanists. "The natural constitution of the human mind," he says, "is twofold. One part consists in appetite, by the Greeks termed *hormē* ('impulse'), which hurries a man hither and thither; the other is reason, which instructs and makes clear what is to be done or avoided; thus it follows that reason fitly commands and appetite obeys." . . . This more or less stoical humanism has entered as an element, often as the dominant element, into many noble lives.

But there have been so many revolts against reason, so many attempts to get rid of this dualism between reason and appetite, that reason in the Ciceronian sense would seem to be inadequate. If the humanistic ideal is to prevail, there is a need for some new element which will guarantee the continuance of an effective dualism.

The second stage in the way to the new humanism is the discovery of the new element. The experience of Christianity and Confucianism, Babbitt appeals to here. A study of these traditions convinces him that

> there has been a curious omission in our modern attempts to construct sound philosophies of life. Behind the problem of the reason, there lurks a far more formidable problem—that of the will. The reason that has the support of the higher will, that, in Confucian phrase, is submissive to "the will of heaven," would seem better able to exercise control over the natural man than a reason that is purely self-reliant.

Christianity has offered this necessary control in the doctrine of grace, but not without supernatural and authoritative sanctions. The question that faces the modern era is, then, how to find, with the positive and critical method, support for a philosophy of life in something higher than reason, something that can take the place of Christian grace and save us from revolt against reason and from the anarchy of private judgment. This support is found in the immediate intuition of a higher will.

My own somewhat limited programme—for I am not setting up humanism as a substitute for religion—is to meet those who profess to be positive
and critical on their own ground and to undertake to show them that in
an essential respect they have not been positive and critical enough. . . .
Though the higher will in man is not amenable to the methods of the
laboratory, it may nevertheless be asserted as a primordial fact—something
of which one is immediately aware.

Babbitt is not unaware of the differences between various experiences
of immediacy of knowledge. He is mainly interested, however, in distinguishing between the true and the false immediacy, or what he calls the
higher and the lower immediacy. His interest in this distinction grows
out of his conviction, deepened by the study of the craving for immediacy
in both Christianity and Romanticism, that it is futile to attempt an
adequate philosophy of life without satisfying the desire for immediacy.
Indeed, he thinks that the important problem is that of discovering the
proper way of satisfying that desire.

It is on this point that Babbitt makes one of the most fundamental
distinctions in his whole system, that between the lower and the higher
immediacy. The first is the immediacy of the primitivist, e.g. Wordsworth, who is "'well pleased to recognize in nature and the language of
the sense' the 'guide' and 'guardian' of all his 'moral being.'" The other is
the immediacy of the saint, e.g. St. Bonaventura, who, "though ready on
occasion to interpret religiously natural appearances, yet affirms finally
that 'the soul knows God without the support of the outer senses.'" Beginning with this initial distinction, Babbitt proceeds to develop the
principal differences between humanism and primitivism.

Assuming, then, that both primitivist and humanist may have an experience of immediate awareness, how does the person of today, lacking
the supports of revealed religion, test the knowledge of which one is
immediately aware? According to Babbitt, there are three principal tests:
First, the immediacy should be "supersensuous," that is, it does not need
the support of the outer senses. Second, it should be "superrational," that
is, it utilizes the distinctions which the analytical reason alone can provide. Third, it should be followed by the "fruits of the spirit." The true
immediacy is not conducive to "cosmic loafing," but rather to ethical
work, *energeia*. Its characteristic virtue is humility, that is, submission to
the higher will and the law for human beings.

Romanticism, Babbitt believes, can pass none of these tests. It usually
involves the sensuous, the subrational, and "passiveness." Indeed, most of

the heresies, ancient and modern, are the result of "certain enormous repudiations" of intuition, reason, or will. Babbitt's humanism is a philosophy of intuition, of rational analysis, and of strenuous purpose. Whether all comers are satisfied as to the nature of intuition or not (they might not be satisfied with the primitivist or the religious account of it either), the important thing is that one's philosophy of life is based on the higher will and upon a belief in the value of rational analysis.

Where does the person who has no immediate awareness of the higher will get effective control for carrying on "the war in the cave"? If we refer to Babbitt's own words, we discover that "this awareness exists in very different degrees in different individuals, so that one encounters in purely psychological form the equivalent of the mystery of grace." Something of a paradox, a paradox to be found in Christianity itself, is encountered here. He answers our question in the spirit of St. John ("He that doeth the will shall know of the doctrine"):

> One may well come to agree with certain great Asiatics, in contrast at this point with the European intellectual, that the good life is not primarily something to be known, but something to be willed. There is warrant for the belief that if a man acts on the light he already has the light will grow. As for the final stages of the path that thus opens progressively, I for one should be content to say with Cardinal Newman [in the hymn "Lead, Kindly Light"], though not perhaps in quite the sense he intended:
>   I do not ask to see
>   The distant scene—one step enough for me.

We have seen, now, what the first two stages in the building up of the doctrines of the new humanism are. The first is the turning to the older humanism. The second is the addition of the "immediate awareness of a higher will." We come now to the third and last stage. Babbitt would add to this experience of immediate awareness, a wise eclecticism, "a mobilization of the sages." Although "wisdom is finally a matter of insight," "the individual needs to assimilate the best of the teaching of the past lest what he takes to be his insight may turn out to be only conceit and vain imagining." Thus, for Babbitt, culture is a preparation for the experience of "immediate awareness" and also its complement.

We have now outlined the stages by which Babbitt discovers "unity all pervading"; rational study of the past, acceptance of dualism, discovery of an immediate awareness of a higher will, and study of the past as a corrective. Here we have the ideas which constitute the principles of unity whereby he interprets human nature and human history, whereby he distinguishes between humanist and primitivist.

In what sense is this philosophy of life really humanistic? Some orthodox Christians have argued that "orthodoxy can alone supply our modern life with the central purpose it so plainly lacks." Babbitt's answer to this question is not, in my opinion, entirely consistent, nor does he take advantage of his own position as a believer in superrational insight. He replies that it does not seem "necessary in order to restore the teleological element to life, to start with dogmatic assertions about God and the soul rather than with psychological observation." In proof of this claim he points to the effectiveness of Buddhism in bringing forth the "fruits of the spirit" without making a place for God in its discipline and without affirming the existence of the soul "in the sense that has usually been given to that term in both East and West."

A man must take his courage in both hands if he is to mention to one of America's greatest authorities a different interpretation of Buddhism. It must be admitted that Buddha was unwilling to discuss the existence or nature of God. He claimed to be indifferent to such questions. But Buddhism conceives a supreme power operating in the world. It is the "law of the deed," an inescapable, impersonal principle of justice and moral retribution. Furthermore, it is perhaps of some significance that Buddha, as quoted by Babbitt, speaks of his illumination as "supernatural knowledge." Hence, Buddhism is not entirely without dogmatic assertion.

And what of humanism itself? It too makes dogmatic and quasi-theological affirmations. We have already seen that the ultimate authority for the new humanism is the body of humanistic standards which, when imaginatively represented, constitute an imitation of an unchanging model supersensuously perceived. Furthermore, does the higher will transcend human nature or does it not? The higher will must be above the human nature, as well as in human nature, or there can be no real equivalent of the doctrine of grace or of humility. If, as a humanist, one is immediately aware of the higher will only within oneself, then one's standards must be only relative. Standards can be universally valid as a norm only if they represent a law above the human being. Humanists must decide, then, whether they believe in a real presence or a real absence of something universal which transcends human nature. In other words, humanists must decide whether they believe in the One or not. Their decision on this question will determine the extent to which their humanism is humanistic.

It may be confidently asserted that Babbitt believes in the real presence of something which is in human nature and transcends human nature. He writes in his essay in *Humanism and America* [New York, 1930, p. 32] that "the measure of the modern man is the perception of the something in himself that is set above the flux and that he possesses in common with other men." In answer to our question, In what sense is Babbitt's philosophy humanism?, we must say it is a humanistic and secular ethics with a religious background. It is not strictly humanism but superhumanism. Babbitt's humanism, then, is not, as M. Mercier has called it, the halfway house to religion. It is already religion.

In answer to T. S. Eliot's question, What does the humanist control himself for?, we must say that it is for the same thing as that for which religious persons control themselves, namely, for the One, for the abiding, for that which is "set above the flux." Recalling Babbitt's familiar statement that there are three levels of experience, the natural, the human, and the religious, we are forced to conclude that his humanism is compounded of both religious and human elements.

Babbitt's appeal is essentially religious. The humanist's point of reference is an "immortal essence," the proper relation to which develops humility. The immediate awareness of it furnishes him the "psychological equivalent" of the doctrine of grace and of the doctrine of original sin. It is precisely because Babbitt's appeal is essentially religious and his humanism involves only a higher will rather than a complicated theology that he has attracted so many serious-minded young students in the past two generations. His claim is, to be sure, that he has not attempted "to formulate what must ever transcend formulation." But if he has not formulated it, he has named it the higher will. Moreover, he has attempted to formulate the standards which the higher will imposes. In spite of his inability to accept a dogmatic and revealed religion, he has worked out a religious view which is based on an irreducible minimum of dogmatic assertion, revealed by the inner light. Does not such a view have affinities with dogmatic and revealed religion?

If these interpretations are sound, it will be inevitable that Babbitt be judged at least in part as a religious thinker. He, of course, disclaims any interest in working out the "unprofitable subtleties" of the doctrine of grace or the higher will. He believes the realities these phrases represent "must simply be accepted as a mystery that may be studied in its practical effects." But we may raise the question as to whether any philosophy of values can long continue to be effective without its implications being examined. The implications will out, no less than murder. F. H. Bradley once remarked that "the modern Christian really worships Jesus Christ, not the Father." One might say that humanism at its present stage of development is based on a belief in a fragment of the Holy Spirit.

That is, Babbitt sees the Abiding, the One, only in its relation to the human being and not in its relation to the whole. And as to his doctrine of grace, a Catholic theologian would say that it is a very much whittled down doctrine. His immediate intuition of a higher will might be equated with the illuminating grace of the intellect (*gratia illuminationis*). But where is the "strengthening grace" of the will (*gratia inspirationis*)? Christian grace saves by illumining the intellect and reinforcing the resident and autonomous powers of human nature. Babbitt's grace illumines the intellect by revealing the higher will, but it does not transmit energy. A Catholic theologian "hot for certainties" would probably present a bill of particulars asking, "Where is actual grace, prevenient grace or cooperating grace, or efficacious grace or sufficient grace?" The point is, Babbitt in claiming to have a psychological equivalent of grace is claiming a great deal more than seems warranted, when we compare his "equivalent" and the Christian doctrine. At best, he can claim to have a psychological equivalent of only illuminating grace. One ought, nevertheless, to be grateful to Babbitt for raising the question of the necessity and nature of grace for many who would not otherwise have recognized it as a fundamental problem. He is helping theology to come alive again.

The present writer believes that humanism has within it the germs of a permanent cultural and religious movement. But if it is to realize its potentialities, it must develop.

First, it must develop a metaphysics. To depend upon an immediate awareness and a wise eclecticism alone will force humanism to rely too much upon the accidental temperaments of its expounders. Moreover, not until humanism does work out a metaphysics can it lay claim to being fully critical, for its implications are now ignored. An unexamined metaphysics is not worth having.

Second, humanism must develop a casuistry. It must discover what the "next step" in the important fields of national life are. The humanist casuistry must also include a technique for meditation and thus put as much emphasis on practicing humanism as on knowing its doctrines. It may be that, in the last analysis, this will involve the problem of institutions, cultural and religious. Babbitt agrees not only with Aristotle but also with the modern psychologists that the good life of a nation is determined by the habits formed in the early youth of its citizens.

But whether humanism develops exactly in the ways here suggested or not, its influence has already become enduring. When we recall the paucity of ideas in American letters at the beginning of this century, and when we remember also how much of writing since that time has achieved what Babbitt calls "the worm's eye view," we must credit the humanists with having in a great measure brought American criticism from a provincial variety to something almost cosmopolitan. Babbitt has also, through his amazingly effective method of teaching ideas and expounding a point of view, exercised a somewhat analogous influence upon the minds of hundreds of his students. A man who has exercised such an influence may speak from experience about being creative.

Humanism has now passed through its period of concentration. If it is to live on as a vital force in American life its next period must be one of expansion. Alfred Orage in his essay on Leonardo da Vinci tells of

> a glorious sentence in one of the Upanishads which is attributed to the Creator on the morrow of His completion of the creation of the whole manifested universe. "Having pervaded all this," he says, "I remain." Not even the creation of the world had exhausted His powers or even so much as diminished his self-existence. When that greatest of works of art had been accomplished, He, the Creator, "remained." Leonardo was, if I may use the expression, a chip off the original block in this respect.

Can as much be said of the humanists? Will they go on being creative?

7 · *Charles Eliot Norton,* Genius loci, *Shady Hill*

We meet today on a historic spot. So fully has Shady Hill entered into the life of the neighborhood and into that of Harvard College that it long ago came to possess a *genius loci,* the distinctive character or spirit of a place. Shady Hill, a white, federal-style house on a fifty-acre tract, was purchased in 1821 by Andrews Norton, in order that he could live near his work at the Harvard Divinity School. The purchase was a part of the bride's dowry, the wife Catherine Eliot being the daughter of the wealthy Boston merchant Samuel Eliot of King's Chapel. Samuel was the uncle of Charles William Eliot, who was destined to become the president of Harvard College. Being born in 1834, Eliot was seven years younger than his cousin Charles Eliot Norton, born in 1827 at Shady Hill.

Almost from the beginning of the Nortons' family residence here, Shady Hill offered hospitality to the intellectual elite of the area. For Andrews Norton, a scholar of formidable theological learning, the love of literature was also a passion. Many an evening was devoted to reading to the children. According to his former pupil George Ripley (of Brook Farm), the elder Norton's "refined and exquisite taste cast an air of purity and elegance around the spirit of the place."

When in 1828 Andrews Norton with his wife and the son of scarcely one year made a six-months' journey to England and Scotland, they visited outstanding literary figures. In the visit to Wordsworth, the poet "took the little Charles Norton on his knee and tenderly gave him his blessing." The poet gave to the father a letter of introduction to Sir Walter Scott. This trip abroad was the first of many for the son.

In later years the guests at Shady Hill included many a distinguished foreign visitor such as John Ruskin, Thomas Carlyle, Arthur Clough, Edward Burne-Jones, Matthew Arnold, Gilbert Murray, and Prince Kropotkin. Add to these illustrious names those of Emerson, Lowell, Longfellow, Parkman, Agassiz, Chauncey Wright, Howells, William and Henry James, Royce, Santayana, Palmer, Barrett Wendell, Nathaniel

The home built by Jim and Margaret Adams in Cambridge, Massachusetts, is located on the original "Shady Hill" estate; the new headquarters of the American Academy of Arts and Sciences is across the street. This essay was published in the *Bulletin of the American Academy of Arts and Sciences* 35, no. 6 (March 1982):11–22. Reprinted by permission.

Shaler, Henry Adams, Babbitt and More, and a host of other American literati.

The Nortons increased the house's fame by accumulating an enormous library, first the father's ample assemblage, and then the son's own library and collection of objects of art. Presumably describing the library, Norton the younger wrote that, "there was at least enough space around the windows for light to get in."

These indicators of the atmosphere of this place gave occasion for Henry James to speak of Shady Hill and the Nortons as "that institution and its administrators." One might say that the Norton accomplishment in this respect amounted to the *poiesis* (making) of this particular space with its *genius loci*. And now it is the new locus of the American Academy of Arts and Sciences. It is appropriate that we add here that Charles Eliot Norton a number of times presented papers at Stated Meetings of the Academy. The remembrance of these things past was inevitably in the mind of C. C. Stillman when in 1925 he established the Charles Eliot Norton Professorship of Poetry, an annual lectureship at Harvard (assigned in 1932 to Norton's relative, T. S. Eliot).

The younger Norton did not follow the academic path of his father. At an early age he became familiar with the New England theology, and later on he would carefully edit many of his father's writings. But this work did not kindle his enthusiasm for the theological disciplines. He graduated from Harvard College at the age of nineteen, having specialized in Greek, Latin, and political economy. At his Commencement he presented a highly commended paper on Santa Croce, a church and convent in Florence. Here he was already anticipating his later writing and lecturing on church building in the Middle Ages, on the art of Egypt, Greece, and Rome, and on the fine arts of the Renaissance, not to speak of his interest in poetry ancient, medieval, and modern. Being independently wealthy, he was able to spend years abroad studying the great architectural monuments.

But Charles Eliot Norton was not merely a chronicler of the history of art. Indeed, we can say that he adapted something of the historical method of his father in that he tried to interpret each period in terms of its manners and morals and of its cultural, economic, and political institutions. He showed little interest, however, in aesthetics. Moreover, philosophy and theology in his view offer only fruitless speculation. Beauty is in the service of imagination and of the higher realities of the spirit. There is no place for the ugly or the coarse in art, whether it be in the visual arts or in poetry. He looked for a direct relationship between higher moral standards and the authenticity of art. He thought that by reason of an authoritarian church, political intrigue, the poverty of the lower classes and their political impotence, and the looseness of morals in the Italian Renaissance, a period of decline came in the arts. He saw greatness in the age of Giotto and Dante, and most of all in the age of Pericles, but not in the Renaissance with its love of luxury and pomp. (St. Peter's dome is "swollen with earthly pride." Italy "had lost the capacity of moral suffering, and she sought relief from harass in self-forgetfulness among the delights of sensual enjoyment.")

It was not primarily in this dimension of his outlook, however, that his influence at Harvard has been recognized, but rather in his having deprovincialized his students and his contemporaries and in his having assisted in rendering the discipline of the history of the fine arts an essential element in higher education in the United States. From Norton's perspective he was articulating the standards of "the civilized mind"—of a universal humanism.

We should observe here that before the time of Norton's retirement a controversy regarding the nature of the discipline was taking shape. Hitherto the discipline had been dominated by classicists and men of letters (and of social status) promoting a "cultivated generalism" for enrichment of the culture. By the 1890s the advocates of advanced specialized research and of the Germanic style of graduate training were coming to the fore. Beginning in the next decade after that, moreover, still another rebellion against the genteel tradition and in favor of innovation and more flexible standards made vigorous claims. Although Norton had been among the first in the 1850s to hail the appearance of *Leaves of Grass* and had been a severe social critic and a vigorous and heroic opponent of the Spanish-American War, and although he had devoted his effort to specialized studies not only in Dante but also in ancient art, he all too easily and glibly was placed by the rebels in the category of a respectable and cut-flower humanism.[1]

Already at the age of thirty Norton had acquired a proficiency in Dante studies, publishing his translation of *The New Life* in 1859, though his prose translation of *The Divine Comedy* would appear over thirty years later. Before 1874, when the Corporation appointed him Professor of the History of the Fine Arts, he possessed an international reputation as a Dante scholar; and subsequently he published a goodly number of Dante studies. Meanwhile, he had assisted Longfellow in his translation of *The Divine*

Comedy. Later on he and Lowell published a two-volume edition of the poetry of John Donne. Norton had previously made a close comparison of all the editions of Donne in the seventeenth century. His students, catching his enthusiasm for Dante, formed the Dante Society of America, which still exists. Longfellow served as its first president, Lowell as its second, and Norton as its third.

Norton's interest in interpreting the fine arts in relation to other features in the culture was by no means a merely historical academic concern. As he surveyed the contemporary scene he noted the contrast between the cultural level in the United States and that of Europe. He was sensitive also to the paucity of artistic creativity in the States. In important respects he belonged to the increasing number of the intellectually alienated.

The late John Lennon was described in a recent obituary as an "inwit." This Middle English term had been given currency by James Joyce in *Ulysses.* The obituary writer meant that Lennon introduced an element of conscience into the youth culture. Similarly, we can say that the intention of Norton was to be the inwit, the cultural conscience, of his time and place. His principal concern was the formation of taste and of standards of criticism. In these respects he is to be compared to Matthew Arnold in England (about whom he was to present a paper at the Academy at the time of the latter's death).

But Norton's conscience ranged beyond the sphere of the arts. It concerned itself with almost all major aspects of the culture, especially with social conditions, the wide extent of poverty, the ravaging of the environment, the evils of bigness, and the crushing of individuality. In the 1850s and 1860s he published scores of articles in the *Atlantic Monthly,* the *Loyal Publication Society* (a forerunner of the syndicated column), and the *North American Review* (of which he was editor for several years). He was also a founder of the *Nation* and for many years supported it intellectually and in other ways. For the *Review* he secured articles from a great variety of contributors in this country and abroad on an astonishing variety of topics, ranging from the arts and foreign literature to historical studies, and on such social problems as prison reform, education of the deaf and the care of the poor, on political leaders, and even on the dime novel. He was a caustic political critic—and not from a distance, for he attended political conventions. He objected to Harvard's granting an honorary Doctorate of Laws Degree to President McKinley, asserting that McKinley was entitled at most to the degree, "Master in All the Arts of Political Corruption."

Norton was much interested in popular education and formed what is believed to be the first evening school in the Commonwealth. He also helped to form associations to enlist citizen participation in public affairs. He wrote articles on all of these subjects. Norton's excellent and critical biographer, Kermit Vanderbilt, has rightly suggested that his "impact" on his contemporaries would have been greater if he had permitted the publication of a volume or two of his fugitive essays.

Norton felt that America could not mature if it could not overcome its Social Darwinism, the self-serving individualism of its economic system, that is, if it could not produce individuals possessing sufficient integrity and character to adopt broad social and cultural concerns and assume corresponding responsibilities. He had little to say in favor of Emerson's social philosophy. His objections to Emerson were not those of his father—on the epistemological level. The young Norton thought that Emerson was an incurable optimist, living a remote distance from the raw realities. In a letter to Thomas Carlyle he wrote that if you took Emerson for a visit to hell, after a few minutes he would say, "Well, it's all for the good." He thought that American "culture" was devoted almost entirely to the cash register and adherent to trivial, mediocre standards belonging to the marketing personality. In principle Norton shared Thoreau's "disdain for the farmer who looked to the fields only for what could be taken from them to market. Such a one would place God on the block if he thought there were a demand and the price were right."

When Norton was nominated in 1874 for the professorship in the history of the fine arts, the subject assigned to him seemed a little queer to the students. His first classes had about thirty-five people, but twenty years later almost all of the students in the College were enrolled at one or another time in his courses. He acquired considerable popularity and became something of a legend, partly because of the distinguished guests entertained at Shady Hill and partly because of his caustic and critical comments on all sorts of things, figures, and events. He frequently remarked on the ugliness and the merely utilitarian character of the buildings at Harvard; he named them one by one. The *Harvard Lampoon* published an article on him, saying that a visitor came to the College and was being shown around by a student. The visitor asked, "Why is this building important?" The student replied, "It is famous because it has not yet been condemned by Charles Eliot Norton." The student impression of his architectural standard appears in the campus tale that Norton had died and was about to enter heaven. "Suddenly he drew back and shaded his

eyes: 'Oh! Oh! Oh! So overdone! So garish! So Renaissance!' He decided
to enter hell instead. But presently he returned, informing Peter, 'You are
over-ornate here, but down there I found I was going to have to put in
eternity looking at Appleton Chapel.'" Only those who are old enough to
have seen that ungainly edifice will fully appreciate the reference.

We have noted the large number of distinguished visitors at Shady Hill
over the years. The number of these guests bespeaks Norton's marked
capacity for making friends, a quality that appears also in his entertaining
of students and especially in his letters. He considered letter-writing to
be an art. His letters are charming and witty, sometimes containing sharp
comment on leading figures and events, but usually running over with
warm fellow-feeling. Evidence of his cherishing the art is ready to hand,
for he published the letters of Ruskin, Carlyle, Emerson and Lowell, nine
volumes in all. In addition, we have the two volumes of his own letters
(edited by M. A. DeWolfe Howe and Sara Norton).

Norton's letters, indeed his whole lifestyle, reflect a historic model of
human being which served him as a guideline, the idea of the gentleman.
I first became aware of Norton's life and work in the classes of Professor
Irving Babbitt. Norton's portrait hung on the wall of his study, and in
conversations Norton's name was often on his lips. I always had the impression that Norton and Babbitt were in firm agreement in their criticism of President Eliot's elective system in the curriculum—in their view
a lamentable relaxation of classical standards, an encouragement of the
student merely to find and follow his own "bent." Norton apparently
discerned here a dissolution of tradition analogous to the loss of common
roots issuing from the individual's movement of residence from the village
community to the metropolis. Norton and Babbitt took special satisfaction in the establishment (under Norton's influence) of the Loeb Classical
Library. At the end of a course of lectures on Rousseau, Babbitt would
recommend returning to the study of Sophocles. It is significant that
neither Norton nor Babbitt showed any serious, continuing interest in
the Bible or in biblical studies. (Babbitt once said to me, a divinity student, that he did not find the Old Testament prophets interesting.) Yet,
both of them had the reputation in certain quarters of bearing the marks
of the Puritan tradition, this by reason of their making too close a connection between the ethical and the aesthetic.

One encounters the idea of the gentleman in strange places in Norton's
writings, sometimes when he wishes to render a passing judgment of
censure on something disagreeable to him, sometimes giving the impres-

sion that the idea of the gentleman is synonymous with "good breeding." In Irving Babbitt's lectures one heard much about the normative idea of the gentleman. As a norm the idea was traced all the way from Aristotle's serious-minded man through Pliny and Cicero ("doctrine and discipline") to the Renaissance courtier to the French *l'honnête homme* to the English version. The gentleman is one who is disciplined by a vital tradition, a person actively concerned with public affairs, with poetry and the other arts, often also an amateur practitioner of one of the arts. In higher education the principal threat to this pursuit of "the civilized mind" is a reductionist specialization, also the "pedantry" of German scholarship which along with the imperialistic natural sciences had invaded the precincts of classical education. The integrating purpose of higher education is to guide the student to a serious use of leisure time toward the end of raising standards of taste and of public life. This context of the idea of the gentleman gave point to Norton's amused report that a neighbor had asked him the question, "What are Pericles?" Norton's was definitely an elitist, aristocratic idea, the leadership of the *Aristoi.* We may recall here that the elder Norton had held that the masses of men should defer to the judgment of religious authorities or experts, such judgment being "beyond the capacity or the opportunities of a great majority of men." In face of this egregious claim, the Transcendentalists had appealed to universally available inner light. The younger Norton was acutely aware of the dilemma created by the egalitarianism of democracy.

Some of Norton's associates did not share his conception of the gentleman. Alice James, who lived down the street, said that Norton was pompous. Norton, who greatly admired Thomas Carlyle, would probably have been surprised if he had known that Carlyle once wrote a letter to a member of his family, saying, "Well, Goosey Norton has been here again." It appears that Carlyle felt that there was a lack of virility in Norton's politesse. On the other hand, it is extremely doubtful that Norton admired the virility of some of the "great men" extolled by Carlyle. On a different level of discussion, the past century has brought about the conflict between the "classical" disciplines and the natural-science disciplines in higher education typified by the debate between Arnold and Huxley. Moreover, in face of the humanism of Norton and Babbitt, T. S. Eliot later on came to the conclusion that their conception of the civilized mind had deprived it of indispensable religious roots.

For Norton the opposite of the gentleman is the barbarian. Probably Matthew Arnold's view was in his mind here, for he had divided society into "Barbarians," "Philistines," and "Populace." Norton identified the barbarian as the self-serving businessman and the merely utilitarian student more interested in getting ahead than getting an education. He would have savored Henry Adams's report of the answer given him by a Harvard undergraduate whom he had asked why he was at Harvard: "A degree from Harvard is worth five thousand dollars more a year to me in Chicago." Norton addressed himself frequently to the barbarism of students, by no means limiting himself to football, which he considered a brutal form of sport. He was chairman of a committee to enforce the rules of football. It is said that Norton once at the beginning of a Harvard lecture on his favorite topic said, "None of you, probably, has ever seen a gentleman."

But we should now turn and allow Norton to speak for himself and at his best reveal the marrow of his work as a historian of the fine arts. I want you to hear a few lines from a paper he presented at the American Academy in 1877, a paper on the dimensions of proportion in the Temple of Zeus at Olympia. Norton had studied the measurements with meticulous care, comparing his measurements with those made by previous scholars, in order to correct the latter, and then finally delineating the basic harmony and the proportions of all parts in relation to the whole. At the end of his paper, which is filled with all sorts of charts and tables, he makes a characteristic attempt to explore interrelations between science and the arts, between mathematics, architecture and music, and their relation to the order of the universe. In doing this, Norton indicates that no one to his knowledge had hitherto observed the possible application of the Pythagorean scale (of music) in any of the works of Greek architecture.

"It is not impossible," Norton writes, "that the architect of the Temple at Olympia may have made an exceptional use of the numbers of musical harmony. He may have been a Pythagorean by training." Then Norton continues:

> It also is not unlikely . . . that the Greek architects recognized a relation between the harmonies of music and those of their own art; and that some of them, adopting the Pythagorean doctrine of numbers as the key of Nature, and the origin of the order of the universe, believed that the most perfect works of their art were to be achieved by the conformity of their designs to the principles of the architecture of the world. The law of harmony must be one for the rolling of the spheres, and for every tone of the lyre or the lute; one for the proportions of the starry habitations, and for those of the earthly temples of the gods.

These are lines from the scholar who held that the nerve of civilization resides in the imagination. One can readily understand why Sir Gilbert Murray, the First Charles Eliot Norton Professor of Poetry, said of him in the opening paragraphs of his first Norton Lecture:

> I met Mr. Norton only a few times and that twenty years ago; but I remember him vividly. Distinguished, courteous and a little aloof, breathing an atmosphere of serenity and depth of thought, he possessed to an exquisite degree the taste that is rightly called classic; that is, his interest lay, not in the things that attract attention or exercise charm at a particular place and moment, but in those that outlive the changes of taste and fashion. His eyes were set toward that beauty which is not of to-day or yesterday, which was before we were, and will be when we are gathered to our fathers. [*The Classical Tradition in Poetry*, Cambridge, Mass., 1927]

These are the words that evoke the *genius loci*, Shady Hill.

Note

1. For a lively, brief treatment of these controversies, see Laurence Veysey's article in *The Organization of Knowledge in Modern America, 1860–1920*, ed. Alexandra Oleson and John Voss (Baltimore and London: Johns Hopkins University Press, 1978), esp. pp. 53ff and pp. 88ff. A recent assessment of Norton's character and stance appears in Jackson Lears, *No Place of Grace* (New York: Random House, 1981), pp. 243–47.

8 · *William James:*
"No Man for Committees"

There could scarcely be anything more instructive regarding intellectual and religious currents of a period than a lengthy, meaty letter from an outstanding theologian to an equally eminent psychologist and philosopher, particularly if that letter were written, as in the present instance, by a learned, cosmopolitan scholar and theologian of the stature of Baron Friedrich von Hügel (1852–1925) to an equally cosmopolitan psycholo-

A letter from von Hügel to James, together with this essay by Adams, were published in the *Journal of the American Academy of Religion* 45, no. 4 supplement (December 1977). The essay, here abridged, is reprinted by permission.

gist of religion possessing the originality and flair of William James (1842–1910), the one being a Roman Catholic and the other a religious liberal. All the more significant is such a letter when the Roman Catholic expresses substantial indebtedness to the psychologist and offers penetrating criticism withal.

The letter from von Hügel to James, dated May 10, 1909, was found by the present writer in the Houghton Library at Harvard, in James's autographed copy of von Hügel's massive, two-volume work, *The Mystical Element of Religion*,[1] an elaborate philosophical and theological study centering attention upon Saint Catherine of Genoa (1443–1510) and her friends. This bulky, handwritten letter had remained for over sixty years tucked into the copy of the von Hügel work sent to James in 1909.

At this time von Hügel was fifty-seven years old, and *The Mystical Element* of 1908 was his first full-length book. Born in Florence in 1852, the son of an Austrian diplomat, he had lived in England since 1866. Previous to the publication of this book von Hügel had published numerous articles (in French, Italian, and English), especially on biblical criticism and also on the current modernist controversy in the Roman Catholic church.[2] *The Mystical Element* received lengthy and laudatory reviews from eminent philosophers and theologians. William Temple later said in the *Guardian*, "It is quite arguable that this is the most important theological work written in the English language during the last half-century."[3] (It is a striking fact that B. H. Streeter of Oxford said that James's *Varieties of Religious Experience* was the most important book on religion in general to be published during that same period.[4]) In 1911 Ernst Troeltsch wrote of the book that it "gives such an insight into the wealth of the component parts which constitute the Christian world of thought as is given in few other works."[5] Michael de la Bedoyère in his biography rightly says, "it is not a treatise on mysticism nor a record of personal mystical experience. Its purpose is typical of his whole approach to religion: to find the right place for the special subject of which he is treating, the mystical element, in man's whole knowledge and experience of his relationship to God."[6]

In working out his position, von Hügel takes into account, extensively and in painstaking detail, major philosophies, ancient, medieval, and modern. As against subjective idealism and as against subjectivism that views the religious consciousness as illusory, von Hügel sees the Object of apprehension as not mind-dependent—in his formulation, it is "given," and it is normative, affirming humanity's highest values. The activity of the mind is seen as instrumental to the critical apprehension of the nature of the Object, though the apprehension can never lead to comprehension of the transcendent-immanent Object. An inexpugnable contrast obtains between the apprehendor and the apprehended, the "Other." At the same time, the contrast does not entail an infinite qualitative difference between Subject and Object. The mystical experience, critically evaluated, is an acute consciousness of, and indeed intimacy with, the "Other."

At the time he received the letter from von Hügel James was sixty-seven and world-famous. He had suffered from heart trouble for some time and was to live for only a little more than a year. There is no evidence that James ever replied to the letter.

The writings of James had already gained attention in England for several decades. Beginning in 1879, partly because of his vigorous opposition to philosophical idealism, he had published numerous articles in the British periodical *Mind*. In addition to the articles, *The Principles of Psychology* had appeared in 1890. Then in 1902 came the publication of the Gifford Lectures, *The Varieties of Religious Experience,* which substantially extended James's reputation on the Continent.

In *The Varieties of Religious Experience* von Hügel saw a major shift of attention from antireligious naturalism to an attitude of openness, not only to a religious interpretation of human existence but also to mysticism and asceticism. Here he appreciated James's "insistence upon the convincingness of unreasoned experience." He approved in James the critical attitude toward a narrow rationalism and also toward the psychologizing of religion which rendered it merely subjective. Therefore he saw in this book a persuasive claim for what James calls "the human ontological imagination," a claim for the objective reality of the divine, thus relating human being and human experience to "the more spiritual universe." Von Hügel sometimes adopted the formulations about "the More." His letter gives numerous page references to *The Mystical Element* where James would find these and related ideas for which he was grateful to him.

Von Hügel goes on to place emphasis on James's essay entitled "Reflex Action and Theism," an address delivered in 1881 in Princeton, Massachusetts, to a Unitarian Ministers' Institute.[7] In his writings von Hügel sometimes refers to James as "Unitarian James." James once referred to himself as "a most protestant protestant," referring probably to his antipathy for every kind of orthodoxy, ecclesiastical, philosophical, or scientific.[8] On this essay von Hügel says, "It is, above all, the 'Reflex Action and Theism' Paper that has become part of me." In setting forth the concept of reflex action, James speaks of it as "the great contribution physiology has made to psychology of late years . . . the great achievement of our generation."[9] Reflex action, he says, "means that the acts we perform are always the result of outward discharges from the nervous centers, and that these outward discharges are themselves the result of impressions from the external world, carried in along one or another of our sensory nerves. . . . The structural unit of the nervous system is in fact a triad, neither of whose elements has any independent existence." Reflex action entails this reflex arc, the intake of the outer world, reflection on this intake, and action of the will.

In writings on von Hügel little attention has been given to his use of the concept of reflex action, even though at the beginning of the chapter in *The Mystical Element* entitled "The Three Elements of Religion," von Hügel says, "I have found much help towards formulating the following experiences and convictions in Professor William James's striking paper, 'Reflex Action and Theism.'" Actually, von Hügel in this chapter and also later on in the work adapts and expands the idea of reflex action so as to make it illuminate the religious life. The triad of reflex action becomes the paradigm for "the three elements of religion." The first element in the religious life is sense and memory, the second is question and argument, and the third is intuition, feeling, and volition. In his description of the first element von Hügel goes beyond James, interpreting it to include religious symbols available in the culture, as well as parent and teacher, and in the end "some more or less self-defined traditional, institutional religion." This inclusion of the institutional factor points to an aspect of human existence and of religion which James generally overlooked or considered secondary to individual experience. In the second element, von Hügel goes on, "it is the reasoning, argumentative, abstractive side of human nature that begins to come into play. . . . Religion becomes Thought, System, a Philosophy." The third element includes "intuition, feeling, and volitional requirements and evidences" and also "the ethico-mystical."[10]

An important difference between von Hügel and James which we have already noticed must be stressed here. In his letter von Hügel asserts that James "has taken religious experience as separable from its institutional-historical occasions and environment and from the analytical and speculative activity of the mind." It must suffice if we deal with three considerations.

(1) First, James's exclusive concern in the *Varieties* is for "the private and the personal." In the second chapter he says plainly, "In these lectures

I propose to ignore the institutional branch entirely, to say nothing of the ecclesiastical, to consider as little as possible the systematic theology and the ideas about the gods themselves and to confine myself as far as I can to personal religion pure and simple." He therefore defines religion, "arbitrarily," as "the feelings, acts and experiences of individual men in their solitude, so far as they apprehend themselves to stand in relation to whatever they consider the divine." Then in the concluding chapter he reiterates, "As soon as we deal with private and personal phenomena as such, we deal with realities in the completest sense of the term." [11] In this fashion, then, he excludes concern for "social salvation" or covenantal religion. He is interested in "what goes on in the single, private man." One may say that this restriction determines the direction and the limitation of James's own "will to believe."

But more must be said here. One should ask why James places so much emphasis on the private and the personal in his interpretation of religion. The answer is not a simple one. His Swedenborgian father's influence has often been noted. Already in 1883 he had expressed in a letter to his wife the desire "to understand a little more of the value and meaning of religion in Father's sense, in the mental life and destiny of man." He was disturbed by the fact that his friends left religion "altogether out." Continuing to refer to his relation to his father, he says, "I as his son (if for no other reason) must help it to its rights in their eyes." Accordingly, his writing of the *Varieties* may be considered to be the fulfillment of a pledge. [12] Moreover, one may say that his father's emphasis on "personal experiences" inclined William to consider "inner personal experiences" to be decisive. But he became convinced that a particular kind of experience was at stake. This conviction is probably to be related to his own personal experiences, for the pivot around which James's work revolves is William James.

James had himself suffered recurrent periods of depression and despair, going back to his late twenties. The deepest depression came in 1870 when he was twenty-eight, following which a more vigorous and optimistic outlook appeared. In the chapter on "The Sick Soul" [13] in *Varieties* he gives in disguised fashion an account of his acute mental suffering, his "bad nervous condition," a "horrible dread at the pit of the stomach . . . taking the form of panic fear." This description may apply to the marked depression he experienced in 1870. He attributed his depressions not only to poor health but also to a feeling of the purposelessness of life. The turning point for him came, he tells us, as a consequence of reading

Charles Bernard Renouvier's second *Essais*. "I see no reason," he wrote in his diary (April 30, 1870), "why his definition of Free Will—'the sustaining of a thought *because I choose to* when I might have other thoughts,'—need be the definition of an illusion." He now became convinced that he could spontaneously recreate his own life.[14] Here we may see the birth of his idea of "the will to believe."

Despite his restriction of attention in *Varieties* to the private and the personal, excluding institutional aspects of religion, James, as is well known, was not lacking in a social philosophy. In accord with his conception of "a pluralistic universe," he favored a pluralistic society, a separation of powers, which would make possible tolerance and openness to criticism and social change. Those who are familiar only with *Varieties* will fail to see why he was called "a militant liberal"; he was "a mugwump, an anti-imperialist, a civil-service reformer, a pacifist, a Dreyfusite, an internationalist, and a liberal,"[15] always for the underdog in politics, science, and religion. Perhaps the most widely known of his more popular writings is "The Moral Equivalent of War." For the most part, however, his interests were microcosmic (centering attention on the individual). His antipathy for institutions caused him to avoid institutional involvement. At the Houghton Library (Harvard) the present writer has come across an unpublished letter to Francis Greenwood Peabody which seems to illustrate James's stance in this respect. Peabody, an early proponent of the Social Gospel, gave one of the first courses on social ethics at Harvard, a course dubbed by students as "Drainage, Delinquency, and Divorce." He at one time invited James to join a new committee on alcoholism. In a typed, undated letter James declined the invitation, and gave his reason, asserting that setting a good example would be more effective than the activity of a committee. The letter concludes, "Excuse the appearance of churlishness that this letter wears. I am no man for committees anyhow."[16] I told Professor Ralph Barton Perry, James's former student and his biographer, that I had found this letter and asked if James's response in it was typical of his attitude toward assuming responsibility in the public, institutional realm. After pondering the question for a minute or two Dr. Perry responded, "Yes, I would say that it is typical." One should remember, however, that in 1894 and 1898 James, for conscience's sake (and to the embarrassment of his colleagues in the Medical School), presented two memoranda to the Massachusetts State Legislature opposing bills designed to require the examination and licensing not only of medical practitioners but also of mind-curers and faith-curers. In his view, the legislation would "hamper the free play of personal force and affinity by mechanically imposed conditions." "Let us not grow hysterical about law-making," he exhorted.[17]

We should observe that, despite his emphasis on the historical-institutional environment, von Hügel in his life and his writings gave little, if any, attention to economic and political problems or to contemporary social problems in general. He was no militant liberal. His quiet militance was confined to concern for the problems of authority in the church. By way of contrast, however, von Hügel in *The Mystical Element* gives substantial attention to the historical-institutional occasions and environment surrounding the life of Saint Catherine of Genoa and also to her active concern for the public weal.

If we look into *Varieties,* however, we find nothing regarding the relation between religious experience and the public realm. When in terms of his pragmatic theory James poses the questions, Does it work? What are the practical consequences of religious experience?, he seeks the test in the private and personal life, not in the area of public, institutional behavior. Here his test is similar to the test Jonathan Edwards proposed in his *Treatise on Religious Affections.* He does not recognize that the pragmatic test should be extended to include the public, institutional realm.[18]

(2) Secondly, consider James's a priori method. The *Varieties* is full of examples, fascinating examples, of religious experience. These examples had to be *chosen* by the author, and it would appear that they were chosen in accord with the presuppositions adumbrated in our preceding paragraph. When in the concluding chapter of the book he summarizes his findings he is really only reporting what he started out to look for. At the beginning of the concluding chapter he virtually asserts this method, an a priori method, to be his. Speaking of his choice of examples, he says, "The sentimentality of many of the documents is a consequence of the fact that I sought them among the extravagances of the subject. . . . You have probably felt my selection to have been sometimes almost perverse. I took these extreme examples as yielding the profounder information."[19] The examples already chosen, then, lead him at the end to speak of his "findings" in terms of the private and personal, of "unsharable feeling," and of the pinch of individual destiny. In short, James did not choose examples that would show the role of an institutional framework or the influence of religious experience upon institutional behavior. He *chose* examples of the private and personal.

(3) More should be said about the contrast between von Hügel's and James's positions. For von Hügel, as we have seen, the first and third elements of the triad include "historical-institutional occasions and envi-

ronment." This aspect of his thought is succinctly suggested by another triad of which he was fond, "the body, history, and institutions."[20] In religion, as in the arts and the sciences, full development requires the recognition of the positive role of the body, an awareness of great figures and paradigmatic occasions, a continuing community, a sense of the past providing standards of a tradition, and the nourishment and stimulus of institutional disciplines. Therefore von Hügel can only lament the fact that in the *Varieties* James separates religious experience from these occasions and disciplines.

In his interpretation of this broad spectrum of "the three elements" von Hügel was closer to Ernst Troeltsch than to James. Troeltsch had stressed the dipolar character of authentic human existence, reliance on the one hand upon the integrity and spontaneity of the individual, and on the other hand upon the guidance, restraint, and responsibilities of dynamic institutions. This polarity Troeltsch stated also in another way by distinguishing between subjective and objective virtues, a distinction that became important for von Hügel's ethics.[21] Here Troeltsch was more directly sympathetic with "Schleiermacher's ethics of objective contents and ends" than with "Kant's ethics of a formal universal validity."[22] Subjective virtues "spring entirely from the bearing of the subjects" and pertain to the individual in immediate interpersonal relations; objective values spring from the claims of institutional concerns and behavior, the family, the state, society, production and property, science, art, and religion. Von Hügel was the first to publish translations of these passages from Troeltsch's *Probleme der Ethik* (1902, 1913), the famous critique of pietistic Wilhelm Hermann, the teacher of Rudolf Bultmann.[23] We see that from von Hügel's point of view James's *Varieties* was exclusively concerned with subjective virtues and experiences. Von Hügel writes with characteristic vigor when he says that James's position led to "an impossible psychology," particularly since James "writes of *all* historical occasions, materials and incarnations as 'historical *incrustations*.'"[24] We may say, then, that the title of James's book is a misnomer, for it fails to deal with *varieties* of religious experience. His conception of psychotherapy was similarly limited.

Recalling now von Hügel's rather broad-gauged critique of James and its affinity with Troeltsch's outlook, we can readily see why he would have strongly approved Troeltsch's critique in his lengthy review of *Varieties*. A concluding paragraph of Troeltsch's 1904 review summarizes much that von Hügel was to say in his letter to James: "From a psychological perspective a critique would have to note above all the undervaluation of the intellectual, the volitional and the ethical in religion as well as the neglect of the psychology of corporate religious life. From an epistemological viewpoint a critique would have to discuss all the basic problems of rationalism and irrationalism, and the universal-abstract and the individual-concrete."[25]

Von Hügel's critique of James is also of significance today. The *Varieties* has been and still is rightly considered to be a classic, indeed to be a work of genius. Probably it has been generally more widely read, and in college courses more widely recommended, than any other modern book on religion. As we have seen, however, it is mainly a sort of casebook in pietistic religion, based on the false premise that "as soon as we deal with private and personal phenomena as such, we deal with realities in the completest sense of the term."[26] The *Varieties* fails to deal not only with collective and institutional manifestations of religious experience; it fails also to deal with the prophetic and priestly dimensions. As von Hügel and Troeltsch have noted, it falls short also in dealing with "the analytic and speculative activity of the mind."

Reinhold Niebuhr held that the crucial deficiency of *Varieties* issues from James's "lack of interest in the collective experiences of men." "For history is always collective destiny. . . . We must worry not only about establishing wholesome relations in the intimate communities of family and friends. We must be concerned about just relations in the increasing intricacies of a technical civilization. Even a genius like James . . . cannot help us with these problems of community and the meaning of human history."[27]

This critique of *Varieties* holds for much psychology of religion and also for pastoral care insofar as it is concerned only with one-to-one or small-group relationships. This pietistic religion which presupposes that privatized religion will itself suffice to produce a just and viable commonwealth is a fateful heritage in American life reaching from John Cotton's Letter to Lord Say and Seal (1636) to Jonathan Edwards to Lyman Beecher to William James to "piety on the Potomac" to the New Narcissism in the age of "the psychological man." This heritage serves as an ideology concealing or ignoring the workings of unaccountable corporate powers political, economic, and social. William James's theory of authentic reflex action was to strengthen the will, but the cult of privatized religion has piously weakened the social will and has reduced the space for corporate responsibility. Small is not always beautiful. The cult of "the psychological man" is a major demonry in both the "religion" and the secularism of American life, promoting a spuriously self-serving abdication of corporate responsibility. It is a form of demonic "possession," a truncated spatialization of piety "in these our nerve-racked, unwisely introspective times." What a difference James could have made if he had not in the *Varieties* defined religion as merely private and personal. Jamesean healthy-mindedness has turned out to be a drug of alienation, illustrating the one-eyed approach of psychology and pietism which relaxes the prophetic tension and the creative, re-creative relationship between personal religion and public theology. Neither personal religion nor public theology is authentic or viable without the other. Either one alone, being season'd with a gracious voice, obscures the show of evil.

Von Hügel's study of Saint Catherine of Genoa and her friends aimed to exemplify a conception that is broader than that of the *Varieties,* a broader conception of the nature and origin, the scope and impact of religious experience. Yet, his letter to James shows his indebtedness to, as well as his criticism of, the Jamesean genius.

Notes

1. Friedrich von Hügel, *The Mystical Element of Religion,* 2 vols. (London: Dent; New York: Dutton, 1908).

2. Lawrence F. Barmann, *Baron Friedrich von Hügel and the Modernist Crisis in England* (Cambridge: Cambridge University Press, 1972).

3. Quoted in Michael de la Bedoyère, *The Life of Baron von Hügel* (London: Dent, 1951), p. 223.

4. Willard L. Sperry, "The Importance of William James," *The Journal of Pastoral Care* 7, no. 3 (1953):148–52.

5. Ernst Troeltsch, *The Social Teaching of the Christian Churches,* trans. Olive Wyon (New York: Harper Torchbooks, Harper and Brothers, 1960), p. 964.

6. De la Bedoyère, *The Life of Baron von Hügel,* p. 225.

7. William James, *The Will to Believe and Other Essays in Popular Philosophy* (New York: Longmans, Green & Co., 1897), pp. 111–44.

8. William James, *The Letters of William James,* 2 vols., edited by his son Henry James (Boston: Atlantic Monthly Press, 1920), p. 169.

9. James, *The Will to Believe,* p. 114.

10. von Hügel, *The Mystical Element,* vol. 2, pp. 51, 52; *Essays and Addresses,* 2d series (London: Dent; New York: Dutton, 1926), p. 146.

11. William James, *The Varieties of Religious Experience* (London and New York: Longmans, Green & Co., 1902), pp. 31, 498.

12. Ralph Barton Perry, *The Thought and Character of William James*, briefer version (New York: George Braziller), chap. 38.

13. James, *Varieties of Religious Experience*, pp. 160–61.

14. James, ed., *Letters of William James*, vol. 1, p. 147.

15. Perry, *The Thought and Character of William James*, chaps. 25–27.

16. The text of the letter is appended to Adams's essay, *Journal of the American Academy of Religion* 45, no. 4 supplement (December 1977), pp. 1118–19. —ED.

17. James, ed., *Letters of William James*, vol. 2, pp. 67–72.

18. James Luther Adams, *On Being Human Religiously* (Boston: Beacon Press, 1976), chap. 8.

19. James, *Varieties of Religious Experience*, p. 486.

20. James Luther Adams, *The Prophethood of All Believers* (Boston: Beacon Press, 1986), p. 66.—ED.

21. Maurice Nédoncelle, *Baron Friedrich von Hügel: A Study of His Life and Thought*, trans. Marjorie Vernon (New York: Longmans, Green & Co., 1937), chap. 3.

22. von Hügel, *Essays and Addresses*, 1st series (London: Dent; New York: Dutton, 1921, 1928), p. 152.

23. *Ibid.*, pp. 153–56.

24. Quoted in De la Bedoyère, *Life of Baron von Hügel*, p. 167.

25. Ernst Troeltsch, "Review of *The Varieties of Religious Experience*," *Deutsche Literaturzeitung* 25, no. 49 (December 10, 1904):3027.

26. James, *Varieties of Religious Experience*, p. 498.

27. Reinhold Niebuhr, Introduction to James, *Varieties of Religious Experience* (New York: Collier Books, 1961), p. 8.

9 · *George Huntston Williams,* *Church Historian*

I

George Williams entered his theological studies in 1936 with the "Horst Wessel" of a goose-stepping Germany ringing in his ears. At that time he became one of my students in the first classes I taught at the Meadville Theological School (Unitarian), affiliated with the Divinity School, the University of Chicago.

Williams and I began our association there out of strikingly similar experiences—he as a student from St. Lawrence University (Universalist), having spent his junior year, 1934–35, at the University of Munich, and I in the next year having joined Dr. Peter Brunner in the underground movement of the Confessing Church's opposition to Nazism. Brunner, now Professor Emeritus at Heidelberg, had previously been incarcerated for some months in Dachau concentration camp.

During the days of turmoil in Munich, Williams became vividly aware of a plumbline in the witness of Cardinal Faulhaber. On one occasion Williams, in a casual conversation in a Munich museum, apparently quite accidentally used a code word. To his surprise he found himself led immediately to an underground meeting of opposition conspirators taking place near the infamous Braun House, only to have the frightened group abruptly disappear when they discovered that he was not the anti-Nazi courier whom they had expected. On another occasion a Nazi student who was absent when Williams brought a Jewish student as a guest into the home for a meal, told him that if he had been home he would have kicked Williams and the Jewish guest down the stairs—whereupon Williams demanded an apology.

Only a few months later I, along with some Confessing Church students in a clandestine seminary in Wuppertal-Barmen, had an encounter with the police who were searching in our pension for a pamphlet published secretly by one of these students, a pamphlet that had been distributed through the post office by sympathetic postal clerks. Later on in Marburg I was apprehended by Gestapo officers equipped with full regalia (including bloodhounds) who had searched in my room for Confessing

This essay is abridged from Adams's "Portrait" of George H. Williams, originally published in *Continuity and Discontinuity in Church History. Essays Presented to George Huntston Williams on the Occasion of his 65th Birthday,* ed. F. Forrester Church and Timothy George (Leiden: E. J. Brill, 1979). Reprinted by permission.

Church documents or other evidence against me, and who required me to face an exhaustive hearing at the Gestapo headquarters.

In the light of our somewhat similar experience in Hitler's Germany Williams and I recognized that we had separately been involved in what the Heidelberg theologian Edmund Schlink was to describe as a unique and important chapter in church history.

Because of our experience in Nazi Germany Williams early took an interest, as did I, in the writings of Paul Tillich, whom we recognized as the crucial theological and religious-socialist critic of Nazism. In his senior year, 1939, at Meadville, Williams completed his B.D. dissertation on Tillich's doctrine of sin, probably the first dissertation on Tillich to appear in English. By virtue of this study Williams became familiar with an elaborate exposition of characteristic demonries of the modern period—for example, imperialist capitalism, nationalism, racism, elitism, sexism, and unengaged intellectualism. He became aware also of the fundamental importance of dissent. I recall reporting to Williams a conversation with Tillich in which he agreed that modern democracy had been of retarded growth in Germany because of the early systematic liquidation of the dissent of the Radical Reformers of the sixteenth century; nonconformity had become thereafter largely alien to the German ethos. Williams in time came to the view that rational dissent is a channel of grace and renewal in human affairs, indeed that when it does not issue from explicitly religious motivation the divine Spirit finds an opening among so-called unbelievers. In any event, the quality of the dissent depends in large part upon the dissenters' grasp of tradition. To be sure, dissent can move in the direction of atavism—or of barbarism, as in Nazism. Moreover, Williams early recognized that ordinarily dissent, creative as well as destructive, requires institutional power in order to be effective in history. He saw also that dissent and renewal very often take the form of reinterpretation of a motif, a doctrine, or an institution that has found earlier articulation. To understand these motifs and their reincarnations the church historian must attempt to grasp the relations between them and the milieu out of which they emerged— priest, prophet, institution, layman, and theologian are to be seen in interplay.

II

In carrying out this task the historian must find a unity of pattern in a variety of particular incidents. When this pattern repeats itself, it becomes a tradition. The church historian dealing with it recognizes with

Goethe that a tradition cannot be inherited, it must be earned. That is, once the main ingredients of a tradition have been discovered, only the words of the historian as artist can give it tangible form by bringing it into focus. Once this happens, it then has the impact of an emblem on the society or the community of faith.

Here we have a preliminary indication of Williams's conception of the vocation of the church historian. One must add, however, that for Williams, the earning of a tradition must be attempted in the context of a growing community of faith in face of historical change. The historian who lives within a community of faith does not sit on a pedestal outside history. He shares the agonies, the frustrations, and the sense of promise in history. Like the jurist, he is aware of precedents of the past which are pregnant with new relevance, new life. Therefore, also in order to take time by the forelock, the historian must participate with a sense of social responsibility in the processes that define current conflicts and policies. The church historian accordingly writes of the past not merely for the past itself, but also for its impact on the present.

When I consider Williams's range of interests in nature as well as in history, in the natural sciences as well as in the humanities, in the variety of languages and literatures, and when I consider his view of the church historian as artist, I think of the paintings of an eminent contemporary artist, Al Held of Yale University. His paintings, black-and-white, are made up entirely of geometric forms (rectangles, squares, circles and the like), some of the paintings being as large as nine feet by nine, canvases of luminous, sprawling complexity. The ingredients of these paintings, the geometric forms, are in consonance and also in tension with each other. Moreover, they lend themselves to a variety of shifting perspectives. At least in its parts this congeries of forms is amenable to rational scrutiny and ordering. In some instances a form seems to extend beyond the edge of the canvas into an indeterminate future or into patterns that are to be lost. The forms do not present simply a pathless forest. Major paths are signalled by heavier, thicker lines. The forms, moreover, are depicted on different levels or layers within the depth of the painting, the lower levels being seemingly earlier partial manifestations of later forms, all of the forms in juxtaposition lending themselves to a variety of perspectives. Moving from one point of vantage to another and then to another the perceptive eye comes to recognize that, although no embracing order is discernible, there are in the house of reason (and unreason) many mansions seeking permanence, each mysteriously and independently related to others in unresolved tensions and in evanescent and partial integration. These are the dimensions of George Williams's depiction as church historian of the human scene, though (unlike Held) he discerns within and beyond the polarities "a deep purpose in the universe," an ecology of grace, an ecology that warns against premature closure or utopian expectations. Yet, the whole is more complex than human reason can embrace; it out-tops our knowledge.

Because of the vastness of the canvas and the complexity of detail, many historians tend to carry on research as specialists, largely confining their attention to carefully limited areas or problems. From early in his career Williams resolved to work as a generalist, here following the venerable model of the German Professor Ordinarius of Church History. Williams thought of the work of the generalist as providing an introduction to Western civilization. He also considered it an opportunity to study all types of Christianity.

When in 1952 he was appointed at Harvard Divinity School, Dean Willard L. Sperry informed him that as successor to Professor George La Piana he was to have responsibility for church history up to the Reformation. Williams was unwilling to confine himself to this, wishing rather to assume responsibility for ancient, medieval, and modern church history, with the exception of American church history. His major course, attended by large numbers of students from the College and the Graduate School (including future members of the Harvard faculty) required two years of four semesters. As in his earlier work at the (Unitarian) Starr King School for the Ministry and the Pacific School of Religion in Berkeley, the breadth of scholarly concern always included his maintenance of familiarity with source materials, manuscripts, and monographs in a variety of languages. But the question was to nag him, how was he to do all of this without becoming a dilettante?

He found some of the answers to these problems under the tutelage of the eminent medievalist Ernst Kantorowicz at Berkeley and also under his previous Chicago teacher, Wilhelm Pauck, who in his work traversed the full arc of historical theology. Kantorowicz was a scholar who in political preference remained a monarchist and who was so deeply immersed in the life and literature of the Middle Ages as to make the diligent student feel that he was living in that period, in "its native surroundings, its time and space." Kantorowicz gave structure to the period by rendering luminous certain dominant themes such as the traditional liturgical tricolon of the "Medieval Ruler Cult": "Christus vincit, Christus regnat,

Christus imperat," displaying "as it were the cosmic harmony of Heaven, Church and State, an interweaving and twining of the one world with the other and an alliance between the powers on earth and the powers of heaven." To be sure, this harmony is all too often broken. These shifting transcendent concepts were used to sanction the exercise of power, to legitimate established or changing distribution of power. The "Ruler Cult" with the old acclamations was traced by Kantorowicz into modern nationalism down to National Socialism and Fascism, not to speak of its revival in papal triumphalism. The "human and Christian virtues were perverted to intoxicate people into fighting for unjust causes." Williams was able to supplement his background in the Social Gospel and in the sociohistorical method he acquired from Chicago with the knowledge of specific ways in which forces for change are perverted in the course of history.

Stimulated by these studies, Williams began to map out major routes through church history. For him these routes or trenches are irrigation ditches (Thomas Mann called them "coulisses") which vitalized the landscapes through which they passed. Sometimes the characterizations by the historian provisionally assume the form of a cartoon, offering the intense visual dynamics of simplified line and color and providing an effective pedagogical device. Williams has said that the characterization of a route in history may acquire the forcefulness of a Japanese print with its few brush strokes. The heavier lines of Williams's canvas became such motifs as church and state, the ministry and the sacraments, the role of the laity, justification by faith, atonement and sacrament, the Radical Reformation, the reluctance to inform, the idea of the university in Puritanism, wilderness and paradise, and attitudes toward nature. They are never presented as merely the organization of data in terms of an integrating idea. In Troeltschean fashion Williams colors in his ideas, fills out their basic outlines in relation to institutions, places, and historical figures. Thus he gives to statistics body, locale, and voice. Moreover, these recurring motifs of the iconography are seen also as analogues of the birth and rebirth of individual figures. In short, these outlines aim to trace the transmutation (and perversion) of values, the Phoenix-like death and rebirth of motifs which sometimes go underground and then reappear under new names and guises.

Williams's pathos for particularity is especially evident in his sense of the genius of place. The thick lines of his canvas are always delineated topographically. Maps, maps, maps are always in evidence. Nicaea or

Kiev or Warsaw or Trent is a place on a map of a particular period. Such mappings of church history are not unilinear, precisely because they do not represent undisturbed balance or symmetry. In fact, they acquire multidimensional form through the discernment of polarities which strive for resolution.

III

Williams's fundamental personal commitment as an individual and as a church historian is to the church universal and to the prophetic obligation of rational dissent, stemming from his family heritage and his experience in the local congregation. His sense of the Body of Christ is informed by the richness of communal experience which comes to a focus in liturgy and sacrament and in the prophetic moments when the church as a corporate entity shows its sacrificial concern for the world and its transcendent independence of the world. I have heard him say that when he is in a worship service he feels almost a physical pressure on his temples by reason of his awareness of the community of faith. In large degree he has chosen the iconography he has delineated because of his interpretation of the perennial and current needs of the community of faith. He says that when he made the decision to resign his pastorate in Rockford in order to accept a teaching position in Berkeley he wept and then wrote an individual letter to each member of the congregation. His wife, Marjorie Derr, who cherished the teamwork with him in the parish, shared this lament, and has continued to perform pastoral duties as a vigorous church member, serving also in numerous community enterprises.

On his traveling fellowship from Meadville he first went, as I had done previously, to study at L'Institut Catholique in Paris under the historical theologian Le Breton who was giving his lectures on the doctrine of the Trinity, all in Latin. (Wilhelm Pauck at Chicago had sometimes teased Williams by saying that as a "birthright Unitarian" he would not be able to understand this doctrine.) From Paris he transferred to Strasbourg because he would find there both a Protestant and a Catholic faculty. Later, as Acting Dean of Harvard Divinity School he aimed to introduce an ecumenical pattern which previously had been neglected.

When he served from 1962 to 1965 as an official Observer at Vatican Council II, he noted that the liberals and the free churchmen were often among the most positive in evaluating the progress of the Council. He was dismayed by the comment of a Heidelberg theologian who said, "It is more pleasant to feel the warmth of fraternal embrace here than the

acrid heat of inquisitional flames—but the purpose is the same!" The
open-mindedness on the part of liberal Protestants toward Catholics was
not entirely new. In his sermon on the Council entitled "A Time to Rend
and a Time to Sew" (December 1962), Williams recalled that William
Ellery Channing was a friend of Bishop John Cheverus of Boston, who,
on later becoming a Cardinal Archbishop of Bordeaux, was a factor in
making Channing's writings on social justice and toleration known in
France. Especially noteworthy for Williams, in addition to the stress on
collegiality and on the lay apostolate, was the recognition in the Council
that the church can be truer to her mission if she is independent of the
state, not only of the Communist state but also of the democratic state.
Equally important for all was the renewed emphasis on the de-
Europeanization of the church and on a pluralistic ecumenism.

This ecumenical thrust was seen by Williams as working not only
against the demonry of nationalism but also against the racism which he
had opposed in determining to attend the inner-city East High School in
Rochester and, later, in marching in Montgomery. He believes that in
America and in the Third World a new more inclusive conception of covenant is being engendered which will bring political as well as religious
renewal. Asa Davis, one of his doctoral students, unbeknownst to Williams, brought the young Martin Luther King to one of his lectures at
Harvard. In this lecture he predicted that the next great theologian would
be a black.

When Williams in 1968 visited Russia at the invitation of Metropoli-
tan Nikodin of Leningrad and under the auspices of La Société Européenne
de Culture he found special satisfaction in becoming personally acquainted with churchmen who were suffering under the heel of Soviet
oppression, though he felt constrained to lament to the Baptists that they
had lost their savor as dissenters.

Williams's ecumenical outlook found singular expression many years
earlier in the days of the Scopes trial of 1925 in Tennessee. At the age of
eleven he was in full sympathy with Scopes's position—his claim to freedom to teach the theory of evolution—but he deplored the contemptuous
attitude of those who made fun of Williams Jennings Bryan and the fundamentalists whom he represented in the court. He felt that sincere conviction deserved respect. Years later when in 1978 he testified before the
Supreme Court of Kentucky he came to the defense of the fundamentalists
in their maintenance of private schools. He took this position in the name
of cultural pluralism and in opposition to the encroachments of the state
in its oppression of civil liberty and of freedom of association. To be sure,

he made it clear that he was opposed to racial discrimination in private as well as in public schools.

Although a liberal in religion and politics, Williams has the independence of mind not to adopt every allegedly liberal tenet. Despite his years of support of the American Civil Liberties Union, he has expressed in numerous articles his impassioned opposition to abortion on demand. In his formal statement on February 26, 1971, before the Massachusetts House Judiciary Committee, he rejected the view that opposition to abortion on demand represents the attempt of a sectarian faction to impose its restrictions upon the public domain. The ground of the rejection of abortion on demand, he said, is not sectarian, nor is it peculiarly Christian, it is humane. It asserts the inherent right of embryonic being, once conceived, to be brought into the world. The claim that freedom of decision for the mother is a matter of private morality is invalid. The issue is one of public morality, and it belongs to the public authorities to safeguard whatever new life may issue from privatized sexual activity, and thus to protect the civil liberty of the unborn. In ancient Rome, he said, the sire could abort the fetus in his wife or servant without their consent. This claim to sire-sovereignty has long ago been rejected. Yet, there is no ethical difference between the ancient sire-sovereignty and the present claim for the sovereignty of the mother over the life in her womb.

In the period of McCarthy-inspired anti-Communist hysteria Williams's alertness to the dangers of statism became cogently evident in his article "Reluctance to Inform" (1957), an article drawing warnings from church history and showing the similarity between former ecclesiastical oppression and the present punishment of journalists and others who refuse to divulge sources of information. From Supreme Court Justices Earl Warren and Felix Frankfurter he received letters of thanks for this article, indicating that the Court had been influenced by it in its deliberations.

Numerous other activities of Williams attest to his sense of social responsibility as citizen and churchperson, such as his participation in 1967 with William Sloane Coffin and others in the ceremonial supporting those who burned their draft cards at Arlington Street Church in Boston, as well as his joining in the antidiscrimination protests in Alabama and elsewhere, and in an antipollution campaign in his suburban town.

IV

These examples of Williams's combination of pluralistic ecumenicity and the prophetic freedom of dissent and social criticism gives occasion to recall his keen interest in the writings of Frederic Henry Hedge (1805–

1890), who was probably the first American theologian to use the term *ecumenical* in its present sense. A Christian Transcendentalist and for a time the president of the American Unitarian Association, Hedge served as the first professor of ecclesiastical history (1857–1876) at Harvard Divinity School. In this position he was, then, one of Williams's predecessors.

It would be difficult to find in the nineteenth century any American theologian, except perhaps Philip Schaff, who stressed the ecumenical ideal more than did Hedge. "The church," Hedge said, "must be catholic, it must embrace the whole, it must gather into one all the elements which are scattered abroad." It is not surprising, therefore, that Williams's brochure of 1949 on Hedge is one of his most suggestive essays on the doctrine of the church, and specifically of the liberal church in its concern for social justice and in its relations to the various types of Christianity in past and present.

Since the doctrine of the atonement is one of the principal items in his iconography, Williams finds much to his liking Hedge's adoption of a form of the doctrine. Hedge's doctrine of at-one-ment serves as the basis for his conception of the reconciliation of differentiating elements in Christian history. In his view this reconciliation comes as the interpenetration of the transcendent and the immanent. Interpreting the atonement in corporate terms rather than as merely the "particular redemption" or election of the individual, Hedge urged the churches to yearn for "a public grace of which the individual becomes a partaker through his social relations and not by private negotiations, and the realization of which is society itself in the measure of its moral and Christian progress." This is the nerve of Hedge's "social gospel." One is reminded here of the view of Hedge's famous German contemporary, Friedrich Julius Stahl, who held that conversion and salvation belong to institutions as well as to individuals. Hedge for his part aimed to recover the Pauline social conception of atonement (and at the same time perhaps to pay his respects to Hegelianism). Accordingly, any radically sectarian movement was to Hedge inimical to the working of the Holy Spirit in its engendering of a variety of authentic witness and in its reconciling of these differentiations in the unity of the Spirit.

From Williams's perspective it is this sectarian spirit that causes him to qualify radically his assessment of the Radical Reformers whom he has dealt with in unprecedented amplitude. They cultivated the inner disciplines that nourish conscience and independence of the world. Moreover, through their separation of church and state they prepared the West for the modern world. But insofar as they promoted the temper of withdrawal they failed to maintain the Constantinian legacy entailing the churches' sharing of responsibility for the character of the society as a whole. The Radical Reformers who did not surrender this legacy were those of the aggressive sects which, like the Levellers and others in England and America, initiated the movement towards the dispersion of power and responsibility in society as well as in the churches, thus giving impetus to the democratization of the organization of the church, the state, and education, and finally also to the laborers in the work force. Williams saw in Channing not only the insistence upon rationality in approaching religion and the Scriptures ("the liberal intellect") but also the maintenance of the Constantinian legacy, as in his classical statement on "Religion as a Social Principle." These themes are all freshly examined in Williams's work on the Polish Brethren of the sixteenth century [*The Polish Brethren*, parts 1 and 2 (Atlanta: Scholars Press, 1980)].

Having emphasized the variety of the forms of Christianity, Hedge was concerned also to find a classification of these differentiations. Here again Hedge's approach is of special interest to Williams, who, as we have noted, possesses a strong sense of the genius of place. Hedge's classification of the types of Christianity is accomplished in terms of place or space. We should recall here that having in his youth studied in Germany for four years under the tutelage of the future American historian, George Bancroft, also a Unitarian, Hedge was familiar with (and later published translations of) the writings of the philosophical idealists on philosophy of history and of church history. Schelling, for example, had developed a chronological scheme, dividing church history into three stages, the Petrine (Catholic), the Pauline (the Reformation), and the Johannine (the coming Age of the Spirit).

Hedge envisaged the major segments of historical Christianity in terms of space and not of time. He identified the different types of Christianity according to their principal geographical areas—eastern, western, northern and southern sectors. In almost misleading simplicity we can note that for Hedge the East represents stability, conservatism; the West, mobility, innovation, progress; the North, internal activity (the inner life), idealism, mysticism; and the South, external productiveness, ritual, symbolism, and ecclesiastical organization. Particularly significant for the New Englander is Hedge's view that Unitarianism and Congregationalism combined the dissenting heritage of sectarian localism, and the view of the church as a territorial establishment promoting a "public theology," entailing the church's sense of corporate responsibility for the character of the society as a whole—the best of the polar opposites, sect and church, as Troeltsch called them.

The elements in Hedge's composite, geographically mapped-out sectors of Christian history past and present appear in Williams's landscape with its many "trenches," but one sector is missing in Hedge, "our neighbor the universe." Williams, a lover of nature since boyhood, includes a theological interpretation of the embedment of the human and religious enterprise in the context of nature as well as of history. Christianity is part of something larger than itself. The God who acted in Israel and in the raising up of Jesus in the prophetic line works in all peoples and their religions. Especially significant for Williams is the relationship between Christianity and Islam and modern Judaism. His positive interest in the State of Israel and his active participation in her support has been noteworthy in a multitude of ways, some of them being highly dramatic.

But the attitude toward nature must also be taken into account. In his elaborate history of attitudes toward nature in Western history [*Wilderness and Paradise in Christian Thought*, New York, 1962] he traces the antinomies suggested by seven sets of Scriptural passages. The great achievement of the covenantal religion of Israel was to disengage itself from the cults of fertility of the Canaanites and to think of the human being as in this sense overcoming nature. In our time American Protestant Neo-orthodoxy has tended to overstress the view that God is to be understood not so much as the Creator of nature as the redemptive Lord of history.

Williams has not been willing to put to one side the theological concern for the cosmos and for the earth and its diversified world in which all creatures have a precious place in God's eyes. There is grace from below as well as grace from above. We are both a part of nature and are separated from it. "There is surely a piece of divinity within us," says Sir Thomas Browne, "something that was before the elements and owes no homage unto the sun." We come from below in one sense: the very salt solution of our blood corresponds to that of the salt density of the sea. We are nevertheless brought out of the water and the seas and lifted up to be reborn as rational, responsible creatures sustained by grace. But the water and the seas are still a part of us. Indeed, water becomes in baptism a symbol for creation and re-creation, of spiritual birth and regeneration through grace from above. In this sacrament, and also through the elements of the Lord's Supper, nature is brought into the history of salvation in a community of faith. Sight, sound, touch, and the olfactory all belong in the liturgy and the sacraments, that is, in the liturgy and the sacraments that do not submerge us in the subhuman, the biological sphere.

Yet, we again and again in our corporate life face the temptation of reverting to a naturistic religion, as in Social Darwinism and in Hitlerism. In the first, "survival of the fittest" becomes the criterion; and in the second, race is raised to demonic prominence.

The authentic religious community is the only community in which we are protected from the demonries to which flesh is heir. Only in this community are we completely human because we have transcended the limitations of our biological provenance. Nor can we be saved by reason alone, for reason must itself be saved. With the help of a superior power whom we address in prayer and in anguish, we prepare for the grace of "regeneration which makes us purposeful, illumined and whole in the community of faith."

V

Despite the originality of his concern for a philosophy of church history, the writings of Hedge on church history are not numerous. If we look for an American church historian who was a generalist possessing a temper similar to that of Williams, we can readily see a kindred spirit in Philip Schaff (1819–1893). Although their philosophies of church history are not the same, they both stem in large measure from a Calvinist heritage, and they are similar in their search for a better understanding of the various types of Christianity. Both of them have worked for reconciliation between these types, though they have recognized that adjustments can be only partial and temporary. Both of them have exhibited a profound interest in liturgy and sacrament, both have cultivated a consistent respect for minorities, both have allowed for diversity of education as well as urging cooperation in all that pertains to the commonweal of humanity. Both of them have promoted appreciation for the worth of every confession. Yet, as was once said of Schaff, of Williams too it may be said that his is "a devotion to Christianity which rises superior to all denominations." They belong to John Bunyan's House of the Interpreter, offering light and guidance and warning to the pilgrim "in the difficult places he meets with in the way."

Both men, I doubt not, would accept with alacrity Nicholas of Cusa's "icon of God" (1454), an omnivoyant portrait which, regardless of the quarter from which the pilgrim regards it, "Looks upon him as if it looked on none other," each experiencing the directness of its gaze, each being precious in its sight but none claiming to possess the icon as his own prerogative, and each knowing that "it taketh the same most diligent care of the least of creatures as of the greatest, and of the whole universe."

10 · *Ernst Troeltsch and Harold Berman on Natural Law*

The Spanish Cardinal Merry del Val once said that for the Protestant the Bible is a wax nose to be twisted any way you please. Something similar could be said of the concept of natural law. Indeed, at one time the Roman Catholic solution with respect to natural law as well as to the Bible was to provide ecclesiastical guidance. In the Syllabus of Errors (1864) appears the papal declaration, Let him be anathema who asserts that natural law may be determined without the guidance of the church. It is difficult to conceive of anything more nonsensical than this demand. Canonists have told me that the encyclical was not of permanent validity but was intended for the immediate situation.

The idea of natural law may be traced back to ancient Greece and Rome and has been a centerpiece of discussion for over fifteen hundred years. Indeed, Julius Stone in a conversation has suggested that the idea has been a "basket" for value theory for a millennium and a half.

Natural law has generally made the claim to provide a rational ethical standard that is discoverable through human powers of apprehension and thus does not depend upon special divine revelation. It is not surprising therefore if its meaning has been subjected to diverse and even to contradictory interpretations. Because of this, and especially because of the ways in which the idea has been made the weapon of special interests, it has been abandoned in wide circles. The conception even of positive law has undergone radical change.

Abridged from an essay originally published in *The Weightier Matters of the Law: Essays on Law and Religion, A Tribute to Harold J. Berman,* ed. John Witte, Jr. and Frank S. Alexander (Atlanta: Scholars Press, 1988). Reprinted by permission.

The legal realists assert that law is what the judges decide it is. In this view the positing of natural law is only a sign of human vanity. As a protest against this vanity Justice Oliver Wendell Holmes, Jr. reminded his students that man is in the belly of the universe, the universe is not in the belly of man. By law he meant no metaphysical truths or grand moral principles but rather "the incidence of the public force through the instrumentality of the courts." Nevertheless, a version of natural law in one form or another has been adopted in recent years (for example, by Jerome Frank, Lon Fuller, and Harold Berman). Of special significance is the fact that in Nazi Germany a conception of natural law was appealed to by judges who were opposed to racist views of "justice." In certain quarters this conflict gave rise to new interest in and respect for the crucial function of natural law as the ground for the criticism of positive law.

The history of the idea of natural law has filled libraries for centuries, as is readily evident in the massive work of Otto Gierke, *Natural Law and the Theory of Society,* portions of which have been translated by F. W. Maitland and Ernest Barker. The development of natural law, and the contradictory views of it, is a recurrent theme in Harold Berman's *Law and Revolution: The Formation of the Western Legal Tradition* (1983).[1] Here we see that in the face of great social and legal change canon law was created as the first European legal system. In all of this the church was the principal carrier of natural law theory. Berman therefore gives considerable attention to the scholastic dialectic.

TROELTSCH: ABSOLUTE AND RELATIVE NATURAL LAW

Probably no scholar has provided a more comprehensive account than Ernst Troeltsch of the development of natural law from the beginning of Christianity through modern secularization and then to its decline. For an understanding of the ways in which Troeltsch spells out the emergence of a natural law doctrine in early Christianity one must first take into account his interpretation of the character and dynamic of primitive Christianity. His whole outlook in these matters was something he had to struggle for in the context of the theological and philosophical conflicts of the latter part of the nineteenth century in Germany.

Ernst Troeltsch (1865–1923) was one of the most original and penetrating cultural analysts of his time. Along with Max Weber, his colleague at Heidelberg, he was a pioneer in the burgeoning discipline of sociology of religion. He was especially aware of the ethical and philosophical problems characteristic of a pluralistic society with its tensions between church and state. But not only tension was evident. That could be present at any time. More significant was "the anarchy of values" following upon the decline of the traditional faith community with its obsolete supernatural sanctions inherited from the Middle Ages. This "anarchy of values," a phrase from Wilhelm Dilthey, was evident on all sides, particularly as a consequence of positivism and relativism. One could not expect guidance from the church theologians who were terribly at ease in Zion, partly because in Germany they were coercively supported by the state and partly because they hugged the shore of their orthodoxy and their Bibliolatry. The new, relatively liberal theology of Albrecht Ritschl (1822–1889) attracted Troeltsch, but eventually he became convinced that its social gospel of building here and now the kingdom of God was not supported by historical studies. The liberal message was something subjectively read into the Gospels. In this view Troeltsch was speaking as a member of the Religious-Historical School; indeed, he was recognized as the dogmatic theologian of this school. He found in the Gospels no social philosophy of the kind promoted by Ritschl (or later by the Social Gospel in the United States). On the contrary, Jesus proclaimed an apocalyptic gospel affirming the coming of a new age. He offered no plan for overcoming oppression or for social reform. The conflict he waged was against false religious leaders. There was here also a profound mystical element (though Jesus "was himself not a mystic"), relating the individual immediately to God and at the same time combining this individualism with a universalism. Since the churches were waiting for the Second Coming, primitive Christianity possessed no social philosophy for ongoing history. It therefore appropriated from Stoicism elements analogous to its own ethos; it adopted a conception of moral natural law, the source of legal rules and institutions. In Stoicism this was viewed as a law that rules the whole world, the divine reason. For the Stoics as well as for the Christians this moral natural law was rooted in the divine will.

Amos Wilder goes further than Troeltsch in finding in the teaching of Jesus elements or equivalents of natural law. Here he finds natural law to be "implicit in the world view of Israel and of Jesus." Through a careful analysis of texts in the Gospels he delineates equivalents of natural law in the teaching of Jesus.[2]

In the history of the idea of natural law one finds considerable variety of content. The Stoic view excluded coercion, the differentiation of power or social class and private property which gives rise to such differentiation. This included the idea of humanity construed as a community of totally free people—all of this issuing from the divine reason. But none or little of this was practicable in the world's present state.

Consequently, a distinction was made between an absolute and a relative natural law. The former was realized in the Golden Age at the beginning of human history, the proton, but its realization was thwarted by the rise of human passions, greed, the lust for power, egoism, and violence. The Christians could readily discern the analogy with the biblical conception of the Creation and Fall. But they had a more exalted conception of the eschaton. Moreover, they did not renounce the absolute natural law so completely as did the Stoics. On the other hand, they knew from the biblical tradition that a standard was required for the present harsh order of state and law, the protection of property by law, war and brute force, slavery and domination. This Troeltsch called relative natural law. It presupposes the Fall, and it restrains and heals sin by means of rationally ordered organizations of coercion. For inventing the term "relative natural law" Troeltsch was criticized by Emil Brunner. But Ernest Barker follows Troeltsch by adopting the term. It is worth noting that Gierke, in discussing Ulpian's (circa A.D. 220) twofold conception of natural law, speaks of the distinction "between the 'absolute' and the 'conditioned' dictates of reason. The latter is the only form of natural law in which it could be applied to the real world."[3] For the Christians the relative natural law was identified with the Decalogue, "the expression of divine reason manifesting itself under the present conditions of the state of sin."

TYPOLOGY OF NATURAL LAW CONCEPTIONS

There have been numerous attempts to classify conceptions or interpretations of natural law. Troeltsch, the sociologist, devised a comprehensive scheme in terms of his typology of religious associations, the church type, the sect type, and the mystical. This typology appears and reappears in his writings with a richness of formulation, notably in *The Social Teaching of the Christian Churches,* in the essay on "The Stoic-Christian Natural Law and Modern Secular Natural Law," and in the essay on "The Social Philosophy of Christianity." These ideal types are for Troeltsch not merely abstract, transhistorical concepts. They serve as the basis for periodization in Christian history and for identifying the dynamics of the Christian movement in history. They also indicate different types of organization and membership, in terms of which the Christian movement related itself to the surrounding world, the larger society. We can give here only abbreviated formulations of these widely familiar concepts.

The most important and central sociological form is the church-type, best illustrated by the medieval church. Here salvation is something given with the divine decree of salvation, as something in principle already realized, independently of personal achievement and perfection. One is born into the church. It is for the masses and for all classes. This type can compromise with existing structures of society which persist in the state of sin and in which the members have to live. Relative natural law is characteristic here.

The sect revolts against the church. The point of departure for the medieval sects was the Gregorian reform and revolution within the church. The sects are rigorous in their application of the evangelical ethic. They do not base their arguments upon learned Patristic or Aristotelian researches into the Law of God but upon the plain Law of Christ or the Sermon on the Mount, the absolute law of nature. This conception permits a good deal of variety of interpretation, forms of inequality as well as of equality. By the appeal to an absolute natural law the sects give to their biblicism "an illuminating reason and a passionate sentiment." The sect does not build upon an objectively and institutionally available grace. The members belong mainly to the lower classes. The "note" of the typical sect is the piety of the members. The sect refuses to surrender to the general state of sinfulness. Compromise is rejected, and therefore relative natural law is rejected. One is a member of the sect by choice. Therefore, the sect substitutes the voluntary association for the institutional church. In general one may say that an orientation to absolute natural law is characteristic.

The sects may be divided into two main groups: the withdrawing sect avoids state and law, often forming small groups separated from the world; the aggressive sect attempts to transform the world (even by force). Far the most important here are the Anabaptists and their progeny who form independent, democratic congregations such as among the English Independents and the American Pilgrims. Gradually, however, the radical natural law feature is pushed into the background. Yet some of these groups become forerunners of modern socialism with an egalitarian natural law which in certain quarters gradually loses the religious foundation.

Mysticism constitutes a third type. Here the aim is immediacy in the experience of one's relationship to God. The historical and institutional elements are at best merely a stimulus and a means to the inner or suprahistorical communion with the divine. This mystical type can appeal to the doctrine of the Spirit in the New Testament, especially to John and

Paul. It tends to remain aloof from the world and society, entailing a disjunction between the inner and the outer worlds. Consequently, it is not concerned with institutional organizations. Ultimately, then, mysticism is a radical, noncommunal form of individualism. Natural law scarcely plays a role. This sort of mysticism may be found in all periods, interwoven with church and sect. These three types appear in successive periods of Western history, finally coming to fruition in the Free Church. Here we see the advent of the denomination as a type. This concept is not explicitly delineated by Troeltsch, though it is always just under the surface. So much for the theory of periodization. We must now turn to a consideration of Lutheranism and Calvinism.

Reformation Conceptions

Troeltsch writes at length on Luther's doctrine of natural law. Under the influence of the rediscovery of Aristotle, the Thomistic doctrine of natural law is formulated, furnishing a precondition for theocracy, or the universal rule of the church. Liberty, equality, and common property are regarded as the true Christian ideals, but these ideals belonged to the original state in Paradise. Since the Fall, relative natural law prevails as a punishment and as a restraint of sin. In relative natural law, sanction is found for the monogamous family with patriarchal power of the man; for the state with the rule of force, of war, and of law; and for the regulation of the just price and for the condemnation of wholesaling and usury. One can see here that at one time the church conservatively protects the power structure and at another progressively protects the rights of the individual. The church claims to serve the entire society. The state, the product of sin, becomes the bulwark of order and liberty.

Luther rejects Roman theology and the canon law. He does not accept the dual morality of Catholicism, the distinction between a lukewarm mass-Christianity and a monastically inclined élite. For the same reason he does not recognize the hierarchical structure of society with its steps leading from nature to grace, from the forms of life ruled by natural law to the realm of grace in the church. He cannot, therefore, set the natural and the Christian law side by side, but must draw the one into the other. He has to realize the Christian law immediately within and by means of the forms of life ruled by natural law. He accomplishes this by means of the doctrine of vocation. In accordance with natural law, society is divided into a system of vocations and classes. But something more is needed.

The vocational division of labor based on natural law must be inspired by the spirit of Christian love through the preaching of the word.

In accordance with natural law, big business, speculation, and a credit economy are excluded, as well as any revolutionary spirit. The relative natural law is therefore extremely conservative. All order and welfare depend upon obedience to the authorities—whoever they may be at a particular time. Even when the authorities abuse their power they must be obeyed. Resistance destroys the social order based on natural law. The authority is based upon reason and the divine will—the relative natural law. Therefore, Luther could oppose the peasants when they made their demands for reform. In this way he did away with the Stoic and rationalist elements of natural law, even though he did view the Decalogue as equivalent to natural law. Troeltsch concludes his presentation by saying that Luther "glorifies power for its own sake."

This whole view of Luther has been vigorously disputed, for example, by Karl Holl, who asserts that Luther presented a new conception of community in both the secular and the religious realm, an organic view of the community analogous to the Pauline view of the body of Christ. Yet because of sin there is a need for law and coercion. But the nature of community—like God's own nature—is to love and to evoke love.[4]

Calvin took over the Lutheran-Catholic natural law but with an important difference: He did not adopt the Lutheran transmutation of natural law into a law of divinely sanctioned authority. He therefore retained the ancient Catholic natural law with its mixture of rationalistic-individualistic and irrational-authoritarian elements. Calvin forbids the private individual to resist duly constituted authority. It is reserved for a subordinate authority. If the highest authority fails, the subordinate authority may step into its place and carry out the natural and the divine law. We may call this the institutionalization of dissent, but it is a dissent belonging to a constituted group authority. The control of power is a corporate control. In short, we have here a corporate constitutionalism. Clearly, we see in Calvin not only a theologian but also a trained lawyer.

In later Neo-Calvinism constitutional dissent could spread within the society in a democratic direction. Here natural law becomes popular sovereignty. Authority rests with the people, not with private individuals, but through duly constituted corporate representatives. Another deviation from Luther and from Catholic natural law is to be seen in Calvin's declaration that usury and commerce are permitted by natural law. As a consequence of this (urban) ethos Calvinism was able in good conscience to form alliances with the countries and the social classes representing the rise of the capitalist economy.

Even a more far-reaching transformation of Calvinist natural law occurs in the English Revolution of the seventeenth century and in America under the influence of the Independents, whose orientation was Anabaptist and sectarian. To be sure, Cromwell resorted to force. But in the democratic direction, relative natural law of the sinful state was replaced by a conception of democratic equality and self-government, an approach to absolute natural law.

Viewing this variety and taking into account the separation of church and state, Troeltsch asserts that the general distinction between the church and the sect has been wiped out. Looking back over the whole period to the Middle Ages he finds only two fully elaborated social philosophies, Roman Catholicism and Calvinism.

But more must be said here. We can discern a great difference between Calvin's position as a whole and that of Luther and Lutheranism. Calvin speaks about the identity of natural law with the Decalogue, but the whole Old Testament law and the history of Israel are viewed as illustrations of natural law. The state is never regarded as a mere antidote to the fallen condition and a penalty for evil. It is chiefly regarded as a good and holy institution appointed by God. Moreover, private property likewise seems to be a directly divine institution. Indeed, political and economic institutions are regarded as divine institutions for the purpose of preserving social peace and harmony. For Calvin, then, the relative natural law is a divine institution. We leave aside here a discussion of Calvin's use of the Ten Commandments, apart from noting that the moral law which has permanent validity is chiefly associated with the Commandments that inculcate the worship of God and the mutual love of men.

ROMANTICISM AND THE HISTORICITY OF LAW

Another possibility (a surprising one indeed) is realized—the decline of universal natural law. This takes place under the rubric of Romanticism. But there were several kinds of Romanticism. A. O. Lovejoy used to speak of "Thirteen Romanticisms." Schleiermacher and Novalis in mystical vein emphasized inwardness, immediacy, and individuality. In the lecture delivered only a few months before his death, "The Ideas of Natural Law and Humanity," Troeltsch sees Romanticism as bringing about the demise of natural law in nineteenth-century Germany.[5] This essay gives a remarkable, synoptic view not only of natural law with its history but also of the Romantic turn in the direction of historical jurisprudence in the *Volksgeist*, the spirit of the people. This Romanticism centers attention not on the universal, the idea of humanity, but on the positive, the particular, the individual, the unique, the spiritually organic, superpersonal creative forces belonging to a *Volk*. As Ortega y Gasset today describes this view, the human being has no nature but only a history. This whole movement separates Germany from Western Europe. With its appeal to the old Teutonic poetry of the Volsungs (which inspired Wagner) it leads finally to a curious mixture of mysticism and brutality. One could say here that Romanticism was dehumanized to go on all fours, "brutalizing romance and romanticizing cynicism." It makes law something that lies outside the moral boundaries, a demoralized law. This entails a total and fundamental destruction of any idea of a universal natural law. With a basic philosophy of pantheism this German view adopts what has been called "the principle of identity": it discerns a spiritual and divine essence inherent in a new kind of community supported by a stern realism. In this new community the state in following its "legitimate political interest" is elevated to the position of a sort of deity. The consequence is a contempt for the idea of a universal humanity. Here we encounter a blind worship of power and success. Uniqueness has become what we might call "uniquity." Bismarck, the "Iron Chancellor," is its symbol and incarnation. These pages are a severe indictment of an ingredient of German culture by a German. In reading them one can see an anticipation of the Third Reich of the Nazis.

Despite these demonic perversions of individuality, this toad, ugly and venomous, wears yet a jewel in his head. Troeltsch asserts that by virtue of the very idea of individuality the German theories have contributed to historical investigation and to the understanding of history. They have created the historical sense as a "specific and definite thing." What is needed, however, is not merely the historical but the universal historical. And this is to be found not in Germany but in the great representatives of Western Europe. This does not mean, however, that we turn in this direction with an uncritical eye. The ideas of Western Europe, especially capitalism with its lopsided individualism, are today under a new scrutiny at the hands of socialism (which has its own limitations). The needed return to the West is a return to natural law. In the context of his philos-

ophy of history Troeltsch looks for a new dynamic synthesis to be created
not by an individual but by a generation of cooperation.

BERMAN'S CONCEPTION OF NATURAL LAW

We turn now to a discussion of Harold Berman's treatment of natural law.
Like Troeltsch, he laments that law has become increasingly secular, pragmatic, and political. But partly due to his centering attention on jurisprudence he takes a path somewhat different from that of Troeltsch. In
his 1980 address at the Divinity School of the University of Chicago,
entitled "The Crisis of the Western Legal Tradition," he says that law "no
longer seems to be rooted in an ongoing tradition and guided by a universal vision." What has been lost is a sense of the rootedness of law in
the moral order of the universe and a sense of its transcendent qualities,
the sense that it points to something beyond itself, to something dealt
with by theology. In place of this rootedness, law is viewed as something
"wholly instrumental, wholly invented, wholly pragmatic." Along with
this attitude has come finally also a deep skepticism about law as a manifestation of justice. Equally mistaken is the antinomian view that confuses
law with legalism. Here Berman would probably approve of T. S. Eliot's
words that "the spirit killeth, the word giveth life."

These views are far distant from the "medieval marriage of jurisprudence and theology" (the title of an unpublished essay by Harold Berman). In the generations after Gregory VII, the symbol of a revolution in
the history of the church, a distinction was made between divine law and
human law, and with human law a distinction between ecclesiastical and
secular law. The link between divine law and human law was natural law,
which helped to determine the priorities between enacted law and customary law. The subordination of positive law to natural law was re-
enforced by the dualism of secular and ecclesiastical law. According to
Gratian, the laws of the church itself were to be tested by their conformity
to natural law.

But how did the breakdown of the marriage come about, the divorce
between jurisprudence and theology? Berman sets forth the singular view
that the divorce began with Anselm (1033–1109), who thought it possible to prove "by reason alone" what faith knows through divine revelation. Although Anselm held that faith enlightens reason, the latter has
its own principles of operation. This strategy, calculated to persuade the
unbeliever, also purported to harmonize articles of faith. In jurisprudence

of the period one sees the same reliance on reason alone. When later on the principal law-making and law-enforcing functions were transferred to the sole jurisdiction of the national state the foundation was laid for the separation of jurisprudence from theology and ultimately for the complete secularization of legal thought. This process did not take place all at once. It reached its fruition in the crisis of the twentieth century.

In Berman's view not only adherence to natural law was lacking but also adherence to the historical school. At the same time the regnant school is the positivist school, which treats law as essentially a particular type of political instrument, a body of rules "posited" by the state. Probably Berman would consider Troeltsch's presentation of the Romantic historical outlook as a perversion of the historical school. In any event, his presentation gives major attention to jurisprudence.

Berman laments the fact, however, that the historical orientation has almost been lost. He therefore spells out the historical jurisprudence stemming from Savigny, "the most important German legal figure of the nineteenth century." His theory of law was directed against ideas prevailing in France after the Revolution. Legislation was viewed as the primary source of law. In this view the legislator is obliged to protect "the rights of man" or "the greatest good for the greatest number." But these views leave out of account traditions of the past with their "prerogatives and prejudices," words that reflect Burke's conception of the nation as a community of generations. Law is therefore considered to be an integral part of the common consciousness of the nation, "internal, silently operating powers." It must never become merely a body of ideal propositions [natural law] or a mere system of rules promulgated by the state [positivism]. It must always be an expression of the *Volksgeist,* a particular expression of the social and historical consciousness of a people at a given time and place. Berman compares this conception to that of the American "unwritten constitution," the national ideals, "the community values." Savigny's historical school held that the ultimate source of law is the older Germanic tradition of popular participation in law-making and adjudication, as well as the more modern German tradition of scholarly interpretation and systematization of the common law, the *jus commune.* This common law, like the English common law, traditional unenacted law, had been the common consciousness of the nation as it had developed through the generations by virtue of the *Volksgeist.*

We should note here that, as with positivism and natural law, significant criticisms have been made of the historical theory. I assume that the questions press upon us, How does one determine the *Volksgeist?* Does it include the Romanticism that in Troeltsch's view separated Germany from Western Europe and which suppressed natural law? Are we to assume that a judge in deciding a technical point in contract law is reflecting the *Volksgeist?* In any event, one must recognize, as Berman emphasizes, that the common memory is highly selective, as in post-Nazi Germany.[6]

Integrative Jurisprudence

Now we come to the pièce de résistance. Berman's address in January 1987 before the American Society of Christian Ethics is entitled "Toward an Integrative Jurisprudence: Politics, Morality, and History." The term "integrative jurisprudence," it turns out, was used previously by Jerome Hall. In this scenario Berman proposes something similar to Troeltsch's demand for a dynamic synthesis. We should recall here that in *The Interaction of Law and Religion* (1974) he suggested that we may be entering a new period to replace the period of particularism and fragmentation. In this new period one may encounter a new synthesis, interaction between and within all spheres, between the immanent and the transcendent, between the individual and the community, between and within the academic disciplines.

The 1987 lecture proposes to bring together three main schools of jurisprudence—positivist, historical, and natural law. They became separated from each other in the eighteenth and nineteenth centuries when legal philosophy was divorced from theology. Since that time each of these schools has developed in various directions. Berman agrees with Hall that the three can be brought together only by giving a broader definition to law than that which is usually adopted. He therefore defines the *actualization* of law as its essential feature. It is a type of social action, a process in which rules and values and traditions—all three—coalesce and are actualized. Pre-Enlightenment Christian writers from Aquinas to Blackstone, though characterized as natural-law theorists, were also positivists and historicists. The common source of these three they found in the triune God.

In proposing integrative jurisprudence, then, Berman asserts that it is not a new thing. It has already appeared in Western legal theory. But, as we have seen, he holds that an authentic integration will require a recovery of the historical dimension. Germany in the 1920s and 1930s forsook historical jurisprudence and adopted an extreme positivism, thus also abandoning natural-law theory: the rule of the state was glorified and made supreme over both history and the moral law of justice.

On the other hand, the historical school has found an echo in such figures as Maine and Maitland in England and in certain ways in Pound and Llewellyn in the States. But a major trend turned attention to instruments and processes of legal development. More and more this trend issued in a sociology of law.

Yet, in England and America judges have applied a historical jurisprudence combined with principles of reasonableness and fairness. Here again we encounter an integrative jurisprudence. In the United States outstanding examples are Joseph Story and Benjamin Cardozo.

In recent decades the integration of the principal schools has been sidetracked by the decline of the historical approach. A spurious, a blind historicism centers attention on what has been said by lawmakers of an earlier time, in the belief that law expresses what has been said in past formulations of the spirit of freedom and equality. These views turn out to be futile attempts to repeat the past. Berman speaks of them as historical positivism and historical moralism. The essence of historical jurisprudence is not historicism but historicity. Law is an ongoing historical process developing from the past into the future. A genuine historical jurisprudence helps to determine the scope of freedom of legal action, the standards according to which law should be enacted and interpreted, and the goals toward which the legal system strives. Therefore, hope is the nerve of this move into the future.

Looking toward the future, Berman sees the possible development of world law. The West is no longer the center; the West is in the larger world. He spells out in considerable detail the possibility of a broader law than the national law. Again the need for an integrative jurisprudence is stressed. Accordingly, he asserts that history alone—and especially national history alone—is as futile and as demonic as politics alone or morality alone. What is needed is the sense of history, the sense of destiny, a sense of mission in America and throughout the West. As against current nationalism the idea must be emphasized, that the body of law is binding on the state.

In all of this one must recognize that a revolutionary as well as an evolutionary element has appeared in the development of the Western legal tradition. Every nation looks to its revolutionary past. This means that historical jurisprudence must be alert not only to the living past but also to the times in which we live. To know the times is essential to any healthy jurisprudence. And a healthy jurisprudence will call for an integrative jurisprudence that seeks what both Troeltsch and Berman have defined as a new synthesis. Berman would agree with Troeltsch in holding that the human obligation is a response to a more-than-human truth and justice.

For a theological interpretation of the needed interaction between the philosophies of law we turn to Paul of Tarsus. In the *First Epistle to the Corinthians* [12:14ff.] we read, "The body does not consist of one member but of many. If the foot should say, 'Because I am not a hand, I do not belong to the body,' that would not make it any less a part of the body." This is true also of the ear and the eye. "If the whole body were an ear, where would be the sense of smell?" In short, any philosophy of law that is isolated from the others brings about distortion, for "if one member suffers, all suffer together."

This twelfth chapter of the epistle is followed by the encomium of love. Accordingly, Harold Berman in an address given in 1963 at the Episcopal Theological School in Cambridge concludes that "law is a process creating conditions in which sacrificial love personified by Jesus Christ, can take root in society and grow."

Notes

1. Otto Gierke, *Natural Law and the Theory of Society* (1881, Eng. tr. 1934). For a critique of Berman's *Law and Revolution* see the review by Peter Landau, *University of Chicago Law Review* 5 (1984):937–43.

2. Amos Wilder, *Journal of Religion* 26 (1946):125–35. This article came out of a two-year study of natural law by Protestant theologians in the Middle West. It was published along with an article by the present writer, "The Law of Nature in Graeco-Roman Thought," *Journal of Religion* 25 (1945):97–118.

3. Gierke, *Natural Law,* p. 233.

4. We have given here only a suggestion of Holl's critique of Troeltsch. For an extensive account of this critique see the Introduction by Walter F. Bense to Karl Holl, *The Reconstruction of Morality,* Eng. tr. 1979, ed. James L. Adams and Walter F. Bense.

5. Gierke, *Natural Law,* Appendix.

6. See Ernst Fraenkel, *The Dual State* (1941), for an account of the conflict in the courts of Nazi Germany between Nazi racist law and rational natural law.

11 · *John XXIII: The Pope Who Would Go Window-shopping*

In the opening ceremony of the Second Vatican Council, the *Kyrie Eleison,* from the opening section of the mass, was the first choral piece that we heard—with the great organ in the Baroque cathedral of St. Peter and the choirboys singing from the cupola. To be able to recognize one of those boys lining the balcony you would need a telescope!

The sentiment of the *Kyrie Eleison,* "Lord, have mercy upon us," is always pertinent in a worship service but was especially pertinent then, when we consider what has happened as a consequence of the Second Vatican Council. This part of the mass suggests that the first act of the worshiper is to ask for the divine mercy and forgiveness for those alienations, those separations, among us and between ourselves and God.

You will recall that it is said that, when Pope John XXIII was asked about the purpose of the Second Vatican Council, he went to the window, opened it, and said to the reporter, "There, perhaps some fresh air will get into the church." In a more formal announcement, John XXIII said that the purpose of the Council was to renew the inner life of the Catholic Church, to bring the church into relationship with the modern world, and to remove obstacles to her accord with other Christian churches, especially "our separated brethren." But no formal statement can adequately express the spirit of that remarkable man.

After very elaborate preparations, and briefings as to what we Protestant observers were to do in our first audience with the Pope, we appeared almost an hour before the Pope himself was to appear, and arranged ourselves in a circle in the large consistory of the papal palace, the Vatican. At the end of this large room there was a high throne, obviously the place where the Pope normally sits for audiences of this size. At the appointed moment we saw the Pope come in. I happened to be sitting rather near the door through which he entered—he sort of toddled or waddled along—with his retinue. He came, shall we say, bouncing in and, looking around, saw us, turned and saw the throne, and immediately began to expostulate. We soon found out that he was saying to the assistants, "I'm

Revised from a lecture on Vatican Council II, presented at the First Unitarian Church, Syracuse, New York, May 10, 1964.

not going to sit up there. No, go and get me a chair. I'll sit with my brethren." They had to rearrange everything—pull the loudspeaker system down from the high throne, bring a chair in—then he sat down among us and proceeded.

That's a rather effective way to make friends. I want to say that our hearts were irresistibly opened to this remarkable human being. Let me give you another example, to indicate his mentality and spirit—a story that came to me from a former professor, under whom I studied for a term at the Sorbonne in Paris, namely the Roman Catholic lay historian of medieval philosophy, Etienne Gilson.

Gilson was a friend of Cardinal Roncalli's, so it was only natural that, after Roncalli became Pope John XXIII, he should visit him at the Vatican. In the course of one of their conversations Gilson finally said, "Well, now, John, how do you like this new job, anyway?" Whereupon the Pope responded, "It's a very interesting job, a fascinating job, but I have my problems." "For example?" said Etienne. "Well, some of those problems are very difficult and some are perhaps a little trivial. You know, Etienne, this is not so important, but it bothers me. One of my favorite relaxations is window-shopping. Wherever I have lived, in Paris or Venice, when I have had free time, the thing I loved most was to go window-shopping. I like to see what the new gadgets are, and I like to see what the new styles are that the ladies are wearing, the hats and shoes and dresses. But now that I have this new job, if I go down in Rome on the streets there is such a tumult of people climbing all over each other—trying to see what he looks like! They tell me here at the bureaucracy that I can't do it anymore. It's not so important, but by this job I have been deprived of my favorite relaxation. I can't go window-shopping any more."

"What about a more important one," asked Etienne. "Yes, you know, Etienne, every day I think more and more about the martyrdom of us priests." "Martyrdom?" "Yes, it's martyrdom, I tell you it's martyrdom. You know we priests have to live in singleness all our lives. We can't marry. We're vowed to celibacy. So we can't have any of the joys of family life or conjugal love, or having children or rearing children. I say that's martyrdom." And then he said to the professor of medieval philosophy, "You know where we got that, Etienne? You fellows from the Middle Ages imposed it on us. And I can't do anything about it. But worse than that, it isn't in the Bible. It isn't in the Bible."

The man who speaks in this spontaneous, direct fashion—even to members of the Vatican curia—has communicated something of himself to many participants in the Vatican Council. I would venture to say that it is partly due to John XXIII's character, quality, and spirit that the American cardinals—who on the whole were supposed to belong to the conservative group—showed themselves finally to be much more on the progressive side than was anticipated.

Pope Paul VI, following John XXIII, has maintained something of the spirit that was engendered by him. His address to the Protestant observers was also warm and frank. He acknowledged that there is no hiding the differences that separate Protestants and Roman Catholics, and he reminded us that in his earlier address he had begged forgiveness of non-Roman Christians for past acts of the Church which had alienated them. He said, "We dare not approach each other except in the spirit of Matthew 5:23, the morning Scripture lesson: 'Therefore if thou bring thy gift to the altar, and there remember that thy brother hath aught against thee, leave there thy gift before the altar, and go thy way; first be reconciled to thy brother, and then come and offer thy gift.'" Paul VI went on to say, "We must look not alone to the past but also to the present and the future." And he adopted one of the phrases that was used by a spokesman of the observers, "Together we are on a road."

Now we are very much aware of the obstacles that stand in the way of new understanding and of new cooperation, obstacles that have been reared from both sides. There have been four and a half centuries of division and persecution, sometimes at the hands of Roman Catholics, sometimes at the hands of Protestants. Jakob Burckhardt, the Swiss historian, has given a brilliant account of the thesis that the form of Christianity, Protestant or Catholic, that prevailed in any section of Europe was determined by who had the strongest battalions. Force has been used for the establishment of one or the other—the Reformation or the Counter-Reformation.

This history is one obstacle, and there are others, among them, obviously, the doctrine of papal infallibility. From the point of view of the academic community and even of Roman Catholicism in this century, this doctrine is extremely difficult to define. Precisely when was the Pope infallible? Most of us beyond the Roman pale have difficulty seeing how there can be any fundamental spirit of cooperation with such a view in force; this conception is a form of idolatry which we, in good conscience, must remain opposed to.

Or the doctrine of transubstantiation, the belief that the bread and the wine are by a miracle of God transformed into the body and the blood of

Christ, and that by partaking them in the mass one receives an infusion of grace. There are aspects of this doctrine that Protestants actually could learn something from, but in its major articulation the doctrine does give us some difficulties.

Or the doctrine of the Virgin Mary and her bodily assumption. Or the doctrine of the immaculate conception of the Virgin Mary. Or the historic claim of the Roman Catholic Church to ecclesiastical monopoly: there may not properly be freedom for "error"; the Roman Church contains the Truth as the deposit of faith, and in a truly Christian society it may not properly allow public expression of heretical opinions. This view still obtains in certain countries that are ostensibly Christian Catholic countries. Or we could mention the very organization of the church, with its centralization of power in the Vatican, or attitudes toward censorship, or attitudes toward birth control, and so on.

But certain things of great importance have been happening within Catholicism. There are many evidences of a kind of emancipation from traditions that are associated with the Council of Trent and the Counter-Reformation—the attempts of the Roman church to deal with emerging Protestantism. There are several significant developments that will, however, take a long time to come to fruition.

Firstly, there is the demand for greater freedom of the bishops—a decentralization of the power of the Vatican. One even hears the word, from time to time, de-Italianization. This principle of the decentralization of authority in the church is one that goes back to the sixteenth century and the Radical Reformation.

Secondly, there is the question of the place of the Bible in the Catholic church. The progressives are insisting that the Bible must take priority over the intervening tradition. A related issue of extreme importance, here, is the freedom for critical study of the Bible according to modern methods of historical criticism, and of cooperation with non-Roman Catholic scholars.

A third matter, suggested by the quotation I cited earlier from Pope Paul VI, is a new evaluation of the Reformation and of the way Catholicism has dealt with it. I have met professors at the Gregorian University in Rome who are trying to teach courses on the history and theology of Protestantism with a newly objective spirit, at the same time that they attempt to re-evaluate their own tradition. In this connection we see a new tendency to give a larger role to the laity in the church and to find new ways of cooperating with non-Roman Catholics.

Despite all of these things that I have referred to telegraphically, there is another side to the story. Those who publicly attack policies of the church are likely, even more than in the past, to be called anti-Catholics. There is a danger in the new spirit that emanates from John XXIII, insofar as it makes people say, "We must be quiet now, we mustn't have open, frank discussions. It rocks the boat, you see, to do this. We should only talk about the new spirit." But we cannot do that.

Consider, for instance, the play by Rolf Hochhuth, "The Deputy," that has caused such a stir in Europe and New York. The Roman Catholics are actually fortunate that this play centers on what Pope Pius XII did not do, namely, make a clear statement attacking the Nazis for the extermination of the Jews. If the play had centered on the things Pacelli did before he was pope, it would have aroused much more of a stir. For this gentleman, Pope Pius XII, was a major figure in turning central European politics in a reactionary direction, in a certain fashion paving the way for Hitler.

This is the kind of thing that Roman Catholic magazines in Europe are themselves bringing out today. That they are doing so is itself an aspect of the new spirit. I asked one of the major authors of these articles—he is a devout Roman Catholic and has been attacked for these writings—why he was doing it. He said, "We must learn the lessons of Nazism, for if we do not realize the sins of our church during that time, then all of that was in vain. I want it to be known."

The situation will continue to be marked by embarrassment and tension. But it is also a situation in which, it seems to me, there appears the spirit of devoutness, the spirit of penitence suggested by the *Kyrie Eleison*—a willingness to learn from each other and to grow through the mutual stimulus of openness, enabling Protestants, too, to learn something from the other side.

I conclude with a statement by an old friend of mine, the distinguished Roman Catholic theologian Yves Congar, whom I've known for about thirty years. He said, "The spirit of the Council is the spirit of freedom and liberty, free of all servility and of all consideration of personal interest. . . . It is an evangelic and apostolic spirit, a spirit of respect and love for people, anxious to uphold their liberty and their dignity. It is a spirit of open-heartedness to others, relieved of any spirit of theological or clerical triumph, and an intense attentiveness to God, who speaks through these new happenings." I say that if this spirit grows in the Roman Catholic Church and is also responded to corporately by us, it might be that eventually some fresh air will enter even into our Protestant churches.

12 · *Reminiscences of Paul Tillich*

This evening I shall have to practice what Ben Jonson called "blotting." "The art of writing is the art of blotting," he said, that is, of omitting. I hope I'll be able to show that capacity here, taking into account the invasion of Father Time. By the way, I was interested to learn recently that the idiom, "To take time by the forelock"—to take Father Time by the little tuft of hair on his balding head—is attributed to the first Greek philosopher, Thales.

My talk does not have the intention of offering revelations. I wish that Hannah and Mutie Tillich could be here to supplement—or correct—what I have to say. Mutie could tell us, for example, of difficulties her father encountered when trying to help her with her algebra lessons when she was a girl. I shall not discuss Tillich's mannerisms, apart from saying that I was always struck by the fact that he wore white socks—no matter what the color of his suit, white socks—and that in conversation in his office, he always had a little paper clip in his hand. Grace Cali, who was Tillich's secretary, told me a friend was so much aware of that paper clip that he offered to buy him a golden one.

I want to deal with Paulus primarily in terms of his relation to others. A scattering of impressions and stories is on the agenda, but I think I can relate each of them to one of Tillich's associates.

Let me start with Tillich's appreciation and critiques of Martin Heidegger. In an unpublished essay on the German philosopher Tillich asserts that Heidegger really did not have ethical norms; his major thrust was simply for *resoluteness.* On the other hand he asserts that Heidegger more successfully than anyone else in this century brought ontology to the fore. In the course of a conversation one day in Cambridge a student in Tillich's hearing questioned whether one should study Heidegger, since he had collaborated with the Nazis. Tillich replied, "If you adopt that as a criterion, you will be obliged also to exclude Plato, for he served the tyrant of Syracuse."

I was long interested in that fact that in his earlier writings, in the 1920s, Tillich referred to himself as a voluntarist. I once asked him,

Edited from an address at the meeting of the North American Paul Tillich Society, in Cambridge, Massachusetts, on December 4, 1987; recorded and transcribed by H. Frederick Reisz, Jr. Reprinted by permission from the *Newsletter* 14, no. 4 (1989) of the North American Paul Tillich Society.

"Where did you get that term, 'voluntarism'?" He couldn't say. Many times when I asked him a question of this sort—for example, about the source of the stimulus for his *The System of the Sciences*—he couldn't, or wouldn't, say. He was good at covering his tracks and he didn't want anybody uncovering them. At any rate I found that the term was first introduced by the sociologist Ferdinand Tönnies to refer to any outlook or philosophy that gives primacy to the will. (I have dealt with this in my article on Tönnies in the *Encyclopedia of Religion*.) Tillich was of course familiar with the writings of Tönnies; in *The Socialist Decision*, for example, he adapts Tönnies' corollary, *Gemeinschaft* and *Gesellschaft*—society and community.

Let me turn to another figure, Karl Barth. Tillich frequently expressed his appreciation for Barth, but he was equally critical. A couple of years ago a Professor Williams, who taught a seminar on Tillich at Trinity College, Oxford, walked into my study and handed me a document. "Did you ever see this before?" he asked. I looked at it and recognized my own handwriting in the margin. It was Tillich's original introduction for the *Systematic Theology*, but it had never been published. He speaks about the forgiveness that is required for one who would presume to write a systematic theology, saying, "I am aware of the fact that if I am going to do such a presumptuous thing, I should ask forgiveness, and I do." After discussing Barth in another context a page or two later, he speaks about theologians who insist on using hundreds of biblical quotations in a systematic theology. This is a spurious method, he says, for these passages are often taken out of context, abstracted, and then put into a new context where they have different meanings. Barth tends to ignore this and seems to be satisfied, since they are Holy Writ, to cite these hundreds of quotations.

I had many conversations with Tillich about the Barmen Declaration [of the Confessing Churches in Germany during the Nazi era]. For a time I had lived in Barmen and was for more than a year in personal contact with the Confessing Church group. Tillich criticized Barth and the others who put together the Barmen Declaration for their failure to attack anti-Semitism and to demand the rights of Jewish anti-Nazis, unless they were members of the church! Barth, we know from Eberhard Bethge, was warned about this by [Dietrich] Bonhoeffer.

I should say a word here about Erich Fromm and Tillich. They were good friends, and I knew Fromm almost as long as I knew Tillich. I had translated Fromm's small book *The Dogma of Christ*, not for publication but to whet the appetite of graduate students for Christology. When talk began about getting it published, Tillich—and we'll see another example of this presently—said, "Oh, don't publish it! It will kill his reputation." In this book we find a Neo-Freudian and a Neo-Marxist interpretation of the major Christologies, from Adoptionism to Nicaea. And the strategy worked; the students' appetite was kindled, for they wanted to investigate to see if Fromm was correct. Tillich agreed with the general thesis as little as I did, as Fromm knew very well. My translation was finally published without my prior knowledge.

Tillich's opposition to the publication gives me occasion to speak of what, at the time, was a surprising experience for me. Initially I had reached an understanding with Tillich regarding which essays I would translate for *The Protestant Era,* including "The Class Struggle and Religious Socialism." But when Tillich looked at my translations and came across this essay, he said, "You can't publish that! Oh, no, no," he expostulated, "it's too Marxist." So it was not published. I promised [Gustavo] Gutierrez, whose lectures I heard recently at Boston College, that I would send him a copy, and it is being published in a volume on creativity in Tillich's writings, edited by Jacqueline Kegley.

Helmut Thielicke, for whose work *Theological Ethics* I had found the translator and the publisher, was my host when I lectured in Hamburg some years ago. Tillich had a standing invitation to lecture at the University of Hamburg; one year he happened to be there on his birthday. Frau Thielicke baked a cake and put candles on it for a little party—she told me that Tillich loved this *Gemütlichkeit.* Afterwards the two theologians repaired to the study for a little wine (required for any symposium). Thielicke, who was something of a prankster, said to Tillich, "You know, I'm professor of systematic theology in this university and I try to keep up on things. I keep running into books on Paul Tillich—the name is on any list of the great theologians of this century. But I came to an embarrassing moment in reading of the writings of Herr Doktor Tillich. I found that other theologians, including contemporary theologians, have a doctrine of the angels. But I don't find any such doctrine in your writings, Paulus. Don't you have an angelology?" "Oh, yes, angelology—well, Helmut, you see. . . ." "Yes?" "I, uh, mmm, well you know, I always loved those Greek gods and goddesses. They're the Christian angels!" "Paulus, I'm sure there has not been in history any such angelology as the one you're suggesting now. Amazing! The Greek gods and goddesses are Christian angels?" "Yes, yes." Then suddenly Tillich said, "Well, now, do you hear them, Helmut? Don't you hear those angels? They're singing now! Look at that gorgeous tree out there in the garden—I always loved that tree.

There they are, right there, dancing in that tree!" Thielicke then said, "Paulus, I have now seen the miracle, and I'm ready to go on to my greater reward. I have seen the miracle. Paul Tillich here not only hears but even sees angels, after only one flask of wine!"

When Reinhold Niebuhr [in 1936] persuaded Tillich to come to the United States to join the Union [Theological School] faculty, its members agreed to sacrifice five percent of their salaries in order to pay Tillich's salary until it could be accommodated in the budget the following year. It was at that time that Carl Voss met regularly with Tillich to tutor him in English. One day much later on, when I complimented Tillich on the style of a recently published sermon of his, he said, "Jim, you know, in studying English I learned that it is not necessary to be obscure in order to be profound."

One day when he and I were conversing on the difficulty of his finding a public in a strange land, I told him about conversations I had had with T. S. Eliot. I told Paulus that Eliot had said that as a young poet he had to decide whether or not he would try to meet a demand already obtaining among those accustomed to the poetry of Tennyson and Browning. No, he said, he would adopt his own style. But if he did so he would have to create his own public, and that would take some time. Whereupon Tillich said, "That applies to me. Certainly it will take me time to create a public, especially over here." Later, Wilhelm Pauck told me he used to tease Tillich because of the Germanisms in his vocabulary, but Tillich replied, "My public likes it, they like it!"

Grace Cali once gave me an article she wrote on Paul Tillich and jazz. She spent the good part of a summer lending records to Tillich. At first she thought he was just trying to be nice to her, but she was pleased by his continuing interest. By the end of the summer he had decided on his favorite, Charlie Parker, whose improvisations especially impressed him. I used to play recordings of Schoenberg for him, relevant to interpreting *Doctor Faustus*.

Wilhelm Pauck often spoke of Tillich's love of fellowship. It was especially evident in his participation in the National Theological Discussion Group. About twenty or twenty-five theologians were present for our yearly meetings at the College of Preachers adjacent to the Washington National Cathedral. Tillich quite obviously enjoyed Pauck's authoritative conduct of the meetings, always insisting that people keep on the track. On one occasion, a guest theologian presented an elaborate paper on Jesus' Ascension. When he had finished Tillich said rather sternly, "I cannot

believe that you take this story seriously and without qualification."
Whereupon, instead of defending his paper, the poor guest shriveled and
sat quietly in his chair for the rest of the meeting.

At another meeting we had an extended discussion on how to deal with
the Resurrection. Tillich here used the term "deliteralizing," which he
preferred to [Rudolf Bultmann's term] "demythologizing." When the
meeting was a little more than half over he said, "I tell you, I'll stay here
as long as anyone else will. Let's stay here and settle this matter, how we
should deliteralize the Resurrection."

This incident reminds me of a time when Tillich and Gustav Weigel
were dual lecturers at Harvard. (Weigel had commended Tillich to the
Catholic public. Later on I had the satisfaction of becoming well acquainted with Weigel when he was the interpreter for us, the "separated
brethren," at the Second Vatican Council. Once in the midst of a discussion he whispered, "We are learning one thing here—that Latin is not a
universal language. That last fellow's accent was so heavily Belgian I
could hardly understand him." I spent pleasant afternoons with Weigel
between sessions of the Council, in particular discussing Catholic theology in the United States. He entertained little hope for it so long as the
Irish are in control. I mentioned a number of writings that showed originality, but in each instance he promptly said the idea came from Europe
and was already cold porridge.)

As I was saying, Tillich and Weigel gave a dual lecture at Harvard to
a packed audience. In the question period a student somewhat aggres-
sively said, "I want to ask a question, and I don't want any qualifications.
I want a Yes or a No." Whereupon Tillich rose and said, "Well, sir, what
is your question?" The student said, "I want to know, do you or don't you
believe in the bodily resurrection of Jesus Christ?" There was something
of a stir in the house; each of the lecturers bowed to the other, as if to say,
"You take it first, Alphonse." Presently they agreed that Tillich should be
the first to respond. His answer was brief and unambiguous: "The answer
is simply No. How can a modern person believe in the bodily resurrection
of Christ?" Applause ran through the hall. Then Weigel took his turn,
saying, "Of course I believe in the bodily resurrection of Christ. My
church, the magisterium, teaches me to do so. Do not ask me to give
further explanation. I believe in it because my church teaches me to
do so."

Everyone here is familiar with Paul Tillich's warm reception among the
students at Harvard. In good weather the students formed borders for the

sidewalk as Tillich approached for the lecture in Emerson Hall. It is said, however, that some members of the Department of Philosophy did not recommend Tillich's courses for graduate students.

During this period someone made a comment that reached Tillich's ear. This person had said that, now that Tillich was here, it was possible to mention the word God and to remain respectable. On hearing this, Tillich was said to have raised his arms in dismay and say, "He knows not that God is a consuming fire!" [cf. Heb. 12:29].

Let me say a few words at this point about Jane Blaffer Owen. She has constructed a Tillich Park in New Harmony, Indiana, where Tillich's ashes now repose. From any part of the park one may see the familiar bust of Tillich which dominates the park. At the end of each path one encounters a large granite stone on which some aphorism of his is carved. Let me read one of these sentences to you: "He who tries to be without authority tries to be like God, who alone is by himself, and, like everyone who tries to be like God, he is thrown down to self-destruction, be it a single human being, be it a nation, be it a period of history like our own."

I am reminded of the story about Tillich's approaching a young lady, a student, on shipboard, and asking in what century she would prefer to have lived. He then gave his answer, "I would prefer to have lived in the theonomous (that is, the High) Middle Ages."

I want to conclude these reminiscences by telling of an encounter with Paulus and Hannah in their home at Union Theological Seminary. Since I was working on translations of Tillich, one evening when I arrived in New York I telephoned him to make an appointment for the next day. Immediately he said, "I want you to come out now, to be here with the guests who are here." When I entered the apartment I found it full of people seated on folding chairs. Noticing that Tillich was in the midst of a lecture, I said that he should not stop for introductions. But presently Hannah came in and called him out of the room for a telephone call. I spoke to the woman in the nearest chair, and she explained, "We are a group of psychiatrists. The other evening we heard Tillich give a lecture downtown on the meaning of faith. It was an absorbing lecture. We asked him if he would spend an evening with us. If anyone had told me a month ago that I would spend an evening in the home of a theologian, I would have told him that I was still in possession of self-control, indeed that he was a little crazy. But here we are!"

I am reminded of the description of Tillich given years ago in the Barthian journal, *Zwischen den Zeiten*. The author spoke of him as "an apostle to the Gentiles." Not caviar for the regenerate. On an occasion when Tillich took my daughter Eloise to luncheon, he told her, "I am pope of the heretics."

When Tillich returned from the telephone call he decided to change the direction of the conversation. "Here is my friend Jim Adams from the Divinity School of the University of Chicago. I want him to tell you what he has been doing recently." Knowing that I was the head of the Independent Voters of Illinois, he assumed, I think, that I would tell them something about politics. But I said, "Recently I have completed reading Thomas Mann's *Doctor Faustus*." Tillich was a little embarrassed. "That book has been on my desk for several weeks," he said, "but I haven't had time to look at it. Tell us about it." I said, "I can tell you one thing that is quite clear. The first fifty or sixty pages could have been written only by someone familiar with the writings of Paul Tillich. Mann's point of departure is certainly Tillich, such as the account of arguments among theological students and the descriptions of theological professors."

Tillich and the guests listened eagerly, whereupon he said, "Let me tell you what happened. Thomas Mann wrote to me to tell me that he was now preparing to write his *Doctor Faustus*. He asked me to send him a memorandum on what theological students and professors were talking about, were excited about, when I was a student. So I sent him a somewhat lengthy memorandum."

As soon as the meeting broke up I told Tillich that I would much like to see that memorandum. Certainly, I said, there will be Ph.D.'s in the future who would make hay out of it as a literary source for *Doctor Faustus*. But Tillich could not find the memorandum. Later I wrote to the widow of an old friend, Professor Fritz Kaufmann, in Zurich, asking her some day to go to the Thomas Mann Archives to look for Tillich's memorandum. Within a short time she sent a copy of it to me. A translation of this document is now available in several publications; Gunilla Bergsten in her book on the sources and structure of the novel has placed passages in the memorandum alongside corresponding passages in the novel, finding that Mann sometimes abbreviates Tillich's paragraph or changes an adjective or an adverb or the order of words in a sentence.

I have spoken of Tillich as "an apostle to the Gentiles." But of course he was not always successful. Somewhere in an essay by Edmund Wilson the following passage appears:

At one of Tillich's seminars where the theologian, charming as the devil and at least as slippery, spun his notions about faith, those of us listening felt that the idea of a personal God—the God we had rejected, the only

God we knew—kept fading further into the distance. I asked Tillich: "You say religion rests upon a sense of awe before the 'fundament of being.' Does that mean that if, on a starry night perhaps out at sea, I find myself overwhelmed by the beauty of the scene, and become acutely aware of my own transience before the immensity of things, I am having a religious experience?" My intent, of course, was to distinguish between mere cultivated sensibility and religious belief; but Tillich, suave dialectician that he was, seized upon my question and said, "Yes." Even though I called myself a skeptic I had provided "admirably"—he grinned—a description of religious experience. He had turned the tables on us, and we sat there uncomfortably—until from the back of the room there came the Wilsonian rumble, "Mr. Tillich, you're taking away our rights!"

Presumably taking away the right to be an unbeliever.

In other more sympathetic milieus Tillich was able to offer a persuasive interpretation of religion for the alienated. Through my association with the American Academy of Arts and Sciences, I became acquainted with the president, the atomic scientist Victor Weisskopf, and with his brother, Walter, the economist. Both of these men said that it was through Tillich's writings that their outlook on religion and human existence had been changed. On one occasion Victor beckoned for me to come aside and said, "I want the membership of the Academy to be exposed to Paul Tillich. Will you please get out a book on Tillich for members of the Academy?" Soon thereafter the Academy secured a grant from the National Endowment for the Humanities, resulting in the volume entitled *The Thought of Paul Tillich,* edited by Wilhelm Pauck, Roger Shinn, and myself [Harper and Row, 1985].

It is not often that a theologian is cited in a Supreme Court decision, though one may recall the extensive correspondence between Felix Frankfurter and Reinhold Niebuhr (*Journal of Law and Religion* 1, no. 2 [1983]). But Tillich achieved the distinction of being cited in Supreme Court decisions.

In the nineteenth century the Court seemed to settle on traditional criteria in the determination of religious faith, for example, "the establishment of some relationship between Deity and believer which demands particular forms of ethical behavior." In the Arno Jacobson case (1963) the defendant in the defense of resisting the draft cited his belief in a "Godness" to which the individual may have a direct vertical relation. On this basis Jacobson rejected war and violence as morally repugnant. In the U.S. Court of Appeals, Mr. Justice H. J. Friendly supported his decision in favor of Jacobson by appealing to Paul Tillich, whose theology seemed to "embrace" Jacobson's unorthodox religious views. Here the statutory demand for belief in a Supreme Being seems to be transcended. The Court concluded that Tillich's notion of transcendence, presented in volume 2 of *Systematic Theology,* in which the anthropomorphic "superworld" of divine objects is rejected and God is affirmed as "the ground of being," seemed to be in accord with Jacobson's outlook. Thereupon the judge accepted Tillich's formulations about "the power of being," about "the God above the God of theism," and about faith as "ultimate concern."

Meanwhile, Mr. Justice Harlan in a concurring decision in the Welsh case warned his colleagues that in appealing to Tillich the Court was descending into an "Alice-in-Wonderland world where words have no meaning." James McBride in "Paul Tillich and the Supreme Court" (*Journal of Church and State* 30, no. 2 [Spring 1988]), shows misconceptions that have arisen as a consequence of interpreting "ultimate concern" as merely a subjective "affective attitude."

I think I have now sufficiently updated the reminiscences. Let me conclude with a word from Tillich: "Reconciliation, reunion, resurrection— this is the New Creation, the New Being, the new state of things. Do we participate in it? The message of Christianity is not Christianity, but a New Reality. A new state of things has appeared, it still appears; it is hidden and visible, it is there and it is here. Accept it, enter into it, let it grasp you."

13 · In Memoriam: *Words for Paul Johannes Tillich*

Paul Tillich is one of the great heroes of the mind in our century. Among his fellow countrymen his name will be mentioned along with the names of Ernst Troeltsch and Max Weber. The scope of his interest was like unto theirs in breadth, and the depth of his insight was more profound than theirs. The style of his writing, both in his mother tongue and especially in the language of his adoption, reveals a luminous, numinous quality

A memorial service was held for Paul Johannes Tillich, University Professor, Emeritus, in Memorial Church of Harvard University on November 4, 1965. The text of Adams's memorial address was published in *The Harvard Divinity Bulletin* (January 1966); it is here reprinted by permission.

that is unique. A luminous style I have said. The metaphor is that of light. But the substance of his writing is numinous, for Tillich in principle intended it to be a reflected light, the light of eternity, the light of Numen. In employing this metaphor here I recall a lecture which I heard from Paul Tillich about twenty-five years ago, a lecture on the theory of light of the thirteenth-century Franciscan scholar at Oxford, Robert Grosseteste.

The luminous and numinous quality of Tillich's thought and intention is well illustrated by one of his mentors, the German theosophist of the seventeenth century, Jakob Boehme. The fact that Tillich in significant ways was stimulated by the writings of this Lutheran mystic gives reason for us to recall here the character of Boehme's vision. As he was at work in his shop this shoemaker's glance was one day attracted by a polished pewter dish which with dazzling light reflected the sun. A strange feeling overpowered him, for it seemed as if he were looking into the very heart of reality and beholding its innermost mystery. Speaking of this experience Boehme said, "I fell into great melancholy and sadness when I beheld the mighty deep of this world with its stars and clouds, rain and snow . . . for I saw evil and good, love and wrath in all things, in the earth and its elements as well as in man and beast . . . In this Light I saw through all things and into all creatures . . . Then I had a great impulse to describe the Being of God." Here we see the great themes of Tillich, the darkness and the light, the coincidence of opposites.

Paul Tillich, reared in the household of a Lutheran pastor, served as vicar in a parish in Brandenburg and then later on as a chaplain in the German Army of the First World War. But already before the war, and following upon his classical training in the Gymnasium, Tillich had discovered Jakob Boehme, probably through the study of Schelling. When he was in his early twenties he published his first two books, volumes that deal with Schelling's construction of the history of religion and with his conception of mysticism and guilt, of union with and estrangement from the powers of being. Here, like Boehme, he reveals a vivid awareness of the demonic as well as of the divine elements in nature and in human nature and human history. The theme is also that of Luther, the theme of the love and the wrath of God.

During his three years of service as chaplain in the Army, Tillich, the young theologian, determined to find respite from the bludgeonings of war by devoting his leisure to the study of art. He tells us that from his "pleasure in the poor reproductions that were obtainable at the military bookstores in the fields, there grew a systematic study of art." The early Christian art of Italy made "an overwhelming impression" upon him. "What no amount of study of church history had brought was accomplished by the mosaics in ancient Roman basilicas." These experiences led him on to the study of contemporary poetry and painting. Thus he came to an appreciation of expressionism as a manifestation of "mystical fullness, the form charged with metaphysical import" or meaning. In an essay of that period he adopts the metaphor of light to express his awareness of the numinous. "If we imagine," he said, "the import (or ultimate meaning) to be the sun, and form the orbit of a planet, then for every form of culture there is proximity to and distance from the sun or the import. If it is the power of the sun which is revealed in the nearness to the sun it is the peculiar power in the movement of the planets which is expressed in the distance from the sun; and yet, it is the sun itself which supports both nearness and distance." In these early years he sketched out a theology of culture where the delineation of the divine Yes and the divine No upon culture *and* religion present the leitmotifs of all his later work. Tillich would have liked the question of Francis Bacon, "Were it not better for a man in a fair room to set up one great light, or a branching candlestick of lights, than to go about with a small watch candle into every corner?" He would have liked also another word from Bacon, "Truth may perhaps come to the price of a pearl, that sheweth best by day; but it will not rise to the price of a diamond or carbuncle that sheweth best in varied lights."

During the next two decades Tillich by means of his vision of the one great light attempted to interpret the expressions and distortions of religion and culture "in varied lights." It is an astonishing journey to follow him on this pilgrimage through the study of the plastic arts, painting, and architecture. (In an editorial footnote to an article on architecture by Tillich in the early 1930s we are told that the author of the article is a leading architect!) From a study of the arts he passes on to a substantial theological interpretation of all the sciences, and then to a religious interpretation of social and economic forces, and to a theology of history. This effort brought him into exile among us. The successor of Max Scheler in Frankfurt, he was dismissed from the university by the Nazis. He had not been a quiet one. Indeed, he had been one of the most articulate anti-Nazi religious socialists. In 1931 he became one of the gifts of Hitler to America. The task of learning a new language and of adjusting himself to a new milieu required an enormous expense of energy.

Tillich pursued his vocation as theologian and teacher in the painful conviction that in many quarters, and particularly in the churches, Christianity was moribund, partly because of the bondage of the churches to a class mentality, partly because of their encasement in a rigid theological language that was incapable of speaking with power to the condition of man in our time, and partly because of a narrow ecclesiastical conception of Christianity and a superficial view of potentially vital and unconsciously religious elements in the culture. He was committed to the task of finding a new language and of giving new utterance to the prophetic tradition of Judaism and Christianity. Imagine the shock which he gave to many of his fellow Christians when in 1926 he wrote:

> In the nineteenth century the prophetic spirit broke forth in two places, and each time it was under the banner of a conflict with Christianity: in Karl Marx and in Friedrich Nietzsche. In Marx we find by word and deed the spirit of the old Jewish prophecy, and in Nietzsche the spirit of Luther. Although this battle, in the one case for justice and in the other for the creative life, took its form as a drive against God, it was an attack upon God who had been bound to a standpoint, i.e., of bourgeois society. Naturally, this attack in turn developed into a standpoint, perhaps the highest that was then possible. Almost all that has been possible outside of and beyond bourgeois society has been influenced from these two sources: on the one hand, from Nietzsche—the vitalistic philosophy, the expressionist art and literature, the youth movement, the campaign against bourgeois conventions, the appreciation of aristocratic discipline, Stefan George and his school. On the other hand, from Marx—the philosophy of history, the passionate tension created by concerted effort directed toward the future, the campaign against the bourgeois ethos, against capitalism and imperialism, the ideal of a fellowship-culture, and the protest against the alliance of the churches with the capitalistic sovereign state.

For his own time Tillich sought new symbols for the creative power of the divine fecundity and for the "demonic powers of our age, as the Old Testament prophets, early Christianity, Luther, Marx and Nietzsche had done for their age and time."

We see here the fundamental impulses that pervaded Tillich's whole career. He wished to make the prophetic and the sacramental, the theological and the philosophical traditions relevant to the present historical situation; and he did this by means of a constant dialogue with the creative and critical figures of past and present—from Amos to Jesus and Paul and the Church Fathers, from Anaximander to Aristotle and Plotinus and

Augustine, from Joachim of Fiore to Nicolas of Cusa and Luther, from Kant and Fichte and Schelling to Marx and Nietzsche, and so on down to Freud, with the biblical symbols serving always as touchstone. As we see in his *Systematic Theology,* he drew from this dialogue the resources that could give new expression in architectonic fashion and "in varied lights" to the divine presence that alone can give new life, new courage to be, to see and to act. He carried on the dialogue in such a fashion as to reveal the prism of the divine presence and judgment in all spheres of culture. Although he was not enthusiastic about the life and work of Goethe, an aphorism of Goethe points to the intent of the dialogue. It was Goethe who said, a tradition cannot be inherited, it must be earned.

In his lifelong dialogue with past and present Tillich has sought to do for our time "what Augustine attempted in his own desperate age as Rome's sway was foundering in the West: to confront every warring ideology in the hope of freeing a depleted faith of accumulated dross and of renewing the power of religious symbols so that distracted and alienated spirits" might once again be brought to an authentic "ultimate concern" through sharing the faith of a Luther in the New Being in Christ, a faith that knows both the wrath and the love of God, a faith that "justifies" both the intellectual and the moral conscience of man.

It is difficult to say whether or not Tillich has elicited a following that may be called the Tillichian School. But there are few people who have become familiar with him inside the churches or outside them who have not been quickened to a new awareness of the light to the Gentiles and of the darkness visible that corrupts and enervates the human heart. Certainly, this impact coming from the mind and spirit of Tillich is in large part due to our recognition of the originality and the patient integrity of this man. He was himself a living example of the divinely given power and courage to be; he was a union of Apollonian and Dionysian powers, a marriage of undogmatic humility with the abundance of daring exploration of creative possibility.

Here we have advanced beyond the thinker to the person Paul Tillich. The light he gave was not a cold intellectual light; it was the light and warmth of responsive fellowship. Dialogue was for him a channel of the divine grace, a manifestation of the power of being. Recently we have retrieved from a library in Zurich a letter which he wrote in 1913 to Thomas Mann. In preparation of his novel *Doctor Faustus,* Thomas Mann had requested from Tillich a memorandum regarding theological studies and outlooks in Halle at the beginning of this century. The first section of Thomas Mann's novel reveals the influence of this letter and of Mann's familiarity with other writings of Tillich. In the letter to Mann, Tillich speaks of his appreciation of the lectures of his teacher Martin Kaehler, and he says that he was not engaged by the systematic presentation in the lectures but rather by the "asides," ideas mentioned out of context. He speaks of his own discussions late into the night with his student colleagues, and then he adds, "What I have become as a theologian, as a philosopher, and as man, I owe only in part to the professors, and in a comparatively overwhelming degree to a student association." It was apparently from these experiences that as *Privatdozent* in Berlin he was moved to introduce what he calls "discussion breaks" even during the lectures, a practice that was not customary at that time.

We have all enjoyed these dialogues with him. In these encounters with him those who have known him as students and colleagues have experienced the light and warmth of his person, what Phillips Brooks used to call truth reflected through personality. For this reason his former students and also men and women from many walks of life again and again have sought him out for the exhilarating joy of being with him.

A former student of the great Jewish scholar, Solomon Schechter, of the Jewish Theological Seminary in New York, tells of his first encounter with him when he was applying for admission to the Seminary. When the young man went into his office, Dr. Schechter asked him to read a few lines in the Talmud. This being done, Dr. Schechter said, "Now let me see if you have any common sense. Why do you want to come to the Seminary?" The applicant replied, "Dr. Schechter, I want to come to the Seminary to study."—"Well, I see that you do not have any common sense, because it would be easier and more efficient to study in the library than it would in the classroom. In the classroom you have to move with the pace of the slower students." The young man, baffled and alarmed, then stammered, "Dr. Schechter, why does one come to the Seminary?" And the scholar replied, "One comes to the Seminary to associate with great men. In the library you can find great books, but in the good classroom you find great men."

We who have known Paul Tillich have known greatness. Today many are here who have been strengthened and healed by the light that he shared with us, by the power working in and through him. Many have become newly aware of "the true light that enlightens all men who come into the world." He was more than a hero of the mind. Through him we have come to know better the love that reconciles that which has been separated in the common life, the love that informs and creates the kingdom of God. He now belongs in a new way to the eternal; and we know that neither death, nor life, nor height nor depth, nor any other creature shall be able to separate us from him or from the love of God. The Lord hath given, and the Lord hath taken away. Blessed be the name of the Lord.

Part Three

History and Theology

THE VICISSITUDES OF TWENTIETH-CENTURY THEOLOGY CAN BE traced in the history of James Luther Adams's intellectual development. He has called the process by which he rejected the fundamentalism of his youth and came to the religious stance of his maturity his "deprovincialization." But the theological liberalism at which he arrived was itself under attack, from the early decades of this century, by the "neo-orthodox" movement led by Karl Barth. Adams came to see that American liberalism, especially—marked by optimism without costing commitments, and by individualism without historical loyalties—also needed to be deprovincialized. Hence he pursued theological studies in England, France, and Germany—during the years that saw the rise of Nazism in Germany and a looming sense of cultural and spiritual crisis. The essays in this section reflect Adams's response to the challenges of neo-orthodoxy and the rise of totalitarian ideologies. They also indicate the resources that helped him define his own prophetic-liberal theological stance.

The first essay, "Prophetic Theology: Interrupting the Meeting," vividly portrays the crosscurrents of Protestant thought, with particular reference to two giants of twentieth-century theology, Karl Barth and Paul Tillich. Adams's concise description of "prophetic theology" intimately connects history and theology.

In "Encounter with the Demonic," Adams traces the origins of the German religious-socialist movement in the thought and ministries of Johann and Christoph Blumhardt. The essay exemplifies Adams's contention that psychic ills cannot be treated in isolation from social ills. Where Johann Blumhardt had applied the concept of "the demonic" to pastoral care for individuals, his son Christoph extended it to social analysis. The younger Blumhardt thus anticipated Paul Tillich and others, Adams argues, in his idea of "demonic"—that is, tragically distorted, destructive—social structures.

The essay that follows sets the central themes of Paul Tillich's thought against the background of twentieth-century history. In "The Storms of Our Times and *Starry Night*," his most recent and authoritative interpretation of Tillich, Adams develops the original thesis that *will* is "the nerve of Tillich's thought." Thus Tillich's concept of faith as "ultimate concern" (and as belief only secondarily) gives primacy to decision over reason and to will over intellect.

In a major, previously unpublished essay, Adams explicates "The Existentialist Thesis" (date unknown) in contemporary philosophy and theology. He places existentialism in the context of the ongoing debate between philosophies of will ("voluntarism") and philosophies of ideas ("intellectualism"). Finally, Adams critically examines the correlation of ontological and existential concepts—"being" and "existence"—in Tillich's theology.

"The Chief End of Human Existence" responds to "the isolationist tendency" in neo-orthodox theology—the attempt to isolate Christian "proclamation" from cultural influence and philosophical critique. Arguing that theology cannot exclude philosophy, nor rule over it, Adams invokes a prophetic-social principle—protest against intellectual "pecking orders." Faith and reason belong together.

We are amply familiar with sins, yet we hardly know what to do with the concept of sin. The rediscovery of sin as a theological category is a task to which Adams turns in "Sin and Salvation." If sin signifies brokenness and separation, then salvation signifies healing and reunion; but, beyond this broad statement, salvation receives only "honorable mention" in this essay. After presenting this essay to a study group, Adams said, "The author must at this point accuse the program chairman of having committed a sin in assigning 'sin' and 'salvation' for one paper. Salvation will not fit into the same envelope."

In "The AIDS Epidemic and Palliative Care" Adams compares the AIDS epidemic of our time to other catastrophic epidemics in history. He then discusses several Greek terms, developed in the early Christian community, which can shape patterns of care for persons who suffer: *diakonia* (service), *koinonia* (community), *metanoia* ("turning about" or conversion), and *kairos* (the "right" or opportune time). Sustaining such caring, Adams suggests, is also an institutional challenge to the churches.

A New Testament story tells that Jesus, confronted by a father who desperately implored him to heal his epileptic son, said, "This kind cannot be driven out by anything but prayer" (Mark 9:29). In "Out of Despair" (1950) Adams explores the meaning of prayer in the face of personal and social suffering—for instance, the case of a dying child and his parents, and Jane Addams's despondency for the people of Chicago in a time of social conflict. Thus faith is most pointedly examined when it is tried and refined in existential situations.

Adams outlines the diverse meanings of divine and human love in "God Is Love," which concludes this section. Love as a feeling and love as a commitment are united in his paraphrase of Augustine: "We give attention in accord with our basic will, our basic desire, our basic orientation, or our love. Ultimately our love determines what we give our attention to." Thus Adams connects "the red thread" of his theology, the primacy of the will, with the idea of love as the fullest expression of God's power and good will.

G.K.B.

14 · Prophetic Theology: Interrupting the Meeting

In 1936 I attended in Switzerland an international conference of students
and faculties of Protestant theology, a conference in which the Swiss theologian Karl Barth was a participant. At the very first session of the conference Barth fulfilled every expectation of controversy. The first paper,
presented by a theologian from the University of Geneva, dealt with the
concept of religious experience, and it employed the language of psychology as well as of Christian theology. Before the speaker was well under-
way, however, Barth suddenly arose in the audience, interrupted the
speaker, and addressed the chairman. "I shall not wait any longer. I want
to ask the speaker a question now," he said, thereby of course throwing
the meeting into an uproar of consent and dissent. The chairman replied
that it is customary for questions to be withheld until a paper is finished,
but that he would leave the decision to the speaker. With questionable
judgment the theologian reading the paper agreed to accept the question
immediately. Barth thereupon made a frontal attack. "Is the speaker reading to us a paper on Christian theology or on the psychology of religious
experience? If the paper is on the psychology of religion, why should we
here listen to it? This is a conference of Christian theologians; only the
Word of God, not talk about psychology and religious experience, is appropriate here." Immediately the assembly plunged into heated argument, a debate on the place, or lack of place, of secular science and even
of apologetics in a Christian discourse. The heat of the controversy pervaded the remaining sessions of the conference. Indeed, the Barthian students within the week, I was told, delivered a formal petition to the dean
of the theological faculty at Geneva, pleading for the dismissal from the
university of the beleaguered author of the paper and for the appointment
in his stead of a Christian theologian. The dean did not comply; he could
not accept the presuppositions of the avowedly Barthian framers of the
petition.

The reader may not feel disposed to accept those presuppositions either.
Yet, one must recognize that Barth's interruption of the meeting is typical
of what has been going on in Protestant theological circles in our time.

From the preface to *Dimensions of Faith: Contemporary Prophetic Protestant Theology*, ed. William Kimmel and Geoffrey Clive (New York: Twayne Publishers, 1960). Reprinted by
permission.

From various quarters in varying ways Protestant theology has been trying to "interrupt the meeting" in both the church and the world.

Already, a century earlier, Søren Kierkegaard in his *Attack upon "Christendom"* [Princeton, N.J., 1944] anticipated the present confrontations and tensions by raising a radical protest against the so-called Christian society of his time and its churches. In the face of the established church and the society of his day he rejected their claim to be Christian:

> When all are Christians, Christianity *eo ipso* does not exist. The race of men have found a way to make Christianity comfortable. Gradually the human race came to itself and, shrewd as it is, it saw that to do away with Christianity by force was not practicable—"So let us do it by cunning," they said. "We are all Christians, and so Christianity is *eo ipso* abolished." And that is what we now are. The whole thing is a knavish trick; these 2000 churches, or however many there are, are, Christianly considered, a knavish trick.

Kierkegaard's view was, to be sure, by no means typical of the theology of his time.

In the nineteenth and the early twentieth century many theologians and churches expended their energy in trying to come to terms with the advances being made by the culture. These advances, for example, the emergence of the modern historical consciousness and method and also of the new image of the world that the empirical sciences provided, had to be taken into account if the statement of the Christian message was to achieve new relevance, or if it was to become disentangled from its identification with mere traditionalism. To this end certain theologians "interrupted the meeting," particularly in the churches. Out of this effort came what has been called "Culture-Protestantism," the tendency to identify the gospel with the highest ideals of the age.

The term is a misnomer insofar as it conceals the fact that the movement offered a critique of the prevalent piety that, despite its ostensible orthodoxy, was in its way a Culture-Protestantism of earlier vintage. It is a misnomer also insofar as it conceals the fact that the movement produced the Social Gospel, a prophetic critique of the economic patterns of the culture. Nevertheless, the new Culture-Protestantism was ill-prepared (as was orthodoxy) to confront "the storms of our times": the widespread economic distress, demonic nationalism, and scientism; the world war; and the despairing nihilism born of disillusion. The religion that had appeared in the guise of Culture-Protestantism was now said to be merely a tinsel embellishment of the culture, a deceptive means of self-glorification, a systematic insulation of the human being from God.

Karl Barth in *The Epistle to the Romans* (1919) sounded a thunderous protest against this sort of religion. What is "the Cause of the Night in which we are wandering?" he asked; and he answered: "The Wrath of God is upon us."

> "No-God" cannot seriously be named "God." When we set God upon the throne of the world, we mean by God ourselves. Our devotion consists of a solemn affirmation of ourselves and of the world and in a pious setting aside of the contradiction. Men fall a prey first to themselves and then to the "No-God." Under the banners of humility and emotion we rise in rebellion against God. Against such rebellion there can be revealed only the Wrath of God.

What Kierkegaard named "a knavish trick" was now being exposed anew. Indeed, the Barthian negative critique of the culture was so radical and complete that Adolph von Harnack with some exaggeration spoke of it as a new form of the Marcionite heresy, the assertion of a radical dualism between God and creation, between God and all culture.

Paul Tillich in the early 1920s set forth a more dialectical theology of culture than this, a theology that was able to say both Yes and No to the culture and which insisted upon a discriminating judgment and responsibility as over against merely bringing everything under an abstract negative cipher. Barth, to be sure, had claimed to maintain "subterranean connections" with the current Christian thrust toward social reform, and subsequently he modified his earlier near-dualism.[1] But before Barth had done so, Tillich (with others) made specific and vigorous protest against the rising Nazism, protest accompanied by a concrete analysis of economic maladjustments and idolatries and of ecclesiastical alliances with political and economic demonries, and by efforts towards social-institutional as well as spiritual reconstruction. Accordingly, one of the members of Tillich's Kairos Circle in Berlin called for "a struggle against the church for the sake of the church."

In the face of the easy conscience of Culture-Protestantism, an impressive number of theologians in Europe and America demanded a new self-understanding on the part of Protestantism. They raised afresh the question, What is central in the Christian message? They asked also, What is the proper relation between Christian faith and the church and culture? The concern with these questions led to new approaches in biblical study;

historical and systematic studies of the relation of Christian faith to politics, science, and culture; and the search for new ways of making the response of Christian faith relevant to the contemporary situation. A common presupposition of this theological revival was the view that Christianity, properly understood, is not a culture-religion but rather a prophetic religion.

What is the meaning of the term "prophetic theology" in this context? One of its decisive features has been indicated already—its intention to expose the human assistance, and particularly the religious person's assistance, "at the birth of 'no-God,' at the making of idols." Like the Old Testament prophets, it emphasizes the Commandment, "Thou shalt have no other gods before me." Neither Christianity as a historical phenomenon nor the Bible as a cultural creation, nor culture with all its "riches," nor anything that is of the order of creatures can be the proper "object" of faith. False faith places its trust in such idols. As Augustine observed, it gives to the creature that which belongs alone to the Creator. Thus it becomes a form of self-salvation, denying the need for grace from the invisible Origin. Prophetic theology, therefore, rejects the notion that Christian faith can provide sanction for a culture-religion. It holds that history and culture point beyond themselves to a commanding, judging, sustaining, and transforming reality. Confidence in and response to this reality is the nerve of prophetic faith.

Such confidence and such a response, however, issue in more than a warning and struggle against the idolatry of any attempt to domesticate this reality or power. Prophetic faith asserts that God through Jesus Christ is the Lord of history and of culture. This Lord of history calls men and women into a community of faith. In response to the Lord of history this community of faith takes time and culture seriously, so seriously as to hold that political and social institutions, the arts and the sciences, as well as the individual believer, have a vocation from on high. Indeed, prophetic faith in its critical and formative power serves as the basis for the true and viable autonomy of these spheres. Redemption is for them as well as for individual persons. Accordingly, prophetic theology recognizes the obligation to interpret the signs of the times in the light of the End, that is, of the Reign of God. It aims to speak to the concrete situations in which men and women find themselves.

But prophetic theology in Protestantism does not presume to place limits upon the sovereignty of God by claiming that Protestantism possesses a monopoly on prophetic insight and action. To do so would be idolatry. Moreover, prophetic theology does not look for simple unanimity in the formulation or the understanding of the Christian message. It therefore carries on a dialogue with respect to the meaning of Christian faith in thought and action.

Through this dialogue of interpretation in response to the living God, prophetic theology releases what is not ultimately within its power, the moving, reforming, transforming element in the history of religion and culture. It again and again "interrupts the meeting" in order not only to tell but also to listen. Viewed from the human side, this dialogue as it issues in responsible action is the process whereby Christians in each age achieve new self-understanding in the light of the gospel and in the face of changing situations, with their new demands and new possibilities. In this way prophetic theology acts out of faith in the Lord of history, who moves in mysterious ways and in whose name men and women can prophesy only in part if they are not to assist at the birth of a Grand Inquisitor.

Note

1. In an interview, Karl Barth said, "In Germany, too, I at first joined the Social Democrats. But I was not very active. I had to work long hours in my study. I had better things to do than take part in German politics. But I still identified myself with the left. . . . Only when 1933 came did it become obvious to me where I had to stand and where I had not to stand." Karl Barth, *Final Testimonies,* ed. Eberhard Busch, trans. Geoffrey W. Bromiley (Grand Rapids: William B. Eerdmans, 1977), pp. 38–39. Further remarks on his political involvements are recorded on pp. 25–26.—ED.

15 · *Encounter with the Demonic*

It is surprising that the Blumhardts, father and son, are little known or appreciated in Protestant, indeed even in Lutheran, circles in the United States.[1] Yet, the work of Johann Christoph Blumhardt, the father, marks a turning point in the modern development of pastoral care; and Christoph, the son, is the seminal figure of the religious-socialist movement

This essay originally appeared in *Metanoia: An Independent Journal of Radical Lutheranism* 3, no. 3 (September 1971).

that stems from him and extends through Kutter, Ragaz, Thurneysen, and Barth to Tillich and the Kairos Circle. The young Blumhardt's "Letter to His Friends" deserves a key position in the documents of Protestant social ethics of the past century.[2]

One cannot appreciate the character and significance of this document without an awareness of its roots and of the milieu in which it appeared. Equally important is it to observe the remarkable theological thrust of the document—its adoption and extension of concepts that stem from the New Testament and which through the writings of the Religious Socialists have gained wide currency in our time. It must suffice if we here center attention upon only two of these concepts, the idea of the Kingdom of God and the concept of the demonic—integrating concepts that condition all the other theological-ethical ideas that appear in the writings of the young Blumhardt and which are adumbrated in the "Letter."

"My only desire is to tell everything to the glory of Him Who is Victor over all the powers of darkness." These words epitomize the message of both Johann Christoph Blumhardt (1805–1880) and his son Christoph (1824–1919), Lutheran pastors whose roots were in the Württemberg Kingdom-of-God pietism of Bengel, Oetinger, and Hahn. The words are quoted from the lengthy Report of 1850 made by the elder Blumhardt to church authorities, regarding the "faith-healing" in Moettingen of Gottlieben Dittus, a young woman who, "possessed" by "the powers of darkness," had been "tortured by spirit-like figures."[3] This report recounts Pastor Blumhardt's struggle, one might say, to exorcise the demon of psychosomatic illness suffered by this young woman. It crowned a pioneer work in pastoral care which two years later took the pastor and his family to Bad Boll. For years he had been directing attention to the healing miracles of the Gospels, relating them to the battle of the inbreaking Kingdom of God. Taking over an old hotel building in Bad Boll, he attracted thousands of people seeking relief. The story of Blumhardt's work is still remembered vividly today at Bad Boll, which after World War II became the seat of a widely reputed Evangelical academy.

Blumhardt's report narrates such fantastic phenomena of mental hallucination and bodily distortion that it is scarcely credible. So puzzled was he by these phenomena that he repeatedly called for the assistance of physicians. Here is his description of a climatic episode in an eighteen-month struggle against the dark powers that possessed Fräulein Dittus:

> Foam flowed again from her mouth. It had become clear to me that something demonic played a role here after what had happened so far, and it

hurt me to think that there should be no means of help in such a horrible affair. While in these thoughts, a sort of wrath gripped me. I jumped forward, took her stiff hands, pulled her fingers together with force as for prayer, loudly spoke her name into her ear in her unconscious state, and said, "Fold your hands and pray: Lord Jesus, help me. We have seen long enough what the devil is doing, now we want to see what Jesus can do." After a few moments she awakened, prayed these words after me, and all convulsions ceased to the great surprise of those present.[4]

In the light of this experience and of similar, if less melodramatic, experiences the elder Blumhardt developed a vigorous eschatology, "looking toward a new outpouring of the Spirit in the struggle between the Kingdom and the power of darkness." "To him," said his son, "the Kingdom of God was something immensely greater, more eternal and more effective for body and soul than anything he saw in Christianity." Accordingly, Karl Barth was to speak of him as "the theologian of hope."

"Jesus the Victor" became the watchword of the younger Blumhardt also, who after the death of his father, with some misgiving because of his imagined lack of capacity for the task, took over the direction of the work at Bad Boll. Christoph, like his father, looked for new outpourings of the Spirit, but gradually he began to question the authenticity of a piety that centered attention on individual sufferers alone. He came to see in this sort of piety a kind of egoism, a using of God for private purposes. In his view, says his biographer, Friedrich Zündel, "the kingdom of God was not fulfilled in the satisfaction of private spiritual needs. He saw its goal to be as great and as wide as creation itself." Pursuing this insight the young Blumhardt became "a theologian of hope" in broader range than his father, even in a broader range than Luther. "According to Scripture," he said, "there is much more for us to learn and to practice than what the Reformers were able to give."

R. Lejeune, the editor of the four-volume edition of the writings of the young Blumhardt, has traced the path that led him to call for a new eschatology. This new eschatology, he held, would undermine the fatalism of supposing that the "world" is simply corrupt and is to remain so. The kingdom of God comes bringing unrest as well as hope. To the spiritualizers Blumhardt said, "You set up a God without hands, without a mouth, without any feet, so that we can do simply as we like. No thanks, I cannot believe in such a God" [cf. Psalm 115:5–7]. From these impulses he developed a theological view of history and a political theology, calling also for a recognition of the positive significance of the natural sciences. (Here we are reminded of the embracing vision of Oetinger.) "God so loved the world. . . ." The whole world is the arena of the battle of the Kingdom, not only for the sake of mercy but for the sake of social justice. "We live in a newly created world, a newly created time." Jesus will be Victor.

A new world was in the making, but Blumhardt knew it would not come without dust and heat, and not without the pain of change. After the death of his father the young Blumhardt gained widespread popularity as "the preacher from Bad Boll"; in various parts of Germany his sermons attracted hundreds and even thousands. Yet, he came to the decision that this was too easy a path. He felt "obliged" to "extend the hand to the working class" among these millions. "I want to build and validate the party that elevates these masses." His avowal of concern for the proletariat brought great disappointment to the "old-timers" and to those who were pleased with a renewal that would disturb nothing in the economic-political order. For many, this turn was the beginning of the end of his father's work. For Christoph it bespoke the shock of recognition that the powers of darkness, the demonic powers, inhabit and possess nations, socioeconomic institutions, and even churches. The realm of the demonic he saw belongs not only to the psychosomatic realm but also to the em-bracing social-institutional spheres of class tension, with people strug-gling for bread and justice and dignity and others in the name of God and Christ opposing this struggle or remaining indifferent to it. Where, then, are the demonic powers? Can it be that the churches are "possessed" by these powers, just as was the poor wretch Gottlieben Dittus? Yes, and not only that. The Kingdom of God may at times find itself obstructed by the churches, and God incognito may be working for righteousness pre-cisely among the atheists.

The greatest shock to conventional believers came when Blumhardt joined the Social Democratic Party. He was the first pastor in Germany to do this. Shortly thereafter he began to serve for six years as the Party's representative in the provincial legislature of Württemberg. Ecclesiastical censure followed: he was asked by church authorities to relinquish his service (of thirty years) as pastor at Bad Boll.

It is noteworthy that twenty years later in Berlin, Paul Tillich, an ordained clergyman, was asked by the Consistory of Brandenburg to jus-tify as a Christian his having joined the Independent Social Democratic Party, a left wing of the Social Democrats. In his response Tillich referred to Christoph Blumhardt and his idea that a secular movement battling for social justice may be more responsive to the Kingdom of God than are the official representatives of the churches. On the other hand, Karl Barth at this time abandoned his open adherence to Religious Socialism, in favor of what Tillich was to call undialectical concern for the Word of God. Barth was not to recover a direct theological or practical interest in political and economic issues until after the Nazis came to power. Meanwhile, Tillich, following the general dialectical pattern proposed by Christoph Blumhardt, worked out in more substantial and elaborate fashion the "basic principles of Religious Socialism."[5]

Notes

1. The estimable three-volume work, *Christian Social Responsibility,* ed. Harold C. Letts (Philadelphia: Muhlenberg Press, 1967), does not so much as mention the Blumhardts.

2. Christoph Blumhardt, "Letter to His Friends," trans. James A. Hinz, *Metanoia* 3, no. 3 (September 1971):5–9.

3. This report has recently been published in English as *Blumhardt's Battle,* trans. Frank S. Boshold (New York: Thomas E. Lowe, 1970).

4. *Ibid.,* p. 18.

5. See Paul Tillich, *Political Expectation,* ed. James Luther Adams (New York: Harper and Row, 1971).

16 · *The Storms of Our Times and* Starry Night

The two parts of the title of this essay, like the hound and the horn, seem to be running in opposite directions. "The Storms of Our Times" is the title employed by Paul Tillich for an address that he gave during the Second World War.[1] *Starry Night* is the name of a painting by Vincent van Gogh. It is this contrast, however, that marks the profile of Paul Tillich's chosen vocation as a philosophical and apologetic theologian. In one aspect of this vocation he has been unrelenting in his recognition and de-

This essay was originally published as the introductory chapter to *The Thought of Paul Tillich,* ed. James Luther Adams, Wilhelm Pauck, and Roger Lincoln Shinn (San Francisco: Harper and Row, 1985). Reprinted by permission of Harper and Row, Publishers.

lineation of the disruptions, the storms, of our times. In this sense, he is an existentialist theologian providing a mirror of this "stormy" situation, at the same time that he issues a protest in the name of authentic human being. The dark storms, however, are not to be endured without light in the night. Here we see the contrasting feature of his vocation, in his attempt to find a new and effective word of religion redemptive in its power. In his view one cannot comprehend religion if one does not recognize its inner tensions and even its ambiguity.

TILLICH'S YES AND NO TO RELIGION

Insofar as religion is a "superfluous consecration" of the forces that have given rise to disruptions, "the first word to be spoken by religion must be a word spoken against religion" ["Our Protestant Principles," 1942]. But this word must be also a transforming word that transcends, or rather goes deeper than, the surface realities. Characteristically, Tillich finds transforming elements represented in the arts, and especially in the visual arts, where often he perceives a "powerful word." He views van Gogh's vividly colorful painting as an attempt to "look into the depths of reality, below any surface and any beautification." Van Gogh's *Starry Night,* says Tillich, reveals a "disruption of the creative powers of nature." It plumbs below the surfaces where the forms are dynamically created.[2]

During his lifetime, Tillich witnessed world wars, acute economic depressions, political reversals, revolutions, and incredible holocausts. He served as a chaplain in the German army of World War I, ministered there to countless of the injured, and officiated at the burial of hundreds of the dead. It is not widely known that Tillich, under that stress and largely as a result of it, suffered a temporary breakdown and had to be withdrawn from the front. Following the war, he experienced the rise of Nazism and fascism and became an exile to the United States. This constant witnessing of blood-soaked carnage apparently gave him a sense of the ineradicable anxiety and dread of death in the human situation, perhaps influencing him in the direction of the existentialists. Accordingly, he adopted psychological categories as fundamental not only for understanding human existence but also for reality as a whole. I was told by a student that in a lecture on twentieth-century thought, Donald Fleming of the Harvard faculty characterized Tillich's writings as unique, for the average theologian, Protestant or Catholic, tends to brush aside despair and the darker side of human experience.

In Germany, as elsewhere, the religious crisis with its despair brought about a "return to religion," in Tillich's view an ominous return to sham spirituality. Writing in 1922 at the time of an inflation that nearly wiped out the middle class in Germany, Tillich, discussing the religious crisis, made the following trenchant comment:

> It would be an annihilating judgment about our time, more annihilating than ours is about the "Wilhelmine Epoch," if a future historian would write about it: "At that time people turned again to religion; . . . in spite of the increase in non-spiritual forces through the economic situation, it was a religious epoch." Such a judgment could be annihilating, for it could be saying, "That time lacked God; in His place, however, it had religion. After having tried technology and world politics, after having tried idolizing the nation, or the class, and having failed in these attempts, it tried religion."

Such attempts, he goes on to say, have failed in all romanticism from the time of Julian, the apostate Roman emperor, up to the present. They always imply a way of "tempting God if the attempt is made for the sake of something other than for God's sake; and it is necessarily a failure. . . . In times of a growing affirmation of religion, even more than in times of indifference and hostility, we need to be reminded that God is a consuming fire."[3]

Tillich's warning against turning to religion for the sake of culture was grounded in his rejection of the notion, a rejection that Tillich found in both Luther and Calvin, that religion (or God) is something detachable, something alongside the culture or the world. This spatializing serves to produce and protect idolatry and complacency, that is, to protect the culture from radical criticism, from the consuming fire of prophetic judgment, and also to "cabin" the creative, renewing power of the really real. This amounts, then, to the virtual worship of particular spaces that Calvin and others have called polytheism. Some of these particular spaces, set apart and worshipped, can include religion or the god of the dictionary, "a supreme Being."

Tillich's formulation is ontological when he says that in principle everything participates in Being, though ambiguously. At the center, or rather in the ground or depth of everything, whether material or spiritual, whether individual or corporate, whether secular or sacred, is Being. God is Being-itself, but not a spatialized supreme "highest Being" above other beings. When religion is authentic, it is openness to and directedness toward "unconditional reality," and proclaims its power and promise, at the same time bringing both the sacred and the secular under judgment. For Tillich, van Gogh's *Starry Night* unveils something below the surface—potent, renewing power, unmanipulable, and unconditional. The "storms of our times" are not to be endured without a supportive and creative element. He refers to this "coincidence of opposites" as a "beliefful realism," "realism and faith."

Apostle to the Gentiles

For Tillich there is in God both ground and abyss (Tillich is indebted to Böhme for the meaning of abyss). The demonic, when it appears, is inflated and distorted by the unpredictable, uncontrollable abyss. This appears in primitive art as the exaggeration of eyes or nose or mouth or genitals. In God, just as in human existence, there is this tension between being and nonbeing. God is always struggling against nonbeing. Apparently Paul Tillich had all of these things in mind when he spoke of the depth of reality. The demonic, then, also issues from the depths, and is to be overcome only by a grace that is more powerful. Tillich liked Nietzsche's statement that "will is the power of being in Being."

In adopting this "depth" language, Tillich reveals a certain uneasiness with the vocabulary of height. The word *height* too often suggests flying away from "the really real." In this reference point of depth, Tillich sees all existence and ultimate meaning as unconditional reality, as "grounded in the depths of being itself." In short, Tillich calls us back to ontology, an inquiry concerning the universal structures of being and the meaning of the inescapable reality of that which is beyond all things.

The word *unconditional,* used so often by Tillich, has been a conundrum for many. Karl Barth, in one of his more scornful moments, called it a "frozen monstrosity." Actually, in the history of philosophy it can be traced back even beyond Plato. The term, Tillich says, is a negative symbol for the divine. So far from denoting a frozen phantom, it points to a dynamic, primordial, holy reality, "infinitely apprehensible, and yet ultimately incomprehensible." The adjectival form, *the unconditional,* is preferable to the substantive form, *the unconditioned;* the latter term implies reification, that it is a thing alongside other things. I once asked Tillich if for the sake of bewildered readers he would give a brief definition of "the unconditional." This little-noted definition appears at the beginning of his essay entitled "Kairos" in *The Prostestant Era:*

The term "unconditional" which is often used in this book points to that element in every religious experience which makes it religious. In every symbol of the divine an unconditional claim is expressed, most powerfully in the command: "Thou shalt love the Lord thy God with *all* thy heart and with all thy soul, and with all thy mind." No partial, restricted, conditioned love of God is admitted. The term "unconditioned," or the adjective made into the substantive, "the unconditional," is an abstraction from such sayings which abound in the Bible and in great religious literature. The unconditional is a quality, not a being. It characterizes that which is our ultimate and, consequently, unconditional concern, whether we call it "God" or "Being as such" or the "Good as such" or the "True as such," or whether we give it any other name. It could be a complete mistake to understand the unconditional as a being the existence of which can be discussed. He who speaks of the "existence of the unconditional" has thoroughly misunderstood the meaning of the term. Unconditional is a quality which we experience in encountering reality, for instance, in the unconditional character of the voice of the conscience, the logical as well as the moral. In this sense, as a quality and not as a being, the term is used in all the following articles.[4]

Whatever one may think of the choice of the term *the unconditional,* we must recognize that one of the most creative things Tillich has done is to contrive a series of terms that aim to communicate with fresh power truths whose clarity and relevance were weakened because of careless interpretation and application. Such terms as *theonomy, kairos, demonic, boundary, the Protestant principle,* and *ultimate concern* have become associated with Tillich's thought. His new terms nearly always were embedded in the tradition, uncovered, newly defined, and applied variously in such attractive ways that many of them have been adopted and adapted by other thinkers, often with little concern for placing them in the context of Tillich's entire outlook.

So much has he attempted in this fashion to approach the modern person alienated from the language of the churches that he has been called an "apostle to the Gentiles." For his part, Tillich early in his career came to view much preaching in Germany as a form of laziness. The conservative preacher seems to think that he has fulfilled his vocation if he mainly repeats the word of Scripture. He contents himself by saying that he has preached the Word, that God must give the increase. If a wicked and adulterous generation has turned a deaf ear, the guilt lies there. It is noteworthy that Tillich reproached the Barmen Synod of the Confessing Churches (which in 1934 heroically issued its famous declaration against the Nazis) with having used merely traditional language incapable of speaking effectively to those who in the name of intellectual integrity were already alienated. The Confessing Churches relentlessly purged from their language everything associated with the neo-Protestantism (and liberalism) of the years 1730 to 1930. Tillich spoke of their effort here as "extravagant," though he acknowledged the need for some "self-purification" in face of the past. He early became aware that this group could not unite anti-Nazi Christians against the regime. For one thing, its fixated language excluded the liberals.[5]

In Tillich's view, "the Word of God is any reality by means of which the eternal breaks with unconditioned power into our contemporaneity." It is not a question any longer of a direct proclamation of the religious truths as they are given in the Bible and tradition, for "all of these things are torn down into the general chaos of doubt and questioning." Hence the need for new terms.

Wilhelm and Marion Pauck, in the first volume of their biography of Tillich, writing of opposition at Harvard to Tillich's ideas and vocabulary, report that "one philosopher went so far as to call Tillich's thought 'unintelligible nonsense.'" Nevertheless, the response of students to his magnetic power was enormous. In commenting on the Tillichian vocabulary, the Paucks say somewhat wryly that "he himself had not created many of the terms he used, but had borrowed them from other thinkers and by subtle transformation made them his own."[6] It is not sufficient to say this, because these terms used by Tillich were delicately interconnected with respect to his total outlook. To understand one term is to understand all of them. Every term supposes the background of his ontology, epistemology, philosophy of history, and doctrine of God.

Wilhelm Pauck demonstrates this convincingly with reference to the term *unconditional*. The term was one used by Tillich's teacher, Martin Kähler, at Halle, in ways and in contexts that suggest that Tillich may have adopted the term from him. Pauck writes:

> For example, in discussing "the living God" in contrast to "the absolute" of Schelling's idealism, Kähler writes: "If one conceives the universal as the precondition (*Voraussetzung*) of everything determined, it appears as the unconditioned which conditions everything else. This translation of the presupposition of thought into the ground of being (*Daseinsgrund*) implies the identification of the indetermined and the indeterminable unconditioned or, in other words, the simple, with "the supreme being." Thus everything determined is regarded (or signified) as something less, as

something that in the last resort is not or ought not to be, while that which transcends everything real is considered as that which truly has being (*das wahrhaft Seiende*).

Then, in conclusion, Pauck goes on to say:

This terminology was certainly not the special property of Kähler, but one will not go wrong in thinking that the very fact that he used it must have been of importance to Tillich, who employed it throughout his life. In this connection, it should be noted that Kähler warned again and again that one should not think of God as a being among beings, as if he were an object, and that particularly one should not speak of him as "the supreme being," a phrase which Kähler called meaningless (*Inhaltsleer*).[7]

The Harvard dissenters were by no means the first in America to mark the difficulty of Tillich's concepts. *The Protestant Era* (1948) was rejected for publication by a major American house. After this publisher had held the manuscript for two years I urged that a decision be made. It turned out to be a rejection. Later on I learned that a "reader" for the publisher, a prominent theologian, in advising against publication, said the book contained a lot of "German gobbledygook" that would find few buyers. Pauck and I then took the manuscript to the University of Chicago Press. Fred Wieck immediately made a contract not only for it but also for the entire *Systematic Theology.* Tillich wished the contract to call for six volumes, but the press restricted the contract to three. After the first volume of this work appeared, Professor Arnold Bergsträsser, a learned, exiled German scholar, a political scientist, and an admirer of Tillich's writings, found so much historical, philosophical, and theological lore as well as vocabulary presupposed that he suggested that we prepare an annotated companion volume for each of the three volumes. He was aware of the fact that for decades Tillich had been giving lecture courses and seminars on Western thought from the Presocratics to the present. He wished especially for us to trace the historical lineage of Tillich's conceptual thesaurus.

Tillich himself was aware of the difficulty of his theological language and could rise to humor about it. Once, when we were preparing essays in *The Protestant Era* for publication, I could not fully understand the intended meaning of several paragraphs in his text. When I consulted him about the problem, he looked at the passages for some time and then said, "I haven't the slightest idea what I intended there. Leave them out."

WILL: THE NERVE OF TILLICH'S THOUGHT

Attempts have been made repeatedly to identify the nerve of Tillich's whole outlook. Some such attempt is highly pertinent, so that one may avoid rendering primary that which is derivative or secondary in his thought. That nerve may be seen most clearly if it is sought by placing his outlook and lifestyle in the context of the whole religious philosophical development of the West. Tillich's philosophical education was achieving its maturity and solidity at a time when a topic being discussed most vigorously was the identification of meanings and tensions in the history of Western philosophical and religious thought. Windelband, for example, had considered these questions toward the end of determining how one should write the history of philosophy. Dilthey identified three basic themes found in Western thought: naturalism, the idealism of freedom, and objective idealism. Troeltsch, Tillich's major contemporary and mentor, had devoted a lifetime to the search for "the fundamental idea" of Christian and Western culture, trying to understand the basic changes, the periods or phases of development. In one of his essays he spells out the Western tradition and the contemporary period by defining the essence of "the modern," and Tillich, in his youth, published a substantial essay on the same topic.[8] Recently, Trutz Rendtdorf, a major German Troeltsch scholar, in a public lecture at the University of Chicago (April 1984), attempted to understand and interpret the fundamental differences between contemporary theological positions in terms of how each position has interpreted and reacted to the meaning of modernity.

Tillich, in the midst of the intellectual ferment of his time, with a classical and comprehensive education behind him, recognized that the problems of thought in his time needed to be set in the whole intellectual history of Western culture, ancient, medieval, and modern. As one way of responding to this, he perceived a persistent tension within every generation between those who believed that the will is primary in the nature of reality and those who believed that the intellect is primary. The former could trace their heritage, Tillich believed, from Augustine. "Augustine is the philosopher of will," Tillich writes, "and especially of the will which is love. . . . Love is original being; the power of love is the substance in everything that is." In the Middle Ages, Augustine's ideas were represented by the Franciscans (especially Bonaventura), Duns Scotus, and Ockham and, later, by Luther and Böhme, and then by Schelling at the beginning of the nineteenth century. Those who saw the intellect as primary could claim as their ancestors Aristotle, Thomas Aquinas, the Dominicans, the British Empiricists and, more recently, the positivists and analysts in philosophy. Tillich writes, "These two lines of thought have made the Western philosophical movements full of life and tension." Against this sweeping backdrop of Western thought, Tillich provides a more detailed analysis of the same tension between will and intellect as primary during the nineteenth century. The later Schelling (the philosopher of will, as contrasted with the earlier Schelling, the philosopher of nature) was influenced powerfully by Jakob Böhme, whose writings were called to Schelling's attention by the Roman Catholic theologian Franz von Baader. For Schelling, Tillich writes, "Will is original being. It is being itself. We can describe being most adequately in terms of will. Being is not a thing; it is not a person; it is will." [9]

Schelling was a major influence on Tillich, as also on C. S. Peirce, who once said, when asked to describe his philosophical position, "You may call me a Schellingian." [10] It was Schelling's emphasis on will as the essence of being that drew Schopenhauer's interest, though Schopenhauer, later an important influence on Thomas Mann as well as on Tillich, [11] turned this emphasis in a new direction. For him, will in human life is perpetually restless, always ultimately unsatisfied in its own longing, and finally desirous of its own cessation in a state of resignation. Here, says Tillich, Schopenhauer achieved, quite independently, the vision of Buddhism (overcoming of self in a formless self) and Hinduism (return to the Brahman principles, the eternal ones), and also set the philosophical stage for the later thinking of Freud (death drive) and Nietzsche, who rejected Schopenhauer's "resignation" and affirmed instead the "will to power." [12]

This line of intellectual influence from Schelling to Schopenhauer to Nietzsche, Tillich argues, must be understood as the source of concern for the primacy of the will in the later thinking of Bergson, Heidegger, Sartre, and Whitehead (the century's great metaphysician, according to Tillich).

In this tradition, called voluntarism, Tillich placed himself. For him, this was the basic nerve of Western mentality, the object of perennial attention in its philosophy and theology. The term *voluntarism* recurs in Tillich's writings, sometimes only in passing. Tillich's voluntarism must be understood not only as an intellectual matter but also as an element of his inner experience, his trauma in the midst of World War I, and his new realism, which became a "belief-ful realism." As has been generally recognized, and as was recognized by Tillich himself, his whole philosophical and theological outlook is fundamentally autobiographical.

The term *voluntarism* is only a century old, having been defined by Ferdinand Tönnies as a philosophy in which the element of the will is primary. For Tönnies, the term *will* encompasses the affections as in Augustine. Tillich was familiar with Tönnies's use of the concepts *Gemeinschaft* and *Gesellschaft,* "community" and "society," and used this distinction from Tönnies in his own thought.[13] It seems evident, therefore, that he also knew of Tönnies's views on voluntarism. One of the most elaborate expositions of the idea of voluntarism after Tönnies was by Friedrich Paulsen, who borrowed the term from Tönnies and popularized it in his *Introduction to Philosophy,* which was read widely and which Tillich certainly knew. Paulsen used this conception to present a "voluntaristic psychology." For the English translation of Paulsen's book, William James provided a lengthy introduction asserting that he would like to promote a wide reading of it. "I should be glad if these introductory words of mine would procure for the *Introduction to Philosophy* a readier reception by American and English students," he wrote.[14]

Whitehead has asserted that the first task of the metaphysician is to choose the root metaphor for interpreting reality. He saw the history of modern thought in terms of root metaphors, as the attempt to interpret reality first in Galilean-Newtonian mathematical terms, and later in Darwinian, evolutionary terms. In his own interpretation, Whitehead chose psychological concepts, viewing all of reality in terms of perception (prehension) and memory. His philosophy, as a result, has sometimes been called "pan-psychism." In short, Whitehead may be compared to Tillich in that both of them chose psychological terms for the interpretation of reality—ontological, societal, and psychological—though of course the meanings they attached to these terms differ. In this sense, Tillich also can be called a "pan-psychist."

Tillich goes beyond Paulsen's voluntaristic psychology to a voluntaristic ontology. In doing this, as we have said, he recognizes that the approach is found in classical form in the writings of Augustine. Although Augustine lived in a time of skepticism, says Tillich, "he overcame this skepticism with the experience that in the depths of the soul—of one's own soul—the truth is dwelling, that it is to be found in one's own soul."[15] It must be remembered too that both the Old and the New Testaments are oriented to the will and the love of God. In Rom. 7:22–24, Saint Paul finds within himself two wills struggling with one another: "For I delight in the law of God, in my inmost self, but I see in my members another law at war with the law of my mind and making me captive to the law of sin which dwells in my members. Wretched man that I am! Who will deliver me from this body of death?"

The Augustinian approach rejects the attempt of human beings to penetrate the outer world; that world can be understood only by turning inward with the assumption that in one's own existence one will find the clue to all of existence, indeed to existence itself. Here is an interpretation of existence in terms of inner experience, long before contemporary depth psychology and modern existentialism. It must be kept in mind that for Augustine, evil does not result from the fact that humans are flesh but from perverted will—humans give to the creature what belongs alone to the Creator, and this is idolatry.

Of special significance for later philosophy was Luther's awareness of the dark underground of demonic forces in himself and in society, leading him to the "hell of despair," and to call out for the transforming power of faith. This conflict of wills Jakob Böhme reads back into the mysterious dynamic in God, which he calls *Urgrund*. The cleavage between the wills is rooted in God himself. Through the human abuse of freedom the will of affirmation becomes disjoined from the integrating will in God, and demonic self-affirmation becomes self-inflation. The self-affirmation, however, cannot sustain itself; it requires partial participation in the divine will. In this restricted sense, God may say to rebellious Lucifer, "When me you fly, I am the wings."

Although Tillich interprets the history of thought as a dynamic tension between those who believe will is primary and those who believe intellect is primary, and sides with the former, he nonetheless assigns to reason a variety of functions. He speaks of ecstatic reason, the depth of reason, autonomous reason, technical reason, and technological reason. For him, intellect is not measurable, detached intelligence but the whole range of cognition in its broadest sense of participation in being. It means, following the Latin (*inter/legere*), to "read between" or participate in. It means becoming aware of the structure (*Logos*) of everything that is. The world as will is "instinct, drive, trend, dynamics," a "dynamic element of all reality." Intellect participates in that reality and seeks to discern its structure. Tillich was fond of Nietzsche's aphorism that "Spirit [intellect] cuts down through life," discerning the authentic and the inauthentic in the

midst of sheer vitality. The intellect also discerns the tensions and contradictions in reality as well as the harmonies in its structure. Thus Tillich
sees "the reality" as primary, the intellect (the participation and awareness) as secondary.

In selecting the psychological metaphors will and intellect to interpret
ontology, other metaphors that are societal, political, domestic, and organic are also interpreted within a psychological context, metaphors such
as the kingship of God; the Kingdom of God; the fatherhood of God; God
as a bridegroom as in Hosea; the church as the body of Christ; Covenant;
society as an organism (the dominant metaphor of the Middle Ages); and
the concept of the demonic, one of Tillich's most widely adopted concepts
today.

Tillich's method and concept of correlation is to be understood as a
dynamic interrelating of the powers, dynamic powers in reality and history, ever finding new expression. In Troeltschian fashion, he strives again
and again for tentative synthesis, in contrast to a Hegelian logistic approach. So when Tillich, as apologetic theologian, insists that one must
listen to "the times" he is saying that one must listen to the unique
manifestations of the ontological will, in a truly kairotic fashion. The
word used by Schelling to designate the depth of reality disclosing itself
was *das Unvordenkliche,* that which precedes and transcends thinking, a
word adopted from popular usage meaning "from time immemorial" or
"time out of mind." Tillich's view is close to Schelling's when he writes
that we have only a dim view of the depth of reality because it precedes
and transcends thought so that intellect, in and of itself, even in its broadest sense, cannot encompass and comprehend it.

Tillich envisions our living within being, within this as dynamic will.
That will is recreative but subject to demonic perversion due to the abuse
of human freedom (Augustine again). We must listen to how that will
manifests itself creatively and ambiguously in each new time. That manifestation is *kairos,* being revealing itself in new crisis and new opportunity. One must listen to that, perceive what the *kairos* is, and respond to
it, lest one fail to be timely. Even then, one's response involves risk; the
response may be the wrong one or the time may not be right. This risk is
never absent.

For Tillich, the central *kairos* of history is the New Being, Jesus as the
Christ, but there are, he believes, also other "times," *kairoi,* in which
time is being uniquely fulfilled. The word *kairos* is drawn by Tillich from

Eph. 1:9–10: "For he has made known to us in all wisdom and insight the mystery of his will, according to his purpose which he set forth in Christ as a plan for *the fullness of time,* to unite all things in him, things in heaven and things on earth."

Three nineteenth-century thinkers in the voluntarist tradition created concepts that revolutionized the climate of thought for the twentieth century. Marx (ideology), Freud (psychoanalysis and rationalization) and Nietzsche (resentment) all undercut the bourgeois conventions, laying open the realities of class structure and the depths of human inner experience. Tillich saw himself and his generation as the heirs of that revolution, and he knew that his work must somehow speak to the challenges it presented. Tillich wrote, "I belonged to the first generation; I tried to show what it means for Protestant theology that not the surface consciousness but the underground of human existence is decisive in human experience and relations. The concept of ideology revealed the interest of the ruling classes in preserving their power by producing a transcendent system to divert the masses from their immediate situation of disinheritance." [16] Here is a clear bit of evidence of Tillich's concern to address the implications of voluntarism in both their social and their psychological aspects.

In Tillich's early European career, his emphasis was primarily (not exclusively) on the sociological implications of his theology; in his later American career his efforts were aimed more (but not entirely) at treating depth-psychological implications of the voluntarist principle. His shift of emphasis may be interpreted as a change of focus within his continuing commitment to a voluntarist position. The shift occurred, it seems safe to say, because of Tillich's concern that his work respond to the questions of the changing times that were rising in ever new forms. Before World War II, Tillich saw in the *kairos* the churning energies of social class newly exposed by the application of insights of Marx as they shaped the human experience in both creative and demonic ways. After World War II, after the Holocaust, after the bomb, Tillich perceived that the most haunting human questions had to do with the vacancy or "void" within the human, spiritual experience. He saw numbness, the loss of hope, the depth of anxiety and despair as psychological realities given birth by the disruptions of the twentieth century. For him, then, the deepest question of the postwar *kairos* was the question of the inner "courage to be in spite of" the threatening landscape and the ominousness of the future. In the dark night of the mid-twentieth century, in the face of meaninglessness, Tillich discerned, however, in addition to threats, a creative promise symbolized powerfully, for example, by van Gogh's *Starry Night*.

TILLICH THE APOLOGIST

If we turn now again to Tillich's conception of the apologetic theologian, a false reading must be rejected. The apologist may be a defender of the faith in a sense, but the faith is not available in a neat package except with authoritarian sanctions. Nor is faith to be defended against outsiders. The apologist is engaged in an internal dialogue, a dialogue between himself as Christian theologian and himself as non-Christian. The apologist's inner dialogue is personal and at the same time more than personal inasmuch as each inner voice corresponds to many voices outside the self. Apology, therefore, possesses public relevance when the struggle is first personally authentic.

Early in his career, Tillich identified himself as an apologetic theologian, defining the role as "the art of answering questions." As a young pastor in Berlin, he became aware not only of the nagging doubts of many parishioners but also of the virtual indifference of those no longer troubled by doubts—they simply had rejected Christianity and every other religion. He was convinced that others of conservative mentality identified the faith with the status quo in politics and economics, "a superfluous consecration."

At the age of twenty-six, Tillich, with a young colleague, Richard Wegener, initiated for the laity a series of apologetic sessions to be repeated in several sections of Berlin; *Vernunft-Abende* they called them. In preparation for this enterprise, Tillich write a lengthy, compact document defining the methods and goals of Christian apologetics. He surveyed various conceptions of apologetics from early Christianity to the present day, giving attention, for example, to the ferreting out of the heretic for excommunication and persecution. This thirty-page document (1913), a remarkably mature statement for one his age, is still extant, and its ideas were echoed in later writings down to his third volume of the *Systematic Theology* (1963).

Besides this document we have in the archives manuscripts of five of the lectures presented by Tillich in sessions of those evenings on apologetics. Years later, moreover, Tillich prepared a tentative preface ("A Personal Introduction") for his *Systematic Theology*. For reasons I do not know, he did not use this preface, and it has remained unpublished. It is concerned entirely with a consideration of his systematic theology as apologetic theology, and also systematic theology as the grounding for apologetics. In 1913 he had spoken of theoretical apologetics as a philosophical inquiry and of practical apologetics as a theological discipline.

In this "Personal Introduction" Tillich begins by saying that for twenty years it had been his "passionate desire" to develop and write a systematic theology, but that the project was delayed. Among the reasons for the delay, he speaks of the external situation, the series of wars, revolutions, and emigrations. He does not mention the fact that by reason of his own emigration he was obliged to learn to lecture and write in the language of his adopted country. Instead, he asserts that for the enterprise of preparing a systematic theology a person can never know enough to venture beyond the publication of essays, particularly because of his own "personal and spiritual inadequacy." The attempt at the enterprise indeed is "almost blasphemous," calling for judgment and forgiveness.

On the other hand, the situation presented a favorable element. The same historical events that made normal academic existence nearly impossible "provided experiences and ideas that no amount of learning could ever have given." This variety of experience caused him to live, as he often said, on the boundary, between contrasting positions.

On both sides many other voices participated. The dialogue, however, was conducted dialectically in the teeth of tense experience, not "from book to book." Of this process he says that "through dialectical affirmations and negations truth is discovered." As we have seen, Tillich saw differences of insight as the result of tensions and ambiguities within the dynamic "will" of being itself. The dialectical process, however, is not a resort to relativism. Data do not speak until they are spoken to, and then one listens, finds common ground, and learns to ask the right questions. The new questions arise from the individuality of each historical "situation." Through the questions one discerns the *kairos*. This is Tillich's method of correlation, a way of uniting "message and situation." The process of discovery is learning to listen for truth wherever it appears as a manifestation of grace. The theologian carries within him, as a member of a faith community, the criterion of the New Being.

When considering Tillich as an apologist, one must not forget that he was a Lutheran Christian. That he was not a narrow Lutheran is evident from the strong interest of Catholic theologians in his work (initiated by the Catholic theologian and friend of Tillich, the Jesuit Gustave Weigel and carried on by a host of Catholic theologians in various countries) and the deep appreciation that Jews have expressed for Tillich's courageous commitments to Jews in Nazi Germany as well as for his sensitive treatment of "the Jewish question." Jews were in the Berlin Kairos Circle of which Tillich was a prominent member.[17] Late in his life, Tillich's personal theological horizons expanded even further through his contacts with Eastern cultures. Nevertheless, at the center of his apologetic interest has been an attempt to give meaningful expression to the Pauline-Lutheran doctrine of justification by faith through grace. His approach to the doctrine was influenced by his teacher, Martin Kähler, who taught him that doubt is an aspect of faith and therefore is also "justified." Doubt presupposes meaning and therefore is part of the work of God, thus having theological significance. The apologetic theologian must listen to the voices of doubt within and without. If doubt is suppressed or ignored, the dialectic of faith collapses and the church becomes stagnant.

In Tillich's view, typical neoorthodoxy refuses to listen and is, therefore, nondialectical. It is all too prone merely to "proclaim" the Word, even to the extent of pushing philosophy aside, and of derogating the findings of modern historical criticism as theologically trivial. What comes from on high is decisive. But it is not enough, Tillich believes, to be grasped by the vertical. It must be explicated and applied on the horizontal as well. To be sure, for Tillich the Bible is the primary witness.

In the unpublished preface to *Systematic Theology,* Tillich states clearly that his theology is biblical in character even though he uses few biblical quotations. Biblical and systematic theology must supplement one another. A systematic theologian must refer to and depend on the work of biblical theologians. Biblical criticism (which Tillich calls one of the greatest stories in intellectual history, equal to the growth of science) is necessary and does not diminish the "divine nature" of the Bible, but makes it more manifest.

Many of Tillich's essays exemplify the dialectical method of his listening. As we have observed, in face of the widespread view that religion long ago lost its charisma as matter for art, Tillich has discerned hidden religious import there, spelling out a whole set of ideological as well as social-ethical and mystical categories for the identification of the false and the true. He has examined the many dimensions of *Existenz*-philosophy in similar dialectical fashion. Nowhere else is there such an elaborate comparison and contrast as Tillich's between Marxism and Christianity. He traces these themes from Creation and Fall to the eschaton. Tillich takes delight always in the nuanced multiplication of distinctions and classifications, Yes and No. Even as late as 1948 he published an article entitled "How Much Truth Is in Karl Marx?" [18]

Tillich's relation to Marxist ideas and movements reveals an interesting ambiguity. As a young theologian in Germany, Tillich had been willing to suffer the rebuke of Brandenburg Consistory (of which his pastor-father was a member) after he spoke at a meeting of a Marxist organization. Later in his career in the United States, when we were preparing essays for publication in *The Protestant Era,* after he had approved all essays for inclusion and after I had translated all of them, he changed his mind about including an essay on the class struggle and religious socialism, saying to me, "I can't possibly include this, it would destroy me in this country." Also, Tillich and I were for a time on the board of editors of *The Protestant,* a magazine in which he published many articles. Tillich left the board because he came to believe the journal editor was a sedulous "fellow traveler" with the American Communist party. It must be kept in mind that at the time Tillich was making these decisions about his relation to Marxism in this country, the prevailing national atmosphere here successfully kept American universities from hiring Marxist faculty personnel. In any event, in Tillich's various essays on Marx, one sees how Tillich the theologian dialectically asks questions as well as answers them. In this way he displays what is meant by understanding human being ontologically as the being that raises questions about the meaning of its being.

A word must be said concerning the development of feminist theologies in relation to the influence of Tillich. Since Tillich's death, feminist theologians increasingly have exposed the limitations of male-dominated religion and theology. The theological work of Mary Daly, one of today's most outspoken antimale feminist theologians, has been influenced by the thought of Tillich, as the methodology of her work shows. *Beyond God the Father* is one way of speaking about God above the God of theism. [19]

Beyond God the Father specifically employs (or goes beyond or against) practically every element or category in the Tillichian theology from beginning to end. Apparently, however, Daly does not take into account Tillich's discussion of possible lines for development of the desexing of theology set forth in the final pages of *Systematic Theology,* part 4. Tillich then would find Daly's desexing of theology as wholly appropriate but would agree possibly with other critics of Daly who believe that she, in seeking to right old wrongs, has succumbed to a naiveté about women and a lack of interest in the truths that arise from the male experience.

Notes

1. See Paul Tillich, "The Storms of Our Times," *The Protestant Era*, trans. James Luther Adams (Chicago: University of Chicago Press, 1948), pp. 237–52.

2. See Paul Tillich, "Existentialist Aspects of Modern Art," in *Christianity and the Existentialists*, ed. Carl Michalson (New York: Charles Scribner's Sons, 1956), pp. 128–47. In this essay Tillich examines various dimensions of existentialist paintings of the twentieth century and selects Picasso's *Guernica* as a mirror of the disruptions of our times and a protest against the insanity of a war-torn world. This chapter is one of Tillich's most concise statements of the relationship between religion and art and one of the best that any twentieth-century theologian has written on this matter. See also Wilhelm and Marion Pauck, *Paul Tillich: His Life and Thought* (New York: Harper & Row, 1976), vol. 1, *Life*, pp. 75–79, where the Paucks discuss Tillich's relation to the Impressionist painters, especially Cézanne.

3. Paul Tillich, "Religiöse Krisis," *Vivos Voco* 2 (1922):616–21.

4. Paul Tillich, *The Protestant Era*, trans. James Luther Adams (Chicago: University of Chicago Press, 1948), p. 32.

5. In connection with the events of those same years, it is important to remember that Tillich thought that Karl Barth had betrayed Religious Socialism by remaining quiet on the issue of anti-Semitism while Tillich and others had published public theses on the matter as early as 1932.

6. Pauck and Pauck, *Tillich: His Life and Thought*, vol. 1, *Life*, p. 171.

7. Wilhelm Pauck, *From Luther to Tillich: The Reformers and Their Heirs* (San Francisco: Harper & Row, 1984). Cited with permission from Harper & Row and Marion Pauck.

8. Paul Tillich, "Das Christentum und Die Moderne," *Schule und Wissenschaft* 2 (1928):121–31, 170–77.

9. The issues of will and intellect are discussed at length in Paul Tillich, *Perspectives on 19th and 20th Century Protestant Theology*, ed. Carl Braaten (New York: Harper & Row, 1967), pp. 191ff. The passages quoted here are from pp. 192 and 193.

10. The German philosopher Schelling, a major mentor of Tillich's, proposed a typology of spaces that briefly goes as follows: (1) Orientation to particular, limited spaces (such as a grove, the sea, a territory, a race, a nation), a fixated tradition exempt from criticism—polytheism. (2) Orientation to a changing hierarchy of gods—monarchical polytheism. (3) Radical dualism, bifurcation of good and evil, an unstable schizophrenia—Zoroastrianism. (4) Devotion to one God the Creator of all spaces, yet holding all spaces under a universal judgment—exclusive monotheism. These differentiations prevail across the apparent boundaries of culture and religion. Tillich occasionally refers to this typology. Like Schelling, Tillich conceives of history as a struggle between time and space,

but Tillich goes beyond Schelling, claiming that time can be the corrector of space. The spatialization of time is idolatry, what Tillich called a "demonic sacramentalism." One entire volume of Tillich's collected writings is entitled *Der Widerstreit von Raum und Zeit,* (vol. 6, *Gesammelte Werke* [Stuttgart: Evangelisches Verlagswerk, 1963].) Tillich distinguishes between the sacramental and the prophetic. Sacramentalism is oriented toward the present, while the prophetic is eschatologically oriented. Either can become demonic: Demonic sacramentalism elevates what is finite without criticism while demonic propheticism is false prophecy. Tillich saw in Nazism and capitalism tendencies toward demonic sacramentalism, the elevation of the finite beyond criticism. Even religion can become demonic in this sense of "demonic sacramentalism."

11. There is an interesting connection between Tillich and Thomas Mann as well. Mann, in preparing the manuscript of *Doctor Faustus,* corresponded with Tillich, asking him to describe the climate of theological issues in early twentieth-century Germany. Tillich wrote lengthy answers, many of which were used by Mann in the novel. See Gunilla Bergsten, *Thomas Mann's "Doctor Faustus"* (Chicago: University of Chicago Press, 1963), esp. pp. 34–45.

12. It distressed Tillich that Nietzsche was so frequently misunderstood and misrepresented. Tillich, therefore, attempted several times, as did others such as Heidegger, Jaspers, and Fromm, to correct the erroneous, prevailing interpretations of Nietzsche's concept of will to power, showing it to be much more profound than the vulgar concept that many scholars had associated with the rise of Nazism. For Nietzsche, Tillich insists, "power is the self-affirmation of being. Will to power means power to affirm one's power of living, the will to affirm one's own individual existence." See Tillich, *Perspectives on Nineteenth and Twentieth Century Protestant Theology,* pp. 198–207; and idem, *The Courage to Be* (New Haven: Yale University Press, 1952), pp. 24–31. Tillich has pointed out that Nietzsche proclaimed the death of God but reclaimed God as "creative life." He challenged whatever opposed life, and what challenged life the most then (and still does) is the "objectivating" nature of bourgeois thinking and acting wherein means replace ends and people become objects of analysis and control. See also idem, "Nietzsche and the Bourgeois Spirit," *Journal of the History of Ideas* 4, no. 3 (June 1945):307–9. These concerns of Nietzsche's were also concerns of Tillich's.

13. Paul Tillich, *The Socialist Decision,* trans. Franklin Sherman (New York: Harper & Row, 1977), p. 75.

14. William James, Introduction, in Friedrich Paulsen, *Introduction to Philosophy* (New York: Henry Holt and Co., 1926), p. vii.

15. Paul Tillich, unpublished, undated lecture, on cassettes 1211–12, Tillich Archive, Andover Harvard Library.

16. Tillich, *Perspectives on Nineteenth and Twentieth Century Protestant Theology,* p. 199.

17. The Kairos Circle is a name used to refer to the group of Religious Socialists centered in Berlin after World War I, a group of which Tillich was a prominent member.

18. Paul Tillich, "How Much Truth Is in Karl Marx?" *The Christian Century* 65, no. 36 (1948):906–8.

19. See Mary Daly, *Beyond God the Father* (Boston: Beacon, 1973). Mary Ann Stenger has written a remarkable article on the influence of Tillich on Daly. See Mary Ann Stenger, "A Critical Analysis of the Influence of Paul Tillich on Mary Daly's Feminist Theology," *Encounter* 43 (Winter 1982):219–38. See also Rosemary Ruether's review of Mary Daly's latest book, *Pure Lust: Elemental Feminist Theology,* where Ruether shows that Daly still acknowledges "glimmers of truth" in some male culture, naming Paul Tillich as one of those males in whom there is a "glimmer of truth." *Unitarian Universalist World* 15, no. 6 (15 June 1984): 14. See also Joan Arnold Romero, "The Protestant Principle: A Woman's Eye View of Barth and Tillich," in *Religion and Sexism: Images of Women in the Jewish and Christian Tradition,* ed. Rosemary Radford Ruether (New York: Simon and Schuster, 1974), p. 336. See also Paul D. Hanson, "Masculine Metaphors for God and Sex Discrimination in the Old Testament," *The Ecumenical Review* 27 (1975):316–24. Hanson discusses feminism as a prophetic element in present-day history, as a manifestation of what Tillich would call the *kairos.*

17 · *The Existentialist Thesis*

The story of Little Red Riding Hood may be an incredible story, with its claim that a little girl capable of walking alone through the woods could mistake a wolf for her grandmother. But the story is more than just a tale that is told. As immemorial folklore it reflects emotional needs, anxieties, and hopes that everyone has. It implies an interpretation of human nature and of the human situation. In short the story belongs to the existentialist tradition. If one thinks of the happy ending of the story, one may say that it serves in its way the purpose of primitive magic, of effective ritual, and even of philosophizing: it gives a sense of ultimate confidence before the uncertainties of human existence. If one considers the identification of the grandmother with the wolf, then one may surmise that the story expresses the child's unconscious fear of the grandmother, fear in the face of the ambivalence she feels toward parental figures; or one may see in the story an expression of the child's ambivalent attitudes toward herself. Here we have the characteristic themes of existentialism: the ambiguity of human nature, the sense of the threats and demands of the human situation, the complex of guilt and anxiety, of fate and freedom, the merging of subject and object, the inevitable involvement of the total person in the decisions of existence, the lack of a neat and tidy system.

But the story represents not only the characteristic concerns of the existentialists. The variety of interpretations to which the story lends itself offers an analogue of the variety of outlooks that go under the name of existentialism. Kierkegaard, Marx, Nietzsche, James, Freud, Heidegger, Sartre, Dewey, Jaspers, Berdyaev, Barth, Brunner, and Tillich would each give a different interpretation of the story and of its emotional ingredients as they symbolize aspects of an existentialist doctrine of being and of the human being. Sartre, for example, will assert that existentialism is atheistic humanism—a bold thrust for freedom in the teeth of absurdity; Lukacs as a Marxist, on the other hand, claims that Sartre's bold thrust is only the febrile gesture of an expiring bourgeoisie. Jaspers' existentialism asserts that the human being in the boundary situation encounters Transcendence and acquires confidence in the hidden ground of being. Heidegger, on the other hand, says that in dire anxiety the really existing person confronts absolute Nothingness. Kierkegaard would say that existence demands the leap of paradoxical faith, and James that only a will to believe can cope with our world of booming, buzzing confusion.

There are many differences among the existentialists. But all of them would hold one thing in common, namely, that human existence is an enterprise in which human thinking and believing is to be understood as an aspect of human existing. Existence is not made for pure thinking or pure theory, but rather for thinking and believing as an expression of existing. The existentialists reverse the Cartesian dictum, *Cogito ergo sum;* they make it read, *Sum ergo cogito.*

In reversing the Cartesian maxim, the existentialists have revived certain themes and attitudes that are characteristic of every post-Enlightenment period. Enlightenment periods or tendencies, for example, those of Plato and Aristotle, and Thomas Aquinas and Hume, characteristically promote intellectualism and rationalism; post-Enlightenment periods or tendencies take up subdominant themes of the previous period and turn in the direction of voluntarism. Much of the history of thought in the West could be written in terms of the dialectic between the assertion of the primacy of the intellect and that of the primacy of the will, between the Cartesian and the anti-Cartesian emphases. The thesis of existentialism, then, is nothing entirely new under the sun; it is a variant of a venerable theme, the theme of voluntarism.

INTELLECTUALISM AND VOLUNTARISM

In employing the terms *intellectualism* and *voluntarism* one need not presuppose a faculty psychology. The terms possess a much wider applicability than is immediately suggested by merely psychological concepts, as can be observed for example in Augustine's and Whitehead's radicalization of psychic categories for use in theology and metaphysics.

The tradition of intellectualism or rationalism cannot properly be characterized in a narrow way. The term *reason* should take into account different conceptions of reason, for example, constructive reason, intuitive reason, critical reason, technical reason. Moreover, the modalities of intellectualism and voluntarism cannot be understood as sharply defined traditions that are mutually exclusive; nor do they appear and reappear in complete self-identity.

In general, however, intellectualism emphasizes the objective orderliness and givenness of the world, of a world that possesses a unified, architectonic structure. It holds that the human being through intellect may in a detached critical attitude discern this objective structure. By contemplative reason one may devise a closed system, and by controlling reason, live in conformity with the unified nature of things. Accordingly, the so-called Greek view of life (i.e., that aspect of it which Nietzsche called Apollonian) presupposes the predominance of intellect over all tensions of the will and the feelings; it exalts the cognitive, nonaffective powers of the psyche. The highest of all virtues is knowledge, the dianoetic virtues. Everything emotional is of a lower nature and is secondary to the reasoning faculty. Wherever the will tends, it can only be in a direction which the imagination or knowledge provides; its choice is determined by the primary action of the theoretical faculty. One never errs knowingly or voluntarily but only through lack of insight. The original stimulus is knowledge of the objective order, and the human ideal is soberness, clarity, objectivity. Here an optimistic estimate of the power of reason is the basis for an optimistic estimate of human nature.

In the medieval vision of intellectualism, the faith in reason, the attitudes of distance, and the search for a closed system find new expression. "The prime author and mover of the universe," says Thomas Aquinas, "is intelligence." Human will follows the lead of the intellect, which grasps

THE EXISTENTIALIST THESIS

the world through the mediated forms of nature, society, doctrine, and sacrament. Salvation is mediated; it is not a matter of an immediate relationship between the isolated individual and God. "The way of religion," says Boniface VIII in *Unam Sanctam,* "is to lead things which are lower to the things which are higher, through the things which are intermediate, according to the laws of the universe. According to the law of the universe, all things are not reduced to order equally and immediately; but the lowest through the intermediate, the intermediate through the higher." This medieval hierarchic conception of mediacy found expression in the conception of the hierarchy of being which was the basis for a hierarchic conception of society, of nature and supernature.

The later Enlightenment intellectualism retained the sense of the objective givenness and orderliness of the world and the critical attitude of distance in the face of this objective order, but it rejected the hierarchy of being in favor of a pre-established harmony. At the same time it emphasized the autonomous character of reason—reason became revolutionary in the face of tradition. Science would trace out the laws of nature. Individuals were to follow their own reason, yet the universal reason working behind their back would bring about social harmony. Every monad is a microcosm in harmony with the structure of the world. Here the Enlightenment engenders optimism concerning human nature and concerning the historical process.

Voluntarism, on the other hand, with its assertion of the primacy of will, exalts the noncognitive, affective aspects of the world and of human being. Whether we consider the Dionysian strain in Greek life and thought, or the pneumatic orientation of early Christianity, we find the emphasis placed on something less, or more, than intellect, which determines the operation of the intellect; in Greece an ecstatic experience of the subject is extolled because it achieves an immediacy of communion with and a surrender to the pulsating vitality of life. In Christianity, as Reinhold Niebuhr puts it, following Schiller, vitality is given preference over form. In early Christianity an ecstatic experience of living in Christ, and participating in his death and resurrection, transforms the whole creature so that the mind and heart surrender to the community-forming power of God. The Christian knows well that knowledge is no saving power. One sees the good but one does evil. Sin is not ignorance, it is disobedience that issues from the rebellious will.

A radical evil is loose in the world, controlling the will of the unregenerate person who is caught in a rebellion against God; humans are full of

guilt, subject to constant temptation, and anxious. Only a penitent response to God's love can give release.

Augustine takes up these themes and becomes a key figure for all later
voluntarism: he sees the human venture as an epic in which the drama of
conflicting wills exhibits on the one side an estranged humanity, perverted
in will, and misdirected in love, and on the other a restoring, reconciling
power that redeems humanity and history. The will is the cause of false
perception, it determines our use of intellect and memory, it conditions
the enmity among us.

Certain of these motifs reappear in Scotism, and in another way in the
Reformation view of God as a sovereign will; human reason is held to be
an instrument of self-aggrandizement, used to make idols in the human
image. We are determined either by the self-destructive confidence we
place in ourselves and our own powers and merits, or by a God-given
faith in transforming grace.

Now, in large part, existentialism can be interpreted in terms of this
age-old conflict between voluntarism and intellectualism. It is a revolt
against the intellectualism that relies upon mere cognitive powers. It
turns to the experience of the whole person so as to include its affective
and passionate dimensions. It revolts against the concern for a world of
objective, immutable essences, and it turns towards the realm of becoming, the realm of subjective existence. It revolts against the rationalism
that identifies its mediating, abstract constructions with reality in its
concreteness. It turns to existence as immediately experienced and suffered in all its conflicts and ambiguities and uncertainties, to the world of
Little Red Riding Hood. To think as an existing person is the aim of
existentialism: to be able to say, "I am, therefore I think," rather than, "I
think, therefore I am." This is the thesis of existentialism: that one must
turn from a static contemplation of self and world to a dynamic encounter
and transformation. As Kierkegaard would say, one must turn from essence to existence.

THE TURN FROM ESSENCE TO EXISTENCE

Indeed, Kierkegaard is generally, though wrongly, considered to be the
initiator of this turn in the nineteenth century. A brief reminder here of
the early (and familiar) part of the movement will show the way in which
the cluster of concepts characteristic of existentialism came on the scene.

In turning from essence to existence Kierkegaard expressed his opposition to the Hegelian objectivity and abstract system and stressed the subjectivity and inwardness of truth, the intensity of experience as feeling, the uniqueness of the moment and of the individual. For Kierkegaard, the existing individual is not a spectator of essences but a passionately thinking creature for whom something serious, a sickness unto death, is at issue. The human being is an ambiguous creature, knowing despair and possibility, anxiety and guilt, and facing the necessity of decision. This ambiguity of existence, with its inevitability of decision, is poised between the finite and the infinite where only paradox is possible. Here we have what Höffding has called the dialectic between qualitative identities and contrasts. Inwardness, anxiety, guilt, individual decision, becoming, these are the categories of existence, categories that belong to a creature of disquietude.

Then the human being must choose; one must make the leap of faith if one is to be free.

Another segment of modern existentialism may be traced to Karl Marx, with his existentialist opposition to Hegelian thought on the ground that it contemplates the Idea, it does not encounter reality. For Marx the Idea is not determinative. Existence determines consciousness, not consciousness existence. Considering the miserable state of existence, it is a form of escapism to search for essences. There is no such thing as human essence; the "human essence" is a deceptive abstraction. Human existence is the sum-total of social conditions. We can find no model for a concept of essence in our bourgeois world, for it is a split existence, in society and in the individual. Both Kierkegaard and Marx find that the capitalist world spawns a dehumanized, thingified human being whose subjectivity is destroyed by the machinery of technology and of abstract philosophical systems and religions. For Marx existence is fraught with the alienation of person from person and of persons from themselves, the alienation of class from class. The bourgeois intellect is only an instrument of class interest; it is a false consciousness that creates ideology—a systematic concealment of alienation. In the face of this concealment we must by means of a historical dialectic tear away the veils of bourgeois progressivism and recognize that the bourgeois social forces are driving toward their own destruction.

From the depth of social existence, from the dire needs of the exploited, humanity will find fulfillment in the new thrust that overcomes the cleavages in society and gives expression to the will of history, but no leap of faith is needed; for social science can discern the laws of history. The decision is clear. The proletariat has nothing to lose but its chains.

But existentialism appeared earlier than in Kierkegaard and Marx in the "positive philosophy" of Friedrich Schelling. As against the "negative philosophy" of Hegel, which begins and ends with the Idea, Schelling in his "positive philosophy" asserts that God and the human being are to be understood in terms of will. In God this will is unified but dipolar. The dipolarity of particularity and universality stand in balanced tension. But human beings, whose essence is their fate and freedom to be self-asserting, existing individuals, draw the polarity out of balance; self-assertion becomes destructive as well as creative; it can become demonic. Hegelian intellectualism and mystical transcendentalism discern only the ultimate *unity* between the human being and God, between finite and infinite. In doing so they derogate the elements of individuality and contingency; they also conceal the distance between the person and God, a distance that is manifest in human guilt and despair. In answer to Hegel's "negative philosophy," then, Schelling asserts that "what has begun only in mere thinking can proceed only as mere thinking and never go further than the Idea." It must remain only a scholastic exposition of logical relations. The *I* that thinks about ideas has had experience of reality; the ideas point beyond themselves to that which is anterior and inaccessible to thought; the *I* that lives in existence does not live in a world locked in a logical concept, it lives in a world of contingency. Ours is a world of freedom and uncertainty. Hegel must be inverted, for existence is *prius* and reason *posterius.* In order to penetrate beyond the anxious realm of disquietude to the really real, reason must be lifted outside itself, in ecstasy. It must confront the God who is the Lord of all Being, "the primordial holy power of being." In order to grasp reality one must be grasped by it. By this means, contingency and the ultimately real are united in the individual and in the historical process. Logical dialectic must be ecstatically transformed into an *existential dialectic.*

With this word "ecstatic" we again encounter a psychological category which is radicalized in order to express the way in which existence points beyond itself. Schelling's existential dialectic issues in an ontology of love. Ecstasy and love! Here, as with Kierkegaard later, the feeling-experiences of intense existence provide the basic categories; we have observed also that Marx radicalizes the psychological concepts of alienation and deception. This use of psychological categories appears in the later existentialists as well. It is a fundamental aspect of their protest against the objectivism which they associate with the rationalism of the capitalist era.

In our day the philosophers Jaspers and Heidegger have given new expression to these motifs of earlier existentialism. For Jaspers scientific objectivity and objectivism miss existence. If we are to know ourselves and our existence, we must ask about the meaning of life. The fact that we ask for the meaning is the essence of our existence. But meaning is not found when life is secure, but rather when we come to shipwreck (*Naufrage*) at the boundary of our being-in-the-world; in the face of death, in guilt and anxiety, our being-in-the-world and its meaning are brought into question and we must decide between defiance and devotion to meaning. The leap out of anxiety into freedom becomes possible when we sense a background that is real and from which we derive our reality. At the boundary of the scientifically knowable, the world points beyond itself to the "Origin of being." When we become open to this Origin our thinking becomes an ecstatic, transcending thinking.

The danger always exists that we will try to interpret this Origin in terms of our being-in-the-world, i.e., in objective terms, in unparadoxical terms. Existential thinking is a transcending thinking that transcends the subject-object world through faith in the "All-Encompassing," the other-than-us that envelops us and that is the ground of love.

For Heidegger, as for Schelling, the psychology of anxiety and guilt is a mythology concerning being. Intense anxiety brings us to the abyss of nothingness; we sense that we are existents flung upon the earth; we are finite, we are limited by death, our existence is "a being-for-death"; these things are hidden from us when we are not really existing. We can know our *existence* only by transcending the surfaces of everyday experience; then we recognize our ecstatic openness to or participation in the world, we achieve immediate relation to other existents, and we go beyond ourselves to meet the future. But just because of this transcendence toward the future we are always in anxiety. In our *ecstatic* relation to the past and future, we take upon ourselves our past, our future, and our present, and we affirm our destiny by Resolute Decision. Human existence, because it is without essence, is the risk itself. For Heidegger, then, the psychology of anguish and ecstasy are the mythology of being itself. Existence is the possibility of being oneself or not being oneself, or asserting freedom and incurring guilt, or of losing freedom in conventionality and thus also of incurring guilt. Guilt is inescapable. But there is no norm for freedom.

This is one of the reasons that Berdyaev says that "Heidegger is not an honest thinker, but an able constructor and calculator bereft of ethics and intellectual scruples."

THEOLOGICAL EXISTENTIALISM—PAUL TILLICH

The law of diminishing returns is by now making its ravages upon this rapid-moving survey of the existentialist theme with its variations, particularly since such a survey must fail to give a sense of the vitality that informs the existentialist literature. Yet the résumé does make it evident that the characteristic concepts of existentialism have gathered a certain momentum, and that like a snowball they have gathered also a large body of diverse connotation.

Apart from the reference to Kierkegaard, this résumé has given no account of the existentialist thesis in Christian thought. Barth, Brunner, Gogarten, and Bultmann, and also Reinhold Niebuhr and H. Richard Niebuhr have made the existentialist themes and concepts familiar in varying types of Christian interpretation. All of these theologians have used the psychological categories of existentialism. They vary mainly in their emphasis upon the actuality of guilt and despair or upon the possibilities of freedom, and also in their definitions of reason, paradox, and faith. The fact that Christian theology should have taken an existentialist turn is nothing strange. Rather, it is strange that so many non-theologian and non-Christian existentialists have been concerned with these themes, for the voluntarist background of secular existentialism is in certain fundamental ways Christian. Even Marx, with his stress on the dynamic character of history and on the misery of human alienation, is not understandable apart from the Judeo-Christian background. There is another way of stating the reason for the interplay between Christian and secular forms of existentialism, which has to do with the much overworked concept of dialectic. The dialectic emanating from ancient Greek thought and from philosophical idealism offers a certain parallel with the Christian categories of creation, fall, and redemption—the disruption and reestablishment of an original unity between the human being and God. This parallel between the philosophical dialectic of thesis-antithesis-synthesis and the Christian separation from and reunion with God has been worked out with greatest elaboration perhaps by Tillich, to whom, as a proponent of existentialist issues, we shall confine our attention now.

Tillich's use of the formal parallels between the philosophical dialectic of identity and contrast and the Christian scheme constitutes a part of what he calls the method of correlation. This correlation is possible because unity, estrangement, and reunion are found in both schemes. To illustrate this correlation one may view the story of the prodigal son as a metaphysical parable exemplifying the dialectic, the Yes and No, the unity, separation, and reunion of the human creature who is subject to creation, fall, and redemption. It should be noted that the parable symbolizes not only the relation between God and the person, but also that between subject and object in the process of knowing. The parable points to what Tillich calls the dialectical ontology and epistemology of love.

In Tillich's dynamic ontology of love we discern not only the typical voluntarist and existentialist conception, stemming from Augustine, Luther, the young Hegel, and Schelling, that love belongs to the structure of being itself; we find here the existentialist presupposition that the human being as microcosm is the "door" or clue to the deeper levels of existence. Every special being, Tillich asserts, participates in the nature of love, since it participates in being; it is also estranged from the power of being. *Existentially,* human beings are estranged from the infinite ground of their being; yet they are not *separated* from it, they cannot be separated from it, completely. *Essentially,* they are united with it. Thus reconciliation is possible.

The dialectic of the person in relation to God is the dialectic between essential freedom and existential servitude, between participation in infinite creativity and estranged, isolated finitude. In this estrangement the person suffers the anxiety of isolation in the face of the surrounding abyss of nothingness and annihilation. The courage of creativity is bound up with the anxiety and fear of loneliness and contingency. Because we participate in essential goodness, and yet are in existential servitude, we sense the goodness as a threat, as a criterion, as a condemnation. The demand of goodness or meaning gives rise to despair. It brings us to the boundary situation. The tension involved here expresses more than anything else the cleavage within human existence, individual and social.

The person's participation in the essential goodness and creativity of being, coupled with the estrangement of existential anxiety and despair, finds a parallel in the basic articulation of existence, the unity and separation between subject and object, the unity and separation in human relations and in the relation between the person and nature. The overcoming of the cleavages of the existential order requires, then, not only the reunion of "the estranged" with the infinite ground, but also a reunion that transcends the cleavage between subject and object, a reunion with that which lies beyond existence and essence, beyond potentiality and actuality. This reunion cannot be complete, but insofar as it occurs it involves the awareness of self-transcendence, the ecstatic opening of the self to the "other." Both true knowledge and true community are acts of love. Knowledge is a dynamic process in which the subject as well as the object is fulfilled.

Viewed from the ontological side, reunion between the human being and God exhibits the power of being to unite independent, estranged elements of reality—it is a work of grace. Viewed from the anthropological side, the reunion of the human being and God, and the transcending of the separation between subject and object in the realm of special beings, is what Tillich calls "ecstasy." Like Schelling, Tillich radicalizes the psychological concept *ecstasy* as well as the concept *love*. "Wherever we transcend the limits of our own being, moving towards union with another," Tillich writes, "something like ecstasy ('standing outside oneself') occurs. Ecstasy is the act of breaking through a fixed form of our own being. Only through ecstasy can the ultimate power of being be experienced in ourselves, in things and persons, and in historical situations." It is experienced also when our concepts become ecstatic, that is, opened to the ground and abyss of being.

But it is not sufficient to speak of Tillich's dialectic as "ecstatic." The Tillichian dialectic is also an existential dialectic, in the sense of Schelling, namely, it aims to break through every intellectualist logism; it wishes to express the dialogue between the universal and the unique, between the necessary and the contingent. Tillich accentuates Schelling's dynamic existential dialectic by his juxtaposition of Logos and *kairos*, and of Logos and fate. The dipolarity of particularity and universality in God, stressed by Schelling, reappears in Tillich's interpretation of the historical. Every moment as well as every individual is unique. Every historical situation approaches us as destiny, offering only a limited number of possibilities and demanding decision in freedom. Rationality alone cannot penetrate to the inner power and possibility of history. We must be grasped, as Schelling also put it, we must be grasped by this power as it is manifest in the fact of our historical existence that demands decision. Being grasped, our decision must be twofold: it should be a risking decision that seizes time by the forelock, meeting the limits imposed by the unique situation; but also it should be a risking decision that expresses what is creatively new and pregnant with a meaningful future. The decision is not made by an absolute subject standing above history, it is a decision made in history where creation must emerge from conflict and ambiguity; it is an ecstatic, gracious decision, uniting an existent form and ecstatically opening it up to transformation and new meaning. In the context of the ontology of love, the *kairos* is opened up to Logos and the Logos finds new fulfillment. Tillich's decision for Religious Socialism is intended to be such a kairotic decision. The fulfillment hoped for cannot of course be unambiguous; the Protestant renounces the hope for any such security; both *kairos* and Logos are under the judgment of the inexhaustible, unconditional ground and abyss of being. History brings diastasis along with synthesis. Every actualization of meaning is fragmentary.

But any such kairotic moment of decision and of "being decided" does not for the Christian existentialist occur merely under the aegis of the ground and abyss of meaning and being, abstractly considered. The joining of *kairos* and Logos is oriented to a norm. This norm is found in the unique and universal *kairos,* in the New Being, in Jesus as the Christ. Here the concrete form, Jesus, is ecstatically opened to the Logos. The norm is symbolized in the Cross, where the finite does not immolate itself but rather in confidence makes the sacrifice in obedience to the infinite love. The Cross is both surrender and affirmation. This is paradoxical, but it is a paradox that is not irrational; for it is the juncture of *kairos* and Logos. The Logos becomes history, a visible and tangible individuality, in a unique moment in time. The individual entity or situation is not only an exemplar of the universal, it also adds something new and unique to the universal. The existential dialectic of the ontology of love finds its ecstatic fulfillment in a concrete universal.

At this point we encounter an essential feature of Tillich's method. It would be wrong to suppose that the validity of this norm can be demonstrated by any empirical-inductive or by any metaphysical-deductive method. It cannot be an empirical-inductive method, because "knowledge of revelation, although it is mediated primarily through historical events, does not imply factual assertions, and it is therefore not exposed to critical analysis by historical research" (Paul Tillich, *Systematic Theology,* vol. 1 [Chicago: University of Chicago Press, 1951], p. 130). No historical research, Tillich asserts, could offer anything "disastrous" to Christian faith. Historical investigations "should neither comfort nor worry theologians" (*ibid.*).

At this point, then, in Tillich's position we encounter the apex of his existentialist thesis. The decision that is determinative for the whole theological position is an "original decision." It is not rooted in "formal evidence" or "material probability," nor can it be the result of deduction. It is "an immediate experience of something ultimate in value and being, of which one can become intuitively aware." The verification of this decision, Tillich says, is its "efficacy in life" (*ibid.*, pp. 102–5), but the process of verification is within "the theological circle." In the first instance this "original decision" is a mystical *a priori*. To this mystical *a priori* the Christian theologian adds the criterion of the Christian message regarding Jesus as the Christ who is the unique juncture of *kairos* and Logos (*ibid.*, p. 9).

In the face of this method of combining the universal and the unique we may offer a general observation regarding Tillich's place in the spectrum of Christian existentialism. In contrast to Barth and Brunner, Tillich rejects any deprecation of reason. In contrast to Barth and Niebuhr, he makes a deliberate effort to devise a philosophical theology. This philosophical dimension is particularly evident in his metaphysics, with its elaborate categorical apparatus which in substantial measure is drawn from the Aristotelian tradition; indeed, Tillich speaks of this metaphysics as a dynamized Aristotelianism. In a sense, these and similar tendencies in Tillich make it perhaps correct to say that his outlook is an intellectualized voluntarism.

In conclusion, I should like to pose some brief questions. These questions could also be asked of other existentialists, for in varying ways they also leave something to be desired from the point of view of philosophical method.

The first question implies a qualification of the characterization of Tillich's intellectualism just offered. In his presentation of the doctrine of God, he speaks of the dipolar ground and abyss of being and meaning. He speaks of God as also being beyond potentiality and actuality, beyond essence and existence. These formulations indicate that Tillich would have done well to apply a closer logical analysis, instead of pushing God into a region where nonliteralism or symbolism plays an inordinately large role and where only the concept of Being is literally applicable. It will be recalled that he asserts that one cannot properly say that God "exists"; by this he means that God is not a being alongside other beings. But why are not the terms potentiality and actuality, essence and existence, applicable to God, even more than to finite entities? Do not such formulations remove God from relation to the contingent world of existence?

Second question: In his conception of Jesus as the Christ, what does he *have?* If historical investigation about Jesus should "neither worry nor comfort theologians," then what becomes of the claim that Christianity is a historical religion? Does it not border upon Gnosticism?

Third question: If "formal evidence" and "material probability" are not relevant to the discussion of the Christian existentialist "original decision," then must one not say that this decision is merely fated by the Christian's accidental existence in the tradition of the West? In the face of a different "original decision" presented by an Oriental, is there no basis for discussion? Or must each remain within a distinct "theological circle"? If so, is not Tillich's Christian existentialism a form of relativism, mitigated only by the concession that no one should absolutize one's own "original decision"?

Fourth question: As we have observed, Tillich has exhibited great ingenuity and originality in employing the concepts that have been characteristic of existentialist thought. But the question may be raised whether his method ultimately is essentially anything other than an apologetic method. As a theologian he has studied other disciplines in order to clarify his own position and to gain a better intellectual grasp of it in terms of the current discussions. But his method is not one that in essence sets out to *find* something. It is rather a method for showing the implications of what he already *has*. Is this a method of inquiry? Is the philosophical theologian justified in studying philosophy (or reality itself) in order mainly to be able to indicate a Christian answer already in hand? If so, what place can any empirical method concerned with evidence have for the Christian?

18 · *The Chief End of Human Existence*

Man's chief end is to glorify God and to enjoy him forever.
—The Westminster Shorter Catechism

The doctrine of original sin set forth by the Westminster Assembly no longer holds sway among the spiritual descendants of the Puritans. We refuse to believe that "in Adam's transgression all mankind, descend-

This essay is based on a sermon delivered at Harvard Divinity School, December 16, 1953, and published in the *Harvard Divinity School Bulletin* 19 (1954). Reprinted by permission.

ing from him by ordinary generation, fell with him." But very different has been the reputation and fate of the first affirmation of the Shorter Catechism. Calvinist and non-Calvinist agree that "man's chief end is to glorify God and to enjoy him." Our chief end, clearly, is joy in community; and, as Milton would say, the community is under the Great Taskmaster's eye. When men and women are alienated from the creative and redemptive ground of community, they are alienated from each other; and they are deprived of the joy that is essential to them.

But we of the twentieth century have not witnessed that joy in widest commonalty spread. In our time of troubles we have learned anew that the obstructions to joy in community are legion, indeed they are wellnigh insurmountable. These obstructions assume manifold forms in our individual and institutional existence, in religious as well as secular life; but fundamental in all of them is isolation, the isolation of persons from each other and from God.

I

The isolation may be that of Narcissus. Jean-Paul Sartre's antihero speaks for many when he cries out of his loneliness, "There is no need for hot pokers in this place. Hell is—other people," that is, other people with whom one enjoys nothing significant in common. In the end this sort of isolation leads to the madhouse. Sartre's demand for fellowship is a secularized version of the sovereignty of God. The human being is made for fellowship.

But fellowship itself may be positively perverted by another form of isolation, one that issues from a more aggressive loneliness than Narcissism. The sociologist calls it striving for status. The person who is bent wholly on achieving status cannot enjoy other people or the goods of life for their intrinsic worth. This yearning for status is today felt to be so pervasive that the contemporary psychologist and novelist have virtually rendered it into the revised version of the doctrine of original sin. This version of original sin is the leitmotif, for example, of Franz Kafka's stories which depict the hell that issues from the person's trying to "establish himself." For the depth-psychologist the striving for status is a major source of the discontents of civilization.

The biologists have offered a striking illustration of a striving for status that produces a socially organized form of isolation, the imperium of "the pecking order." They tell us that a group of fowls newly brought together will within a short time form a pyramid of "peck-dominance": at the top of the pyramid one fowl will establish the supreme status of being able to peck all the others without being pecked in return, and beneath this "top hen" there will appear a hierarchy of hens with diminishing pecking privileges; at the bottom of the pyramid is the largest group, the hens that can be pecked by all others "from above" but that dare not peck back. The pecking order forms a social organization, but it is scarcely a community of enjoyment.

Both of these forms of isolation—that of repellent particles and that of the pecking order—are familiar in human affairs. Both deprive us of the joy of togetherness.

A striking fact about the history of religion is that to overcome the first form of isolation the second is frequently offered as a cure, as a way of salvation. This second type provides security of status for all believers. But the security is a spurious security; it renounces the responsibilities and the joys of open community. Instead of the joy of mutual togetherness it provides a hierarchy of domination which puts people into straitjackets that frustrate what is creative in both themselves and God.

In ancient Mesopotamia we find already a religious protest against any love of status which issues in imperialist domination. According to recent findings, the Mesopotamians at one period conceived of the gods as having amongst themselves overcome this form of isolation. Their gods were not arranged in a hierarchy; instead, they were equal and responsive to each other. A god was not a domineering authority. He or she was a member of a divine community of mutual respect. Decisions were made in council, and only after discussion. Indeed, the divine act was conceived to be the act of raising the hand to the ear in order to hear what another god had to say. Archaeologists believe that this conception of the community of the gods was a projection of a "primitive democracy" in the Mesopotamian villages.

In this ancient view of the divine power as responsiveness in community one may see something of the biblical conception of the end of human life: to glorify God and to enjoy God in communion and community. The Gospels are replete with parables and incidents that show the community-forming power of God bringing persons together in recognition of their togetherness and in the enjoyment of mutuality. The divine initiative elicits a new responsiveness that overcomes the brokenness of human relationships to each other and to the divine. Out of the new togetherness which the disciples had experienced with Jesus arose a new *koinonia,* a new fellowship in responsiveness. This new responsiveness was itself taken to be the redemptive work of God overcoming isolation and giving birth to the joy of the Reign of God.

But the old isolation and brokenness were not completely banished. They reappeared to bring separation and striving for status, and even imperialism. Extenuating circumstances, for example, the threat of dissolution at the hands of false prophets and the disillusionment resulting from the delay of the parousia, may be appealed to as an explanation for the partial loss of the outreaching quality of the early Christian *koinonia*. The faith in the community-forming power has been reborn and displaced again and again in the history of Christianity. Indeed, much of this history offers the data for an elaborate phenomenology of peck-dominance, and the forms of dominance bear close resemblance to the familiar power-configurations of "the world."

These forms of peck-dominance issue in institutional arrangements, but they appear also, and perhaps first, at the level of theological debate. Contemporary Protestant thinking exhibits two related types of peck-dominance (and of the isolation ensuing from them) which deserve special attention. The first is what we might call "proclamationism," and the second is today called "kerygmatic theology."

II

"Proclamationism" is a barbarous term, but its meaning is so readily evident that we may be permitted to use it. Proclamationism assumes that the task of the church and of the preacher is to proclaim the gospel by simply repeating the words of the Gospels or of the creeds. It identifies the gospel with formulations which were contrived in an earlier historical situation and that are taken to be the very Word of God. It assumes that the substance of Christian faith is capsuled in a definitive and full expression in a particular historical form; and it makes the repetition of this particular form a work of piety, whether that form brings about effective communication and newness of life or not.

I recall a meeting of American theologians at which a paper was presented which asserted that repentance is appropriate for churches as well as for individuals, repentance especially for not making the gospel relevant to our times. One of the theologians in the group vehemently protested, saying to the author of the paper, "You may well have reason to repent in *your* churches, but I have nothing to repent of. In my church we know what the gospel is; it is set forth once and for all in Scripture. My church has proclaimed this gospel. Far be it from me to ask God to forgive us for having preached His word. Let those who have not preached Scripture repent." He never returned to this ecumenical group. One is reminded of the pastors who during the rise and ascendancy of Nazism held that their responsibility was fulfilled if they proclaimed the words of the Bible or of the creeds without "human adulteration." In the face of the rising tyranny of Hitler they said, "We have preached the pure doctrine, for we do not presume to improve upon divine revelation. We have done our duty, but a sinful world has refused to give heed. May God be merciful to these sinners." Here we see a veritable legalism of the word, if not a belief in the magic of the word. The ox remains in the pit, but the law is preserved intact. Here humanity is made for the word, not the word for humanity. The "proclaimer" is separated from the Original by attachment to the mere words of another time, indeed by identifying the Original with those words and by not permitting new words and deeds of healing to issue forth in a new situation. In doing this, then, the "proclaimer" is separated from the new situation with its unique need for healing and its unique possibilities.

Proclamationism is to be found not only among the orthodox; some liberals become similarly attached to the "progressive revelation" of another time. Proclamationism, both liberal and orthodox, makes its unseasonal proclamation a work of piety. In protest against this proclamationism, Christian "existentialism" (at the hands of Bultmann) has claimed to open a way to overcome the false security of "possessing" the definitive word. Yet, by giving a nontemporal abstract meaning to the essence of the early Christian "myth," it too remains isolated from the concrete, immediate life-situation. In the act of overcoming the proclamationism of orthodoxy it exhibits a new form of isolation.

To be sure, proclamationism has often been impelled by a sound intention. It has aimed to detach itself from and to protest against the idolatry of the seasonal; it has tried to offer an appropriate noncooperation with the spirit of the age. But its "success" is its failure. Culture-Protestantism is not to be corrected by absolutizing the formulations of another age in opposition to the perversions of the present age. This procedure often ends by being a sort of Culture-Protestantism in reverse. Of its protest we may say that nothing is so much like a swelling as a hole. In saying this, however, we do not overlook the fact that, in the face of Culture-Protestantism, the words of another time, and specifically of the Bible, can and often do continue to be a living fountain as fresh and as prophetic as on the morn of their birth out of the Eternal. But they are life-renewing only for those who take the responsibility for consequences in the just community, as well as for purity of doctrine or of intention. Risking revaluation of the old is the price of new relevance. A living tradition is not bequeathed through some law of inheritance; it must be earned, not without dust and heat, and not without humbling grace. Genuine faith is not a faith in one's "faith." It looks beyond itself. It yields to a transforming power, to a power that is only feebly at work in mere proclamationism. Whenever proclamation issues in transformation, something more than proclamationism has been at work.

III

The isolationist tendency that we have discerned in proclamationism appears also in exclusively kerygmatic theology. The term *kerygmatic,* stemming from the New Testament word *kerygma* (proclamation, message), is used to characterize an ordered and systematic presentation of the unique Christian message. That there is a uniqueness in the Christian conception and experience of the transforming power of God and that this must be given intelligible order is the just claim of kerygmatic theology. This claim is made by any church that aims to be Christian. But exclusively kerygmatic theology avowedly renounces every demand that Christian theology should come to terms with philosophy; it renounces the demand that Christian theology should examine its claims in the face of universally valid principles. Centuries ago Tertullian adopted this position when he placed in complete opposition "the follower of the cross" and "the wisdom of men." "Where is there any likeness," he asks, "between the Christian and the philosopher? between the disciple of Greece and the disciple of heaven? What indeed has Athens to do with Jerusalem? What concord is there between the Academy and the Church? What between heretics and Christians?"

In wide circles this view is today attributed to Karl Barth, but wrongly so. Barth has maintained subterranean connections with the philosophers. From the beginning he has presupposed a Kantian philosophical position that renders traditional concern with metaphysics untenable. But not only Kantian philosophy serves him. There are also echoes of Hegel in his outlook. Recently he has been giving a more positive significance to the *Imago Dei* doctrine. In doing so he continues to reject Hegel's trust in reason and also Hegel's panlogism; but at the same time he retains the structure of Hegel's dialectic. If dialectic theology would display a responsible attitude here, it would be obliged to offer a philosophical analysis of its own dialectic, a conception of which in its basic structure is reminiscent of Hegel's theory of alienation and fulfillment as it finds articulation in his logic and metaphysics.

Some contemporary theologians have gone so far as to say that metaphysics, having encumbered Christian faith with supernaturalism, should be abandoned altogether; thus, they say, the Christian theologians should have learned their lesson and should not now try to substitute a naturalistic or avowedly scientific metaphysics. Metaphysics, they say, raises pseudo-questions, and it gives pseudo-answers, answers that point to no verifiable referents. Indeed, in certain quarters it is asserted that logical positivism has demonstrated the bankruptcy of all metaphysics and properly reduces philosophy to meaning-analysis. In line with this outlook is the assertion of a certain type of kerygmatic theologian that religion and theology are concerned only with value judgments and not with theoretical judgments (a dichotomy that breaks down the moment one says that "God is love"). Consequently, it is argued, a greater dogmatism is required to establish a metaphysical position today than was ever necessary to establish a religious position. It is only one step from this view to the notion that the gospel is a scandal to human reason and that it should be proclaimed in all its glorious folly that confounds human reason. In the face of these (actually philosophical) claims one can only say that the sheer necessity of believing something is no basis for any particular belief. Such a claim is thus hoist on its own petard.

This fact becomes the more evident when we observe that this sort of exclusively kerygmatic theology itself points to referents that cannot be verified. It presupposes that the gospel and its interpretation are readily available in Scripture. But this is to overlook the fact that the interpretation of the Redemptive Event is not given unambiguous expression in the New Testament itself. The canon of the New Testament confronts the theologian with a theological problem, for, as B. H. Streeter points out, there are seven different types of religion in the New Testament. Thus kerygmatic theologians have to make a choice, and this choice cannot properly be defended as merely a matter of faith. Nor can they substantiate their theology on the ground that theirs is a biblical, and therefore a completely authoritative, theology. There are several biblical theologies; and, besides, these theologies are human interpretations. Moreover, kerygmatic theologians who stake their faith on the scandal of the gospel must first decide what that scandal is, and they cannot substantiate the claim that it is subversive of human reason. The "scandal" of the gospel is rather that the human being is not capable of self-salvation, that salvation is of God. In many ways, then, kerygmatic theologians come very close to being arbitrary theologians; and they achieve this scandal by renouncing not only philosophy but also responsible and honest biblical criticism; thus their isolation is twofold. Consequently, they demand arbitrary decision and submission; they try only to be heard, they will not lift the hand to the ear.

The alternative to arbitrariness is a philosophical theology that aims to overcome isolation between the theologian and the biblical scholar, and that recognizes that philosophical implications are involved in every theological assertion. These implications require the risk of having to confront the demand for faith. The risk involved in meeting this demand is not so great as that of ignoring it. Actually, kerygmatic theologians in effect concede this fact when they assert that we must distinguish between the three-storied "worldview" of the Gospels and the gospel itself. This distinction presupposes the proximate validity of the science and the philosophy that have rendered the worldview of the Gospels untenable. We see, then, that the peck-dominance of theology over philosophy has been achieved partially by the surreptitious use of either tenable or untenable philosophies.

But it is equally unacceptable to the Christian if a peck-dominance of philosophy over theology is "established." In the end the kerygmatic theologian is justified in asserting that this dominance serves to dilute or pervert the gospel. The proper relation between kerygmatic and philosophical theology is one that recognizes the claims and the limitations of both. Christian faith asserts that the Reign of God is available (as Professor Joel Cadbury has pointed out, this is perhaps the most accurate translation of the saying generally rendered, "The Reign of God is within you"). But the response to this availability does not preclude the demand for truth represented in science and philosophy. On the other hand, science and philosophy aim, with varying degrees of risk, to seek that which is universally valid. Yet this striving is always informed by a faith that has unique historical and experiential provenance. When these two impulses, the one from Christian faith and the other from science and philosophy, are isolated, faith and truth resort to separate maintenance, and finally they sue for divorce; divorce cripples both.

But, as we have seen, Christian faith is not able to avoid philosophy; faith seeks understanding, and in doing so it turns to philosophy. Philosophical reason can be informed by faith; but only if the faith accepts correction at the hands of reason and experience can it be also an informed, a dependable, faith. God moves in mysterious ways, and God's ways are not in human control through either faith or reason.

Yet both faith and reason are God's gifts; each has its divine vocation. To deny its vocation to either of them is to indulge the striving for status—the original sin of the pecking order. Both theology and philosophy in mutual responsiveness are a part of the human response to the divine ground of community. To isolate them from each other is to impair the community among those who live by the confession that the end of human existence is "to glorify God and to enjoy him forever."

19 · Sin and Salvation

The term "sin" may be defined as that state, attitude, or act which is constituted by or results from a wrong relationship to that norm-giving reality which is both the ground of meaningful human existence and the judge of all human attempts to achieve meaning. Thus the term "sin" is not a merely ethical category; it presupposes a metaphysical or theological orientation.[1]

We must, therefore, first indicate the nature of the ultimate orientation—the norm-giving reality—which represents the context within which a wrong relationship (sin) may occur. The creative reality in which we find ourselves as individual, socially related entities may be characterized as dynamic tension between the power to exist and varying degrees or extensions of mutuality. Anything that exists possesses the power of existential affirmation in the context of mutuality. The power to affirm or maintain existence requires some degree of mutuality. When mutuality is absolutely lacking the power to exist is also lacking.

This precondition for existence as such we take to be the ontological basis for "the good." In this sense, "being is older than value." Hence we may say that "being" in the metaphysical sense is both an ontological and an axiological category. *Esse est bonum qua esse;* being is good as being.

This previously unpublished paper was read at a meeting of the Chicago Philosophy of Religion Association in 1948.

Reality is therefore norm-giving in this ontological-axiological minimum. Thus human beings find themselves, in Heidegger's term, "thrown
into" the sort of existence that demands a minimum mutuality, with its
concomitant threat of destruction if the demand is not met. But the reality of which human beings are part, and by which they are confronted,
also offers the possibility of ever increasing mutuality and creativity.

Meaningful human existence involves the exercise of freedom on the
part of persons in their participation in and relationship to the creative
process which is a manifestation of the divine. Human freedom permits
persons to determine in varying ways and degrees the extent to which
they will appropriate the actual and latent resources available to them.
Thus they may extend or reduce the various types of mutuality possible
within the creative process of which they are a part.

. All human beings, by virtue of their humanity, possess the freedom to
participate in this creative process. Indeed, they are fated to be free to
participate, they are fated to make decisions, though it must be recognized that this means also that they may use their freedom not to participate. Indeed, they can even decide to end either their own existence or
the existence of others.

Now all men and women are to some degree aware of these facts, that
is, of the minimal demands of existence, of the possibility of creative
achievement, and of the necessity for decision. Indeed, human beings
characteristically experience frustration in their desire to appropriate the
available resources. They all wish to achieve some sort of status in the
community, and they normally have some sense of their own inadequacy
fully to appropriate resources. Moreover, they posit certain ideals that
serve as criteria for judging their accomplishments and deficiencies in
their vocation, in their relations to the community, in their own inner
development, and in their cultural creations.

Thus they posit one or another set of values by which they measure the
true, the good, and the beautiful. They also discriminate various defec-
tions from these ideals as dishonest, self-deceptive, illogical thinking; as
selfish, shortsighted, uneconomic, illegal, or unintegrated behavior; as
lack of taste; as mediocre talent; as distorted or clumsy artistic expression.
This dimension of human consciousness is usually characterized as culture.

The religious dimension includes these categories but relates them to
a "holy" reality. This religious dimension gives an ultimate orientation to
existence as actual and potential, as well as a sense of immediacy in rela-

tion to this orientation. In the religious outlook, reality and its possibilities are viewed as a divine "gift" and demand, supporting all meaningful existence and at the same time threatening all inappropriate attempts to achieve meaning. That is, existence is interpreted as manifesting a divine purpose and as permitting some degree of fulfillment through human cooperation with or appropriation of the actual and latent resources. Thus the religious outlook finds a divine splendor eminent within the actual, and yet transcending all actuality.

It also interprets the potentiality of existence as a divine promise and not as a merely human possibility. The mutuality and the power of being are thus interpreted as the consequence of divine grace. Even the human capacities that make possible a participation in this power of being with its concentric circles of mutuality are interpreted as autonomous (in the sense that the person exercises a certain freedom of participation) and also as theonomous (in the sense that this autonomy is itself a gift of grace and is thus related to something beyond itself). The possibility of increasing one's participation in the divine purpose of fulfillment is viewed as a divine command and as dependent upon the divinely given resources.

Here it must be emphasized that the divine splendor is never seen as wholly actualized. Existent reality is never to be properly interpreted as a complete manifestation of the divine majesty. To interpret it in this way would be to spatialize the divine and (so to speak) to view it as "exhausted" in some particular manifestation. It would constitute the identification of the absolute with the relative or the contingent. This absolutization can also be improperly attributed to some future historical and contingent state of affairs, such as is illustrated by the utopian conception of the classless society or of the kingdom of God.

To deny this ambiguous character of existence is tantamount to asserting either that humanity is God or that humanity is totally corrupt. In the former instance, evil must be interpreted as illusory or really good, and ethical categories thus also become meaningless. In the latter instance, we are left with the idea of total depravity, a conception which is self-destructive. The concept of total corruption can have no validity if the mind that posits it is totally corrupt.

The conceptions of sin and salvation presuppose some such view of the divine splendor and promise as set forth above. Moreover, the conception of sin is a correlative concept in another sense, that is, it implies a freedom and responsibility which give dignity to the human being. Thus, human existence is ambiguous, for humans at the same time express the "good" of being and some contradiction or perversion of this good. This state of cleavage represents both an affinity with the divine and an alienation from it.

In Jewish and Christian theology the affinity between the human being and the divine is usually described in terms of the doctrine of *Imago Dei*.[2] The various types of alienation are called sin. These types of alienation represent the different ways in which the dynamic affinity between the human and the divine can be frustrated or perverted through human freedom. It should be pointed out that most of these forms of sin could (as Luther suggests) also be characterized as forms of despair, the distrust of God, a lack of faith in God's power or goodness, and an unwillingness to achieve the dignity that comes to persons when they submit to that which would judge them and overcome the alienation. We now turn to a characterization of these types of alienation.[3]

1. Original sin. This term has acquired so many confusing and nonsensical meanings that it should probably be abandoned. Yet, the concept has its value, for it reminds us that alienation from God is not adequately described in terms of freedom alone or of the individual's conscious act of will. Sin is not merely a private affair. The individual person through solidarity with the race shares a universal alienation. Whether we consider the universally egoistic and combative elements in human nature, or the universal operation of the so-called "collective unconscious," or the inescapable participation of all members of society in society's total character, we must recognize that the human being is fated to have a share in the common human condition of corporate frustration and egoism, and to have a share in the universal perversion of creativity and mutuality.

Here we see the operation of determinism as well as freedom. Hence, humans feel themselves to be at the same time responsible and not responsible. Both the fateful character and the guilt of human existence are due to the universal[4] self-assertiveness of beings that contradict their own nature. This basic underivable cleavage in human existence underlies all human history. And thus, as we have said, it would be false to characterize all forms of alienation or sin as simply conscious, deliberate, and individual acts of will. Here, then, is the root of the idea of original sin: the recognition that humans are in a situation which is not what it ought to be, a situation which is given to them (or fated) and yet for which they are responsible.

Indeed, this paradoxical combination of freedom and determinism is present in all of human experience, and even in so-called deliberate, individual acts of will.[5] On account of this, every moralistic system which assigns merit and demerit, praise and blame, merely on the basis of individual performance and without reference to what the individual had to start with or to cope with, must be qualified.

Three familiar attempts to explain original sin should be mentioned here (and rejected). The first interprets sin as merely a residue of our inheritance from the jungle. This view is inadequate, for it overlooks the fact that the frustrations and perversions of humanity are not due merely to uncontrolled instinct which humans will eventually outgrow. The truth is that it is precisely in the operation of the highest human faculties that we find the most destructive perversions and corruptions.

The second view interprets sin as merely the consequence of social conditioning. Hence, it asserts that the human being is naturally good but is corrupted by custom and institutions, or it asserts that the perversion of freedom will cease in the classless society. But, we may ask, why have evil customs arisen, why have we a class society in the first place? The presupposition of this point of view is that humans can be conditioned to conform freely to some established order. Thus it both denies that freedom is underived and asserts that freedom can be got "under control." It overlooks the fact that since freedom is inseparable from individuality it expresses itself in creative or destructive uniqueness of decision. Thus freedom may at any moment be used to transcend or criticize the "perfect" classless society in the name of an allegedly better society, or it may be used simply to assert autonomy as such for the sake of maintaining individuality (i.e., the individual may say, "I don't care if your beehive is perfect; I don't like beehives").

The third view interprets original sin as a historical heritage transmitted from Adam. This makes the human being sinful without responsibility, and through a particular historical event. Sin without responsibility is a complete contradiction, as is a universal sin dependent on a particular event. The frequent denial of original guilt in connection with original sin is evidence of the recognition of the contradictory nature of this third view.

2. *Sin as the identification of the finite with the infinite.* This has usually been characterized as hubris or pride. It is that form of alienation whereby a man or a woman rejects the divine demand that they fulfill their nature by a submission and by an adjustment compatible with their finite, dependent character or creatureliness. Sin is, however, not to be attributed to human finitude; it is to be attributed to the fact that the human being,

who is related to and can participate in infinite creativity, attempts to absorb or domesticate the infinite dimension into the self.

This sin takes a wide variety of forms. (1) The world-denying forms, such as Barthian dualism, which, despite its claims to the contrary, absolutizes the Bible and also denies all intrinsic value to the human being or culture; Christian Science, which exalts the spirit and (in theory) deprecates the material world; that type of mysticism which devises a technique for making the flight to the other world of the spirit; the otherworldliness of certain fundamentalist sects. (2) The world-affirming forms: doctrinaire socialism, communism, bourgeoisism (capitalism), Utopianism (socialist, liberal or Christian), nationalism, racism, Nazism, Roman Catholicism, bourgeois or nonprophetic Protestantism which serves primarily as a divine sanction for the status quo. Other examples might be art for art's sake (aestheticism), and devotion to an established convention, a moral norm (moralism or legalism), or some form of already achieved good. In medieval thought this world-affirming pride, as relating to the individual psyche, was classified in a threefold way, and all three forms were interpreted as self-love. I refer to the familiar *libido dominandi, libido sentiendi,* and *libido sciendi.*

In short, this type of sin identifies the creature, some aspect of the creature's life, or something produced by the creature, with the Creator— it is devotion to a humanly made god, a god made in the image of the human. Thus it obstructs creativity and mutuality and resists criticism. By spatializing and domesticating the absolute it alienates itself from the norm-giving creative reality, God, and attempts to conceal from itself its own ambiguous character. It does not recognize the need for salvation. It already possesses it.

3. Sin as unbelief. The first form of sin as unbelief is indifference to God (secularism). This is the attitude that simply takes the world and existence for granted. It has no explicit sense of the gift of grace manifest in the divine splendor and promise of reality. The world and its possibilities are simply "there." Moreover, the norms of human existence are viewed as merely human desiderata, or as projections, or as merely the contingent expressions of cultural activity, or as expressions of interest.[6] At its best this view exalts human autonomy, but due to its unbelief it eventually degenerates into some sort of heteronomy (authoritarianism of a political or religious character). "There is nothing a jellyfish wants so much as a rock." Or it degenerates in the opposite direction into pure relativism, conscious or unconscious pursuit of "interest," or antinomianism. This form of sin may, of course, be associated with numerous types listed in the preceding section.

It should be pointed out that there are many people who adopt a secular "unbelief-ful" attitude with regard to explicit statements of religious orientation but whose attitude towards values actually is religious; they interpret them as making an ultimate valid demand and sometimes even as having some cosmic ground. These people are therefore really people of faith; through observing theologians who identify themselves or their systems with God (see the previous section) they have acquired a contempt for "religion." Whether they are capable of transmitting their belief-ful attitude without an explicit religious orientation may be doubted. In this respect they may, aside from the influence of their behavior, be sinners of the secularist variety. They are sinners because they do not use their freedom to be creative by developing new and effective forms of thought concerning the divine splendor and promise.

Lassitude is the second form of sin as unbelief. Niebuhr has argued that all sin may be characterized as pride, the demonic desire to become like God. But there is one form of sin that can scarcely be classified in this way, the sin that used to be called accidie. Lassitude, the attitude of "don't care," recognizes neither the divine splendor nor the divine promise. It is thus a form of alienation which is self-centered but without dynamic. Hence it is not demonic alienation; it is enervation and the wish to flee from the fate of making decisions either for or against the basic issues of life and culture and religion. It is what Bergson calls the slide back into vegetability.

All sin is self-destructive. It is on the path that leads to nothingness and meaninglessness, for it is alienation from the ground of creativity and thus also from that which leads to dynamic fulfillment. But this alienation does not bring upon itself the divine judgment from the outside. The wrath of God is in the sin itself, which carries the seeds of its own death and meaninglessness.

But sin also carries within it much that is creative. If it were completely destructive it would lack the support of the power of being; if it were completely lacking in mutuality, it would not be able to exist. Hence, it must be characterized as a perversion or frustration of creativity through the abuse of freedom. Accordingly, it is often difficult to distinguish between a great creative thrust and blasphemy (e.g. Oedipus Rex, the Roman Catholic Church), or between a creative thrust and the destruction of freedom (e.g. communism), or between prophetism and anarchism (e.g. the Anabaptists). Sometimes sin is an "ancient good made uncouth" by a changed historical situation, or it is a stubborn attachment to the best structure of good that has been established.

Just for these reasons the ways of salvation which are pursued are often difficult to distinguish from sin. They represent an overcoming of alienation which prepares the way for a new alienation. The most powerful means of escaping God is "religion." Indeed, "religion" may serve as the best evidence against the view that sin is an atavistic yielding to animal instinct, for it illustrates the thesis that humans do not "fall" through moral failure but by stepping too high. Sin of a personal or a social character is often the result of the elevation of isolated elements, an elevation that brings frustration, conflict, and even destruction. And likewise religion is often simply a means whereby, by using an isolated technique, the spatialization of the absolute, one attempts to make oneself infinite (or one with the infinite). Hence, pseudo-religion is often worse than secularism. It is a form of self-salvation in which a special section of the finite is identified with the infinite. (This concept of self-salvation is drawn from Paul Tillich.)

In practice, the means of salvation—dogmatism and ritualism, for example—become instruments for the will to power of those in possession of "pure doctrine" or of the sacramental means of salvation. Thus salvation by "works"—belief in the "pure doctrine" of the Bible, participation in the sacraments—is the most dangerous form of self-salvation. For the result is that the "religions" develop a death struggle with rival polytheisms; that is, the "religions" making absolute claims develop an inner uncertainty and anxiety which produce fanaticism.

Notes

1. Cf. Luther's statement, "Just as a jurist speaks of man as a legal possessor of his property, just as a doctor speaks of a healthy and of a sick man, so a theologian speaks of man as a sinner." *Werke,* Wiemar ed., XI, sic 2, 327, 11. 17ff.

2. The doctrine of *Imago Dei* has been employed to give ultimate orientation or metaphysical status to individuality, universality, rationality, freedom, self-transcendence, creativity, unconditionality, original goodness of being, divinely given dignity, and the like.

3. All of these forms of sin can also be characterized as self-love, but this term is not used here because it does not directly connote the type of relationship

between God and the human being it represents. Moreover, self-love as such is not sin. Self-affirmation is an indispensable element of self-realization.

4. In connection with the word "universality" as applied to sin, it is well to recall the comments of H. Wheeler Robinson: "The practical universality of sin must not be taken as a single fact, capable of explanation by some single dogmatic hypothesis; it is a collection of facts, covering the widest range. . . . There are many grades of sinners which the mouth-filling word Universality tends to obscure." *The Christian Doctrine of Man,* 3d ed. (Edinburgh: T. & T. Clark, 1926), pp. 303, 365.

5. Cf. the paradox that autonomy is a gift of grace, or that salvation (which involves human decision) is of God and not of the human being.

6. Cf. Durkheim's essay on "Anomie." In contemporary America the most prevalent and distinctive form of secularism is that of the man who considers the world his oyster.

20 · *The AIDS Epidemic and Palliative Care*

Palliative care today confronts a new situation, in which the concern for persons living with AIDS has become a central one. We have become accustomed to speak of the appearance of AIDS as an epidemic, a pandemic. New questions are therefore inescapable.

Such epidemics are of course not new in Euro-America. The Harvard historian William Langer estimated that the Black Death killed at least a quarter of the population of Europe in the years 1348 to 1350, and that in the next fifty years the total mortality rose to more than a third of the population. Florence was reduced in population from 90,000 to 45,000, Sienna from 42,000 to 15,000. The pandemic of 1348 to 1350 was followed by a long series of recurrent outbreaks all over Europe. In London there were at least twenty attacks of plague in the fifteenth century, and in Venice the Black Death struck twenty-five times between 1348 and 1576. In the years 1348 to 1374 the total population of England fell from about 3.8 million to 2.1 million. Eighty percent or more of those who came down with the plague died within two or three days, usually in agonizing pain.

This essay appeared in *The Journal of Palliative Care,* 5, no. 3 (1989), published by the Clinical Research Institute of Montreal. Reprinted by permission.

Those epidemics were often accompanied by severe outbreaks of typhus, syphilis, and "English sweat," a deadly form of influenza that infected both England and the Continent in the first half of the sixteenth century. The bubonic plague in 1665 killed nearly a tenth of London's estimated population of 460,000.

These afflictions of course called for an explanation. Almost everyone in the medieval period interpreted the plague as a punishment by God for human sins. Many blamed the Jews, for example, accusing them of poisoning the wells. John Calvin was convinced that a group of male and female witches, acting as agents of Satan, had brought the plague to Geneva. People crowded into the churches, appealing to the Virgin or to St. Sebastian. As recently as 1830, 60,000 people fled Moscow during a epidemic of cholera, and in 1832 in New York City a fourth of the population took flight in steamboats, stagecoaches, carts, and wheelbarrows.

The appearance of HIV and AIDS is scarcely to be compared in extent to these pandemics. Yet, the cost in suffering and in monetary expense has been mounting. In October 1988 the American Medical Association found that the costs of hospital stays for children infected with the AIDS virus ranged from $466 a day for "boarder" babies—those who have nowhere else to go—to $705 a day for the sickest youngsters. The expense was increased because foster-home placement was difficult. "Average lifetime costs were $90,347 per child," the study reported. Because these children test positive, nobody wants to take care of them either at home or in foster care, so there is no place else for them to go. By September 1988 the Federal Center for Disease Control had recorded 1,185 cases of AIDS among children under the age of thirteen, of whom 672 had died. Far more children (it is known or assumed) are infected with the virus and are expected to become ill in the future.

The first thing the person engaged in palliative care must confront is the patient's sense of guilt. In many instances the patient seeks someone to blame for the suffering. Another way the patient is tempted to take is to say that the suffering is God's will, perhaps because God wishes to punish or, it may be, to bring a wayward soul closer to the divine plan, or closer to God's love.

This sort of "explanation" is familiar in the face of unexpected or acute suffering. I recall a congregational council in Salem years ago in which a young ministerial candidate was being interrogated and tested for his worthiness for the calling. In this large assembly a wiry elderly Scotsman with a stubby red beard posed what he called a hypothetical question in pastoral care. "I want you to imagine that a widow in your parish has scraped through the years to rear her son, her only child. She has eked out a living by taking in dressmaking, or babysitting for other families, and the like. She has enabled her son to manage the hurdles of high school and then of college; indeed, he has just graduated with honors and has secured a promising employment. But now you, the minister, receive a telephone message that the young man has been killed suddenly in an automobile accident. It is your duty to visit the widow and to bring her some comfort. What will you say to her?" The candidate did not pause to reflect about the question. With reckless self-confidence he said that he then would explain that it was all a part of God's way or plan. Perhaps she had shown such single-minded love for her child that God took him from her to bring her closer to God. This answer of course brought a vigorous protest from the congregation, and the candidate was buffeted from all sides. "What kind of God is that? What comfort was the widow to glean from this theological machinery?" Finally, the candidate reluctantly surrendered, and to almost everyone's satisfaction he conceded that he did not know what he would say to the bereft mother. Thereupon the wily Scotsman expressed the regnant opinion. "If, young man, you had said that a half-hour ago, you would have gained unanimous approval, and you would have saved all of us from theological distress." This remark elicited approving applause.

The person engaged in palliative care does not have the obligation to deal with these imponderable questions except perhaps to insist quietly that they are imponderable. They are a constricting net from which the sufferer should be freed. This net includes such questions as "Why me? Why, when I was on the way to achievement or at least to satisfying fulfillment?" Ordinarily, patients do not expect an answer to these questions, or will not be satisfied if such answers are proffered. They are aware of the noiseless foot of Time, and they feel themselves to be alone. Whether they are fully aware of it or not, they want a more fundamentally human response than a resolution of the imponderable questions. They long for the reaffirmation of life, the response of caring.

Here we encounter one of the most precious elements in human existence, the fact of caring, and the comfort that issues from experiencing someone else's caring. Isn't it a wonder and a mystery that living beings can engender this sort of relationship? Human beings are not like billiard balls to push or to be pushed this way or that. They live in and from each other. The greatest wonder of all is that they are *alive*.

Striking and puzzling are the obstructions to caring. One of the most intractable is the intervention of moral or "religious" standards that can insert distance between the caring person and the one who is suffering. Many a child is rendered lonely and burdened by constant reference to these "standards." The concerned parent may so much emphasize the rules that these rules, rather than affection or caring, dominate the relationship. What is needed, also in palliative care, is the courage to care, and to show it. There is nothing judgmental in this sort of caring. This is not a time for judgment but a time for compassion, and this of course requires experience and skill.

The various dimensions of palliative care may be explored through an examination of concepts that are characteristic in early Christianity, though all of these concepts have their rootage in the Old Testament.

Diakonia (service) in its simplest form means to wait at table; or it can mean a new pattern of human relationships that extends even to washing the other's feet. I recall participating in the Lord's Supper in a Church of the Brethren when at the end we in turn washed our neighbor's feet, and then our neighbor washed ours. In the New Testament these actions are viewed as love in action. Worldly rulers lord it over their subjects, but the concern of the disciples is with God's kingdom. Hence, the service of others is service to God. But this service is not the service rendered by isolated individuals. It is the life of a community, of a community bound together in serving God through serving others, and thus in serving the inbreaking kingdom—all of this toward the end of promoting faith and hope and love. T. S. Eliot once said, "Between the true artists of my time there is an unconscious community." The same must be said of those engaged in palliative care. They belong to a fellowship in which there is a sharing of faith, a sharing of gifts of the Spirit, and even a sharing of suffering—a *koinonia*. This sharing can be enhanced by participation in the life of the church.

We see, then, that *diakonia* is a service rendered by people living in a sisterhood or brotherhood. One is not alone in serving; and, besides, the serving is not only a service; one should rather say it is a response to the loving power of God. Therefore, we must say that the person who offers care for the sufferer of AIDS is one who responds not only to the sufferer but also to divine power, a transforming, community-forming power. This response is clearly something quite different from "explaining" the suffering to the sufferer, itself a quagmire to be avoided through *diakonia,* caring service.

An equally illuminating concept is *metanoia.* In the customary biblical version the term has been inadequately rendered by the word "repentance," a translation perhaps influenced by medieval penitential practices. "Conversion" would be a better translation—a turning around. *Metanoia* was familiar in Greek usage, and meant change of opinion, feeling, or purpose, and thus it could mean also remorse or regret. In the Old Testament prophets we find the idea of turning back or returning to God, a turning away from "violence or idols or sin," from unfaithfulness to the covenant. Again we see that unfaithfulness is communal as well as individual. It includes the person offering care. The more positive meaning of the term is peculiarly significant for the AIDS sufferer. The sufferer in "turning" within finds a deeper self; at the same time it is a turning to the divine power. In addition to the ordinary self of passing impulse, the sufferer may find a deeper, permanent self that is experienced as an entering in of the divine power of cosuffering and compassion.

This sense of the cosuffering of God is explicit in the idea of the Crucifixion. It has been set forth in memorable fashion by the German poet Heinrich Heine in his *Pictures of Travel.* After describing in vivid fashion the enjoyment of the Greek gods and goddesses on Mount Olympus with their wine and song, he continues:

> Suddenly there came gasping towards them a pale Jew, dripping with blood, a crown of thorns on his head, bearing a great cross of wood on his shoulder, and he cast the cross on the high table of the gods, so that the golden goblets trembled and fell, and the gods grew dumb and pale, and even paler, till they melted in utter mist. . . . Was it perhaps necessary for miserable and oppressed humanity? He who sees his God suffer bears more easily his own afflictions. The merry gods of old, who felt no pangs, knew not, of course, the feeling of this poor tortured man, who in turn could in his need find no heart to turn to them. They were holiday gods, around whom the world danced merrily, and who could only be praised in feasts. Therefore they were never loved from the very soul and with all the heart. To be *so* loved, one must be a sufferer. . . . Of all the gods who loved in the olden time, Christ is the one who has been the most loved.[1]

But the God of the Bible is not only a sufferer. This God also responds to human suffering. This feature of the divine is memorably expressed in Jewish folklore. Here God is always ready to listen to prayer for forgiveness or for help. According to one tale, the angels became annoyed by

God's ever-loving response. They felt that God was becoming not only soft-hearted but also soft-headed. Therefore they constructed a wall around the throne to protect God from the prayers of the distressed. But God was not to be thwarted in this way, for when the over-righteous angels were not looking he bored a hole under the throne, so that the prayers could be heard and responded to, prayers asking for forgiveness, for new beginnings.

It remains now to refer to the New Testament term, *kairos*. In ancient Greece this term was interpreted in contrast to *chronos*. This latter term referred to clock time measurable by the regular movement of the stars. *Kairos* on the other hand points to a moment single in kind, in which something unique can happen, the right time. It points to fulfilled time, after a process of preparation or anticipation. This is the moment when the person living with AIDS recognizes that death is at hand. The one engaged in palliative care does well to recognize this *kairos,* for it is the moment when the sufferer can think of loved ones and also of final arrangements, things to be taken care of. It is a moment not so much of resignation as of the need for strength, for the recognition of a resource hovering over the *kairos,* a divine resource beyond human contriving. The Old Testament prophet Isaiah evokes just this resource that belongs to *kairos.*

> Hast thou not known? Hast thou not heard, that the everlasting God, the Lord, the creator of the ends of the earth, fainteth not, neither is weary? There is no searching his understanding. He giveth power to the faint; and to them that have no might he increaseth strength. Even the youths shall faint and be weary, and the young men shall utterly fall. But they that wait upon the Lord shall renew their strength; they shall mount up with wings as eagles; they shall run, and not be weary; they shall walk, and not faint. [Isa. 40:28–31]

Our discussion of palliative care has necessarily centered attention on person-to-person relationships, on what is called the microcosmic sphere. The fully relevant discussion would take into account the macrocosmic dimension, the socioeconomic institutional framework, and also the mesocosmic dimension where those engaged in palliative care may cooperate with other citizens to raise consciousness and to promote social change. Here it is recognized that every personal problem is a social problem and that every social problem is a personal problem. Moreover, it is recognized that those who are living with AIDS are not the only group requiring care. Therefore our social responsibility calls for institutional implementation. Our response to need must be both a personal (or individual) and institutional (or group) response. Without institutional change our institutions can become a prison. *Metanoia* is required for institutions as well as for individual persons, a process ever changing, ever encountering new *kairos*.

Note

1. Heinrich Heine, *Pictures of Travel*, vol. 2, trans. Charles Godfrey Leland (London: William Heinemann, 1891), pp. 270–71.

21 · *Out of Despair*

In *Death Be Not Proud* John Gunther gives a moving account of his sixteen-year-old son's losing struggle against death from a malignant tumor. Here the father recounts the desperate attempts of the doctors and the parents to save the boy's life. He tells of the happy, though temporary, triumphs, of the boy's courage and selflessness, and of his eager interest in keeping up his studies. "I have so much to do," the boy confides to his mother, "and there is so little time."

The father tells us that John had never prayed much and that perhaps this was in part an expression of his dislike of compulsory chapel at one of his schools. To counteract this disinclination, his mother from time to time read prayers to him, Hindu and Chinese prayers as well as Jewish and Christian. Once she suggested to him that he should himself think of a prayer—one of his own special kind—he might be willing to tell her. One grayish afternoon he said suddenly, "Speaking of prayers, I did think one up." He called it "An Unbeliever's Prayer":

> Almighty God
> Forgive me for my agnosticism;
> For I shall try to keep it gentle,
> not cynical,
> nor a bad influence.
> And O! If Thou art truly in the heavens
> accept my gratitude

for all Thy gifts,
and I shall try
to fight the good fight. Amen.

The skepticism of this sixteen-year-old is understandable to many of us. It is understandable, because for us certain of the traditional conceptions of prayer are no longer tenable. Yet, this "Unbeliever's Prayer," expressing as it does his sense of gratitude in the face of impending, untimely death, and his compact to fight the good fight, offers us the reminder that the religious impulse keeps alive our sense of dependence upon, and of a divinely given fellowship with, the font of life and being. More than this, however, the boy's disposition to express in prayer his gratitude, his commitment, and even his skepticism, reveals something that we are prone to forget: the fact that the characteristically religious act is prayer.

The characteristic act of the industrial executive or employee is to produce goods or services. The characteristic act of the physician is to minister to the patient's health, of the artist to create things of beauty, of the moral person to act with ethical responsibility. The distinguishing act of the religious person is worship, and the essence of worship is prayer. Other activities, to be sure, are of concern to the religious person. But prayer is the characteristic act of the religious life, though it brings these other activities into its purview.

Wherever the life of prayer is absent, the religious life has become externalized; it is disappearing into formality and routine. Form is confused with substance. This transformation into externalized religion is the fruit of a moribund "faith" that no longer knows the characteristic act of the religious life. By this fruit shall ye know that faith is dead.

Prayer is not itself a fruit of faith. Perhaps we should say that it is the bud. It is nearer to the root, nearer to the awareness of the ultimate ground and resource of faith. By this root shall ye know the genuinely religious impulse. In the "Unbeliever's Prayer" young John Gunther was turning to this root, even in the moment of his asking forgiveness for his agnosticism. His confession of agnosticism was a "centering down," as the Friends would say, in to a root integrity that is ultimately a gift of grace without which there could be no good fight to fight.

There lives the dearest freshness deep down things;
And though the last lights off the black West went
Oh, morning, at the brown brink eastward, springs—
　　　　　　　　　　　　　　　[Gerard Manley Hopkins]

The recognition and the renewal of human fellowship is also a symbol of our initial gift of freedom from God, whereby we may act in some independence from the source and root of our being. We may even become separated from the powers that make for human fellowship and fulfillment; we may become separated even from ourselves in a kind of schizophrenia. But without the freedom to abuse freedom, the act of return would itself be impossible, it would have no meaning. This act of return, this theme of the "lost and found" is set forth in Jesus' profound parable of the prodigal son. The father in the parable is always waiting for the son's return, but he cannot force it. The son must come to himself and remember the riches that are in the father's mansion and in the father's mercy.

So it is when we pray. The act of prayer is our own initiating gesture, our rising and going to the father—the characteristically religious act.

But before we consider this initiating gesture, we must recall what it is that we must arise from. What is it that we are bound to which constitutes our brokenness and which calls out for the re-uniting, re-creative act of prayer? There are of course many things, but they all have one element in common: they are rooted in a sterile soil, in despair, in loss of hope, in loss of vital relation to that which can heal our brokenness. Despair is the loss of sincere desire for a vital relation to the powers within us and beyond us that make for personal growth and widening fellowship with others. Despair, however, is not necessarily listless and spiritless. It may be dynamic and active, full of enthusiasm.

In its listless form despair is bondage to what is recognized or believed to be exhausted. Sometimes it binds us to our distress in loneliness; it binds us to ourselves or, rather, to only a part of ourselves. It leads us hopelessly to believe that our broken lives are doomed to remain in their brokenness. These are passive forms of despair.

In its more spirited form despair is bondage to the actual and familiar, the cherished and accepted-at-face-value, cut off from that ultimate and divine reality which can judge it and transform it. Despair can be a vigorous nerve that with false hope attaches us to what is and that energizes us to indulge a merely possessive love; it can be the lively nerve that binds us to what "they say," to enervating, cramping convention; it can be a pulsating desire that binds us to what is only partial, to the narrow, divisive interests of class or status or race or party—the most destructive enemy of humanity and God. This kind of despair also binds us to the habit of simply taking ourselves and our wants and ambitions, ourselves and "our" world, for granted, "enjoying" in crass immediacy the cornbread with which the mouth is crammed or for which it waters. This possessive despair leads us to believe that what we have is what we want or that we simply want more of it; it leads us to believe vainly that our fragmentary lives are complete and whole, at least in principle. This is the dynamic, energetic form of despair.

Whether our despair is spiritless or enthusiastic, it is a form of inertia, either the inertia after a full stop or the inertia that cannot stop. Indeed, in either the spiritless or the spirited form despair is a kind of exhaustion; for it is bound to the merely partial which has within it the power of death. Both the spiritless and the spirited despair are forms of brokenness and exhaustion without hope for something more. If we see no hope, or if we place our confidence in what is not reliable, we are in despair, for we have lost touch with that which is our proper ground of hope. In short, we despair of God. This is the ultimate blasphemy. From this blasphemy, whether it be spiritless or full of confidence, only faith can bring release, a faith not of our own contriving but rather a faith that is a holy gift. From this blasphemous despair we must arise and go to the waiting father of Jesus' parable. The act of rising, or rather of being raised, is the characteristic act of faith. It is prayer.

Anything that helps us to become free from these bonds, anything that releases us from the inertia of possessive love or from the inertia of despondency and from spiritless exhaustion, no matter whether the release be *called* prayer or not, prepares us for the renewal of outgoing love that is ultimately not of our making, a renewal that belongs to prayer.

But we perhaps rightly reserve the word "prayer" for the more deliberate gesture whereby the human creature reaches out for the cleansing, healing, transforming power that flows from the original Creator to the ever-renewing Re-Creator.

This reaching out requires an initiating gesture on our part. In the first instance it is the gesture in which we confess that we falsely attempt to live from despair. The gesture is of course most insistent when it is desperate, that is, when it bespeaks our awareness that we have come to our own limits.

Whether the prayer be private or public, it is the gesture whereby we move towards detachment from the despair that binds us to the "dated self" and to its tangible securities and insecurities. Those who do not know this despair will scarcely undertake the initial gesture. They will either turn away from prayer or pervert it into despair by seeking in it a buttressing of the natural desires, desires that are particularly vigorous when they bear the semblance of piety.

The striking thing about prayer as we all too often practice it is its feebleness and perfunctoriness, its triviality and unreality. These qualities appear if one does not really "center down" to the ground of one's own existence but also of all existence. To be genuine, prayer must lead to a sense of the ultimate, and yet also to a sense of the intimate out of which deep calleth unto deep, saying "Our Father." This sense of the ultimate and of the intimate requires that prayer shall issue out of a concrete situation and in the end "speak" to a concrete situation. This situation may be personal; it may be social, demanding "concern" for the injustices and demonries of the body politic. Here out of our despair we make our petitions. Not that by petition we revert to magic, impiously attempting to force our will upon God. Nor that we expect our special petitions to be answered in the way we want. Petition is what opens us to the powers that re-create fellowship and that issue in movement towards transformation. Thus the fundamental petition is the one following a confession of despair, the petition for forgiveness and for renewal—the harbinger of new beginnings.

All of these elements inhere in Christian worship and prayer. Yet we often are tempted to say that public ritual only impedes confession and petition, renewal and dedication. The sociologist may tell us that public ritual is only the machinery whereby a group objectifies its myth and thus transmits its distinctive value preferences. The psychologist may tell us that ritual induces a suggestibility that breaks down ordinary rational restraints and releases emotional energy, a substitute for wish-fulfillment. But effective ritual is more than these things. Appropriate ritual, entered into prayerfully, enables worshipers to break with the immediate claims upon their attention and at the same time to bring them under the Great Taskmaster's eye. The worshiper moves through detachment to new attachment.

In surrendering to this new attachment we enter, as it were, the second gesture of prayer, the gesture of the human spirit which meets a corresponding gesture working within the constitution of the person and within the constitution of the universe. This second gesture is the gesture of surrender to that which is sovereign and holy.

Yet, although the power and insight that are released issue from the very depths and not merely from within us, the kind of power and insight received depends partly upon us. We are free to release evil, stormy spirits as well as others. Mary Austin, who spent many years studying the prayer of the American Indians, tells us that the Paiuta Indians believe it is very important that one should in prayer give the proper name of the Power.

Likewise the Christian idea of prayer is based upon the conviction that there is something in the universe that is responsive to the activating principle of humble prayer. But it also recognizes the danger of calling forth destructive powers. For this reason, Christians have characteristically concluded their prayers with the words, "in the name of Jesus." With these words there comes to mind not merely the overpowering sense of the possible newness of life and love to which Jesus gave expression in his proclamation, "The kingdom of heaven is among you" (that is, "The kingdom of heaven is available"); all of this, and more too, is implied when we give the name "Christ" to the ultimate and intimate redemptive power of God. By this name we refer to the reality that manifested itself in the person and work of Jesus and in the new community which was formed in loyalty to him and to the power of which he spoke with authority. In prayer, we, in fellowship with our Elder Brother, seek again this spirit and this power unto salvation.

"Manifestly artificial," the skeptic may say of prayer. "It is patently only a means of 'psychologizing oneself.'" But, actually, it is no more artificial than any other means of releasing energy and insight and new beginnings. The lakes of oil beneath the surface of the earth had to wait for the invention of the combustion engine before their power could be released. So also the abounding grace of "the deep down freshness of things" must wait for appropriation through the self-originating gesture of prayer. There is nothing magical about the process. It is not a means of bringing God under control. It is rather a way whereby the divine is permitted to direct us and to save us from our despair. One does not change God or control God. The process is more like that which takes place when students seek out great teachers. Teachers retain their own essential character, but through their tutelage the students are themselves changed. Thus in prayer our whole existence, personal as well as institutional, is brought before the throne of grace whence issue judgment and healing.

I know of scarcely any illustrations more persuasive of this process than an incident in the life of Jane Addams, founder of Hull House in Chicago. The incident, as she recounts it, appears to be given a purely human setting without reference to any more-than-human power. But the liberation from despair and the release of new healing which she describes are quite analogous to the gesture of genuine prayer and the response to it.

In Chicago in 1894 a great streetcar strike had plunged the city into near chaos. The cars were standing abandoned in the streets, people were milling about, violence was rife, the federal troops had been sent to Chicago by the president of the United States, and their presence there was resented by the governor of the state. Driven almost to distraction, Jane Addams cast about for some means of gaining poise and perspective. What she did is to be explained partly by her own childhood experience. Abraham Lincoln had always been a sort of patron saint for her. He was a close friend of her father's; his name was often in the conversations of the household of her youth. Suddenly in the face of the disturbances, she decided to try something very similar to what we have called the self-initiating gesture of prayer.

> I walked the wearisome way from Hull House to Lincoln Park—for no cars were running regularly at that moment of sympathetic strikes—in order to look at and gain magnanimous counsel, if I might, from the marvelous St. Gaudens statue which had been recently placed at the entrance of the park. Some of Lincoln's immortal words were cut into the stone at his feet, and never did a distracted town more sorely need the healing of "with charity towards all" than did Chicago at that moment, and the tolerance of the man who had won charity for those on both sides of "an irrepressible conflict."

That walk of two miles to the St. Gaudens statue on that hot summer day was Jane Addams's appeal to powers beyond herself, and it was taken in the name of a spirit that has been summoned again and again, long before Lincoln was born.

This is the gesture of prayer, our daily privilege, our ever present need. It is a way that leads out of despair to the richness and power and tenderness that lie at the heart of God.

22 · *God Is Love*

There is no word in our language which has been so much misused and prostituted as the word "love." It has been preached by those who are ready to condone every cruelty if it serves their purpose. It has been used to disguise true motives—to force people to sacrifice their own happiness and submit themselves to those who profit from this surrender. It has been used as the moral basis for unjustified demands. It has been made so

This sermon was given at the Meadville Theological School, Chicago, on November 7, 1947.

empty that for many people love may mean no more than living together for twenty years without quarreling more often than once a week. It is dangerous and embarrassing to use such a word. Yet a psychologist, and especially a minister, may not properly succumb to this embarrassment. To preach love is at best bad taste. But to make a cool and critical analysis of the phenomenon of love and to unmask pseudo-love—tasks that cannot be separated from each other—is an obligation that the psychologist and the minister have no right to avoid.

This obligation rests upon the minister not only because the characteristic basic description of the essence of human existence in Christianity is presented in the word love but also because one of the major conceptions of contemporary depth psychology is the idea of Love. This presupposition of psychology is well stated by Sigmund Freud when he says, "A group is clearly held together by a power of some kind; and to what power could this feat be better ascribed than to Eros, who holds together everything in the world." What is this thing that has been believed to hold the world together since Heraclitus and Socrates and Hosea and Jesus spoke?

It is unfortunate that in most of the modern languages the word for love covers a field for which in Greek at least three words were used. The poverty of our language in this respect is to a certain extent responsible for the confusions in the ethics of love in theory and practice. Without understanding the fine and profound distinctions embodied in the Greek terminology we are unable to interpret the meaning of the words of Jesus. If we are not able to interpret accurately the meaning of these distinctions, we run the risk of succumbing to a self-deceiving feeling of universal sympathy which spoils the clarity of our thinking and the consistency of our acting.

The three words for love in Greek designate three different realms in which the striving of one being toward union with the other one is expressed. The first realm is that of natural love, including body and mind. This is the realm of *eros,* based on the natural unity of the separated members of our world, the desire that makes every being long for other beings and for the true, essential being in order to overcome loneliness, seclusion, anxiety, and error. This longing for union in all beings is the first realm of love, the most natural and the most universal and the most ambiguous because it is based on want and desire and is always ready to be turned around into hate and the will to destruction of the self and of others. It is unfortunate that the word designating this realm, the word Eros, was so abused for the lowest and most distorted forms of bodily desire that the New Testament could not use it at all, and consequently that the relation of Christian love to natural love became an obscured and an unsolved problem in the whole history of the Church. One thing at least is clear, however; from a Christian point of view Eros involves both mind and body, both spirit and mind. Eros is the basic biological, psychological union that maintains the fabric within which and beyond which the other forms of love appear.

The second realm is that of *philia*, friendship in the largest sense, the personal love which chooses and selects on the basis of personal sympathy, of personal affinity. The love of friendship is not separated from the natural love, but it constitutes something new above it. It was that love which the later ancients praised as the highest form of human relations in a world in which all other unities had disintegrated. The word *philia*, love in the sense of friendship, points to a personal preference that cannot be commanded, cannot be viewed as an obligation in any particular instance. Personal friendship is entirely free; it therefore excludes the many and includes the few. The command that we love one another may include the natural love and the love of friendship, but neither natural nor friendly love, neither passion nor sympathy, can be demanded; they exist or they do not exist; they are or they are not.

On the other hand, certain demands may be made with respect to natural and friendly love. In both forms of love, at least two major distortions must be avoided. The command against these distortions is peculiar to both political and religious liberalism. These two distortions are today called masochistic and sadistic love. In masochistic love, one gives up one's self, one's initiative and integrity, to become submerged entirely in another person who is felt to be stronger. Because of deep anxieties that give rise to the feeling that one cannot stand on one's own feet, one wants to be rid of one's own individual self and to become part of another being, thus becoming secure and finding a center that one misses in oneself. Freud calls this the desire to return to the womb. This surrender of one's own self has often been praised as the example of "the great love," notably extolled in the stories of Tolstoy and criticized by Chekhov. It is actually a form of idolatry, and also an annihilation of the self. The fact that it has been conceived of as love or loyalty has made it the more seductive and dangerous.

Sadistic love on the other hand springs from the desire to swallow its object, to make the other a will-less instrument in one's own hands. This drive is also rooted in a deep anxiety, in an inability to place confidence in intrinsic values. Instead of finding increased strength by being swallowed, sadistic love finds strength and security by having a limited power over the other person. The masochistic as well as the sadistic kind of love are expressions of one basic need that springs from an inability to be independent. Using a biological term, we may call this basic need "the need for symbiosis." The sadistic love is frequently the kind of love that parents may have for their children. Whether the domination is overtly authoritarian or subtly "modern" makes no essential difference. In either case it tends to undermine the strength of the self of the child and leads in later years to the development in the child of the very same symbiotic tendencies. The sadistic love is not infrequent among adults. Often in relationships of long duration, the respective roles are permanent, one partner representing the sadistic, the other one the masochistic pole of the symbiotic relationship. Often the roles change— a continuous struggle for dominance and submission being conceived of as love. One can see this struggle in any social group, between husband and wife, between parents and children, between professors and students, between professors, between students. This struggle operates constantly to distort fellowship among persons, to distort fellowship among liberals. Love cannot be separated from freedom and independence.

As we have said, natural love and the love of friendship cannot be demanded in any particular case, though freedom and individual integrity are required for both of these forms of love. But the third form of love can be demanded, whether it applies to the relations between God and the human being, or one human being and another, or the human being and nature. It is the love for the ultimate meaning and destiny of the other being. Therefore it is *caritas*—charity, helping, saving, fulfilling love; it is a caring for the creative forces of life as they express themselves in another being or in other beings. This is the realm in which the demand that we love our enemies has its meaning and reality. We love our enemy when we love his or her ultimate meaning. We may have to struggle against what the enemy stands for; we may not feel a personal and individual affinity or passion for him or for her. Yet we are commanded for this person's sake and for our own and for the sake of the destiny of creation, to love that which should unite us. Even with respect to our attitude toward ourselves this divine love may have to show antipathy for ourselves. We cannot love ourselves ultimately except by loving ourselves in the light of our ultimate meaning, and therefore *in spite of* what we actually are at a given moment. This is the meaning of the divine forgiveness; it is a love in spite of the immediate, momentary merit of the self or the other. We can love ourselves ultimately only in the certainty that we are forgiven. In this sense, in the sense of forgiveness, we can love our enemies; indeed, we in our immediate actuality will ourselves have to be classed in some sense among the enemies. Loving the enemy in spite of what he or she now does or strives for includes loving patience with one's own self in spite of what it now does, in spite of what it has achieved, in spite of its opposition to love. The divine love always has the character of "in spite of" or of forgiveness, whether this love is directed toward our enemies or toward our friends or toward ourselves. The "command" to "love your enemies" has meaning only in unity and with the prayer, "God, forgive them as thou canst forgive me." "Help me to love them as thou canst help me to love myself with thy love." And certainly it is not easier to love oneself in this way than it is to love another or to love one's enemy. One who thinks it is easier to do so wills to ignore the war within one's own cave.

But more than the love of the self's or of the other's ultimate meaning and destiny is implied in Christian *Agape.* Love is the uniting of that which is separated, as Hegel (and Tillich) would say. Love is not only the love of the ultimate meaning and destiny of a self regardless of its merit; it is also the love by an individual of other individualities. Hegel in his youth (in one of his college themes) once wrote: "Modesty is the irritation of love over individuality." His idea seems to be that all persons should feel a certain limitation and humility because of their own individuality; they should feel also a respect and love for the individuality of others. But in the union of individualities there is a transcending of separateness; this sort of union brings fullness or abundance of being. Here, Hegel says, the person does not dominate and is not dominated. There is something separate still, but it is no longer seen as separated. Even in true knowledge of something this sort of union and fullness of being is achieved.

This sort of love, the love of individuality for individuality, the love of one creature for another, the love of one creative being for another, is nothing abstract and merely general; it is the joining together of particular clusters of affirmation with other clusters. Because Anders Nygren [in *Eros and Agape* (Philadelphia, 1953)] has omitted this caring of individuality for individuality, and of one individuality for another, he has missed an important aspect of *agape.* Jesus was not a person who simply blessed all persons without regard for their particular character. The search of the shepherd for the sheep that was lost from the fold of the ninety-nine was a search for a particular sheep. Every member of the community is precious, not merely because of its being an expression of the ultimate creativity of being but also because it possesses its own unique selfhood, adding to the richness of being.

The divine love is, then, not only a love "in spite of" the actuality of the self (another or one's own self); it is also a love because of the particularity of the self. And this love is rooted in the awareness that there is an infinite creativity in being and that there must be a union of particular selves if the ultimate meaning and destiny of each is to be achieved. Love in this sense is fullness of being; it is not self-denial, it is self-affirmation, the affirmation of strength, the union of that which is separated.

This meaning of love may be illustrated from the life and death of Jesus, considered as an expression of the fullness of being. It can be pointed to also in the experience of art, considered as the experience of uniting that which is separated, the experience of affirming individuality joining with another individuality to rise to the ecstasy of fulfillment.

When we listen in full awareness to a noble piece of music, the cosmos is expressing its fullness, bringing together individualities; it is breaking through their limitations and uniting them in the richness of being. The ecstatic moment in natural love, in the love of friendship, in the *agape* or divine love, in the climax of a piece of music, is essentially the same ecstatic moment (redintegration). It is the uniting of that which is separated; it is the affirmation of a new fullness of being. In the moment of greatest enjoyment of music, for example, the forms used by the composer are burst and transcended, and our own individual form is somehow broken through; the song of the stars at the morning of creation is sung in us and through us again. This song of creation is the song of love that is sung through vital and healthy natural love, through the love of friendship, and through the *agape* of the New Testament. The same could be said of the dance, an old religious rite.

Jesus hanging on the cross is the lover who unites that which is separated; he even offers his own life as a sacrifice, not that his individuality may be destroyed but rather that the ultimate meaning and destiny of human existence may be expressed. Moreover, his individuality is not destroyed; it is fulfilled through affirming love, through the strength of abundance. Down through the ages men and women have remembered this man because they have seen more than a good man expressing uncalculating, self-giving love; they have seen in him a highly individual person who formed a community of persons, bringing together that which was separated; they have seen in him the cosmos achieving strength and abundance of expression, not in the submissive love of masochism, not in the dominating love of sadism, but in the free and independent expression of individuality reaching out to individuality, rising through self-sacrifice and self-giving, to that union with others which is fullness of being, the dancing, fulfilling, reconciling love.

They see in him the cosmos singing and even dancing the second-century *Hymn of Jesus* [*Acts of Saint John*]:

> I would be saved, and I would save.
> I would be loosed, and I would loose.
> I would be born, and I would bear.
> I would hear, and I would be heard.
> Grace danceth. I would pipe. Dance ye all.
> I would be united, and I would unite.
> A way am I to thee a wayfarer.
> The whole on high hath part in our dancing. Amen.

Part Four

Religion and Society

RELIGIOUS SOCIAL ETHICS AT THE HANDS OF JAMES LUTHER ADAMS becomes an interdisciplinary field of study and a call to social action. Intellectual history, sociology, and theology figure prominently, and sometimes philosophy, psychology, literature, and aesthetics do, as well. Academic disciplines play a significant role in the shaping of public policy—by providing empirical research and by framing the basic concepts of public discussion. Adams typically does not seek to establish "correct" positions on social or moral issues, but to further the processes of consensus-building by which they are decided in a diverse, democratic society. Thus Adams is centrally concerned with the institutional structures and voluntary associations that invite (or else exclude) citizen participation.

We live in an age of ideologies, secular and religious. The ideological character of supposedly anti-ideological stances, such as the currently popular political "pragmatism," suggests the ambiguities that cling to the term. In the first essay in this section, "Religion and the Ideologies," Adams discusses the prominence of "ideology" in the modern world and the ethical problem of overcoming ideological bias. The religions can overcome their own biases only through a unifying, transcultural stance—"an examined faith" on the level of social consciousness.

Ethics is concerned with human relatedness and intentionality, the necessities of mutuality and purpose in human life. "Covenant" names these necessities in the biblical tradition, thus making ethics central to religion. In "The Prophetic Covenant and Social Concern," Adams develops the idea of covenant as the basis of religious social ethics. Since covenants are historical, they are perennially broken; then the prophetic demand for their renewal is perennially required.

An examined faith requires an examination of religious and ethical language. "Root Metaphors of Religious Social Thought" explores the boundary where language and religion meet, where basic ideas of meaningful human existence are formed. Adams uses Whitehead's idea of "root metaphor" to describe the basic alternatives for interpreting human existence. He contrasts those derived from the private and interpersonal realms with those derived from the public and political realms.

Thus religious social ethics, like the arts, is a form of human creativity. It names and envisions the fundamental realities of the human condition. In "The Arts and Society," Adams explores the moral and spiritual significance of artistic expression. He recognizes that the integrity of art and its power to shape and reshape our perception of social reality depend upon the autonomy of the artist.

The four essays which follow deal with specific areas of social-ethical concern: racism, the mass media, poverty and welfare reform, and peace. In "Our Unconquered Past" Adams responds to the rise of demands for "black power" among African-Americans in the late 1960s. Moving beyond the "colorblind" stance of an older liberalism, he sees black consciousness as the assertion of a positive self-identity. Viewed in a prophetic-ethical perspective, present racial conflict signifies historical judgment on American society—a past that must be "conquered" as the precondition of achieving an inclusive human identity.

The bureaucratic management of poverty is examined in "Exiles, Trapped in the Welfare State." In the demands raised by groups such as the Welfare Rights Movement, seeking redress from the arbitrary application of administrative procedures, Adams identifies a fundamental ethical demand of the poor—to be included in the social covenant.

In "Broken Cisterns and Earthen Vessels," Adams traces, from ancient Israel to the Reformation era, the course of prophetic protest against territorially delimited conceptions of religion. The mass media of communication and the quest for material success exemplify "territorial religion" in contemporary America, he argues, insofar as they are mechanisms of social uniformity and acquiescence to massive poverty—"our devotion to the idols of class and clan."

Ancient and contemporary history belie the easy assumption that religion invariably serves the cause of peace. In "The Religious Problem of Peace" Adams treats peace as a problem *within* religion—reflecting unresolved tensions between sacramental and prophetic elements—as well as a problem *of* religion. The prophetic principle engenders justice and peace by pointing to a transcultural human identity.

Shakespeare speaks of "the uses of adversity," Adams of "The Uses of Diversity." In the closing essay in this section he takes the biblical story of the Tower of Babel as a description in mythic terms of the human condition. The diversity of individual and cultural voices, our Babel, generates not only social conflict but also positive opportunity. The university and the church are faithful to their tasks when they use religious and cultural diversity to enrich the common life.

G.K.B.

23 · Religion and the Ideologies

Walter Bagehot claimed that to understand English institutions, or indeed any institution, one must divide them into two classes: first, those which excite and preserve the reverence of the populace—the dignified or theatrical parts; and next, works and rules. The dignified parts of English institutions Bagehot identified with the Crown and the aristocracy—the means for eliciting the loyalty and unity of the people. The efficient parts he identified with the Cabinet sitting in the House of Commons and deriving its moral and material support from those who wielded authority—the middle class.

What Bagehot has said about institutions applies also to ideologies. His analysis points to a duality in every ideology.

I

What is an ideology? In the face of the conflicting and overlapping meanings attached to the term, we shall use it here to refer to that composite myth by which a society or group identifies itself, not only for itself but also for other societies or groups. An ideology posits the group's goals and the justification of these goals, in terms of which the group deals with other groups and with conflicts within the group; it defines and interprets the situation; it aims to overcome indifference to "the common good"; it reduces "excessive" emphasis on individual action; it makes possible group action.

An ideology may be official, in the sense that it is formulated by authoritarian governmental agencies, as in Soviet Russia and Nazi Germany; or it may be a thing of more wilding growth, contributed to by the more freely playing forces of a multigroup society. In the latter situation the ideology will reflect certain roughly discernible major presuppositions, but it will reflect also a variety of emphases in interplay and tension.

In some quarters today, for example among the "new conservatives," the term "ideology" is in disrepute. The "new conservatives," avowedly following Edmund Burke, use it to signify what they abhor, namely, any oversimplified, "abstract," doctrinaire theory of human nature and history and concrete situations. But this neoconservative conception of ideology

Reprinted, revised, from *Confluence* (Harvard University) 4, no. 1 (April 1955). Reprinted by permission of Harvard University.

is concerned with only one type of ideology, a type with which the neo-conservative ideology carries on a polemical dispute.

In its full mythical corpus, an ideology articulates a myth of origin and a myth of mission—a Whence and a Whither—for the group, not merely in a general way (so as to express the group's sense of values and of vocation) but also in relation to the situation in which the group finds itself. An ideology exhibits the continuity that maintains the self-identity of the group, but in its actual functioning it also purports to be relevant to a given situation, to be "timely." In a relatively stable society the element of continuity in ideology will be most readily evident. But in times of rapid change, of malfunctioning institutions and of consequent conflict, the "timely" dimension of ideology receives increased attention. During the past generation great dislocations in institutional structures have given occasion for a widespread demand for new, "timely" articulations.

Among the Western democracies a sense of the need for a "timely" application of their ideologies is particularly acute. This need for the ideological definition of the new situation is more than a domestic concern in these countries. Before the gigantic and increasing power of Russia and her satellites, the Western democracies, whose ideologies have traditionally been largely for home consumption, now have in some measure a sense of ideological impotence, particularly in the face of the skepticism of the indispensable allies in the Middle and the Far East who retain a bitter taste of what they consider the West's white-supremacy attitudes and imperialist colonialism. At the same time, the West faces in Africa not only a Russian Communist drive but also another growing missionary movement at the hands of Islam. Viewed in historical perspective, the present moves of Soviet Russia and of Islam in the regions mentioned can be described as a reaction in part against the earlier impact of the West, although in each case the manner and the import of the "attacks" have been different.

In the course of these developments, the United States has confronted the necessity of emerging from its relative isolation into the status of a major world-power. The great extension of our defense boundaries—accepted by some sections of the population and vigorously rejected by others—is enough to give us ideological schizophrenia for at least another generation. Thus in both the domestic and the international spheres we see pervasive ideological conflict. In the latter sphere, rival myths of origin and destiny have entered into vigorous mutual encounter. To an almost unprecedented degree, we have become ideology-conscious.

II

We should observe that Bagehot's division of the constitution has not escaped criticism. The Earl of Balfour has argued that the Crown and the aristocracy have shown themselves efficient as well as dignified, in that they serve to give unity to the community. A similar qualification should be borne in mind if Bagehot's distinction is applied to ideology.

As a group develops its myth of origin and mission, the myth will acquire highly dignified interpretations of the group's beginnings, its subsequent course in history, and its outlook for the future. The myth of origin presented in the Declaration of Independence does not exhaust the essential features of the origin and motivation of the American Revolution. Accompanying the "dignified" protest against taxation without representation were "efficient" causes now ignored in the national consciousness: chauvinist and demagogic tendencies and also an interest in the economic advantages that would accrue to Eastern-seaboard financial groups indebted to English creditors and in turn to frontier groups indebted to the seaboard financial groups. The explication of the causes and motives of the Civil War (or, in the variant ideological formulation, the War Between the States), as set forth by either side looking back on the struggle, contains quite different ingredients, each repressing certain "efficient parts" and underlining the dignified elements of its own ideology. It is easy for the unconverted to discern greater distortions of this sort in fascist, Nazi, and Communist ideologies. The dignified, theatrical elects of the ideology accumulate a splendid, though partly brummagem, wardrobe; or perhaps we should say that at some time or other they function as an arsenal of weapons. Burke would have called them "armed doctrine."

The very origin of the concept of ideology, of course, is as a weapon, a *Kampfbegriff*. The main phases in the genealogy of the concept are fairly familiar. Since at least the time of Napoleon, the term "ideology" has borne a perjorative connotation. Napoleon thought of *idéologues* as disturbing, irresponsible theory-mongers. According to Marx (with some qualifications), ideology is a smokescreen of dignified fictions that conceal unsavory realities, protect ruling-class interest, and resist any structural transformation of the *status quo*. For Nietzsche, ideology is a tool of the will to power; in Christian "morality" it expresses the power of resentment, exercised by uncreative, sniveling, conventional piety—a slave morality in which weakness fetters strength. For Freudian psychology of the unconscious, ideology may be a form of compensation or rationalization, even neurotic alienation from reality. Through these successive theories of alienation one may trace a lineal descent: ideology, resentment, neurosis. In each of the formulations there is the presupposition that an alienation in the substructure reappears in the superstructure, revealing a "false consciousness." The "efficient parts" manipulate the "dignified parts." Moreover, in each of these mechanisms religion is included as an expression of false consciousness. Indeed, Marx exempts only himself.

False consciousness supported by special pleading, however, is obviously not the only factor operative in the unfolding of an ideology. History, as von Humboldt declared, is made by tying on to what already is. Ideas and ideologies are not immaculately conceived. They come to birth and grow under cultural conditioning, and this cultural conditioning influences also the intrinsic values that are appealed to. Here fate controls the reins at least in part. This is the insight of ancient Sophism and also of the historicism that has so largely informed cultural analysis during the past century and a half. This insight stresses the fact that individuality is a category for the understanding of history when the sense of the meaning of existence is involved. Meaningful group individuation, then, along with ideological taint, is expressed in the creation and transformation of ideologies. As Whitehead would say, definition is the soul of actuality.

Some anthropologists, adopting the cultural relativism that is the concomitant of historicism's stress on the individuality of cultural creativity, have held that a cultural ethos can make only an arbitrary claim. Thus they have told us that incompatible value-systems are equally valid. We leave aside the question as to whether a value judgment is not implied here, a judgment favoring integrated functioning within a cultural system.

Among civilized beings an ideology cannot remain efficacious in the long run unless it appeals to values, that is, to sanctions that make a greater claim than the arbitrary claim that "they are simply 'ours' and that's the end of it." The question that must be pressed is whether the complete relativist, in the face of Nazi aggression, for example, expects to be taken seriously if he or she asserts that resistance to Nazism can make no claim for itself other than that it adheres to an equally arbitrary, culturally conditioned preference.

Rather than adopting a position of this nature, we make better sense if we assert that group individuality, if it acquires the strength to elicit free cooperation, must participate somehow in universality. It must have spiritual power or meaning. It must be oriented toward something beyond itself. On the other hand, spiritual power must have its roots in individuality. As Tillich has observed, the demand is paradoxical. Spiritual power depends upon a conviction of intrinsic truth, and at the same time it must fulfill some deep-seated "interest" or vital tendency in the group. In other words, dignified and efficient parts must give aid to each other.

Spiritual power, however, with the aid of ideology, all too often becomes psychic violence, thus degenerating into force. To Whitehead's aphorism that definition is the soul of actuality, one should add that narrow definition is the evil genius of provincialism and fanaticism. After the Cromwellian period it was said that "there is nothing so dangerous as a Presbyterian just off his knees." This crusading mentality is an inheritance from the venerable religious practice of promoting tyranny in the holy crusade against the infidel. One can discern it in some of the current religious crusades against secularism. On the other hand, in the modern world where the nation has replaced the church, fanatical ecclesiastical "orthodoxy" might well say to the faithful in the new church, "When me you fly I am the wings." This overweening confidence in the righteousness of one's own cause is the most dangerous element in ideology as well as in religion. It can perpetrate tyranny in the name of moral absolutes, or of "Christian civilization," of or "the democratic way of life" (which for many includes white supremacy or "dropping some atom bombs on those Russians"). German Christians gave vigorous support to Hitler; and the hour of worship on Sunday in the United States, as the cliche has it, is the most segregated hour in American life. But if the danger of fanatical particularism as well as ideological taint attaches to religion as well as to ideology, the question arises: Is there no difference between ideology and religion?

III

If religion and ideology are understood to belong to the same genus, then religion has no special contribution to make in the explication or application of ideology, except to add to the complexity of the conflict or to increase its intensity by inserting the self-justifying appeal to divine sanctions. In large measure religion has just this effect. (We should note here that the ensuing discussion will be restricted to the primary religious tradition of the West, Judeo-Christianity.) Because of the very difficulty of distinguishing between religion and ideology in their customary performance, we must say with Marx that the beginning of all criticism is the criticism of religion. In order to take into account the full range of religion, however, the criticism must be of religion as a cultural phenomenon by religion that looks to a transcultural orientation.

It is now practically a commonplace for cultural anthropologists and sociologists to assert that religion in general is concerned with the "reinforcement of prevailing moral norms" and with promoting the "docile acceptance of these norms"; or that it effects "reconciliation with inferior status and its discriminatory consequences"; or that under certain circumstances it "provokes rebellion against inferior social status." Thus it is assigned an immediately functional character, and only that. Precisely because of these features of "religion," prophetic figures and movements in Judaism and Christianity have criticized "religion" as well as ideology. The Old Testament prophets castigated these features by calling them "idolatry," as did Paul; Augustine said of this sort of "religion" that it gives to the creature what should be reserved for the Creator alone; Luther spoke of it as putting one's "faith in man-made gods," and in his elaboration of this view he anticipates in certain respects Marx's conception of ideology.

Augustine's formulation is of course reminiscent of the language of the Old Testament; it presupposes the mythological distinction between Creator and creature (a distinction that does not necessarily imply a supernaturalist objectification of the Creator). Max Weber, commenting on the cultural implications of this distinction as interpreted by the Hebrew prophets, observes that it was the basis for their attack upon the *status quo:* the created order was subject to change and therefore should be subject to criticism. Yet, Weber also notes that the prophets were not the direct proponents of the oppressed classes; they were as strangers, remaining in a certain isolation from the people. This otherworldly dimension of the prophetic outlook was the basis of the criticism that they directed at "religion" and at its "reinforcement of prevailing norms" and at the "docile acceptance of these norms." These norms as articulated at a given moment are but contingent creations of fallible creatures. They do not present the divine will in capsule form. The religion that transcends "religion" promotes a certain relativism that rejects the absolute claim of *any* "religion" or ideology. From the point of view of this radical prophetic criticism, "religion" is the major promoter of sin insofar as it merely reinforces prevailing norms.

A positive evaluation of individuals and groups is derived from the doctrine of creation when it is supplemented by doctrines of sin and redemption. Creatures as such are essentially, though not existentially, good; and as creatures they are unique individuals. Indeed, individuality is a condition of their existence. But this individuality involves limitedness, and when this limitedness assumes that it is self-sufficient, it presumes in effect to be God and it enters into demonic struggle with other individualities. Redemption from this demonry does not issue from individuality itself; it has the same source as creation. The divinely redemptive power can work only when individuality in its uniqueness and its limitedness recognizes the demand for mutuality in community with other individualities in their uniqueness and limitedness.

The ecumenical movement, beginning with the Stockholm Conference of 1925, has recognized the pride of individuality which has caused the separations among the churches themselves, separations that involve doctrines and orders and conceptions of society. It has not attempted to achieve a super-church but to bring the different churches into mutually respectful conversation and into new forms of cooperation. The differences between the churches, differences rooted in venerable traditions, are almost as great as the differences between the ideologies that prevail today; indeed, the leaders of the ecumenical movement recognize certain homologies between many aspects of these variant church traditions and the ideologies of the corresponding territories.

The official report issued by the Evanston Assembly of the World Council of Churches (1955) states, with respect to the social-ethical implications of the Christian faith, that they hold that evangelism should aim to transform the whole person in the social context of life. This view is in accord with a principal emphasis, to be observed also in earlier conferences, upon the conception that "the responsible society" is not held to be "an alternative social or political system, but a criticism by which we judge all existing social orders."

IV

Bagehot's distinction between the dignified and the efficient parts of the constitution is somewhat similar to a distinction that must be made in analyzing a religious system. The doctrines of God, humanity, and salvation can symbolize the unity of a given group, and in this respect they are dignified parts of the religious system. But the influence of a system upon social policy is to be discerned primarily in the organization of the church. This is an efficient part, a visible locus or medium of power.

An instructive index to the meaning of a theological system is the kind of community developed or desired by the faithful. A doctrine of God or humanity or salvation is not understood fully if it is grasped only in its metaphysical dimension or in its personal implications; its social efficacy reveals itself ultimately in the impersonal institutional precipitate. This institutional dimension of a religious system involves not only the religious group's own form of organization; in the end it will affect social policy as well. The reverse process, of course, also takes place. Ecclesiastical organization can be affected by nonecclesiastical forms and influences.

An excellent illustration of the institutional implication of a theological idea is the principle of organization—the separation of church and state—derived from Jesus' statement, "Render to Caesar the things that are Caesar's, and to God the things that are God's" [Mark 12:17]. An equally striking illustration is to be observed in the historical fact, much stressed by Ernst Troeltsch, that the types of social philosophy that have emanated from the churches tend to reveal a correlation with the types of ecclesiastical organization represented in the respective church types. The Roman Catholic Church and the churches of the Magisterial Reformation have shown a preference for the hierarchical articulation of society. The churches of the Radical Reformation, particularly the aggressive sects, demanded a dispersion of power, the rejection of the concept of *Corpus Christianum*, the separation of church and state, local autonomy for the congregation, an increase in responsibility for the laity, the permission of a loyal opposition. The first type, the church type, has tended to favor a monistic society. The second type, the sect type (with its descendant, the denomination), has favored pluralism, including toleration for infidels and freedom of association in general.

Analogous secular theories of social organization have, in the modern period, very often followed chronologically upon the ecclesiastical theories, revealing the latter's direct influence. Saint-Simonian, Comtean, and Marxist conceptions of centralized hierarchical authority closely resemble Roman Catholic conceptions. On the other hand, the conceptions of society and social organization preferred in the democratic societies of the English-speaking countries are largely the outgrowth of the Radical Reformation, from the congregational polity of Independency in seventeenth-century England and America. Indeed, *laissez faire* economic theory must be said to have similar roots, for the left wing ecclesiastical theorists and the economic theorists held analogous presuppositions regarding a pre-established harmony not requiring deliberate attention. It is likely that the ecclesiastical theorists were influenced in turn by conceptions of social organization promoted by the emerging small-business leadership.

The tensions between the theory of the negative, minimal state and the theory of the welfare state (or of the planned society) which are characteristic of our time remind one of earlier ecclesiastical controversies respecting the doctrine of the church. The increasing demand for social control of the economy and of the repercussions of industrialization must meet especially vigorous resistance from people (church members or not) whose background is the tradition of congregational polity. A group of American Congregationalist laity and clergy are today defending *laissez faire* and the negative state in opposition to proponents of the welfare state. At the same time, the churches of the Radical Reformation as well as the Roman Catholic Church have long shown ready sympathy for theories of the welfare state or of planning.

Here we see, then, the ways in which religious conceptions and ideologies inevitably affect each other. The contrasts and tensions referred to here constitute the major tensions in contemporary ideology not only *between* the ideologies but also *within* given ideologies. Ideological taint, group individuality, and group fanaticism are all involved in the conflict. The religion that transcends "religion" brings all of these claims under judgment.

In the face of these conflicts over theories of society and of social organization, the report of the Evanston Assembly would appear to be an attempt at mediation, for the conception of "the responsible society" set forth gives no exclusive sanction to either side in the controversy which began, according to Gierke, in the late Middle Ages. On the contrary, the report attempts to see the virtues and the dangers on each side. Consequently, the ecumenical movement may enable religion to make a constructive contribution to the conversation between the ideologies as well as between the churches.

In any event, both the dignified and the efficient parts of religious systems as well as of ideologies would appear to require continuing reinterpretation or revision if both freedom and order are to be tolerably maintained in the defining and shaping of new situations. Today the importunate question is whether, in the face of the quickly changing East, the ambiguous democracies of the West can perform this task with the requisite speed.

24 · *The Prophetic Covenant and Social Concern*

There is no such thing as a completely isolated being. Human beings are in relationship, and bonding is a characteristic feature of this relationship. Bonding is the development of attachment, loyalty, affection. It generates the collectivities that function in history. In bonding, human beings develop a sense of the past and of the future and even a philosophy of history.

BONDING IN NATURE AND HISTORY

There are varieties of bonding. The most familiar and perhaps biologically inevitable kind of bonding is familial. One cannot come into existence except through heterosexual activity. The fact that the most intense hatred as well as the most intense affection can appear within the family shows something of the ambiguity of bonding. Another kind of bonding which has been of interest in Western culture from ancient times is friendship. My professor of Greek at Harvard used to say that the paradoxical thing is that one should find much in ancient Greek literature on the idea of friendship, and yet it is practically impossible to find any examples of great friends.

Another kind of bonding is the type that the Nazis attempted to consolidate, namely the bonding of pigment. The Nazi ideology was based on *Blut und Boden,* blood and soil, a philosophy of nationalism and racial supremacy. But they had no monopoly on racism. One of the most disturbing chapters in Arnold Toynbee's *A Study of History* [London, 1936], deals with the birth of racism in Anglo-American culture. His thesis is that after the publication of the King James Version of the Scriptures one book after another picked up the Old Testament idea of "the chosen people" and adapted it to the British. It became a kind of biblical nerve for British imperialism and especially for the idea of white supremacy. Bonding of pigment has been a vital feature also in American culture; it continually provides occasion for conflict and for new attempts at reconciliation—for attempts to transcend the accident of pigment and to achieve bonding in the name of something more universal.

This is the first of three lectures given at the Meadville/Lombard Theological School, Chicago, in January 1977; revised, 1990. Edited from the transcription of Alice Blair Wesley. Reprinted by permission.

A few years ago I discovered a letter from Karl Marx to one of his friends, complaining about his wife and daughter putting on their best Sunday-go-to-meeting clothes to go off to a Methodist chapel. He said, "I've tried to be tolerant with them, but I really had an outburst last Sunday. I said to those two ladies, 'If you are so much interested in religion, I suggest one Sunday you stay home and read the Old Testament prophets, and you'll see what it is!'" The kind of bonding you have in some forms of Marxism, which has so much changed the planet, could not have occurred in Western culture without the background of the prophets. Marxism presupposes prophetism.

To understand this tradition, I want to perpetrate some generalizations. George Lyman Kittredge, the Shakespeare scholar, used to say that the art of teaching is the art of telling a lie and then qualifying it. I'm going to tell some "lies" of oversimplification and then make qualifications.

HISTORICAL RELIGION

The Western religious outlook may be characterized as a historical point of view. In Judeo-Christianity since the Old Testament prophets, and even before, the center of attention is upon *events* in history. The historian Williston Walker, asking why Christianity triumphed in the early Mediterranean period, answered that it had an event to point to, namely Jesus Christ, the Incarnation. The other religions, he said, had myths and legends and nonhistorical figures. Jesus was a historical figure, a cardinal event that could be pointed to. A historical religion is oriented to events that happen in history, to processes that raise one above history, and not to an inward, narcissistic journey. Even when it is nonreligious—when the old myths have died and it is secularized—the Western outlook on life is not one that promotes a merely mystical transcending of history.

Western religion, then, is oriented to events in history. One has to understand existence in terms of events, their processes, their outcomes, their catastrophes. This means also that a historical form of religion sees history as being formed by groups. Individuals are not isolated, but enter into bondings in history. These bondings, as they affect history and maintain some kind of continuity in history, find institutional forms. So historical religion is ultimately one that sees history in terms of persons in groups and in institutions. The idea of the person achieving fulfillment without participation in groups, without relatedness and responsibility in the face of institutions, is a form of escape from history and away from authentic, historical religion.

Further, in a historical religion the sense of the past is important, because events, groups, and institutions become the occasions and the sources of achieving personal and social identity. Let me give an illustration.

I remember seeing Robert Sherwood's play, "Lincoln in Illinois," when it was first presented. At the climactic moments one could feel the entire audience identifying with Lincoln. Here was an interpretation of the past, highly idealized but also deeply meaningful, for in that event I felt a sense of group identity in terms of a meaningful past.

A historical religion is oriented also to the future; it is eschatological. It understands the meaning of life in terms of the pursuit of a goal, to be realized in the future, for groups and institutions. A historical religion, then, has a sense of the past and also of direction towards the future. It is in this sense that many people have said that Marx represents the old prophetic and Messianic idea of a drive toward the future. The meaning of history is going to be achieved by a fundamental change of institutions.

A further feature of historical religion is that history, with its events, groups, and institutions, is understood in terms of periods. That is, there is a sense that what is going on now has had a past, but the present also has its peculiarly unique features, and one's social responsibility must be related to those unique features of the present.

The classical writer on this subject is Ernst Troeltsch. He said there are two characteristic features of a historical point of view. First, it is concerned with events. It tries to give meaning and direction to events, which are unique. As Oscar Wilde said, "History does not repeat itself. Only historians repeat each other." But history is related to events within the context of institutions. Troeltsch attacked the idea of writing history merely in terms of individual persons as carriers of ideas, since persons exist in groups and in institutions.

Second, Troeltsch said that a theory of periodization is characteristic of the historical point of view. People seek to understand themselves by identifying and describing the unique features of the present and the unique problems and responsibilities that the present calls for. It is interesting to observe the awareness of historical uniqueness and of periods in American fundamentalism. I was reared on the *Scofield Reference Bible,* in which the footnotes organize history according to "dispensations" running from the

Creation to the Last Judgment. By the time I was eleven years old, I could rehearse these dispensations—the whole organization of history in periods.

The first appearance of such a philosophy of history is to be found in the book of Judges. George Foote Moore, professor of Old Testament at Harvard a generation ago, made one of the great scholarly discoveries of the twentieth century. He pointed out that the same stories appear in the books of Judges and Joshua, but that in Judges the stories are lined up in periods. The writer has tried to understand what is happening to the people of Israel and works out three periods. First is a period of military conquest, with the assistance of Yahweh. Then comes a period of betrayal, marked by a lack of adherence to Yahweh's law and by consequent military defeat. Finally, there arises a judge, who brings a return to Yahweh and to military conquest.

To use a farmboy's metaphor, Moore's thesis is: If you take the book of Judges and put it through a wringer, what comes out in the old-fashioned washtub is a series of "tags," as he calls them—periods marked by faithfulness, unfaithfulness, and the coming of a judge. These tags come through again and again. We may note that a major source of Marxism's appeal has been its similar theory of periodization: the original rule of the aristocracy; the present rule of capitalism, fraught with contradictions; and the "messianic" rule of the proletariat, to come.

Origins of the Concept of Covenant

Human social existence requires the achievement of a means of communicating about social existence, a characteristic feature of which is the invention of concepts. Concepts do not come down from heaven; they have to be invented. The poets are the legislators of humanity, as Shelley asserted at the end of his "Defence of Poetry," in the sense that it is by poetic imagination that the great concepts that interpret human experience have been devised. To be sure, the earliest poets, such as those who invented the concept of covenant, are unknown to us.

You recall the story in Genesis about Yahweh's instructing Adam and Eve to name all the flora and fauna. In the history of Jewish thought "naming" is one of the great theological themes; human beings, to achieve self-understanding and communication, have to name things. So in his commandment to name things, God was commanding something absolutely indispensable if they were going to be human. The story is told that Adam and Eve did their best, working for some time naming all the flora and fauna. Finally they sat down in the shade of a tree, thinking with some satisfaction, "Well, we've done what he asked—we've named them all," when suddenly something came hopping through the grass which they hadn't seen before. "What's that?" asked Adam. "I've never seen that before." Eve, who was the creative figure, seeing this thing hopping around, said, "Ah, ha! It looks like a frog to me." She named it.

One of the great namings in the history of Western culture, and one that represents a major thread in biblical literature, is the concept of covenant. It is interesting to observe how this concept was invented and the implications of the initial occasion of its invention. As generally happens, theological discourse here picks up a concept from ordinary experience and gives it a new and expanded meaning. A concept that originally applies to one aspect of existence is reinterpreted to explain the whole of existence. We call this process the radicalizing of a concept.

The concept of covenant was taken from the political realm and applied to the theological realm. It was made the basis of understanding the relationship between humanity and God, of understanding the nature of ultimate reality in terms of bonding. A political metaphor, in contrast to a metaphor drawn from interpersonal existence—a personalistic metaphor—has the broadest applicability. It interprets the whole of human existence; everybody is in the political order. In this case it becomes the key to understanding the life of a people.

The political background of the concept of the covenant was first worked out by the American scholar George Mendenhall [in *Law and Covenant in Israel and the Ancient Near East* (Pittsburgh, Pa., 1955)]. He studied scores of treaties between a sovereign and smaller jurisdictions from the ancient Near East, going back as far as the fourth millennium B.C.E., and found analogies between them and the idea of covenant in the Old Testament. He showed that there were six ingredients of most of these ancient treaties, or covenants, which long predated the children of Israel's leaving Egypt: (1) a preamble—a historical prologue describing the past that has led up to this moment; (2) stipulations with regard to the agreements between the sovereign and the smaller jurisdictions; (3) the provision that the agreement must be periodically read in public and (4) must be kept in a sacred shrine; (5) blessings invoked on those who loyally maintain the agreement and (6) curses on those who are not loyal to it. In the literature of the covenant in the Old Testament, Mendenhall then finds very specific illustrations of each element.

THE MEANING OF COVENANT

We may say, then, that in the Old Testament concept of the covenant the meaning of life is found in the processes and the responsibilities of history, namely in maintaining an agreement that provides order and continuity in the society. The meaning of life is rooted in a sense of obligation. Now I want to offer a series of propositions, those "lies" that have to be qualified if they are to take account of human experience with full adequacy.

I. The concept of covenant in the Old Testament prophets is the covenant made at Sinai through Moses. The first characteristic of human collective existence is commitment, that is, making an agreement, a promise. Promising is a characteristic feature of meaningful human existence. Richard Cabot, in *The Meaning of Right and Wrong* [New York, 1933], argued that meaningful thought and life require making agreements; further, the growth of individuals or cultures is seen not only in their loyalty to but also in their improvement of past agreements, including those which persons make with themselves. Martin Buber speaks of humans as promise-making, promise-breaking, promise re-making creatures; the making of promises and commitments Buber sees as essential to human nature.

II. The meaning of life is found in the processes and responsibilities of groups and institutions. The entire people, in this covenant view, is responsible for the character of the society. This is one of the great insights in history, namely that one is related to the collective in such a way as to be responsible for the consequences of one's actions and for the consequences of collective action. Institutional and not merely individual behavior is an indispensable aspect of human existence.

III. We see the Old Testament prophets' repeated emphasis on the idea that fulfillment of the covenant requires concern for the weak and the deprived. This is one of the most remarkable things in the Old Testament, an idea that has reappeared recently in John Rawls' influential study, *A Theory of Justice* [Cambridge, Mass., 1971]. This third point is to be connected with the second: the collective is responsible for the character of the society. Responsibility for promoting mercy and justice, especially for the deprived, requires criticizing those who have power in the society.

IV. The covenant is for the individual as well as for the group. We see this especially in the liturgical Psalms, in which individual meditation, prayer, and commitment are prominent. But they are never separated

from institutional responsibilities. It is remarkable that the idea should
have developed that the interior life, the prayer life, entails collective and
not only individual responsibility. But equally remarkable and puzzling
is our capacity to forget this.

V. The biblical idea of covenant is what I call a covenant of being. That
is, the Old Testament asserts that the people's covenant is a covenant with
the essential character and intention of reality. It is not merely a covenant
between human beings; it is a covenant between human beings in the face
of reality. The fundamental demands and possibilities of reality are not
created by humans but exist in its very nature. The understanding of
reality is appropriate only when it is seen in terms of an ethical covenant.
The covenant is with the creative, sustaining, commanding, judging,
transforming Power. This is the ultimate theological orientation of the
Old Testament idea of covenant.

VI. The covenant includes a rule of law. It recognizes that meaningful,
collective existence involves a consensus and a commitment with regard
to what is right. It is a legal covenant. The desire for justice can be
fulfilled only through collective concern with law as the major agency of
social control. But there is a second part to this proposition:

VII. It is not only a covenant based on adherence to law but also upon
trust and affection. One maintains responsibility for the collective, not,
finally, because it is the law, but because of love. The responsibility is
motivated by affection. Thus the breaking of the covenant is not merely
a violation in the sense of criminality but in the sense of breaking faithfulness, of violating the affection that was the ground and nerve of the
covenant in the first place. It is through God's love, God's grace, that we
receive the covenant.

VIII. The covenant was produced by a prophetic criticism and carried
within it a continuing need for the freedom of critical dissent. Prophetic
criticism is a radical form of dissent, pointing again and again to the
faithlessness, the betrayal of the covenant, by "the children of Israel."
Thus the prophetic outlook becomes the major thrust for self-criticism in
the culture.

We might say that Socrates brought judgment in Greek culture
through dialectic—by asking the Yes and No of tough questions. Prophetic criticism directs its questions to the sins of the collectivity. In his
book on ancient Judaism, the sociologist of religion Max Weber said that
the prophets were precursors of the modern free press. I would say it this
way. Old Testament prophetism institutionalized dissent and criticism

and thus initiated the separation of powers. The prophets said that the culture was not under the control of centralized power; viable culture requires the institutionalization of dissent—in other words, the freedom to criticize the powers that be.

SOCIAL RESPONSIBILITY

The covenant of social responsibility, then, is one that is rooted in a historical conception of the meaning of human existence, and not merely in a conception of personal religion. Personal religion, though it may have its own uniqueness and insight, gains adequate meaning only in relationship to the larger context of existence. The concept of the covenant is one of the great conceptual inventions of our ancient forebears for defining identity. We achieve authentic identity through an understanding of history, of our place in institutions, and in the claim that this is precisely the essence of reality, of being itself or God. The divine power liberates humanity through this sense of social responsibility, of dissent and criticism. We have here a major form of bonding.

Please observe the contrast between the form and character of this bonding and that of Nazi bonding. Bonding in Nazism is rooted in elements of nature, namely in one's own blood and soil and territory. The intention of Nazi religion is to enforce that bonding, regardless of law or universal standards, and to suppress every kind of free criticism. Nazism is oriented to nature. The prophetic covenant is oriented to history—to the demands of history and the achievement of meaning in history through social responsibility. The orientation to nature is of course not excluded. To make such a futile attempt to exclude it would be to ignore the hand that feeds us. Today we are beginning to recognize the imperative demands of ecology, requiring an extension of covenant—leading us again to the covenant of being, requiring also a reconception of the political symbolism in the direction toward organic symbolism. In other words, these different symbols and perceptions confront the demand for "creative interchange."

RESTRICTED COVENANTS

It is easy enough in a homiletic mood to speak of a covenant of strength and love. But in many a human group there are other kinds of covenant—"restricted covenants." We are all too familiar with the restriction that aims to prevent "undesirable" races or classes "invading" the neighborhood.

Besides those covenants there has been and is an equally pervasive, restricted covenant—the male sexist restriction that has kept women in a subordinate status and role, except perhaps inside the family.

Lamentably, scriptural sanction (especially Pauline) has been appealed to. In the fundamentalist church of my youth, women by sacred command were required to be silent in church meeting, even though they were the hustlers who kept an eye on the budget. They, and not the men, were required to cover their heads in church or during prayer (at home). These are examples of pious male-domination, yet they are feeble examples in contrast to the discrimination practiced in the marketplace and, in large measure still, in politics. It is still inconceivable that today a woman could be president of the United States, although in Britain a woman has been prime minister for years. This is one of our forms of apartheid.

It is significant that well over a century ago American feminists recognized their derogated status to be analogous to that of blacks. Here the relation between gender identification and the body could not be ignored. But times have been a-changing. In wide circles the feminists in the United States have been crying protest, making their claims, and forming voluntary associations to support them. We must say that their literature and public actions have been in advance of what is called "liberation theology" (such as has been promoted in Central and South America).

But as with the restricted covenants imposed upon the blacks and the Hispanics these covenants imposed upon women are still widely pervasive, particularly in the economic sphere (with respect to executive authority and to salaries and wages). Like children, they are supposedly not entitled to adult monetary remuneration.

In short, a long pull will be required before our apartheid is overcome and before anything like equality is achieved for either blacks, Hispanics, or women. This dismal situation is even more readily evident if we consider the large number of women who in addition to working are obliged to keep the home-fires burning. All the more dismal is the situation for women who are single parents.

In our search for equality for women the emphasis might well shift to a recognition of the complementarity of man and woman as intended by the Creator (already expressed in *Genesis*). Respect for each other flows naturally from the Creator's original purpose and could affect the quality of sensitivity to values within our present culture. Such a shift could prove to be pregnant with possibilities for an enlightened equality.

25 · Root Metaphors of Religious Social Thought

At a recent farewell dinner for the poet W. H. Auden on the eve of his return to England one of the guests posed the question, "Mr. Auden, do you agree with the poet Shelley's dictum that the poets are the unacknowledged legislators of the world?" After a pause Mr. Auden in his gruff way replied, "The legislators of the world—are the secret police."

Another contemporary critic has called Shelley's dictum "a notorious piece of hyperbole . . . merely a misunderstanding arising from the manifold character of Apollo."[1] Some of you may charge me with a similar misunderstanding if I venture here to adopt Shelley's view, that is, to extend its application to the creators of root metaphors of religious symbolism which give meaning and direction to social thought and action.[2] Root metaphors such as the covenant with God or the Reign of God may not have been devised by people whom we call "poets." Yet, these and similar images are manifestations of *poiesis,* that is, of "making"—of creative imagination. In Greek the word *poet,* literally, means *maker.*

I

The root metaphors of the Bible or of early religious symbolism are not poetic in the ordinary sense. As Kierkegaard would put the matter, they come not from the genius who proudly displays his own creations but from the apostle who points beyond himself. That is, they are kerygmatic in intention; they are the saving word, the sacred word, for the religious community. Moreover, they are generally the essential ingredients of the cultic acts of a religious community. Unlike poetic images (which "supervene on life"), the root metaphors "intervene" in life—they *aim* to affect behavior (Santayana). Hence, the "makers" of these metaphors are in a sense to be counted among the unacknowledged legislators of the world. Certain of them, in fact, had to suffer encounters with the police when in prophetic protest they appealed to the sacred sanction. A news item in the *London Times* reported: "A new saint has appeared in the Ganges Valley. The police are after him."

This essay is Adams's presidential address for the American Theological Society, originally presented on April 13, 1973; revised and abbreviated, 1988.

This element of conflict seems to belong to the genesis of the great root metaphors. They generally come to birth—or to rebirth and new interpretation—in times when the community is questioning old moorings and seeking new ports of call. We see this readily in the shift from polytheism to monotheism in the Old Testament, or in the advent of monasticism, or in the Reformation. Many of these "makers" in the past are not only acknowledged, they are also unknown—lost to us in the "dark backward and abysm of time" [Shakespeare]. One of them, however, is known to us as a historical figure, indeed also as one of the most influential "makers" of the West. I refer to Augustine. Although he was an academic figure and thus unlike the "makers" of biblical antiquity, he should be mentioned here at the outset, and that for three reasons.

First, because he exemplifies the crisis-oriented situation in which a new root metaphor achieves acute relevance. He lived in a time of historical crisis when Rome, the capitol of the Empire, was sacked by Alaric and his Goths and "when fugitives from Rome came flying to Carthage in the wake of the news." People were asking, was the fall of Rome, "the eternal city," the result of abandoning the old civic gods? Was the fall due to the victory of Christianity, the new faith? In the teeth of this historical situation Augustine ventured boldly to offer an answer.

The second reason is that in doing so he became a new "maker," or rather he adapted old and familiar concepts, the concept of drama and the concept of the City, in order to interpret the meaning of history past, present, and future. The concept of the City was a thousand years old as a cosmic symbol, but it had lost much of its power. Augustine gave it new birth in the conception of the Two Cities, the heavenly and the earthly.

We come, then, to the third reason for referring to Augustine here. In speaking of *two* Cities he recaptured the metaphor in a special way by uniting it with another metaphor. In the years before his conversion Augustine had been a professor of rhetoric. In this profession he had devoted his attention to analyzing the *poiesis*, the "making," of the pagan dramatists. When he came to formulate a new theology of history he drew upon these poets. In the Greek and Roman tragedy he had found a protagonist and an antagonist. Accordingly, he now interprets human history as the perennial drama of Two Cities; thus he combines the literary metaphor of *drama* with the political metaphor of the *city*. The Two Cities are the City of God and the City of Earth, the "heavenly city" of *sojourners* in the world and the city of those who are "at home" in this world and wish to live after the flesh. These two Cities are in dramatic conflict. In this dichotomy faith and unfaith become the organizing principles.[3] In terms of this drama he sketched out a philosophy of history, past, present, and future, a drama in seven acts or great periods.

There is a third reason for considering Augustine here. He not only restored and gave new life to familiar metaphors, illustrating the fact that the great root metaphors are subject to restoration, to rebirth; he also had the audacity to draw his metaphors from the pagan and not from the Christian past, at the same time that he integrated them with a Christian ethos.

In this "making" for a social group, the Christian community, Augustine exemplifies several aspects of the function of the root metaphor. It aims to help human beings understand their environment and themselves in the face of that environment. That is, it offers a description of the environment and the appropriate response. So Augustine provides a symbolization that defines the human condition in history, that is, in terms of institutions as well as of persons; and he gives the group and the individual meaning, orientation, and motivation in relation to the penultimate environment and also to the ultimate environment, the Source and End of salvation. The symbolization underlines what is viewed as most important, and it gives hope for the future. This process of symbolization delineates the self-identity and vocation of a religious community and renders the "poet" the legislator of whom Shelley spoke. This "making" that defines the human condition and human destiny and also defines self-identity with vocation performs a major function which Alfred Schultz calls "typification," that is, it offers a "system of motives for action, of choices to be made, of projects to be carried out, of goals to be reached."[4]

These characterizations of root metaphors in religion of course inevitably bespeak a hermeneutic method, a cultural hermeneutic. It is pertinent here to refer to Rudolf Bultmann's delineation of major dimensions of hermeneutic method to indicate something of the scope of our present intention to deal with these metaphors. Bultmann's exposition is concerned with the interpretation of biblical texts, but it can apply also to the interpretation of root metaphors in a culture. According to Bultmann, there are four possibilities.[5] First, texts may be interpreted in order to reconstruct past history. Second, the object of interpretation may be established by psychological interest; third, by aesthetic interest, and finally, and most important, by an existential interest, when the inquiry is governed by the possibilities for ongoing human existence. In this fourth aspect of hermeneutic method Bultmann stresses the idea that the biblical text of the gospel drives the human being to the necessity to decide about his or her own existence; indeed it drives the person to recognize that the necessity for decision is the essential quality of being a person. In short, the crucial text "brings judgment to the world and opens up for men the possibility of authentic life."[6]

Now, none of the four possibilities mentioned by Bultmann is to be excluded from the hermeneutic enterprise. In the examination of root metaphors, however, we envisage a fifth possibility, namely, that the interpretation may be established also by a sociological interest, when the inquiry is governed by the possibilities and responsibilities offered for our social institutional existence, that is, for the widely mingled decisions required of us as historical beings. The recognition of the need for this fifth dimension of hermeneutics amounts to a radical criticism of Heideggerian as well as of Bultmannian privatistic existentialism. This fifth possibility aims to discern a public theology rather than a merely privatized theology of individual authenticity. The feminist Beverly Harrison has called this "a hermeneutic of justice." We shall return to this matter later.

II

In his act of symbolization, Augustine, as we have observed, employs for his theology of history a dramatic metaphor combined with a political one. In doing so he has made a selection. He might have selected other metaphors, but he did not. This *selecting* of a telling metaphor is the characteristic "making" of *poiesis*. The poet seeks "a bright, particular star." In the history of root metaphors this kind of "making" exhibits a wide-ranging imagination. But selection is always present. One is reminded here of Whitehead's assertion that the first task of the metaphysician is to select a ruling metaphor. According to Whitehead, such a selection enables the philosopher to discern and characterize a connectedness or coherence, a kind of rationality, in the world.

The selection of a symbol for *religious* discourse presents, as we have observed, a special problem. The symbol or root metaphor as a form of communication must point to the divine, must relate the divine and the human, the transcendent and the immanent. The "maker" doth glance from heaven to earth and from earth to heaven. But this poet does not have available the language of heaven. The pointer, the vehicle of communication, must come from earth. One must select an image, a morphe, from the realm of ordinary experience. A particular image is selected from a segment of experience and is then "radicalized" by being applied to the whole of reality, to the divine and to the relation between the divine and the human—to the root of everything. The symbol drawn from the earth must point beyond itself, thus becoming an "ecstatic" image (as Schelling would say).

But since it must be drawn from earth, that is, from some segment of earth, certain limits are imposed. It can be drawn only from a conception of the embracing cosmos, or from the inanimate order, or from the biological, or from politics, or the family, or personal existence. What else is there, unless one adopts a negative theology renouncing all symbols?

The criticism is often directed at religious symbolism that it is anthropomorphic. If some form, some morphe, is required, and if anthropomorphism is rejected, should one then prefer an image drawn from the subhuman sphere, say, from the movements of the heavens? Should one automatically prefer a mechanomorphic symbol? Nathan Soderblom long ago reminded us that primitive humanity had already tried subanthropomorphism, having seen the divine in *mana,* a power similar to electricity.[7] Obviously, anthropomorphism can interpret a much wider range of experience and meaning than can kinomorphism, a symbol representing sheer energy, *une force qui va.*

Religious symbolism, then, represents a selection from the spectrum of human possibilities, for, as Calvin reminds us, the essence of God is inaccessible to us. "Our capacity," he says, "cannot endure the fullness of God's infinite glory. It is therefore necessary when He appears to us that He put on a face adapted to our capacity." Thomas Aquinas makes a similar claim when he asks, "Whether Holy Scripture should use metaphors?" He replies that "these things are not literal descriptions of divine truths."

III

What, then, are the major types of root metaphor in Western religious tradition?

My attention to this question of classification was first aroused at Marburg University in Germany years ago in discussions with Heinrich Frick. In his *Vergleichende Religionswissenschaft* (1928), he had presented a typology of metaphors in terms of orientation to time and orientation to space. In the growth or seed parables of Jesus regarding the coming kingdom he saw an orientation to time, whereas in the Fourth Gospel the eschatology is spatialized, for there the Gospel writer makes a contrast between earth and heaven, between here and there. These metaphorical figures, Frick noted, are not mutually exclusive. In the Lord's Prayer, for example, both time and space play a role: "Thy kingdom come, thy will be done on earth as in heaven." Frick did not develop this time-and-space typology. There may be good reason for this. The distinction is of limited scope for differentiating major biblical images.[8]

Of the major symbols there are relatively few types. Indeed, for our purpose we can reduce the number to four, namely, political metaphors, domestic metaphors, organic (or body) metaphors, and personalistic metaphors. The contents and interpretations of these types, to be sure, vary considerably in their full historical development, giving expression to a variety of pieties and polities. Moreover, the major types are not by necessity mutually exclusive. Taken together, they provide a reservoir of metaphors which in the course of time are drawn upon in extremely varied ways.

First, let us consider political symbolism as it appears in the Bible. Paul Lehmann has asserted that "the formative biblical images that point to and describe the divine activity in the world are *political* images, both in the phenomenological and in the fundamental sense of the word."[9] Among these political images are the kingship of God, the Messiah (or the Christ), the kingdom of God, the kingship of Christ and the covenant. In the Old Testament these political metaphors provide the ingredients of a political theology.

What are the main features of this political theology? That is such a large question that we may do well to glance first at a simplified version of an earlier period, a version that has been called a "politicized cosmos." In his studies of religion in ancient Mesopotamia, Thorkild Jacobsen finds a symbolism which he describes as that of a "primitive democracy."[10] He shows in considerable detail how the council of the village elders was projected into a council of the gods. In this view, the gods of the council, like the elders on earth, were obliged to enter into discussion before any decision was taken. No true god would make a decision on his own advisement. If he became a deviant, sanctions would be imposed by the other gods of the divine council. Accordingly, one might say that here the sign of a true god was his ability to lift his hand to the ear and attend to what the other gods in the council were saying about considered policy. Here Jacobsen, then, finds political metaphor and political theology.

An analogous politicomorphism is characteristic also in ancient Israel. It appears in the conception of Yahweh as lord, sovereign, ruler or king, over his servants. We need not pause here more than to observe in passing the initial rejection of kingship and its symbolism. God is also described as judge, warrior, law-giver, the source of equity. The sociomorphic pattern throughout was that of the ruler and servant, the latter referring eventually to the individual as well as to the people as a collectivity.[11]

The metaphor of covenant is likewise a politicomorphic symbol, drawn from the sphere of international relations. Although some scholars point out that the term *covenant* does not appear as often as has been assumed, it has entered into Western consciousness as the sign of a commitment to and a promise from Yahweh, a commitment to work for a society of justice and mercy. If Socrates brought philosophy from heaven to earth, the prophets brought the religion of Israel from an exclusively cosmological orientation into the arena of history, maintaining the Exodus motif of liberation from bondage in Egypt. They made it into a "historical religion" wherein the acts of God in history provided a norm for *judging* the acts of the people and their kings. Thus "God hath a controversy with his people." The metaphor of king and covenant made Yahweh sovereign over the whole of life, over every aspect of individual and social existence.

In reminding the people of the lordship of God the prophets managed to establish themselves in some independence of the monarch and the cultus and the people—a sort of separation of powers. In contrast to the situation in Babylon, the Hebrew prophets were not members of the court on expense accounts. Max Weber has suggested that they prefigure the modern free press. In the name of the lordship of Yahweh and in the name of the covenant they criticized the monarch and the people.

The covenant brought with it a law to be obeyed. Yet it was not a merely legalistic metaphor. Like the covenant, it was a gift from the mercy of God, engendering gratitude and trust. Violation of the covenant was not so much a legal crime as a betrayal of trust. This aspect of the covenant introduces an affectional element.

Moreover, the covenant had an institutional thrust. It assigned the individual responsibility in the context of the people's responsibility for the behavior of society. Like the concept of kingship, the covenant's jurisdiction is over the entire territory, not merely over the cultus or over the inner life of the individual. If one scrutinizes the sins the prophets excoriate, one discovers that for the most part they are the sins of institutional misbehavior, the sins of the monarch, of the palace guard and the bureaucracy, sins in money matters, such as bribery and exploitation, and especially the neglect of the poor at the gate. The prophetic theology is a political, a public theology. Moreover, it is oriented to the future. The eschatological metaphor of the coming of the Messiah underscores the element of hope. So much for the essential features of Hebraic political metaphor.

Alongside the politicomorphic symbolism is what we may call domestic metaphor, drawn not from the political territory but from the sphere of the family—father and child, bride and groom, brothers, sisters. It is customary to consider political symbolism as strongly impersonal, in contrast to the more personal quality of domestic symbolism. As we have observed, however, the affectional element belongs to the covenant metaphor. Yet, the personal, more intimate quality of domestic symbolism becomes evident in Hosea's use of the metaphor of bride and groom, husband and wife. Israel is a faithless wife, but despite her faithlessness Yahweh the groom pursues her to say to her, Nevertheless, don't you understand, I love you. Here we see a certain contrast with Amos' sole emphasis on righteousness and judgment. The reuniting of the separated husband and wife transcends the past in the renewal of covenant, opening the way to new possibilities in the nation. This is the meaning of forgiveness. In Hosea, the political metaphor of covenant is presupposed, and the domestic metaphor seems to be subordinate.

Both political and domestic symbolism appear in the Gospels. Indeed, they are joined in the Lord's Prayer: "Our Father who art in heaven . . . Thy kingdom come." Because of the acute eschatological tension, that is, because of the expected imminent End of the Age, the Gospels are often said to have no social-institutional theology. It is significant, however, to recall Shailer Mathews' little book, *Jesus on Institutions,* recently reissued. In any event, the political metaphor, the kingdom of God, remains, though in paradoxical form—the kingdom is coming but it is already breaking in to form a new community. In the spirit of Old Testament prophetism, moreover, the Gospels maintain and stress the affectional element, now called *agape.*

The political metaphor, however, is not confined to the Gospels. It appears later in the metaphor the kingship of Christ; the kingship will become fully manifest only in the Eschaton when Christ will present to the Father not only the redeemed souls but also the redeemed institutions of the social and political spheres. In the Gospels, however, we find also the emphasis on the person, on integrity of motive, on purity of intention, on inwardness of spirit.

If we concentrate attention on this feature of motive, spirit, and inwardness, we approach a different type of metaphor, which we may call personalistic. God's transforming power becomes manifest in the working of his Spirit through *metanoia*—change of heart and soul and mind—what in the Old Testament was called "turning back" to Yahweh. On the divine side the Father yearns for the return of the prodigal, the shepherd seeks for the sheep that is lost. *Metanoia* is the appropriate response with its quality of right motive and inwardness.

When this element is extracted and separated from the political metaphor of collective election and responsibility; when, for example, it stresses individual repentance or conversion to the exclusion of collective responsibility, the outcome will be a pietistic conception of salvation, a one-to-one process between God and isolated human beings, an escape from the conflicts of the political sphere.

But the personalistic metaphor can be joined to others in a unique way, e.g., to the political, as we see in the seventeenth century when the doctrine of the spirit and the doctrine of covenant give birth to congregational polity—and ultimately to modern democracy.

We have now spoken of political, domestic, and personalistic metaphors. It remains to mention a fourth type, the body or organic metaphor (which is anticipated in the Old Testament). We see it also in Plato's conception of the state as the individual, the psychophysical organism, writ large. In the Pauline Epistles the metaphor of the Body of Christ becomes a major motif. Perhaps, as with Augustine's metaphor of the Two Cities, Paul's metaphor of the Body of Christ gains its power through its merging of two metaphors, the organic and the political, though in this instance the political metaphor is reduced in its jurisdiction, due to the impossibility of applying it to the political order under the control of Caesar. In terms of the organic metaphor, all members of the church, all parts of the body, are under one directing and coordinating head. Through grace (*charis*) and Spirit (*pneuma*) they are given charismatic powers— apostles, teachers, administrators, women, and slaves, as well as men. The Body of Christ as the corporate entity has the vocation of a new Israel, and each of the members under the umbrella of this general vocation has his or her own vocation. Note, then, what has happened here; the political, the organic and the personalistic metaphors have been combined.

The four types of metaphor here delineated may seem at first blush to be a closely limited number, but this view is misleading. For these metaphors as they function in history assume a multitude of forms. Here we see the essential mobility of concepts and symbols and metaphors. This mobility is due in part to what Schelling calls the infinity of the idea.

Metaphor lends itself to manifold inner development, stressing or expanding now this and now that ingredient. H. Richard Neibuhr's study of *Christ and Culture* shows the variety of dimensions contained within the political metaphor: Christ above, against, within, and transforming culture. The mobility may be seen also in the inclusion—or exclusion—of sexism, classism, and racism. Here we see the ambiguity attaching to religious symbols, an ambiguity that despite the initial intention may leave the way open to demonic perversion.

This unfolding mobility of metaphor Troeltsch speaks of as latency. So he finds in the New Testament seeds of quite different developments—in the church type, the sect type, and the mystical type of religious association, each type assuming a different form of social organization. These changes, however, may not be entirely the consequence of inner latency; they develop also in response to a changing historical situation. But each of these types of association may be concerned with differing spheres.

IV

We are now ready to generalize and to say that there are three areas in which a root metaphor may find application: the macrocosmic, the mesocosmic, and the microcosmic, that is, the sphere of general theology or metaphysics, the sphere of social institutions (the transpersonal sphere), and the sphere of the individual person.

Any root metaphor is likely to be capable of defining or illuminating the cosmic or general theological orientation. But if a root metaphor is personalistic, it may fail to define the mesocosmic sphere of institutional behavior and obligation. The late William Warren Sweet was wont to describe revivalism in this way. The American economy, he held, was reaching the end of the frontier period and confronting new social-institutional problems. Revivalism was a way of escape: it offered the nonpolitical solution of individual conversion. Give your life to Jesus, and other problems will take care of themselves. This kind of solution we might call the demonic pretension or inflation of a metaphor, in this instance of the microcosmic metaphor. It presumes to perform the functions of the microcosmic and macrocosmic spheres. This demonic pretension is possible with all root metaphors; and for this reason they need the correction of each other.

To be sure, the microcosmic thrust of pietism, both religious and secular, is in part a healthy protest against the rigidities of dogmatic formulation or of political or ecclesiastical bureaucratism. This protest was evident in the Great Awakening. Yet it is clear that Jonathan Edwards showed little positive or constructive interest in the mesocosmic sphere of social institutions. His writings are largely confined to the macrocosmic metaphors of the history of redemption and to the pietistic microcosmic metaphors of the individualist metanoia of religious affections. In these respects he was moving away from the mesocosmic metaphors of Calvin (whom Troeltsch called the first Christian socialist).

Here we see an ever-present use of root metaphor. It may have begun in a struggle of liberation, but it is later used to legitimate the status quo. The organic metaphor has been used repeatedly to entrench established authorities, for example, in the Middle Ages and in eighteenth- and nineteenth-century conservatism. John of Salisbury in literalist fashion tries to draw an analogy between every part of the anatomy and specified functions and institutions in society, from the eyelashes to the toes, all under the close supervision of the temporal and spiritual powers.

These examples find their counterpart in the various interpretations of the covenant used in defense of such extremes as totalitarian society and spiritual anarchism. Here we see the spectrum containing two poles, the emphasis on institutional nourishment or guidance and the emphasis on individual spontaneity. This breadth of scope indicates the variety of value systems that may find shelter under root metaphors.

The most creative use of root metaphors seems to occur when they are extended to the liberation of the deprived and the neglected at the gate. The Exodus motif and the trek towards the Promised Land were given powerful expression by Martin Luther King, Jr.

The present seemingly moribund state of biblical root metaphors is perhaps due to the fact that in the churches they exhibit little of this dynamic of liberation. They have been privatized if they have not been entirely neglected. In this fashion they become primarily self-serving for the believer. The term *covenant* becomes familiar in the phrase, restricted covenants.

It may well be that the renewal of the vitality of religious root metaphors must come from outside the churches, as happened when the French Revolution stimulated social reform among the Methodists in England, or when the socialists in the nineteenth century moved certain church leaders in the direction of religious socialism. Marxism today is making a sufficient appeal in Catholic circles in Latin America to elicit a warning from the Vatican. The demand for black liberation today is coming mainly from the outside, as is the movement for women's liberation. This situation obtained in the sixteenth and seventeenth centuries when the middle classes were emerging from below, and the ensconced intellectuals faced a prophetic protest even to the point of anti-intellectualism.

Again and again we see that renewal comes from the least expected quarter, namely, where the eyes of the blind are being opened and where the captives are being released. Who knows? It may be that the powerful root metaphors of the next age will appear through symbols drawn from Latin America or the Third World, joined with symbols drawn from Jewish-Christian sources. The Marxist concept of alienation has already been domesticated in part in Christian theological writings.

In short, it is plausible that the future lies with the ecology of the root metaphors in which the interplay of political, domestic, personalistic, and organic imagery joins the macrocosmic, the mesocosmic, and the microcosmic, bringing forth treasures both new and old. In all of this we recognize that the unacknowledged legislators of the world are the "makers," the poets. Robert Louis Stevenson could have had this in mind when he said the human being lives not by bread alone, but also by metaphors. And the greatest of these, as we have seen, link heaven and earth in the tie that binds.

Notes

1. Michael Oakeshott, *The Voices of Poetry in the Conversation of Mankind* (London, 1959), p. 54.

2. I use the term "root metaphors" in the sense of "organizing images" suggested by Frederick Ferré; they function for those who use them "to give structure, interpretation, and emphasis to experience," in this way "affecting our apperception of values" and influencing our behavior. See "Metaphors, Models and Religion," *Soundings* 51, no. 3 (1965):331–32.

3. Heinrich Scholz, *Glaube und Unglaube in der Weltgeschichte*, chap. 3, "Das Drama der Weltgeschichte" (Leipzig, 1911).

4. Alfred Schultz, *Collected Papers* (The Hague, 1971), vol. 1, pp. 59ff. In this theory of meaning and typification Schultz makes use of ideas drawn from Weber and Husserl.

5. Rudolf Bultmann, *Essays, Philosophical and Theological* (London, 1955), pp. 240ff.

6. Rudolf Bultmann, *Kerygma and Myth* (New York, 1957), p. 39.

7. Nathan Soderblom, "Macht: I. Religionsgeschichtlich," *Die Religion in Geschichte und Gegenwart* (Tübingen, 1929), vol. 3, p. 1812.

8. See also Ernst Topitsch, *Vom Ursprung und Ende der Metaphysik* (1938), and Heinrick Gompers, "Problems and Methods of Early Greek Science," *Journal of the History of Ideas* 4 (1943).

9. Paul Lehmann, *Ethics in a Christian Context* (New York, 1963), p. 90.

10. Thorkild Jacobsen, "Primitive Democracy in Ancient Mesopotamia," *Journal of Near Eastern Studies* 2, no. 3 (1943):159–72.

11. G. Earnest Wright, "The Terminology of Old Testament Religion and Its Significance," *Journal of Near Eastern Studies* 1, no. 4 (1942):404–14.

26 · *The Arts and Society*

We are inclined to smile at the dictum of Stuart Pratt Sherman that "beauty has a heart full of service." Art is supposed to be autonomous, and beauty to be an end in itself. Consequently, when beauty's heart is affianced, beauty becomes captive to something alien to it. Indeed, it is corrupted. This corruption is evident when art is made captive, for example to didacticism and moralism. Moreover, didactic art is never enduringly successful. It is always short-lived, and it seeks new brummagem existence in each generation. Its failure is a sign of resistance to the bondage of beauty.

If art, on the other hand, is separated from all other concerns, it becomes trivial and meaningless, for then the creation and appreciation of art have no relation to the process of responding to and judging human experience. The price of separation is as great as that of bondage. In both separation and bondage, the price is nothing less than impotence. The theologian is familiar with an analogous dilemma in the relation and the tension between revelation and reason. If revelation is separated from reason, it becomes arbitrary; if it puts reason into bondage, it becomes alien to intrinsic meaning.

Beauty is not an isolated entity. Just as every shape in a painting affects every other shape, so a work of art is somehow conditioned by or related to other aspects of the culture and in turn affects the culture; for art is a communication rooted in the human situation at a given time, and the response to this communication is elicited in a particular cultural situa-

Abridged from an unpublished paper presented to the Theological Discussion Group, Washington, D.C., in 1955.

tion. In this cultural process beauty in artistic creations shows itself to have "a heart full of service."

This "service" is not necessarily utilitarian, yet it is inevitable that beauty should take the form of a servant. Longinus hinted at something like this when he defined poetry as "the echo of a magnanimous mind." Goethe was more explicit when he asserted that the Muse is a good accompanist, but a poor leader.

The strictly aesthetic aspects of art and of the evolution of art are not readily amenable to sociological interpretation in terms of class structure and social control. Yet there are aspects of both the form and content of art which exhibit the influence of general social forces, or which reveal art to be either in the service of existing social controls *or* in protest against them. In primitive societies, with their rigid kinship systems, political art—especially the art of revolt—is practically nonexistent. The class structure where it exists (in embryonic form) is a fixed entity, and the art "serves" to support the position of chiefs and other ranking figures; it does not even remotely approach criticism of these authorities and their sanctions. The Marxist contention that realistic art reflects the productive intercourse between humanity and nature and that idealistic art attempts to conceal class relations by employing religious or other delusive symbols, finds little application to primitive art. If primitive art reflects struggle, it is not class struggle but rather struggle between secret societies, or between kinship or age groups. At the same time, a variety of styles and motifs may appear which employ multiple symbolism. All of the symbols provide the artist and the beholder an occasion for participating in totemistic supporting realities.

When we turn to civilized societies, the social system is of course greatly altered in a variety of ways, for example, with respect to the division of labor and the overt competition of rival authorities. Yet, despite these changes, the artist may not stand in tension with the society but may "serve" the regnant authorities. Indeed, a symbolism that has "accompanied" a quite different "leader" in a contiguous society or tradition may be appropriated for the purpose of enhancing the power of the local authorities. Religious symbolism that in a different historical tradition has served to ignore, limit, or devaluate the power of worldly authority may be turned into a weapon of domination.

Ideological art is a form of repression, a form of social control through domination. It may appear in subservience to political or economic or ecclesiastical power, or to combinations of these powers, albeit subtly.

Viewing the great Byzantine mosaics today, we may rightly be impressed by the numinous qualities that transcend every particular social system and that express a sense of creatureliness. But in the social situation from which they emerged and to which they spoke, the Byzantine mosaics in their numinous power served also to enhance absolute political and ecclesiastical authority, though the beholder is given a sense of participating in the supporting, commanding power. In this respect the mosaics remind one of primitive art. In the Pantocrator, for example, one must recognize art to be in large measure in the service of caesaropapism. The symbol and the style endow the ecclesiastical-political power with a cosmic aura. Here we find art of a high aesthetic quality, but art that has a heart full of repression.

Insofar as art serves to enhance the regnant powers in the society we may be justified in speaking of it theologically as the art of creation; or more precisely we may call it the art of the orders of creation. In contrast to it we should then look for the art of the fall. I do not here refer to the art that extols the indulgences of the prodigal son in "the far country." I have in mind rather the art that exposes the meaninglessness, the frustration, the anxieties of the created, existing world. In a minimal sense this art is prophetic. That is, it proclaims doom. This art is in the service of protest against the actual.

T. W. Adorno has suggested that the devils' heads, the gargoyles, and the other grotesque figures which adorn the Gothic cathedrals express impulses of resistance to the Catholic *ordo*. In the Romantic period, perhaps the idealization of nature in the depiction of landscapes or of still lifes may be interpreted as a protest—if not against the orders of creation as such (as in the Rousseauist ethos), then against these orders as they have been distorted by the rising industrialism. Both the gargoyles and the Romantic landscapes may be viewed, then, as at least in part a protest against repression. In an oversimplified pedestrian way one English critic (cited by Edith Sitwell) has suggested these dimensions of protest, along with an appeal for the archaistic, by characterizing Grey's *Elegy* as "a plea for decentralization, recalling the over-urbanized ruling class to its roots in a rural society."

The art of protest against repression has close affinities with the sectarian mentality. If for typological purposes we call the art of the orders of creation the art of the church-type mentality, we may speak of the art of the fall—the art of tension with the world—as the art of the sect-type. Wilhelm Fraenger in his study of Hieronymus Bosch, and S. S. Kayser in his study of Matthias Grünewald, have shown the close affinity between the ethos of these artists and that of the sectarian reform movements— Bosch employing Adamite symbolism and Grünewald having sympathy with the reform movement of Geiler von Keiserberg and also perhaps with the "bitter-Christ" doctrine of Thomas Münzer.

The "sectarian" art of protest has reappeared in our own century, not among the Protestant sectarians but rather among their secular spiritual kin. Much of the art of the present century is a protest not only against inherited aesthetic conventions but also against the enervating, repressive, and destructive forces of the actual world. One finds a strong plea for "revolt against the past" and for "the transformation of sensibility" in the manifestos of Marinetti and the Futurists. Very striking is the protest of André Breton and the Surrealists against "the mediocre face of reality," against a civilization that feeds on banalities. The major motifs of Breton's explication of Surrealism remind one of the ancient Gnostic rejection of the created order and also of the Gnostic search for the reality that is beyond the unrealities of this prison of the soul. The Surrealist holds that there is no satisfactory basis for art in the existing society; "We must struggle against our fetters with all the energy of despair," says Breton. Even more convinced of the fall is George Grosz, who has recently asserted that he sees no meaning in life. One can document this sense of despair and of tension with the world in the paintings of the "tough-minded" Fernand Léger, with his "refusal to make concession to sentiment, to charm, or to decorative function," and also in the discordant and chaotic tensions of other practitioners of nonrepresentational painting.

If in the face of this art of the fall we ask about the relation between the artist and society, we receive the answer, "The artist is what our torn world has made him," in the words of Herbert Read. Here the artist feels at odds with the world and with the social system. So far from offering participation in the ritual of redemptive powers, the artist points to "the absent God," in Simone Weil's phrase, of the Gnostic.

It is not surprising that Gauguin, having asserted, "Sadness is my forte," should long for a positive religious experience and should, in *The Yellow Christ,* try to participate vicariously in a Breton peasant's act of worship. Nor is it surprising that Henry Moore in *The Madonna* (a work commissioned for the Church of St. Matthew, Northampton) should in his lack of a sense of ritual participation "take refuge in rusticity, . . . a tactful compromise."[1] And it is not surprising that Picasso in seeking to depict suffering in all its intensity of resistance to the demonic should, in his *Guernica,* recapture the "bitter-Christ" motif from Grünewald's *Crucifixion* (the Isenheim Altarpiece).[2]

To be sure there is an art in our time that extols creation as undisrupted. Van Gogh, out of "the desperate violence of his spiritual hunger" in the face of the ruptured meanings in human society, speaks of "a terrible need for—shall I say the word?—for religion. Then I go out and paint the stars." With blue and cobalt, he might have added, I try to paint the "dear deep-down freshness of things" (Hopkins). Some people have asserted that the unbeliever Matisse turned to religious painting only in his old age. His answer was, "In my work I have always sung the glory of God and His creations. . . . The past sixty years had no other meaning than to lead me to this chapel" (at Vence). He might also point to those many paintings in which he has sought to uncover the intrinsic powers of sheer line and color. Like Chagall, he has sought to depict "universal forms" "abstracted from nature" and "endowed with inexhaustible significance" (Chagall). In Cézanne we see the artist who in the face of the vitalities of nature attempts to fuse inner ontological vision with objective being which, in its form-creating power, is allowed to speak for itself. (The analogy with phenomenology here has been noted by disciples of Husserl.)

But is there an art of redemption in our time? In an important sense art as such is redemptive. It represents an ontologically grounded drive toward personal and social integration of the parts and the whole. Matisse expresses this integrating feature of art. "Suppose I set out to paint an interior: I have before me a cupboard; it gives me a sensation of bright red—and I put down a red that satisfies me; immediately a relation is established between this red and the white of the canvas. If I put a green near the red, if I paint in a yellow floor, there must still be between this green, this yellow and the white of the canvas a relation that will be satisfactory to me. But these several tones mutually weaken one another. It is necessary therefore, that the various elements that I use be so *balanced* that they do not destroy one another."[3] He says, in speaking of his work at Vence, "This is not a work that I chose but rather a work for which I have been chosen by fate."

But there are different levels of the redemptive work of art, levels characterized by the relations between form and content, and by the presence of religious style.

Thus the question may be asked, What is redemptive in what we have called "the art of the fall"? Kandinsky, commenting on the doubt and despair of the present age, says we are like an ancient and badly cracked vase dug out of the earth. But, he continues, it is not the primitive shape of the vase which is significant; it is the crack. In this crack—that is, the refinement of the struggle and suffering of passing through this age—the seeds of the future will grow.

Probably, then, it is where this suffering has been felt most poignantly that the art of redemption will appear. One sees it in Rouault's "Son of Man," his flesh "flame-scorched, as rent with the thousand eyes of the peacock," in Marcel Brion's words. But in an age when the artists are impatient with the burden of the past, the art of redemption may perhaps be expected most unimpededly to appear in the nonrepresentational arts, in abstract painting, in architecture, in sculpture, and in music. If I may express a personal preference here, I would point to the music of Stravinsky, for example the *Symphony of Psalms,* where creation, fall, and redemption are all expressed. The redemption was intended from the foundation of the world, but also the redeemed shall always *have been* fallen.

In Alban Berg's *Violin Concerto,* with its twelve-tone scale, one discovers a still greater poignancy in the tragedy of existence, for that tragedy is the work of Death. Here we encounter a realm that appears at a deeper level than the problem of "the arts and society." But here again, art shows that it does not exist for its own sake alone. It has "a heart full of service." And what it serves is ultimately not a matter of calculation but rather of grace.

Notes

1. Edgar Wind, "Traditional Religion and Modern Art," *Art News* 52, no. 3, (1953):21.

2. Michael Ayrton, "A Master of Pastiche," in *New Writing and Daylight,* ed. J. Lehmann (London, 1946).

3. Henri Matisse, *Notes of a Painter,* p. 411.

27 · *Our Unconquered Past*

On Labor Day weekend [in 1967] in Chicago, the National Conference of New Politics held its first meeting, and at this meeting the conference was confronted by a black power caucus. Believing that this conference was to be only "another white, middle-class lib-lab gathering," the members of this caucus abandoned the assembly to meet separately. They framed their own resolutions, and then on Saturday they reappeared at the conference and presented thirteen demands on a take-them or leave-them basis. They also demanded that they be assigned fifty percent of the voting power, even though they numbered less than fifteen percent of those present. The preamble of their demands began:

> We, as black people, believe that the United States' system is committed to the practice of genocide, social degradation, to the denial of political and social self-determination of black people, and cannot reform itself. There must be revolutionary change.

The demands called for immediate reparation for the historic, physical, sexual, mental, political, and economic exploitation of black people. I do not need to rehearse the specifications here; they are already familiar to many. The conference, made up largely of whites, voted by a three to one majority to approve the demands, and without very much discussion. Some of the comments by dissenters have been severe, namely that the method of the black caucus was authoritarian, bludgeoning, and humiliating. "White leadership," said one of the delegates, "never knew what hit it, but learned that black power means white impotence."

This fall I have participated in a [Unitarian Universalist] church conference in New York City where essentially the same tactics were used. In this instance an almost equal proportion of blacks and whites were present. When the assembly attempted to discuss the demands made by the caucus, which had not participated in the previous deliberations of the conference, it was told that discussion was unnecessary: what was called for was unqualified approval of the demands. When a discussion nevertheless ensued, a black woman danced a ritual up and down the aisle, chanting imprecations upon old-fashioned white liberals. The assembly shortly thereafter approved the demands by an overwhelming majority, in

This sermon was delivered on October 13, 1967, at Appleton Chapel, Harvard University. It is reprinted, by permission, from *The Unitarian Christian* 23, no. 3 (Fall 1967).

order to transmit them to the denominational authorities for negotiation and action.

Now I do not propose to consider here the pros and cons of the arguments for accepting or rejecting this kind of procedure. You will not be surprised to learn that some of the dissenters said that the assembly simply exhibited racism in reverse. A comment that has been made regarding the Chicago convention is equally pertinent for the New York church conference: "The convention was an educational experience bordering on shock."

An educational experience it was. Everyone present was made properly aware of the resentment of the deprived blacks in our society. Everyone recognized anew that the processes of democratization in our society have been miserably and intolerably slow and inadequate. When the black power caucus demanded that significant positions of administrative authority be given black members of the churches, we experienced "the shock of recognition" that actual administrative power in the churches as well as in the universities and the government has continued to be decisively white—and racist. As was said in Chicago earlier, "The walls of the convention room began to drip with guilt."

Leaving aside here the question of the validity of black power caucus tactics, we must, it seems to me, affirm that the new ethos implicit in black power reveals a new self-image emerging among the blacks of the caucus mentality. They intend to belong fully to our society and to engender the respect and power due to them both as citizens and as church members. On the other hand, we see that it is high time that whites develop a new self-image that more seriously takes into account what we have actually been and done, and what we have not been and not done. The ghettos are a part of us, they belong to any realistic self-image. When we think of ourselves, we must put alongside suburbia and Harvard Yard the deteriorated neighborhoods and the rats, the white violence and the police brutality, the continuing discrimination in employment and unemployment, the sense of dependency and the sense of humiliation that are nourished and maintained even by the social welfare system. In short, our self-image must somehow include what is across the tracks where the deprived whites as well as blacks and other ethnic minorities live and die. Our white self-image must take into account the fact that the black caucus people do to us what they feel has been done to them. You may say that the black power tactic is something less than a creative thrust; but for the whites it is nevertheless an educational experience that we ignore only to the common detriment. Certainly it will not serve as an educational experience if it gives rise only to a white backlash.

Post-Nazi Germany may provide us with a warning. In some quarters in Germany the memory of the Nazi period has elicited only rationalizations that aim to explain away the evils of the Nazism and responsibility for them. In attacking and revealing these evasions of responsibility the more healthy-minded Germans have asserted that the rationalizations are bound to leave Germany corrupt, indeed to make it more corrupt. These healthy-minded Germans insist on reminding Germany of what they call its unconquered past, *eine unbewältigte Vergangenheit*. If we Americans recognize that ours is the only industrial democracy where one may count upon having riots every summer, we may be willing to admit that we, too, have an unconquered past. But nothing is improved if we only let the walls drip with guilt.

Black power is a gesture, perhaps a ritual, pointing toward a new self-identity for the deprived, yet courageous, black person. It is a thrust in the direction of self-respect, and it surely also aims to elicit respect. It is also, to be sure, in danger of becoming a means of oppression. Yet it can give rise among whites to a broader and more realistic self-image. But neither of these identities is properly more than a transitional phase. If they are to bring healing, they must be pervaded by the spirit of which Erik Erikson speaks, the spirit that "gives the opponent the courage to change even as the challenger changes with the events."

What we all seek is a new and common self-identity that is inclusive and that can be shared, an identity that is determined not to leave the past unconquered. That unfinished business of American democracy obviously calls for the recognition of guilt, but more than that it calls for new works that are meet for repentance, in short, for new beginnings. The power of God is the power of renewal and of reconciliation.

An oracle of Isaiah addresses peoples who had been at strife with each other, the people of Judah and the people of Moab. Yet in the face of catastrophe for Moab, the prophet Isaiah in the name of the Lord of history asks Judah to take counsel and grant justice. And he then points to the promise of the future [Isa. 16:4]:

> When the oppressor is no more
> and destruction has ceased

and he who tramples under foot
has vanished from the land,
Then a throne will be established in steadfast love,
and on it will sit in faithfulness
one who judges and seeks justice
and is swift to do righteousness.

28 · Exiles, Trapped in the Welfare State

In the Old Testament we find an account of one of the first protest marches in history, following upon the freedom march that took the children of Israel out of Egypt and across the Red Sea. But now the protest is not against Pharaoh, it is against Moses and Aaron. Korah and his colleagues, spokesmen of the protest march, say to Moses and Aaron, "You have gone too far! You take too much upon you, seeing all the congregation are holy, every one of them, and the Lord is among them. Why then do you exalt yourselves above the assembly of the Lord?" [Num. 16]

What is remarkable about the story is the reason given for the revolt. Korah and his associates argue that authority should lie with the whole congregation, "for all the congregation are holy, every one of them, and the Lord is among them." That is, all members of the assembly may approach the altar. There is no justification for setting aside certain privileged officers to approach Yahweh. Apparently the protest represents a sort of lay movement, an affirmation of the priesthood of all believers.

If we read the further account of the wanderings in the wilderness we come then chapters later upon the report, "Notwithstanding, the sons of Korah did not die" [Num. 26:11]. And, certainly, they did not. The argument of Korah has been repeated again and again through the centuries. Indeed, the recurrence of the protest traces a red line through history. Again and again the Korahs have been swallowed up only to rise again. Their arguments appear in a variety of formulations, but generally they aim to broaden the basis of community, or to disperse authority and power, to make possible a wider participation.

This essay was originally published in *The Unitarian Christian* 22, no. 4 (Winter 1967). Reprinted by permission.

THE PROPHETIC TRADITION

In important respects, the Old Testament prophets are in the line of Korah. They protest against the aloofness of the monarch, the callousness of the palace guard, the rigid class stratification, the neglect of the poor. Some scholars find anticipations of democracy in various tendencies of the Old Testament period. Whatever may be the validity of this claim, the prophets stressed the responsibility of the entire community for the character of its institutions. The Lord, they said, hath a controversy with the whole people. The entire community is responsible for social injustice.

We cannot say, as was asserted earlier in this century, that the New Testament community was a democracy. It did not even protest against slavery. But it did attempt to humanize the institution of slavery. Moreover, the early Christians insisted that slaves should be eligible for offices in the church; and they emphatically enhanced the status of manual labor. They assumed the responsibility of paying for the vocational training of orphans. They even established credit unions. They also admitted to membership people of all races, giving these people offices within the congregation. Of equal importance is the fact that the constituency of the first Christian congregations was largely from the lower classes. The New Testament scholar F. C. Grant has characterized the early Christian movement as one of the greatest agrarian protests in history. These churches soon extended themselves to embrace other classes. Again we meet the principle of Korah. Besides transcending race and class, the early Christians assigned to the whole congregation the responsibility of recognizing and confirming (or rejecting) the authenticity of the working of the Holy Spirit in those leaders who claimed its sanction. For this reason the early Christian congregation, formerly characterized by liberal scholars as democratic, is now spoken of as pneumatocratic (from the word *pneuma*, meaning spirit-directed). The Spirit that directed the community was believed to be available to the whole congregation. In the words of Korah, "all the congregation are holy, every one of them," slaves and all. More than this, St. Paul insisted that God hath tempered the body of the community together, "that the members should have the same care for one another. Whether one member suffer, all the members suffer with it; or one member be honored, all the members rejoice with it" [1 Cor. 12:25–26].

The main line of the churches through the Middle Ages and the Reformation period followed the policy of Moses more than that of Korah. It was the "heretical" sects that stressed the equality of church members.

Some of these sects insisted that elders and preachers should be elected by local congregations. In the seventeenth century in England they asserted that every member (man and woman alike) had the right and the responsibility to participate in shaping policy. We require a church, they said, in which the Spirit may blow where it listeth, and especially in which the concerns of the minority shall receive a respectful hearing. Indeed, they in some instances asserted that it is precisely through a minority that the Spirit of God is likely to find utterance. The modern democratic idea, as Lord Acton (the Roman Catholic historian) has said, was born in these small heretical conventicles. By analogy from the doctrine of the free church, the idea of the democratic political order came to birth. It is not too much to say that certain of the constructive principles of the Constitution of the United States issued from these sectarian movements. This movement from the seventeenth century to the twentieth served in important ways as the midwife of the middle-class, a new class struggling for liberation from the status-bound social order of feudalism. Thus the seventeenth-century religious movement had consequences for economic as well as political life. Of special significance for political life was the new impetus given to the demand for new rights, particularly to the demand for the rule of law, even for the monarch. The Levellers in England, for example, demanded a written constitution, regular elections, the extension of suffrage, and equality under the law. John Lilburne, the leader of the Levellers, in making these demands, had the benefit of the influence of the towering English jurist Sir Edward Coke.

One of the most dramatic events in the history of English law was Sir Edward's protest, under James I, that the King "cannot properly take any cause out of any courts and give judgment upon it himself." On another occasion, Sir Edward confounded and offended the King by citing Bracton, saying "that the King should not be under man, but under God and the Laws." Sir Edward reports that on this occasion the King "fell into that high indignation as the like was never known in him, looking and speaking fiercely with bended fist, offering to strike him. Which the Lord Coke perceiving fell flat on all four." As Catherine Drinker Bowen comments, "It was a tremendous scene: a king's fist raised against a judge. . . . Very likely, Coke did fall on his face. It was that or a cell in the Tower. . . . But the next morning a new prohibition, under Coke's seal, went out to the High Commission from the Court of Common Pleas." Sir Edward Coke did end up in the Tower. "Notwithstanding, the sons of Korah did not die." The Boston Tea Party and the Declaration of Independence were of their doing.

We have adumbrated three seminal principles: the principle of Korah that all persons may approach the altar as equals, the prophetic principle that the community is responsible for the character of its institutions and that "members should have the same care for one another," and the principle of Sir Edward Coke and the seventeenth-century Protestant "heretics" that all persons should be equal under the law.

THE EMERGENCE OF THE WELFARE STATE

Bearing these principles in mind, I would like now to turn to the contemporary scene. In 1911 Great Britain established a limited program to insure low-income groups against some of the high costs of illness. Less than a year later, Louis D. Brandeis, then a lawyer in private practice, urged the National Conference on Charities and Correction to support a program of social insurance. During the presidential campaign of 1912 the Progressive Party, under Theodore Roosevelt, adopted the proposal and made national health insurance one of the main planks of its platform. This action was of small moment at the time, but like a mustard seed it grew into a mighty tree. Indeed, it turned out to be only a branch of a larger tree, one of the branches of later vintage, for Medicare legislation has been enacted only recently. Meanwhile, we as a nation have developed the so-called welfare state, and all of us, people of all classes, live under the increased security of the tree, even if we do not rest entirely in its branches. I do not need to rehearse the description of all these branches. We can stress the fact, however, that in the past half-century an enormous change has taken place through the qualification of the older bourgeois individualism and through the advent of what the World Council of Churches two decades ago began to call the social ethics of "the responsible society." This change is an expression of what the lawyer calls an extension of liability. A recognition of the responsibility of the whole community for the character and consequence of institutions and for at least the minimal welfare of all citizens has gained wider and wider acceptance from year to year. Meanwhile, also, a new strength has appeared among blacks, the strength to give shape to an importunate demand for the extension of civil and social rights, to the demand that they be permitted to enjoy social and economic and legal equality. The sons of Korah are on the march again. And there are those who would like to have the earth open her mouth and swallow them up.

If we consider current developments in the welfare state we observe a tendency that is so familiar in human affairs that we may speak of it almost as a law of human behavior. Stating it in colloquial terms, we may liken this tendency to what happens when we try to carry a crowded bag of potatoes in an imperfect paper poke. The paper bag tears, and we quickly try to prevent the potatoes from falling out. But soon after we have stopped this breakthrough, another tear appears, and out go the potatoes again.

So was it in the period of individualism. Just when the successful people thought full prosperity was only around the corner, cyclical unemployment and other structural maladjustments supervened. And so it is in the welfare state. Having remedied the worst feature of the old laissez-faire economy, we are now beginning to see deficiencies in the structure of the welfare state. We are entering a period in which these failures are giving rise to fundamental criticism, not the criticism from the diehards or from the John Birch Society, but criticism from within the welfare state itself.

The welfare state in its origin and development has been a response to the demand for "the responsible society." It has grown out of the recognition of collective responsibility for at least a minimal social security. As a consequence, enormous changes have been introduced in the areas of public housing, education, minimum wage, farm-price support, Medicare, and equal voting. Not all has gone well. In some instances the failures have been due to racial discrimination, as the demonstrations and the riots remind us. And the end is not yet here.

But there is one deficiency in the administration of the welfare state which has little to do with race discrimination. It is almost a built-in deficiency; and it discriminates against white and black alike. This deficiency has not yet gained general public attention. What is fundamentally at stake here is the equal protection of the law. What is at stake is that for the sake of which John Lilburne, the Leveller, was whipped through the streets of London, and for which Sir Edward Coke allowed himself to be imprisoned in the Tower.

Equal Protection of the Law

I have said that those who suffer from this lack of equal protection are both black and white. A notorious example of this general discrimination against the poor is the systematic exclusion of a large number of citizens from eligibility for social welfare benefits because of legislative requirements regarding length of residence. Another example of discrimination that affects people of all races is the imposition of ceilings on public-welfare grants in such a way as to penalize large families, ostensibly to depress the birth rate among the poor. Yet the children of a large family can be just as hungry as the children in a small one. In some states, parents suffering from these restrictions have been brought into court on charges of physical neglect, and the children have been forcibly removed from their homes.

Probably the most obvious abuses of the poor result from administrative practices, either because legislative definitions are vague or because the administrators are given very broad discretionary powers. These discretionary powers inevitably leave room for arbitrary and inconsistent decisions. The vagueness of the legislation is often due to the legislators' lack of any clear concept of social welfare. The task of interpreting the statutes therefore falls upon the welfare bureaucracy or upon the individual social worker. In many instances the administrators may abuse their discretionary powers in order to express their unfavorable moral judgments with regard to poverty. In these instances the social-welfare agency becomes punitive. These punitive actions are by no means constitutional, for they violate the principle of equal protection.

The American Civil Liberties Union in Chicago has made a study of abuses in the administration of welfare benefits among the poor. The most frequent complaint among people on welfare relief is that payments have been withheld. Recipients often do not know, and cannot find out, why their checks have been withheld. Add to this the difficulty of being admitted to the relief rolls. One must send away for a marriage certificate, one must demonstrate the amount of the previous year's income, one must meet demands for information regarding possibly responsible relatives. I shall not detail the frustrations that arise if the children are illegitimate. Punitive treatment is readily possible here. Most notorious of all are the after-midnight raids carried out by the police in search of a cohabiting man.

Richard Cloward, professor of social work at Columbia University, prepared for the national conference of the American Civil Liberties Union a document regarding the unjust treatment of the poor under the present social-welfare system. It reveals that the constitutionality of many policies is in question, that the broad discretionary powers are abused arbitrarily, and that thereby the agencies save money. Moreover, social workers sometimes fail to inform the poor of what they are entitled to in services, food and clothing, and emergency help. Commenting on the hostile attitudes of some social workers, Cloward cites the finding of the Moreland commission in New York: "Observations in the offices and evaluation of handling of clients . . . revealed an attitude of annoyance and disregard of human factors, and in many cases almost an 'adversary' rather than a helping relationship." One of Cloward's most severe indictments is that the poor are denied one of the elemental rights of a citizen, the right to a hearing.

Recently the Civil Liberties Union in New York City has proposed establishing a civilian-complaint review board. In the statement proposing this, the CLU asserts that "violations of individual rights by Welfare Department officials can be divided into two categories: first, deprivation of benefits and services which the client is entitled to receive, and second, personal indignities that may be directed against clients, often in violation of the clients' constitutional rights."

As we have already observed, a basic complaint throughout the nation is that the constitutionality of many types of administrative decisions remains untested; and the repeated demand is for the right to a hearing. In Massachusetts a new group of mothers organized a march to the State House on Beacon Hill in Boston. Mothers for Adequate Welfare they call themselves: M.A.W., pronounced *maw.* And what are their demands? They not only request more money for food, housing, and clothing; they also claim the right to know the rules under which society pays them, the right to privacy in discussing their problems with welfare workers.

The original Social Security Act of three decades ago made provision for fair-hearing procedures for all federally aided assistance programs, but apparently the states have not actually adopted the procedures or they have been extremely slow in doing so. The President's Advisory Council on Public Welfare, in its admirable and extensive report published in June [1966], gives detailed recommendations regarding "the rights of individuals under public welfare" and then states that "there is a great urgency for the emphatic assertion of public welfare's responsibility for the protection of individual rights, and for the scrupulous observance of the individual rights, and for the scrupulous observance of the individual rights of the people it serves." In 1773 it was the Boston Tea Party; in 1966, the Mothers for Adequate Welfare marching on the State House to ask for equal protection under the law. These mothers are the daughters of Korah, saying "You have gone too far, seeing that all the congregation are holy, every one of them."

REMEDY

It requires no fertile imagination to recognize the consequences of the frustrations of which I have given only a few examples. The principle consequences are apathy, cynicism, and despair—the soil of irrationality, criminality, and violence. A sense of inferiority, felt as a consequence of being relatively deprived of rights others enjoy, engenders anger, and it turns inward in the form of self-hatred, or of violence against family members and neighbors. The drama, in short, is a tragic one. "The essence of tragedy," as Alfred North Whitehead has observed, "is not unhappiness. It resides in the solemnity of the remorseless working of things." The remorseless working of things I have been describing has produced in the midst of our society a host of exiles, of trapped exiles, in the welfare state, exiles from the benefits of dignity and the equal protection of the law. But the remorseless working of things does not end in self-hatred. It can explode outward against the entire system.

The remedy that is being suggested, namely, the equal protection of the law through the extension of the right to a hearing, the development of a procedure for airing grievances, will of course bring new problems. It will require a proliferation of rules and of new personnel to apply the rules. But this is what has been required in the court system that obtains in other sectors of the society.

Professor Cloward thinks the system of welfare he has described is incorrigible. Human dignity can be restored, he thinks, only through the abolition of the entire system and the introduction of a guaranteed income that will permit people to be autonomous and to exercise the control of the consumer. The end purpose is to stop treating the poor as *things* and to treat them as *persons*. At the other side of the spectrum from Professor Cloward is the conservative economist of the University of Chicago, Professor Milton Friedman, who recommends the introduction of a negative income tax in order to eliminate the welfare system. These and other remedies are on the agenda for much future discussion, especially as poor whites and blacks become better organized to present their grievances. One should by no means deplore the fact that they are beginning to organize. That they are doing so is an assertion of human dignity, a sign of a new self-identity, a sign of the vitality of democracy. It can be a step in the direction of increased social participation and responsibility.

> We been down so long
> we ain't got no way to go but up.
> Go tell it on the mountain,
> to let my people go.

At the present moment our obligation is to see the reality and enormity of the prototypical problem of our welfare state, to recognize that the

Establishment is confronted again by the sons of Korah and that the earth will not open and swallow them up. They are asking to be brought out of their exile into a fuller humanity. As we hear their demands we may recognize that like Lord Coke these exiles are asserting that "the King is not under man but under God and law." But more than that, if we see these exiles in their plight, we may be able to hear in a new way the words of St. Paul, that God hath tempered the body of the community together, that the members should have the same care for one another, "whether one member suffer, all the members suffer with it, or one member be honored, all the members rejoice with it."

29 · *Broken Cisterns and Earthen Vessels*

> *They have forsaken me,*
> *the fountain of living waters,*
> *and hewed out cisterns for themselves,*
> *broken cisterns that can hold no water.*
>   Jeremiah 2:13

> *But we have this treasure in earthen vessels,*
> *to show that the transcendent power belongs to God and not to us.*
>   II Corinthians 4:7

In the Second Book of Kings is recorded a remarkable and instructive story that very well symbolizes one of the major religions of humanity, a religion against which prophetic religion must always struggle. Naaman was a commander of the army of Syria, and a mighty man of valor; but he was also a leper. In search of a cure, he made a pilgrimage to Samaria to appeal to Elisha. In response to his plea Elisha told him to dip himself seven times in the River Jordan. Naaman obeyed the instruction. "He went down and dipped himself seven times in the Jordan; and his flesh was restored like the flesh of a little child, and he was clean." Out of gratitude Naaman now returned to Elisha and offered him a present. But Elisha would accept no gift. Then Naaman made a strange request. He asked that he be given two mules' burden of earth, saying that henceforth

This sermon, previously unpublished, was given at the Vassar College Chapel in Pough-keepsie, N.Y., on February 18, 1965.

he would not offer burnt offering or sacrifice to any god but the Lord of Israel.

Why did Naaman wish to take with him to Syria two mules' burden of soil from Samaria? The answer is that he, like his contemporaries in Samaria as well as in Syria, believed that in order to worship the god of any country it was necessary to stand on earth taken from that god's territory. The gods of the time were territorial gods.

The belief in a territorial god we call primitive. Nevertheless, it is a belief that in some form appears among all "civilized" peoples. We may trace its heritage not only from preprophetic Hebrew religion. The heritage stems also from the civic religion of the ancient pagan city-state, in which each city had its own gods and its own local cultus. The tendency of all religion is to be or to become territorial. In our own time we have seen territorial religion most conspicuously in Nazism, the religion of blood and soil. Here we encounter territorial religion at its worst—in a totalitarian fanaticism that enforces absolute uniformity. Not all territorial religions have been so absolute in their claims.

In the view of the prophet Jeremiah, territorial religion—the worship of Baal—puts its confidence in broken cisterns that can hold no water. It knows not the Lord of all history who seeks a universality that lets "justice roll down like the waters." It tries to live from a narrow self-enclosure that cuts it off from the judging, transforming power of God. Jesus likewise took up the struggle against territorial religion. In the face of the pagan city-state the early Christians appealed to Jesus' words, "Render unto Caesar that which is Caesar's, and unto God that which is God's." They asserted that there is an authority higher than that of Caesar and the territory. But territorialism was not permanently overcome. Indeed, it was restored by the church itself. The Swiss historian Jacob Burckhardt reminds us that even in the period of the Reformation the confessions of Christianity were determined strictly according to their territory. These confessions ostensibly repudiated any merely territorial concept of religion. Nevertheless, they reverted to it in their competition with each other. Whether Catholic or Protestant, the religion that prevailed in each territory was established or protected by force. In 1526, eleven years after the beginning of the Reformation, the principle was adopted into what we call the throne-and-altar tradition.

In the period of the Reformation the individual believer was confronted by a distressing choice. One could adopt the religion of the prince, or leave the territory, or suffer persecution. Social stability, it was held, required this policy. As a consequence, the Reformation turned out to be a period of migration, of exile. The Pilgrims migrated from England to Holland, and thence to Plymouth. Many of the exiles who came to America brought with them the mentality of territorial religion. This territorial mentality obtained in all of the colonies except Baptist Rhode Island and Quaker Pennsylvania. In the eighteenth and nineteenth centuries all of the American colonies adopted religious pluralism, and the principle of voluntaryism replaced the old territorialism. They came to see that the stability and strength of the commonwealth, so far from requiring uniformity, demand freedom and diversity of faith.

The protest against the territorial conception first appeared decisively with the advent of the Protestantism of the Radical Reformation. Here we encounter the demand for the separation of church and state. Political influences were to be eliminated from the church, and ecclesiastical control from the state. These radical reformers rejected also the old concept of Christendom, the view that a civilization can be Christian, and that a nation in its entirety is the constituency of the national church. They denied that the individual becomes a Christian by merely being born and confirmed in so-called Christian territory. Membership in the church, they held, must be a matter of individual choice. For this reason they rejected infant baptism. We have given here an oversimple, abbreviated account. But we have indicated what the radical Protestants had in mind when they rejected the principle: The religion of the prince is the religion of the territory.

One other important thing must be added to the story. Territorial religion, even though it claimed to be the religion of all the people of a territory, from time immemorial served the welfare of only a part of the people. In many instances the protest against territorial religion bespoke the demands of people who previously had been suppressed, of people who had been prevented from playing anything but a subservient, passive role. It asked for social reform. This protest is already evident in the proclamations of the Old Testament prophets. The New Testament scholar F. C. Grant has spoken of the early church as the expression of "one of the greatest agrarian protests in history," a protest against the domination of the ruling classes in the cities, the bureaucracy in Jerusalem. An important segment of the Radical Reformation in its turn represented the emergence of hitherto suppressed classes into a new freedom and into fuller participation in the common life of church and society. Indeed, modern Anglo-Saxon democracy as we cherish it came to birth and developed under the aegis of radical Protestant protest against the bureaucratized elite of territorial religion.

We see, then, that a veritable epic of religious and political struggle may be conjured up from the ancient story of Naaman who asked Elisha for two mules' burden of earth. Viewed from the perspective of human effort, this heritage of prophetic religion is no mean accomplishment; it appeared on the stage of history "not without dust and heat." Viewed from the perspective of Judeo-Christian faith, however, the heritage is not so much a human achievement as it is a response to the judging, transforming power of God. The judging power of God destroys faith in the broken cisterns of human contriving, in the false and enforced securities of territorial religion. The transforming power of God engenders the faith that we have the treasure of life in earthen vessels whereof the transcendent power belongs to God and not to us.

Now, we would like to believe that the attitude prefigured by Naaman no longer obtains among us. We would like to believe that our religion today depends primarily upon individual freedom of choice, and that it is not bound to a territory. But, in fact, we must recognize that in one way or another certain features of territorial religion remain or reappear. One could, for example, easily defend the thesis that the modern nation-state is the successor of the old territorial church. Actually, there is a wide spectrum along which new forms of territorial religion can appear. Let us consider two important points on this spectrum: first, the territorial religion implicit in that new mechanism of uniformity, the mass media of communication, and second, the cramping burden of poverty imposed upon those excluded by top-heavy territorialism.

A new and pervasive form of territorialism has been brought upon us in the past half-century by the modern revolution in communications. The radio, television, the moving pictures, and the newspapers constitute the almost perfect machinery for achieving widespread uniformity. This uniformity is producing among us something akin to a new territorial religion.

Community after community has witnessed the taking over of its newspapers by syndicate publishers and has suffered a marked reduction of independent editorial judgment. This centralization of power in the idea industries has a marked influence in politics. The moving pictures are similarly controlled by a small number of major producers. The product reminds one of the definition of mass media given by Gilbert Seldes: "repetitive gestures on the producing end, and passive enjoyment for the consumer." The motion picture is the last place where criticism of the so-called American way of life can be expected. As one critic has asserted, the motion pictures try to show that Americans are happy because they are "stuffed with turkey, God, and new models of automobiles." It has become a major concern of public policy to determine how to reduce the export of the typical American motion picture and to promote films that present something other than crime, sex, and spectacle. Fortunately, one can find American films of artistic integrity and moral realism.

Television, dominated by the advertising agencies, joined the drive towards uniformity and conformity by producing what David Susskind has called "trivia and pap," which are "reducing us spiritually, emotionally and intellectually." On even a higher level this mass medium tends to produce conformity by avoiding controversial issues, issues that might reduce the effectiveness of the advertising. Fairfax Cone, an executive of a leading advertising agency, has succinctly stated that the test is "how much the public can stand of the very same stuff; how many westerns, how many private eyes, how many guessing games, how many situation comedies."

Regardless of the superior quality of some programs, the general effect of television and of the cinema upon the national mentality derives from a characteristic feature of these mass media. As a one-way form of communication they produce a sort of narcotic apathy. I know of no more devastating description of television than the one offered by the psychiatrist Dr. Eugene David Glynn—that in the main it prevents our being adults, it encourages infantile dependency. The characterization reminds one of the status of infant baptism in traditional territorial religion. Television, he says, offers a mother-substitute by providing "warmth, sound, constancy, availability, a steady going without ever a demand for return, the encouragement to passive surrender and envelopment." By means of television, he says, our age is becoming "the oral age, the age of intake and being fed, when the mouth is the vital organ in relation to the world . . . the counting on someone else to supply satisfaction and security, not glory, comfort in the group, not individual prominence." Dr. Glynn, of course, does not consign television wholly to the devil. He urges that it be used in such a way as to elicit audience participation and to liberate people from conformity and dependency.

You may ask, what has all this to do with religion? The answer is that the ethos, the value preferences, the characteristic sensitivities, the tacit philosophy of life of the population, including the church population, are defined and largely determined by those mass media. These definitions of ethos and sensitivity are on the way to becoming our territorial religion.

Viewing the mass media as a whole, we must see in them an illustration of the old principle, the religion of the prince is the religion of the territory. Our princes of the mass media are the principal purveyors of our increasingly uniform territorial religion. These purveyors, to be sure, claim to give the public what it wants, but the claim cannot conceal the compulsive desire of the purveyors to define what the public wants.

What the public wants is what the purveyors define, or at least what the purveyors do not want the public to want. For over a decade I have watched "Days of Our Lives," because it is available at lunchtime, and occasionally "General Hospital" in the afternoon. One must distinguish between what is provided in the morning (for the middle-class or upper-middle-class housewife and the elderly) and what is available in the afternoon (primarily for teenagers). In the morning the daytime serial, or "soap opera," is often a moralistic tale indicating the evil consequences of male infidelity at the office. Here the integrity of the family is by implication extolled, it hopes and its anxieties are disclosed.

In the afternoon the teenagers receive their full quota of attention. It is estimated that eleven million teenagers watch "General Hospital" five hours each week. Consequently, nothing can be scheduled at this time at the school. Parents know that at this hour most of the teenagers are somewhere watching television.

Certain subjects to be sure are excluded. Procter and Gamble's monitors (or their like) make sure that nothing about high prices, nothing critical of the socioeconomic system, is shown; nothing of literary quality intrudes, for this would give the viewer a sense of inferiority; and certainly nothing about seemingly attractive alternative conceptions of society, nothing, for example, about socialism, appears.

Generally, one finds in a soap opera three or four subplots or triangles; heterosexuals irresistibly fall in and out of love—it just "happens," and one cannot control it—practicing what might be called "serial polygamy." All of this appears in the *mise en scène* of suburban America.

What are the positive, evaluative elements of the soap opera? In the first place, we should agree with Margaret Mead who held that the primary interest is not entertainment. This may be the manifest interest, but the latent, and more pervasive, interest is in the depiction of a variety of life-styles (to be sure, a strictly limited number of them). In her study of the response of teenagers Margaret Mead found that the girls' sophistication was about two years in advance of boys of the same age; the girls noticed the style of clothing or the hairdo, or they noted and compared the actors and actresses. The boys of the same calendar age were primarily interested in the plot and in the hero in conflict with the villain. Some years ago the researchers for CBS started on the assumption that the young teenagers "identified with" the Lone Ranger, thus "compensating for" their dependent status in the family. To their surprise, these boys "identified with" Tonto, thus revealing "a heart full of service" to the follower and helper of the Ranger.

The daytime serial, then, seems to provide personae with some of whom the viewer may identify. I became fully aware of this when in "Days of Our Lives" Marlena, the admirable psychiatrist, a sort of moral anchor person along with the grandparents, was reported to have been killed. I could not control my emotion, and wept. On the next day one learned that not she but her (absent) sister had been killed. Of course, if one misses the scenario for a week or a month or two, monthly plot-summaries are available in *The Soap Opera Newsletter.* Unlike "legitimate" drama, the soap opera has no beginning, middle, or end. It runs on for years, thus giving little room for the catharsis that clears away the "accidents" of human being in order to reveal the essence.

But there is another side to the daytime serial. I noticed in the *New York Times* that the rating of "Days of Our Lives" had been going down. I therefore watched to see how the rating would be recovered. The answer to my question seemed to be quite clear in the sequel; there was an increase of violence and of sex in bed. It should be noted that for years one of the figures in "Days of Our Lives" has been a gentleman criminal.

The daytime serial is definitely for the middle class or the upper middle class. Poor people are not presented, and there are no gas-station attendants or even characters with middle-class occupations such as that of a plumber. The cast of characters belongs to an achieving, a consumer, society, not to the unsuccessful or the neglected. No twinges of conscience emerge in this area.

Something of what I have said here was already meticulously analyzed forty years ago by my former colleague, the anthropologist-sociologist W. Lloyd Warner of the University of Chicago (see *Genetic Psychology Monographs,* February 1948).

A question remains for me. Why are these soap operas not studied in theological schools or in courses on religious education? For there we find an important ingredient of our territorial religion.

We come now to a second segment on the spectrum of territorial religion. As we have already observed, the religion of the territory has always tended to be the religion of certain groups within the territory. It has not represented as broad a constituency as the term implies. In each age the territorial religion has decisively expressed the concerns of only a segment of the community. In one age this segment is the nobility; in another it may be an economic hierarchy. From the time of Amos and Jeremiah prophetic religion has tried to expose the pretensions of the dominant groups and to arouse concern for the needs of the neglected and the rejected. Prophetic religion in our time still has a mission to perform in the face of territorial religion.

I have just been looking into a memorandum on poverty in the United States, an unpublished document of the Committee on Economic Development, prepared by economist Howard Bowen, President of Grinnell College. In this document we find what we rarely hear about through the mass media, or even from the pulpits.

What should one select as typical from this substantial and extensive report? On one page we read that two and a half million dwellings are occupied by more than 1.5 persons per room. On another page that, according to a 1948 tabulation, 21.4 percent of all manufacturing workers received less than $1 per hour (or $2,000 per year on an annual basis, assuming full-time employment); on still another page, that in 1950 ten percent of all persons twenty-five years of age and over had completed less than five years of school. The condition of a large segment of the farming population is appalling. 1,670,000 families have a cash income of less than $1000 per year. This poverty is a part of *us*, the part concealed by the territorial religion of the successful or the nearly successful.

We recognize that the overcoming of poverty as such is not equivalent to the advent of the kingdom of heaven. A rise in the standard of living is no guarantee of improved standards of life. But this truth does not conceal the price exacted by territorial religion that preaches comfort to the comfortable and that cultivates blindness to the brokenness of our cisterns. Nor does it conceal the stupendous difference between the size of the military budget and that of the anti-poverty program.

We have spoken of some of the ravages of territorial religion as they have thwarted human freedom in the past and in our own time. Our description is of course incomplete. Here there is ample room for disagreement. But it is clear that territorial religion continues among us, in our submission to the religion of the prince and in our devotion to the idols of clan and class. We are still like Naaman, worshipping on two mules' burden of local soil.

What is wrong with territorial religion? It is a commitment to blood and soil. It represents the spatialization of religion. It is a major form of idolatry. It is a mechanism for protection against criticism. Karl Marx has astutely observed that whenever the economic system is under attack one protects it by wrapping the flag around it. Winston Churchill tried to oppose the Labor Party by claiming that it was alien, that it was un-British.

Faith in the Lord of history, the Lord of all nations who has made us all of one blood, demands that our earthen vessels be open to that which is beyond them, to that which breaks open the self-styled holy race, the holy nation, the holy economic system, the holy *status quo*. From on high comes the command, Thou shalt have no other gods before me.

St. Paul viewed the powers that enslave humanity as cosmic powers. Our bondage to them, however, was due to our guilt as well as to our fate. Everyone makes a contribution to their rule, to our reliance on broken cisterns. But Paul bears witness to a power that resists and overcomes these hostile powers. It is not a visible thing like the worldly powers. It is a treasure, he says, hidden in earthen vessels, to show that the transcending power belongs to God and not to us. This is the power that calls us out of enslavement under the "weak and beggarly element" into a new community of faith, into a transforming community that seeks independence of the principalities and powers of this world. This is the perennial thrust of prophetic religion. We can test our own grasp of this prophetic religion. The test is our awareness of the judgment that lies upon the gods of our territory. It is the quality of our independence in faith and of our response to the transforming power that opens the way to renewal and to a community of justice and humanity.

30 · *The Religious Problem of Peace*

The story is told that during the years of his exile Dante was once apprehended in a small village through which he was wandering and was hailed
into a convent court as a vagrant. When the officer of the court asked him
what he was looking for, he replied in a wistful tone of voice, "*La pace*" —
peace. In speaking this word, Dante expressed the aspiration of the saints
and the prophets of the ages who, recognizing humanity's exile into a far
country, have longed to be at one with God and with humanity. To Dante
himself the word "peace" was no accidental or whimsical reply. It is the
word that appears in that memorable line of *The Divine Comedy* which
Matthew Arnold singled out as one of the touchstones of great poetry: "In
His will is our peace." Manifestly, peace was for Dante a problem of religion. Indeed, his unhappy state of mind when he was brought into the
court was no doubt due in part to the fact that he was in exile from
the city of Florence precisely because of the religious strife of the time,
the struggle between the Guelphs and the Ghibellines.

We have here an epitome of much of the history of religion, an illustration of the paradox of religion as it has been known. Religion exalts
peace but is itself caught in the toils of religious strife. It offers peace
only as the reward of struggle and suffering. Was it not the Prince of
Peace himself who said, "I bring not peace but a sword," and, yet again,
was it not the man of sorrows who was to be crucified on Golgotha who
said, "My peace I leave with you"?

RELIGION AND CONFLICT

The close association between religion and conflict, of course, is a commentary not only on the nature of religion but also on human nature. "To
fight," says George Santayana, "is a radical instinct; if men have nothing
else to fight over, they will fight over words, fancies, or women, or because they dislike each other's looks, or because they have met walking
the opposite directions." One is reminded of the account of the two Maori
tribes, one of which sent a message to the other in the middle of a battle:
"We have no more ammunition. Unless you will send us some, we shall

This essay, here abridged and with a new addendum, was originally published in *New
Perspectives on Peace*, George B. Huszar (Chicago: The University of Chicago Press, 1944).
Reprinted by permission.

have to stop fighting"—a request that was promptly granted. The request has been made and granted in other times and places, too.

Conflict is of the essence of life. Without conflict, neither individuality nor social change is possible. War may be a dispensable invention, a transient institution; but, even if it were to disappear as an instrument of social policy, new modes of conflict and change would soon be devised. For that matter, peace is itself a dynamic process, an orderly mode of resolving conflict.

Since conflict is of the essence of life, it is perforce an inextricable aspect of religion. Except in stagnant civilizations, religious movements have usually had their beginning, their middle, and, alas, their end in strife. There has been a deep conflict with Christianity itself, not to speak of the conflicts between Christianity and Judaism and between Christianity and the other religions. Indeed, the contentious element in the Christianity of the sixteenth and seventeenth centuries became so repulsive to the people of that time that there arose a widespread skepticism concerning all religion.

In ordinary parlance, religion is identified with an explicit belief in God, or in some higher power, with a belief in some creed that sets forth a theory of the creation of the world, of human estrangement in sin, and a method of salvation from sin. The distinguishing mark of religion in this narrower sense is an explicit orientation to what is conceived to be the Controller of Destiny. It is, of course, understood that this orientation is supposed to affect the believer's major choices and preferences in life.

But such a definition is far too narrow for understanding modern piety. A broader definition is needed which will take into account other orientations of an essentially similar function. Accordingly, the word "religion" has today taken on a wider meaning than that of the traditional definition. In current discussion the word "religion" is no longer interpreted exclusively as a belief in the supernatural. In its wider connotation the term may be said to signify any explicit or implicit orientation to whatever is regarded as worthy of serious and ultimate concern. Since everyone entertains some conception of "the totality of things conceived as a realm of meaning," everyone may be said to be religious in this broader sense of the term. That is, all persons are religious in actuality if not by intention, for all persons tend to regard something as worthy of serious and ultimate concern.

According to this broader definition, we are in a situation somewhat similar to that of the bourgeois gentleman of Molière's play who discovered that he had, without his knowing it, been speaking prose all his life. To be sure, many individuals seldom articulate the ultimate principles by which they live; yet some principle or principles are the covert presuppositions of their thought and action. They are woven into the social tradition in which personality structure is formed.

Thus the difference between the narrower and the broader definition of religion is that one describes an orientation that is overtly and explicitly religious, while the other includes what is implicitly religious. The one orientation is religious by intention; the other is religious not by intention but in substance. In some instances it is, of course, difficult to draw a sharp line between the overt and the covert types of religion. Thus, communism, fascism, racism, intense nationalism (such as 100 percent Germanism or 100 percent Americanism), or attachment to a particular social, economic, or political system, may in varying ways assume an explicitly religious character. Hence, some critics of National Socialism have characterized it as an "ersatz religion," that is, a substitute religion. We also frequently hear such phrases as "the religion of democracy," "the religion of science," and "the religion of communism."

Fundamentally, religious attitudes are present in a society even though that society may seem to be secularized, for all orientations at bottom claim some sort of ultimacy; they claim some decisive role in determining basic preferences and choices in human life. They relate the human being to the Controller of Destiny or to that which is worthy of ultimate devotion. In short, they point either to God or to that which serves in God's place. For this reason it is correct to say that theology still reigns as the queen of the sciences. It is the science concerned with ultimate orientations.

Sacramental and Prophetic Religion

Now, in approaching the problem of peace as a religious problem, we must bear in mind not only the ultimately religious character of all basic orientations in human life but also the wide variety of orientations possible. We cannot here attempt to give even a bare outline of this variety. It must suffice to observe two principal types of orientation, which I shall call the "sacramental" and the "prophetic." These two types of orientation are found in both the overt and the covert, in both the ecclesiastical and the nonecclesiastical, religions.

The sacramental type of orientation is the dominant type all over the world and throughout human history in both the overt and the covert religions. It finds the supremely worthful, the central meaning of life, the holy, in certain finite forms; that is, it regards particular realities and forms as the bearers of the most meaningful, the holy. Certain things and acts receive a sacramental quality. In these particular natural and social realities the individual finds the ties that give security and a feeling of belonging and being rooted somewhere. In primitive societies these sacramental realities take the form, for example, of totemic worship, with its concomitant "collective representations" and social patterns. In more highly developed societies also, the sacramental rootage is found in the symbols, institutions, and rituals that give support and character to the general personality structure of the constituent members of the society. These natural and social realities are what are known as "primary ties," and they find expression in the patterns and symbols of a social or ecclesiastical system. John Dewey centered his attention on this type of orientation when he said: "Intellectually, religious emotions are not creative but conservative. They attach themselves readily to the current view of the world and consecrate it."

The sacramental aspect of religion provides a sort of consecration of reality as given, whether it be the nation, the race, the authoritarian church, the bourgeois church, or a fixed social system. In all these instances the holy reality tends to be viewed as once and for all delivered. Security and richness of life are promised to all who will conform. Through conformity the individual and the society are provided warm, nourishing support and a sense of at-homeness in the world. Thus habit, the great flywheel of society, and obedience, the centripetal force in that flywheel, are maintained. Radical criticism is taboo. This does not mean, however, that no sense of tension is possible in the sacramental attitude. The surrounding society may be subjected to criticism, but the faithful will be exhorted to return to the lost, or almost lost, securities and holy realities of an idealized past.

It would seem, then, that the sacramental attitude is both indispensable and inadequate—indispensable for its umbilical primary ties, and inadequate because of its tendency toward self-deification. One is reminded of William Hazlitt's remark that "the trouble with the man of one idea is not that he has an idea but that he has no other."

Protest against the domination of the primary ties gives rise to the second basic religious attitude—the prophetic attitude. This protest may take the form of rational criticism and skepticism, as with the Greek sophists, or it may take the form of prophetically and explicitly religious criticism, as with the Old Testament prophets, primitive Christianity, Muslim reform movements, radical Protestantism, and eighteenth-century religious liberalism. It may be revolutionary in its implications, or it may adopt the tempo of gradualism. In any event, it presupposes a sacramental attitude in the surrounding culture, and it subjects the sacramental realities, the consecrated and established mores and institutions, to untethered criticism and discussion. It protests against the destructive consequences of the traditional loyalties and points to new forms of fulfillment, and then it presses its criticism deeper by unveiling the blasphemous, the ideological, or the irrational character of the accepted sacramental attitude.

The prophetic attitude turns against the particularism and deification of certain accepted sacraments. It demands a higher obedience that calls into question every finite form and thus every sacrament. It establishes a tension that transcends all the tensions between the sacramental attachments; that is, it establishes a tension between the actual and the demanded. In its covertly religious form it appeals to universal reason, in its overtly religious form it appeals to the sovereignty of God. With these appeals comes the demand for a just social order, for a knowledge purged of the arbitrary and the superstitious, for a new era in history, when old sacramental realities will be transformed and will take their proper place in the larger kingdom of the good.

This prophetic principle is the moving element in the history of religion, but it is also the rarer of the two attitudes. It stresses the demand for change, it questions established sacraments, and it takes the risk of open discussion. But it, too, is subject to perversion: it can absolutize the newly demanded form. Through its depreciation of the supporting sacramental attitude it can so radically break the connection with the primary ties as to lose contact with the supporting powers of nature and history. Thus it becomes utopian, irrelevant, or even destructive.

Hence these two attitudes, the prophetic and the sacramental, are complementary. The sacramental attitude alone leads into the iron grip of attachment to the given; the prophetic alone leads to a detachment that is irrelevant, to a loss of contact with the actual historical process. The sacramental attitude and the prophetic attitude together provide the dialectic of attachment and detachment which alone can find meaning in and through and beyond the given and the demanded—the marriage of security and adventure.

PEACE AS A RELIGIOUS PROBLEM

This leads to certain general conclusions concerning peace as a problem of religion.

1. Preaching in favor of peace and the conditions requisite for it can be effective only when it is accompanied by a severely critical and prophetic attitude toward the sacramental devotions that engender war. A just and lasting peace will come only in the way in which war comes, that is, when it is inevitable. It will come only when there is a strong enough prophetic sentiment to demand it and get it. The demand for an attack on the evils of racialism, statism, isolationist national sovereignty, economic monopoly, and selfish exploitation of human and natural resources constitutes a demand for a new meaning to inspire the transformation of present sacramental attachments into more inclusive sacraments.

It may be, then, that the old Greek adage to the effect that wisdom comes through suffering has some bearing on the problem of peace as a problem of religion. Our extremity is God's opportunity, and we will probably not really mend our ways until we realize that we have reached our extremity. America has become so closely attached to its established sacraments that much more suffering than we have yet encountered may be required before we shall as a nation become convinced that fundamental changes in attitude are necessary. When that time comes, the sacramental realities that now promise security will be enlarged or put into a new framework of meaning and adventure.

2. This new meaning, if it is to be powerful enough to be the basis for maintaining international structures (economic and political), must emerge from something already existing. Prophetism must strike root in common tradition. It cannot be extemporized. It must find its roots in prophetic attitudes that are at the same time incipient in the respective countries and mutually understandable among the nations most concerned. In both secular and religious circles there are a number of people who are inclined to seek a common tradition in the idea of the law of nature[1], a religioethical and legal concept that has a centuries-old history in the West and for which analogies can be found in the East.[2] With its roots in the Greco-Roman as well as in the Judeo-Christian tradition the idea of natural law has long served in political and social life as a source of both stability and flexibility. It is a part of the secular as well as of the religious tradition, and it is closely bound up with the Protestant as well

as the Roman Catholic heritage. It has been vigorously (and quite consistently) repudiated by the totalitarian countries.

Some contemporary prophets have suggested that the next phase in the larger cultural development of the planet will usher in a synthesis between East and West similar to the earlier great synthesis of the Middle Ages. Already in the sixteenth and seventeenth centuries certain Jesuit missionaries in China utilized the idea as a point of contact between Christian and Chinese thought. Modern liberal Protestant missionaries as well as secular leaders in various countries of the Orient have long given attention to this problem of synthesis. Similar attempts at *rapprochement* between Christianity and Islam and between Christianity and Hinduism have also received attention.

3. On the other hand, the new meaning as it affects either the sacramental or the prophetic attitude should not be envisaged as something requiring absolute identity of form. Unity does not require identity. The West, to be sure, will be affected by the East, and the East will be affected by the West. But on both sides growth must be in terms of local sacramental and prophetic traditions. Any attempt of the United Nations to *impose* their ideas upon each other or upon other cultures will not be successful. Certain groups within the World Council of Churches have attempted during the past decades to bring about unity among Christian churches on the basis of a creedal formula. The attempt has not been a conspicuous success. The same result will ensue if the Western democracies attempt to propagate their particular conception of democracy or society, either as a system of ethical ideas or as a system of political institutions. We must recognize that "in my Father's house are many mansions." The nations of the West have no monopoly on the forms of democracy.

4. In any event, progress must be slow if it is to be sure. Prophetic religious sentiment whether overt or covert is, however, prone to become utopian. Particularly liable to this evil are those sentimentalists (both in the churches and outside them) who ignore the necessity for organized power for the maintenance of peace. Sacramental attitudes, on the other hand, are prone to become arbitrary and to ignore basic ethical demands. Alongside these two perversions is the attitude of the cynics who profess to take neither the prophetic nor the sacramental attitude seriously. Any maturely religious attitude—that is, any attitude that is aware of the tragedies and perversions of history and that is aware of the high cost of

civilization at any time—must therefore guard against all three of these false sentiments, that is, against utopianism, particularism, and cynicism.

Perhaps the greatest contribution that religion, whether over or covert, can make is to maintain the attitude that peace *can* be achieved even though it may come hard. With the disillusionment and distress that will ensue "when peace raises her ugly head" and the nations are catapulted into new conflicts within and between them, there will be the grave danger of a "failure of nerve." Arnold Toynbee, the British historian, has indicated the disastrous consequences that might ensue if the nations of the West should leap into war again within another generation. It would, he says, become a great opportunity for the continuation of the Fascist counterrevolution, for the English people might in despair refuse to fight again and would thus yield to totalitarianism. Toynbee's comment stresses the great importance of *decisive* policies for peace. If there is any health in our religion now, we must say that peace *can* be made. Hope is a virtue, and it must be cultivated if it is to function.

5. But if these age-old imperialisms are to be restrained and if a new spirit of cooperation is to be engendered, we must look forward to struggle and sacrifice and not to quiescent peace. Strife among humans will continue so long as they are human; on the one side of the struggle are those who enter into relations with their fellows with the view of *imposing* their ideas or institutions, their prophesies and their sacraments, and on the other side are those who consider it their religious duty to admit that they are human and fallible and that a truth and a goodness are possible among men and women which have not yet been brought to birth. This is the age-old struggle of the religions. Not until religion inspires a willingness to forego the sort of divine sanction that incites people to social or ecclesiastical imperialism will religion be made safe for democracy and for the world.

On the basis of our analysis, it would appear that the lines of division are not between those who are usually called the religious and the irreligious people. On the contrary, the lines cut across the churches and on through the unchurched portions of society. They cut across the overt and the covert, the organized and the unorganized, forms of religion. In all groups are to be found the people who want peace without sacrifice and the people who want peace. Peace, which as we have shown is always ultimately a problem of religion, demands a new attack on the common enemy in ourselves. Our task lies not between the nations but within each nation—yes, within the heart and mind and will of every person. This task calls for continuing renewal.

Over forty years after the present essay was published I attended the 350th anniversary celebration at Harvard University. On this occasion we heard the address of Charles, Prince of Wales, in which he summoned us to recall a word of the ancient Greeks, "*metanoia*," which he appropriately in the university setting translated "knowledge that transforms," and which in the New Testament appears as "change of heart and mind and soul." He in effect merged these several meanings when he concluded the address: Could the institutions of higher learning "re-explore the religious dimension which primitive people called the great hunger, that overwhelming and inexplicable impulse which brought man out of the remote and dangerous past to where he is today through passions of the spirit? It was a hunger to provide a sense of meaning and the life of meaning which conducted him in the search for truth in all dimensions—both material and spiritual. Thus, however well these institutions may serve an existing social order, if their vision of themselves ends there they will diminish and perish. If they succeed in serving not just the immediate needs of the present, but something greater than themselves yet to come, the chances are they will not only renew themselves, but help to renew their ailing societies."

So we end as we began. Peace is a problem within the religions as well as a problem of religion. The instrument of lasting peace is the sword of the spirit which can boldly and yet humbly divide the word of truth; and the hope of lasting peace lies with the peacemakers who are willing to wield that sword even against their own "religion."

Notes

1. "The origin of this general philosophy is to be found in the later period of classical antiquity—in the Stoic theory of Greece and Rome, and especially of Rome; in Cicero and in certain elements of Roman Law; and finally, and above all, in the combination of these factors with a Christian outlook to form a Christian system of Natural Law. The fundamental conception is that of the dignity of the common element of human Reason, as it appears in every individual; and this conception, in turn, goes back to that of a 'common law,' pervading all nature and the whole universe, and proceeding from a divine principle of Reason which expresses itself increasingly in the successive stages of created beings. The

true nature of man is assumed to be the divine Reason operating in him, with its sovereignty over the sense and affections." Ernst Troeltsch, "The Ideas of Natural Law and Humanity in World Politics," trans. Ernest Barker, appendix I of Otto Gierke, *Natural Law and the Theory of Society, 1500–1800* (Cambridge, 1934), p. 205.

2. C. Paul Masson-Oursel, *Comparative Philosophy* (New York, 1926), p. 160.

31 · *The Uses of Diversity*

De Tocqueville, the French observer of American ways, over a century ago remarked, "I know of no country in which there is so little independence of mind and real freedom of discussion as in America." More recently Lord Northcliffe has said, "America is the home of the brave and the land of the free where each man does as he likes, and if he doesn't, you make him." In filiopietism we of course might reply that America is a land of contrasts and that a good many things, even contradictory things, may rightly be said about it. Turning to the other side of the ledger, for example, we could cite the German theologian who, after a recent visit to this country said, "The odd thing about you Americans is that in a discussion you assume that the other fellow might be right." This judgment, like the less favorable ones, could no doubt be confirmed if one looked in the right place at the right moment.

Whatever the whole truth in these matters may be, we in this place, in a university and in a divinity school, accept as valid the criterion implied in both the unfavorable and the favorable judgments I have just cited. We cherish the open mind and freedom of discussion. We are committed to "the uses of diversity" for the common life and for the academy as well as for the church, though of course a unity within the diversity is also imperative. The sanctions we appeal to in favor of diversity vary according to the context in question. If the context is political, we may appeal to the Federalist Papers where a system of checks and balances is extolled for the sake of protecting a multiplicity of interests. If it is social,

Adams was appointed the Edward Mallinckrodt, Jr., Professor of Divinity at Harvard Divinity School in 1957. This essay is an abridged version of his convocation address, given that September at the Memorial Church in the Harvard Yard. It was published by Harvard University and is here reprinted by permission.

we urge somehow the imperative of equality; we deplore snobbism. If the context is economic, we may appeal to the principle of the consent of the governed as represented by the free market. If it is academic and pedagogical, we speak of freedom of inquiry. If it is ecclesiastical, we affirm the freedom to worship or not to worship. In all of these spheres we expect and promote a diversity, and even a conflict, of interests and values. This conception of cultural pluralism is an outlook and a heritage that have been wrought through a long period of time, and not in America alone.

But all is not well with this heritage, from the point of view of either our performance or our principles. In conspicuous and lamentable ways America has shown itself unfaithful to the heritage. We do not firmly possess the substance of democracy even where we retain ostensible forms of it. One needs only to mention certain familiar phrases to indicate the jeopardy in which the heritage stands: the age of conformity, the mass society, the thingification of industrial workers, pressure groups, ordeal by Congressional "investigation," ghettos North and South, and white-pigment college fraternities. But apart from the matter of performance good or bad, questions regarding principles press upon us. Is cultural pluralism only a fancy name for the dissolution of culture, for riding in all directions at once, for an empty secularism? Certainly, mere diversity in itself cannot create a community of integrity, for example, a community of genuine scholarship or a community appropriately to be called the Christian church. As Santayana remarked, freedom, like the air we breathe, is necessary for existence, but it is insufficient for nourishment.

I

What, then, are the right uses of diversity? This is a large question in its scope. The ultimate ground and goal of diversity are not necessarily evident in the institutional arrangements required by the concept of checks and balances, or by the ideal of equality, or by freedom of inquiry, or by the "laws" of the market. From the Judeo-Christian point of view, the ground and goal of diversity are not in our control. They belong to the divinely given creative and redemptive forces to which the Old and New Testament bear decisive, if not exhaustive, witness, forces that grow not old and that elicit a living faith that is not attached to temporal "securities."

Within the context of the biblical conception of the creative forces of human existence, the story of the Tower of Babel [Gen. 11] by its negative implications offers a partial index to the nature and justification of diversity. The people who erected the Tower of Babel, according to the legend, wanted thus to build a city with its top in the heavens. In face of this demonic storming of the gates of heaven, the Lord is represented as saying, "Behold, They are one people, and they have all one language; this is only the beginning of what they will do; and nothing that they propose to do will now be impossible for them." Whatever the original source and import of this legend may have been, it says something essentially theological; it suggests that absolute unity and conformity in the cultural enterprise will present a threat to viable and meaningful human existence, that the absence of diversity (when it is not simply a sign of exhaustion) is a denial of human creatureliness and also of human individuality and freedom. The legend also offers an interpretation of the role of language. "The whole earth," we are told, had only "one language and few words." This paucity of language is apparently taken as a mark of self-destructive tribalism, or at least as a tempting condition for it. The legend seems to assert that the Lord, in order to keep human beings aware of their dependence upon something not their own and in order to make them the more free from the danger of tyranny, had to *scatter* them and to give them many languages. By implication, then, we may discern in this conception of "scattering" a striking interpretation of human individuality, indeed a theological interpretation of individuation as a category of the human condition. Diversity of place and perspective and language is appropriate for creatures that under God are scattered, individuated, incomplete.

Alfred North Whitehead was fond of saying that "definition is the soul of actuality," by which he meant that particularity and limitedness condition every entity, yet that each entity partakes of the soul of being. This view recalls the prophetic outlook of the Old Testament. For the prophets, the once-happening individuation and scatteredness of human existence, the creatureliness of man and society, imply that everything finite is subject to criticism. At the same time, the particular, the individual, the concretely limited, is related to a Creator that transcends the particular, the individual, the limited. Here, then, is a positive, if qualified, evaluation of individuation. As an evaluation it is quite different from the unmitigatedly Greek tragic view—for example, from the view of Anaximander for whom individuation as such involves a metaphysical guilt to be atoned for only by return to the abyss of the unlimited. The biblical outlook is critical, but it is less radically pessimistic. From the biblical prophetic point of view, the limitedness of individuation characterizes all human groups and also the cultural creations of individuals and groups. This limitedness characterizes religion itself and even the words that point to creation or salvation; it characterizes the institutions that transmit these words and the theologies that bring these words into systems. Human beings are not gods, they are "scattered" and their language is legion. On the other hand, within the very individuation or scatteredness a divine purpose can be served. Scatteredness is of the nature of things, and yet it possesses a derived dignity and a creative possibility. Where diversity is suppressed, blasphemy and distortion ensue.

Accordingly, the first use, the religious vocation, of diversity is to keep human systems and institutions and languages open; it is to protect people against the weakness of their own strength; it is, in short, to maintain responsiveness to the freedom of God as Creator, as Judge, and as Redeemer. In the face of the human inclination to heaven-storming and also of religion to denying human scatteredness by driving toward the uniformity and conformity of a Tower of Babel, prophetic biblical faith places a special demand upon a divinity school. The demand placed upon us is not only the maintenance and protection of diversity but also the use of diversity for a positive purpose. Devotion to a purpose, then, is the second use of diversity—devotion to a purpose that does not deny the scatteredness and that nevertheless promotes a viable integrity. What is this purpose?

Here we encounter a delicate problem of definition, a problem before which we must be patient of diversity of answer. A radically Protestant divinity school as an institution promoting learning and piety is committed to encourage and give expression to diverse insight and sensitivity in response to God's manifold activity and also in face of questions posed in a changing world and in a free university. Moreover, in its relation to the variety of churches it serves, a nondenominational divinity school cannot properly claim to possess a fixed formulation of the faith and purpose that inform or should inform its activities. Particularly, it cannot identify itself with any formulation characteristic of some one denomination. On the other hand, it cannot properly define its purpose in terms of a lowest common denominator. Quite the contrary. A divinity school aims to open the way to enrichment, not to impoverishment. In the light of this commitment I would like to suggest that within the context of prophetic Christianity and also of the free university, a divinity school should be as much concerned with questions as with answers.

II

I have always been intrigued by the account of a singular crucifix that is said to rest on the altar of a church in Toronto. On entering this church and looking toward the chancel, one at first gets the impression that this crucifix is a question mark. This question mark of course confronts not only the individual worshiper. It confronts also the church itself, the church as a corporate body representing a historical tradition. And beyond this it confronts the whole culture of which the empirical church is a part. Perhaps we may say that a divinity school, like the churches themselves, serves its proper purpose when it lifts up this question mark before itself and before the churches, and also before the university.

But this particular question mark is not a floating apparition without content or substance. It presupposes the affirmation that God in this man on the cross has revealed the power unto salvation, the power that in love and judgment comes to us as a servant to live with us and suffer with us, at the same time calling us to be its servant—the power that brings reconciliation between God and humans and between humans as neighbors. This power is the love that will not let us go, for it is ever seeking new community. It must be responded to anew by each generation, by each denomination, by each church, by each individual. But the response is not to a merely hypostatized power, and certainly not to a compendium of copybook maxims. The response is a response of persons to a Person.

Who is this person to whom we respond? The answers that have been given to this question have been legion. Fifty titles are available in the New Testament alone, and still others appear in the historic confessions. The titles are not the person, not even all of the titles taken together.

If it is claimed that Scripture or tradition offers us the touchstone, we must affirm that Scripture and tradition are not simply and readily to hand for some sort of automatic appropriation. Scripture itself reflects a diverse response to the person of Christ. This diversity is to be observed not only in the titles given to him. The diversity appears also more generally, for example, in the variety of theological categories that constitute the semantic response to revelation which is preserved in Scripture. The writers of Scripture, unlike the tribe of Babel, did not have merely "one language and few words." They were themselves among the scattered. Because of this diversity a certain deception is latent in any claim made in behalf of some unified biblical theology. Among scholars there is in actuality no homogeneous biblical theology. A variety of categories newly understood and newly related to each other in each generation constitutes the history and the future of biblical theology. The categories of biblical thought—the Son of Man, the Messiah, the kingship of Christ, the covenant, the kingdom of God, justification by faith, atonement, love, God the Father, the Son, and the Holy Spirit—have been understood in a variety of ways through the centuries, and except through exhaustion or under the psychic violence of coercion, the variety will persist. Moreover, the New Testament, not to speak of later tradition, presents around the Christ a variety of pieties. St. Paul, viewing some of these diversities, did not demand a ready-made doctrinal conformity. "There must be factions amongst you," he said, "in order that those who are genuine among you may be recognized." And, surely, Pauline Christianity does not exhaust the "genuine" witness. As Calvin was wont to say, we are benefactors of "a diversity of grace."

The sign of the vitality of Christian faith is to be observed in new and newly relevant response to the power of God brought near and made uniquely available in Jesus' word and deed, in his life and his trust in God the scatterer who is the Creator, the Judge, and Reconciler. The power of God resides precisely in its continual self-surpassingness in the human scene. The church, the ecclesia, is called out of the world, that is, out of every self-sufficient fixation, to witness to the power of God that brings judgment and that opens the way to new beginnings. In response to this power unto salvation, a divinity school, especially, should be a disturber of every provincialism, systematically repudiating every identification of the revelation in Jesus with any particular human response to it, whether that response be found in Scripture, in the ancient church, in the Reformation, or in the denominational traditions. Our faith is not in these "creatures." We are called to seek the unity of fellowship that issues from our together confronting the questions that have been raised by the diverse traditions and by our own experience, and from our together testing our answers in thought and in life, under the Great Taskmaster's eye.

III

This testing process, for us, takes place not only in the context of the churches. Our divinity school does its work within a university, another enterprise of questioning. The university is not to be understood in a merely abstract way, as a routine promoter of free inquiry or as a catalogued program for the education of youth. A university possesses a symbolic power that has gathered about the whole enterprise since its inception centuries ago, an enterprise that is a partnership embracing many places and times and perspectives. This becomes clear if we recall the meaning of *universitas*. Here again we encounter diversity. In the Middle Ages the generic term *universitas* meant a plurality, an aggregate of persons. Thus it referred to a corporation: guilds, municipalities, and scholars and students. In its association with the university and its *studium generale* the term came to have a more special meaning: it was a school that attracted students from all parts who formed themselves into "nations," and at this school there was a plurality of masters from far and wide.[1] Although the university initially developed under the aegis of church or state (or both), it has achieved its stature as we know it through freeing itself from both ecclesiastical and political subservience, in short, through the process of "scattering" or individuation. This has been necessary in order that it might enjoy the uses of diversity, of a diversity promoting the untethered pursuit of truth by means of the humanizing disciplines.

This diversity is to be observed in the composite historical origin of the university. We have referred already to the medieval origins of the university. The New England fathers even sought these origins in biblical times. From the researches of a member of our faculty we know that in early New England the university was given a biblical sanction, the first universities being traced to the prophets of ancient Palestine.[2] Members of the university were called "sons of the prophets." A Dutch scholar in 1602 traced the lineage to an even earlier time than that of the prophets, asserting that the first university was founded by Noah "as means of spreading knowledge of good letters and so preventing another flood!" Apparently, the university was, from the beginning, supposed to raise questions, here questioning the reliability of the rainbow covenant! This lore was adopted from medieval tradition. The university, however, has humanist Renaissance sources as well as medieval ecclesiastical ones. It is the Republic of Letters. The study of *bonae litterae* was not introduced under biblical sanction, nor for that matter was the study of the Greek and Hebrew languages so introduced. Renaissance ideals were at work here: a liberal education was for the free man. An Italian humanist, Vergerio of Padua, defined a liberal education as one that "calls forth, trains, and develops those highest gifts of body and of mind which ennoble men, and which are rightly judged to rank next in dignity to Virtue only."

The ideal of a liberal education figured in the Puritan beginnings of Harvard College. This is sometimes forgotten. The statement in the early pamphlet, "New England's First Fruits," is familiar to all: "After God had carried us safe to New England, and we had builded our houses, provided necessaries for our liveli-hood, rear'd convenient places for God's worship, and settled the Civil Government: One of the next things we longed for, and looked after was to advance Learning, and perpetuate it to posterity, dreading to leave an illiterate Ministry to the Churches, when our present Ministers shall lie in the Dust." This statement, inscribed on one of the gates of Harvard Yard, can give the wrong impression, namely, that Harvard College initially was designed only for the training of a learned American clergy. As Samuel Eliot Morison has reminded us, Harvard College, and the other colonial colleges, "attempted as best they could, with the scanty means at their disposal, to provide a liberal education in the accepted Renaissance sense of the word—an education that would introduce youth to the best thought and literature of the past, sharpen his mind to a keen instrument for the acquisition of knowledge, discipline his intellect and form his character so that he would be both able and ready to play a prominent part in the affairs of men."[3] It is abundantly clear from her curriculum that Harvard was not a divinity school, but a religious College of the "Liberal Arts." The University, as we know it, developed on the base of the College, preserving in the community of scholars the earlier diversity and expanding the freedom of inquiry in the context of professional education and of highly specialized scholarship.

Diversity is of the essence of the university. Indeed, diversity of perspective is the life-blood of free inquiry. To be sure, there must be agreement to search for adequate method in the use of evidence, but in the interpretation of evidence variety is indispensable to the advancement of learning. This variety of interpretation is the occasion for creative conflict and the prerequisite to the finding of new fact. A university in which there is complete consensus of interpretation is dead; it is not a university.

IV

Ours is a multiple church. The churches are "scattered" and individuated, possessing many languages. In some instances these churches have denied their scatteredness; they have tried in sectarian spirit to build their own Towers of Babel. But the true church cannot be identified with any of these ecclesiastical Babels or with any other particular tradition. This view is an offence to many ardent souls. As John Calvin asserted, there are many people "who are not satisfied unless the church can always be pointed out with the finger." But, said he, that is something that cannot be done with assurance; the whole question as to the dimensions and limits of the church of Christ must be left to God, "since he alone 'knoweth them that are his.'" So, far from pointing it out with the finger, we must say that the church is scattered in the diaspora and using many languages.

In the face of this diversity of our scatteredness we are tempted again and again to long for a restful unity, forgetting that such a unity would be more enervating and destructive than vitally integrative. The scatteredness of the churches is not only an expression of the limitedness of each. It is also the occasion for diverse richness of piety. Wilding growths there are, but mere uniformity, mere conformity, can lead only to deformity. On the other hand, nonconformity for its own sake can lead only to "uniquity," a demonic attachment to uniqueness—a Tower of Babel upside down, but a Tower of Babel. Strangely enough, these contrary motions, the one toward conformity and the other toward uniquity, lead to the point where the extremes meet in deformity. Obviously, no simple, foolproof formula is available for protecting us against these extremes and for guiding us to a unity beneath the differences. It would seem clear, however, that a divinity school, rooted as it is in the diverse life of the churches, has the vocation of developing sensitivity to the intrinsic qualities and the persuasiveness of diverse pieties and traditions, and also of bringing them into dialogue with each other, thus opening the way at the same time to newly relevant innovations and to newness of fellowship.

The uses of diversity, therefore, are themselves diverse, but overarching them is the striving for fellowship, for that fellowship which the Tower of Babel distorts. To be sure, the lurking danger is that we shall erect an Eiffel Tower, projecting the false belief in the perfectibility of human being through reason, science, and democracy.

What binds us together is at the same time the ground of our individuality and the ground of our common identity. This dialectic of individuality and identity has seldom been more persuasively envisaged than by Nicholas of Cusa in the fifteenth century. In the opening pages of his book *The Vision of God,* Cusa speaks of a portrait that has the peculiarity of omnivoyance; it looks directly at the observer no matter what the observer's location before it; indeed, it seems to be looking directly and simultaneously at everyone who stands before it. In love and judgment God looks at each onlooker wherever he is; God looks toward each onlooker as she moves; and God looks at all onlookers at the same time. God supports the nearness and the distance. Cusa thinks of the portrait as God's vision of humanity. We might venture to consider it God's vision of the multiple, scattered church, and at the same time as the image which before

God the churches may have of themselves. The application of Cusa's allegory to a doctrine of the multiple church serves to stress not only the potential significance of individuation and scatteredness but also the fact that individuation secures its integrity by looking toward the countenance of God.

But perhaps Cusa's allegory overstresses the separateness of the individuals who seek God's countenance. The relation between the individuals and God and between the individuals should be conceived in a more dynamic fashion. The divine working is a gathering as well as a scattering. John Bunyan paradoxically envisaged the gathering and the scattering in a more dynamic image than that of Cusa: "Christians," he said, "are like the several flowers in the garden, that have upon each of them the dew of heaven, which, being shaken with the wind, they let fall their dew at each other's roots, whereby they are jointly nourished, and becomes nourisher of each other."[4] Through a sort of divine ecology God gathers what God scatters. It is a pity that we allow ecclesiasticism to impede this divine ecology. It is perhaps the peculiar advantage of a nondenominational divinity school that it can transcend the separating barriers and yet respect the individuality of the scatteredness of the churches.

In our view of the multiple church, then, we see the churches as responding to the fullness of the divine reflected in the variety of Scripture, as discovering truths and forms of piety that were only latent in Holy Writ, as permitting themselves betimes even to become acquainted with Deity at first hand. Through this diversity they reflect, albeit in a refracted way, the dynamic that obtains within a living and not a static God. Jeremiah Burroughes, one of the Independents of the middle of the seventeenth century, gives us a vivid pictures of the providence of God manifest in the refractions:

> God hath a hand in these divisions to bring forth further light. Sparks are beaten out by the flints striking together. Many sparks of light, many truths, are beaten out by the beating of men's spirits one against another . . . If you will have the cloth woven, the woof and the warp must be cast across one another. If you will have truths argued out, you must be content to bear with some opposition for the time. They who are not willing to bear some trouble, to be at some cost to find out truth, are unworthy of it . . . We may well behold men's weakness in these divisions, but (we may) better admire God's strength and wisdom in ordering them to his glory and his children's good.[5]

A divinity school in face of the churches and in the matrix of a university is given the vocation of responding to the providence of God which works in just this fashion, protecting diversity and yet seeking unity in diversity.

But in the end the fulfillment of this vocation is not in the power of humanity; we can only prepare for it as we wait upon the Spirit. The people of Babel were caught up by a demonic suprapersonal power that drove them into blasphemous unity. By way of contrast, the Christian church had its forceful and missionary beginning at Pentecost. The Holy Spirit then raised persons above themselves not into a Procrustean conformity but rather into a community where many languages were heard and yet where everyone heard the others speak in one's own language, where persons retained their own individuality and yet through the Spirit were open to the others, where the common relation to the universal engendered unity in diversity. Here we find the paradigm of diversity as a gift from the divine fecundity. May we not say, accordingly, that the true uses of diversity are in the hands of God, leading us again and again from our pretentious and self-destructive Towers of Babel to ever new Pentecosts, which let the wind of the Spirit blow where it listeth "that God may do with his own what he pleaseth and to what persons and when and where he pleaseth"?

Notes

1. S. E. Morison, "The History of Universities," *Rice Institute Pamphlets* 23, no. 4 (1936):212.

2. George H. Williams, "Translatio Studii: The Puritans' Conception of Their University," *Archive for Reformation History* 57, nos. 1–2 (1966):152–81.

3. Morison, "The History of Universities," p. 247.

4. *The Life and Writings of John Bunyan,* ed. H. E. B. Speight (New York, 1928), p. 218.

5. Jeremiah Burroughes, *Irenicum* (London, 1646), pp. 242–45. Quoted by Winthrop H. Hudson, "Denominationalism as a Basis of Ecumenicity," *Church History* 24 (1955):40.

Part Five

Liberal Christianity

THE ESSAYS IN THIS SECTION DEAL WITH THE LIBERAL CHRISTIAN stance that Adams has adopted, criticized, and sought to redefine. In several works he interprets its meaning, its history, and its future prospects; in others he enlists liberal Christian perspectives to interpret human existence. By denomination a Unitarian Universalist, Adams has long worked in thoroughly ecumenical circles: "Ours is a multiple church," he says. Within his denomination he has been a critic of sectarianism and complacency, a prophetic voice of social-ethical concern, and (like St. Paul and Paul Tillich) an "apostle to the gentiles." Never one to shun controversy, he revels in Edwin Wilson's acerbic comment on a theological pronouncement he once signed. Alphabetical order put "Adams" first among a group of thirteen Unitarian ministers. Said Wilson, a humanist leader, "It's Jim Adams and the twelve."

In "Neither Mere Morality nor Mere God," Adams succinctly defines his liberal Christian perspective. He affirms the unity of religious faith and moral responsibility; as the title of this volume indicates, he holds that an "examined faith" necessarily includes ethical commitments. He also affirms the converse, that a thoroughly examined ethics necessarily includes faith—a confidence in righteousness and a humility in the face of the temptation to self-righteousness.

In "The Liberal Christian Holds Up the Mirror," Adams first details the historical significance of liberal Christianity, then holds up the mirror to its "blemishes." Close examination reveals losses of depth, identity, and historical mission—losses not to be recovered, he believes, apart from a renewed understanding of historical roots and a deeper engagement in socially prophetic associations. "By their roots" and "by their groups," he has said, "you shall know them."

Conscious of his own religious roots, Adams is critical of religious liberals who lump together (and condemn) all Christian "evangelicals." In "Liberals and Evangelicals" he distinguishes those at the fundamentalist and reactionary end of the spectrum from those at the "new evangelical" and radical end. Religious liberals have a (seldom recognized) affinity with the latter and, Adams holds, have much to learn from them about commitment and the social meaning of the gospel.

The essay that follows, "Liberal Religion and the Phoenix," calls attention to the thought of Henry Nelson Wieman, the American philosopher of religion. Consistent with his liberal and inclusive approach, Adams does not sharply distinguish a biblically rooted Christian theism from a philosophically grounded naturalistic theism, such as Wieman's. The central issue, for Adams, is to liberate "liberalism" from bondage to its inherited cultural forms and class loyalties; in this effort Wieman is a resource for the renewal of liberal religion.

In "The Ages of Liberalism" Adams proposes three periods in the history of liberal Christianity: the eras of the Radical Reformation, the Enlightenment, and the yet-to-be-named twentieth century. He names these three ages, as Joachim of Fiore, the early medieval theologian, named the three ages of world history, after the Persons of the Holy Trinity. But Adams's order is different from Joachim's, for he suggests that for liberalism the age of the Son, the Mediator, comes third. Many will find the suggestion astonishing; but it is historically insightful. "The Age of the Mediator" is seen in contemporary theology's accent on hermeneutics— the mediation of religious meaning by story and symbolism. It is seen also in Adams's own accent on voluntary associations—mediating structures of social-ethical vitality.

"The Grotesque and Our Future" exemplifies a similar turn of historical and intellectual thought. Adams celebrates the founding of the American Unitarian movement and calls for a renewed commitment to social reform. He takes grotesque representations in art as symbolic of gross moral disorder, representations which should awaken protest and move the churches to action.

The final three works in this section concern the ministry of the church—its corporate vocation, which also defines the professional vocation of the minister. In each of these works Adams uses a biblical symbol to interpret contemporary existence. "Covenants of Strength and Love" takes Israel's covenant with Yahweh—broken, and yet to be made new— as a symbol of the calling, failing, and renewing of religious community in history. Here Adams uses secular examples, from the detective story and soap operas to modern dance and architecture, to illustrate the human hunger for meaning. Religion, he says, is "loyalty to that which is considered ultimately reliable," and God is that which "brings into being and maintains a community that is consciously dedicated to achieving righteousness in the community at large." Thus Adams invites us to examine our faith in a radically new light.

"In the Beginning Is the Word" uses theological ideas in a similarly liberating way. Starting with the biblical symbol of the divine Word, Adams discusses the universality and the religious significance of human communication: the creation of meaning through dialogue. The recognition of Jesus' rhetorical genius (Mark says he "did not speak without parable"), and the theological identification of Jesus with God's creative and redemptive Word, serve to focus the meanings of the ministry and the vocation of the church.

The spoken word, then, signifies a desire to originate meaning, or to make a new beginning; a biblical symbol of the end and aim of human existence underlines the final work in the volume, "The Messianic Banquet." Adams interprets this notably social metaphor with reference to the work of Rudolf Otto, the German scholar and friend to whom this book is dedicated. Otto saw in the biblical accounts of the Last Supper a symbol of future hope, anticipated in the present. In this deeply moving sermon for a communion service, Adams rejoins his characteristic dichotomies—the personal and the social dimensions of life, the prophetic sense of "not-yet" and the sacramental sense of divine presence. The image of the Messianic banquet evokes awareness of a grace that is both near and far, present and future—a unity of human fulfillment that is at once both intimate and ultimate.

G.K.B.

32 · Neither Mere Morality nor Mere God

The late Dean William W. Fenn of Harvard Divinity School used to tell of a snatch of heated conversation between two students he once overheard as he passed through the corridor of Andover Hall at the Divinity School. Attempting to bring an argument to a triumphant conclusion, the one student said, "All you have is *mere* morality." To this the other student replied scornfully, "And all you have is *mere* God."

These two epithets, "mere morality" and "mere God," adumbrate two aspects of the religious mentality which, as each of the students from his perspective implied, should never be allowed to stand in simple opposition or separation. These epithets are of course little more than polemical weapons; but they do point to a fundamental and perennial question, that of the relation between fact and value. Are the high values that elicit human commitment merely human, or are they more than human in their rootage and sanction?

The British philosopher F. H. Bradley once commented on Matthew Arnold's claim that "religion is morality touched with emotion." In fairness to Arnold it should be recalled that he went beyond this definition in his description of God as "the power not ourselves working for righteousness." But here is Bradley's comment on the definition of religion just cited:

> "Is there a God?" asks the reader. "O, yes," replies Mr. Arnold, "and I can verify him in experience." "And what is he then?" cries the reader. "Be virtuous and as a rule you will be happy," is the answer. "Well, and God?" "That is God," says Mr. Arnold, "there is no deception and what more do you want?"

Then Bradley goes on to say:

> I suppose we do want a good deal more. Most of us, certainly the public which Mr. Arnold addressed, want something they can worship; and they will not find that in an hypostatized copy-book heading, which is not much more adorable than "Honesty is the best policy," or "Handsome is that handsome does," or various other edifying maxims which have not yet come to an apotheosis.

Abridged from Adams's introduction to a series of essays in *The Unitarian Christian* 15, no. 1 (October 1959). Reprinted by permission.

Religious commitment issues from the declarative into the imperative mood, from recognition of divine Fact that defines and redefines and sustains virtue. This is the sense of Baron Friedrich von Hügel's assertion that "religion has primarily to do with is-ness and only secondarily to do with ought-ness."

This pointing beyond "ought-ness" to "is-ness" is characteristic not only of religion. Science is also concerned in the first instance with fact. Scientists as such are not primarily interested in the social change for good which their scientific discoveries will make possible. That interest belongs to the applied sciences. Scientists are primarily concerned to know the truth about the world as they find it, and they are not as scientists primarily concerned with what they ought to do with or about it. Religion and science in their differing ways seek reliable fact.

Accordingly, religious faith is a response to that which is held to be ultimately reliable. Christian faith finds the ultimately reliable fact in the meaning-giving, sustaining, fellowship-creating, transforming power to which Jesus of Nazareth responded and which is available ("near at hand") in the Reign of God. This "object" of faith is neither "mere morality" nor "mere God" if they are viewed as opposite or as separate. It is just because of this that Dean Fenn was fond of telling his story.

Christianity is not "morality touched with emotion." Nor is it, strictly speaking, a mystical religion. It is a prophetic, that is, a historical religion; it summons men and women to an encounter with, a response to, a living God, the Lord of history, who has "spoken and speaks" to and in history; it points to an initiative that is not of human making and to a response that is concrete and incarnational in the perennial struggle against the forces of evil in humanity and in history. Its mode is existential more than it is discursively argumentative. We should dwell for a moment here on the prophetic sense of urgency with respect to this demand for the concrete.

In a recent poll at Harvard College a substantial proportion of undergraduates, according to *The Harvard Crimson*, "presented a God whose substance is so tenuous and vague that, like certain very rare gases, it becomes highly enigmatic to say that He is 'there' at all. Such a being certainly seems incapable of having much more of an effect on human life than the normal inhalation of argon." This kind of God is no longer a concrete presence. It is the dead end of the alley of pale abstraction. Actually, however, the abstractionist conception of God can point to a noble, if erstwhile forgotten, heritage. Rational clarity and consistency again and again, in the very name of a God of order, must enter the scene in order to correct the arbitrariness, the naive anthropomorphism, the superstitions, of "faith." On the other hand, this rational thrust can create the vacuum that the writer in *The Crimson* describes. Arguments about the existence of God can end up here. But the vacuum of abstractionism generally does not last. It gets filled with half-gods. Some concrete, commanding power such as the nation, the white pigment, or the flesh pots of suburbia, will project and occupy a throne. A new superstition becomes the subject of faith. Thus humans show themselves to be incurably, and even self-destructively, "religious."

One can observe in the history of the ancient Hebrew religion this oscillation between devotion to a distant, if universal, God and the demand for something more immediate and concrete. The German philosopher Schelling, recognizing this oscillation in the history of religions, called for a transcending of the *universality* of abstract monotheism and the idolatrous *concreteness* of polytheism. He found this in the New Testament. Martin Buber has frequently commented on the viability and power that the Christian conception of God enjoys by virtue of the centrality of Jesus in Christian devotion.

The liberal Christian outlook is directed to a Power that is living, that is active in a love seeking concrete manifestation, and that finds decisive response in the living posture and gesture of Jesus of Nazareth. In a world that has with some conscientiousness turned against this kind of witness and its vocabulary, the effect of this witness will in a special way depend upon the quality of its costingness in concrete action and upon its relevance to the history that is in the making. To say this is only to say that the truly reliable God is the Lord of history and also that our sins will find us out. Yet, this Lord of history has given us a world in which the possibility of new beginnings is ever present along with the judgment that is always upon us. To this Lord of history Jesus responded with his message and demonstration of hope in concert with sacrifice.

33 · The Liberal Christian Holds
Up the Mirror

One of the recent developments of research in the area of biology has been the study of social organizations among the animals, and particularly among the fowls. Some of the social scientists have been studying, for example, how long it takes a group of fowl to form a social organization. As I recall the findings, only eighteen to twenty-four hours elapse before a group of chickens hitherto unacquainted with each other form a tightly structured social organization, a flock.

The social organization turns out to be a rigid hierarchy. At the top is one chief hen who by dint of pecking the other hens has established her prestige: she is able to peck any other hen and none other dares peck back. Immediately beneath her in pecking rank will be three or four hens who are second in command; they have established their power and "right" to peck all the other hens in the yard except Number One. And then gradually the hierarchy broadens out to *hoi polloi,* the common hens, who may be pecked by any of the hens in the higher echelons but may not peck back. Food and other privileges become accessible in accord with these rankings. This hierarchy is called a "pecking order."

A hierarchy of this sort is to be found also among other animals. Among horses, for example, there are "kicking orders." Squirrels, monkeys, and even cows establish comparable pyramids of authority. And we all know that something similar is to be found among human beings, a social organization in which authority is centralized at the top and in which some kind of patterned obedience is required of others.

A PROTEST AGAINST PECKING ORDERS

Liberal Christianity, in its religious and social articulation, might be defined as a protest against pecking orders. It began in the modern world as a protest against ecclesiastical and political pecking orders. Protest in the economic sphere also soon appeared. One of the principal sources of liberal Christianity is what is today called the left wing of the Reformation or, as Professor George Williams calls it, the Radical Reformation, a com-

Originally presented at All Souls Unitarian Church, Washington, D.C., in 1956, this essay was published in *The Unitarian Universalist Christian* 32, nos. 1–2 (Spring/Summer 1977). Reprinted by permission.

posite movement that in part originated as a protest against the authoritarian organization of the churches that were ruled from the top down. Another source is the Enlightenment, with its demand for individual, rational self-determination. (Subsequently, Romanticism emphasized individualism still more, and uncovered something deeper than reason—intuition and feeling.)

In interpreting the character and source of liberal Christianity in this way, I presuppose that in order fully to understand any religious movement—and indeed, any secular ideological movement—one must include the answer to the question: What consequences do the ideas held by the group have in the sphere of action? A belief is effective when people are prepared to act in accordance with it. "By their fruits shall ye know them." We are accustomed to applying this pragmatic test to the behavior of *individuals*. The test may be applied also to groups' behavior, and specifically to religious movements. We can extend the test to religious groups by raising the question: What difference do the ideas of the religious movement make in social organization? What kind of social organization do the "believers" prefer? How do they want authority articulated? Do they favor a pecking order or some other kind of "association"?

Although there are other tests of meaning, this pragmatic test is revealing when applied to theological doctrines. We determine in part the meaning of belief in God or in Christ as held by any group, by answering the question: What does the believer in God want changed in the society? And what is to be retained? The questions raised by this pragmatic sociological method do not imply that a belief that claims to be an index to the way of salvation will provide important perspectives for all aspects of life and thus also for institutional structures. It is not appropriate to interpret religious ideas in terms of their effect upon the individual as an isolated entity. In fact, such an entity is a myth. Everything must be understood in terms of its relations, and so also the human individual. One determines the meaning of a religious idea, then, by examining its implications for individuals in their relatedness, that is, for their institutions, family, church, state, economy, and voluntary associations.

Liberal Christianity, as we have noted, has its roots partially in the Radical Reformation. The radical wing in England—the Independents, the Friends, and the shapers of congregational polity, for example—rejected the notion that the cosmos is a hierarchy and that society must be organized on the pattern of hierarchy controlled by priest and monarch. They insisted that the state should not use coercion in matters of religious belief and that the ecclesiastical authorities should not interfere in the political order. Accordingly, proponents of the radical wing demanded the separation of church and state. They offered various theological defenses for this position. A typical antihierarchical view appealed to the belief in the freedom of the spirit: "The Spirit bloweth where it listeth." The radical wing also insisted that the church is a layperson's church; it is not to be controlled by the clergy. Every child of God has his or her own individual conscience, for the Holy Spirit is available to every child of God. As applied to church order, this view has been called the principle of radical laicism. Indeed, the Friends have held that there should be no "hireling priestcraft." Every member is also a minister. In various ways the radical wing found a sanction in the New Testament for their conception of the Holy Spirit and of church organization.

In the Radical Reformation one finds also the view that religious fellowship does not require uniformity of belief. A religious fellowship should rather be the place where the members, respecting each other in mutual confidence, will hear from each other and will test what the Holy Spirit prompts; thus the fellowship, and also each member of the fellowship, is to be enriched. As Rufus M. Jones says in *Mysticism and Democracy in the English Commonwealth* [Cambridge, Mass., 1932], "There is something more in each individual than there would be if he were operating in isolation. He becomes in a real sense *over-individual,* and transcends himself through the life of others." In this fellowship, a minority position was to be protected in the very name of the Holy Spirit. According to this view, God works in history where free consensus appears under the great Taskmaster's eye. Thus the sanction for the maintenance of freedom was held to be a covenant between the people and God. The idea of the covenanted fellowship with a high degree of local autonomy is the essence of what is called congregational polity.

Out of these ideas and others like them, political democracy was born. Basic to this whole development was the demand for co-archy in place of hierarchy. This demand was first applied to the church and then also to the state. Thus some proponents of the radical wing considered their free church to be a model for a democratic state. The political conceptions were drawn *by analogy* from the conception of the free church. What were originally elements of a doctrine of the church appeared now as ingredients of a political theory: the consent of the governed, the demand for universal suffrage, the rule of law over the executive, the principle of loyal opposition. The conception of the democratic society, then, is in part a descendant of the conception of the free church.

In the Enlightenment of the eighteenth century, new influences affected the emerging liberal Christianity. Here a vigorous antitraditionalism, a belief in the perfectibility of humanity through progress, in freedom of inquiry, and in the test of reason were characteristic emphases.

From these sources, liberal Christianity gained its major thrust. In the face of the traditional pecking orders, liberalism developed its characteristic feature, namely, the conviction that human beings should be liberated, indeed should liberate themselves, from the shackles that impede religious, political, and economic freedom and which impede the appearance of a rational and voluntary piety and of equality and justice for all. Here we can discern vigorous reformist (and even utopian) elements that were already strong in certain branches of the radical wing.

There are, of course, other ways in which liberal Christianity's origin and development could be described. One could, for example, stress liberalism's confidence in humanity and human capabilities. Here one would need to expound its protest against the doctrine of total depravity. One could stress its promotion of tolerance. Here one would need to recall its thrust against sectarianism, its demand for universality, a demand that has engendered a new attitude of sympathy and openness toward other religions. Or one could bring to the fore its passion for rationality and rational discrimination. Here one would recall its battle against rigid and arbitrary traditionalism and against obscurantism, a battle that has brought historical understanding of the tradition and especially of the sacred literature. Here one would stress also its eager encouragement and appropriation of the values of culture and science. All of these things have belonged to liberal Christianity. In earlier days before the outlook had lost some of its luminous glow, they were summed up in the magic symbol "progress." A concurrent theological symbol was "progressive revelation."

AMBIGUITIES OF LIBERALISM

But liberal Christianity has its blemishes. These blemishes have appeared not merely because its performance has fallen short of its intentions. Some of its blemishes have issued from its character. One must add, however, that criticisms of liberal Christianity have come not only from hostile critics. They have been made also by the liberals themselves. Indeed, in our undertaking here to hold up the mirror, we as liberal Christians may look critically at ourselves, and thus aim to vindicate the method of liberalism. Liberalism lives partly from its criticism of itself.

Before we consider some of the criticisms of liberal Christianity, we should note certain ambiguities that attach to its definition. These ambiguities arise from the fact that a tension inevitably develops within liberal Christianity and within liberalism in general. This tension is an aspect of the morphology of ideas and of social movements. Alfred North Whitehead has pointed out that when we examine the intellectual agencies that function in the adventures of ideas, we find a rough division into two types, one of general ideas, the other of highly specialized notions. As an example of a general idea he cites the ancient ideal of the intellectual and moral grandeur of the human soul; as an example of a highly specialized notion he cites the ideals of early Christianity. The distinction is pertinent for an understanding of the tensions and ambiguities within liberalism and within liberal Christianity.

An analogous distinction may be made between the general idea of liberalism and the more highly specialized notions of liberalism worked out in the eighteenth and nineteenth centuries. Liberalism's "general idea" has been to promote liberation from tyranny, provincialism, and arbitrariness, and thus to contribute to the meaningful fulfillment of human existence. This aspect of liberalism we may call its progressive element: it is critical of the status quo and seeks new paths of fulfillment. A "specialized notion" of liberalism has developed during the last two centuries, namely a doctrine of pre-established harmony coupled with the laissez-faire theory of society. Under the conditions of early capitalism, this doctrine was vindicated in economic progress, but beginning a century ago, progressive liberalism became critical of this "specialized notion." From the point of view of progressive liberalism, the laissez-faire society was producing new pecking orders that frustrated both equality and justice. Accordingly, the more general idea of liberalism has come into conflict with a specialized version of it. Progressive liberalism has criticized laissez-faire liberalism as closely bound up with the narrow interests of the middle class, and also with the dogma of political nonintervention in the economic sphere. Progressive liberals have protested against the status quo that was defended by laissez-faire liberals. In support of the crescent labor movement they demanded a more responsible society—a political intervention for the sake of the disinherited. So great has been the tension between the general and the specialized forms of liberalism that the strategies of progressive liberalism (working in the direction of the welfare state) have become almost the opposite of those of laissez-faire liberalism. We see, then, that there is an ambiguity in the meaning of the word *liberalism,* and that it is the consequence of a tension between two related versions of liberalism. Indeed, the ambiguities are even more complex than we have indicated. New tensions and ambiguities have appeared in recent years as progressive liberalism has moved on to become critical of an exclusive devotion to the pattern of the welfare state. Here progressive and laissez-faire liberalism has moved nearer to each other. Thus the ambiguities in terminology continue to appear.

But there are still other ambiguities to be taken into account. Liberal Christianity is not identical with liberalism considered either as a generalized or as a specialized notion. Liberal Christianity is explicitly oriented to the ultimate resources of human existence and meaning discerned in the Old and the New Testaments and in Christian experience. At the same time, liberal Christianity has been associated with several kinds of liberalism both generalized and specialized. Indeed, because of its intentional entanglement in the secular order (in contrast to orthodoxies that claim to remain aloof), liberal Christianity is never in its actuality easily to be distinguished from one or another of these forms of liberalism, except perhaps in terms of its ultimate orientation. Accordingly, liberal Christianity has aimed to be critical of these forms of liberalism. The relationships of creative involvement and of critical tension are roughly analogous to those which Paul Tillich takes into account in his conception of the "Protestant principle," a principle that is creative but that also brings under judgment every actualization of Protestantism. Thus liberal Christianity may be understood as a continuing dialogue not only between these and alternative nonliberal outlooks. The very persistence of these dialogues is indispensable for the viability of liberal Christianity. But it also gives an inner tension and an ambiguity of direction to any liberal Christianity or any liberalism that is not single-mindedly and piously driving towards self-destruction.

THE LOSS OF DEPTH

In order to consider some of the criticisms of liberal Christianity I want to employ a somewhat pedestrian analogy. Every viable social movement or philosophy requires several dimensions, for it must have body—amplitude of form or shape. In short, it must have the dimensions of depth, breadth, and length. I shall interpret the criticisms of liberal Christianity in terms of these dimensions.

First, then, we shall speak of depth. Liberal Christianity, in the initial forms emanating from the Radical Reformation, placed great emphasis on the sovereignty of God, the view that the whole of life—not merely the inner life, not merely the life of the individual, but the whole of life including social institutions—is to be brought under obedience to the righteous, sovereign God and in response to the promptings of the Holy Spirit. We have noticed already how these conceptions, as articulated by the Radical Reformation and by the Enlightenment and Romanticism, involved the rejection of the hierarchy of being and of the traditional church and society based upon this hierarchy of being.

In the nineteenth century there appeared new conceptions of historical development and new knowledge from the sciences. The earlier ideas of progress were merged with the idea of natural and social evolution. Here the liberal Christians made a laudable effort to take seriously the new insights emanating from Darwinian biology and from other historical research. The Bible was subjected to a new criticism. Previously the idea of miracle had been rejected. Now the history of religion and society was seen to be in constant evolution. Partly from this insight came one of the great accomplishments of modern times—the higher criticism of the sacred literature.

At the same time, however, a misreading of the Gospel ensued, and with it the loss of depth in the religious interpretation of God, man, and history. The conception of God became purely immanental; we humans were believed to be gradually becoming better and better as God unfolded himself in evolving humanity, and history was viewed as the arena of unilinear progress. Enlightenment conceptions of the human being as a rational being and the Neo-Darwinian view of human evolution progressing "onward and upward forever" were alleged to be implicit in the New Testament. These ideas, seen in succession, were taken to be evidences of "progressive revelation."

Father George Tyrrell, the Catholic modernist of a generation ago, indicated cryptically the error in this modernization of the gospel when he said that the liberal Christian looks down the deep well of higher criticism, sees his own image, and calls it Jesus. This particular form of modernization of the gospel was not only objectively false, it issued in a reduction of tension between the gospel and "the world," between the gospel and the natural human being. The overweening confidence in the natural propensities of human nature and in the upward grain of history was a superficial view, and it could not be maintained before the facts of life.

Much has happened to call in question this optimism about human nature and history. In our century of rebarbarization we have witnessed a dissolution of values and the appearance of great collective demonries, the nihilism that Neitzsche predicted. Progress is now seen not to take place in the moral and spiritual realm merely through inheritance. Each generation and each person must anew win insight into the ambiguity of human nature and must in changed circumstances give new relevance to moral and spiritual values. This renewal does not take place in technical progress—with each succeeding generation standing on the shoulders of previous achievement. It requires a realistic appraisal of human foibles and a life of continuing humility and repentance. At the depths of human nature there are potential divine resources, but there are also ever-powerful forces working for perversion and destruction. In the New Testament view, the Reign of God brings all persons under judgment; it is not sanction for what Thoreau called "improved means with unimproved ends." Albert Schweitzer, near the beginning of the present century, showed the wide distance between certain modern conceptions of progress and the New Testament conception of the Reign of God. Since his time and particularly through the New Testament studies of Rudolf Otto, contemporary liberal Christians have discovered new depths in the biblical teachings regarding history and the Reign of God. The tragic dimensions of history were missed by those liberal Christians who interpreted history as unilinear progress. The appreciation of the depth of perversity, as well as of the resources available to humanity, lies beyond the purview of the "modern" doctrines of progress.

A corresponding loss of depth is to be observed in a related aspect of liberal Christianity as it has come to us from the nineteenth century. Under the influence of utilitarianism and also of Kantianism, liberal Christianity in wide sectors has tended to identify religion with the good life. Here we have the thinning out of liberal Christianity into moralism. Other forces, to be sure, were operative in liberal Christian thought—for example, the heritage from Schleiermacher which emphasized the transmoral character of religion and specifically of the Christian religion. But from Kant and also from the "practical" bourgeoisie, many liberal Christians have learned to reduce religion to the observance of ethical precepts. Thus again the depth dimension was lost. Moralism replaced the deeper relatedness to the divine source of and judgment upon our moral "values." In the old liberal Christianity, Jesus was viewed as primarily a moral teacher and model. Thus the divine ground and source of meaning as disclosed by Jesus and the Old Testament prophets were lost sight of. The protest against the Christ of the creeds was a justifiable protest against a dehumanized Christ, and it was also a justifiable attempt to give Chris-

tianity a new ethical relevance. But ignoring the problems dealt with in
biblical theology and in Christology could only lead to a narrowing of
sensitivity. This reduction is to be observed also in the interpretation of
Jesus' parables as primarily ethical parables, whereas modern liberal
scholarship has reminded us that they point to the more-than-human resources of human existence, to the Reign of God "that grows of itself"
and not ultimately by human devising. Here again the writings of the
liberal Christian scholar Rudolf Otto have been of signal importance.

Something further must be said regarding the loss of depth consequent
upon the waning of interest in theology. In addition to the influence of
forces already mentioned, this tendency has been promoted by scientism,
an illiberal imperialism of method. It has been promoted also by the
implausible conceptions of God that have been entertained not only by
the orthodox but also by merely traditionalist liberal Christians. Whatever the cause and whatever the justifications of these tendencies may be,
the outcome in some circles of liberal Christianity has been deplorable. A
whole range of perennial problems for the religious consciousness has been
ignored. In effect some liberal Christians have said in response to those
concerned with theological inquiry, "We must tell you that you are dealing with pseudo-problems. You are an orthodox Christian, perhaps without knowing it. Liberal Christianity has emancipated itself from concern
with these pseudo-problems." The paucity of thought and of piety here is
blatantly evident today in the lack of a theological interpretation of the
great social issues. This kind of "religion" is neither liberal nor Christian.
It is a superficial provincial backwash of "progress," impotent to deal intellectually and responsibly with the deeper, ultimate issues of life. Hap-
pily, there are countervailing tendencies among liberal Christians, hinted
at in our previous incidental references to certain liberal Christian leaders.

THE LOSS OF IDENTITY

In some respects we have already anticipated the discussion of the dimension of breadth. One of the characteristic features of liberal Christianity
has been its intention to maintain familiarity with and participation in
the best thought and practice of the secular world. This feature of liberal
Christianity has roots not only in the idea that Christian faith is more
than a repetition of traditional words and practices. It is rooted also in
the conviction that God's truth is by no means restricted (if granted) to
those who praise God's name. This conviction is not of recent vintage
among liberal Christians. We now know, as we did not a generation ago,

that the relation between religion and science two and three centuries ago was not one of mere hostility ("warfare" was John Draper's description in his long-familiar book). The Protestants, and particularly the liberals, long ago defended and protected scientists whose findings were at first blush believed to be inimical to Christian faith or to biblical revelation. The methods and findings of the natural and the cultural sciences are of concern to liberal Christianity. It holds that these methods and findings must take their place within the integrity of knowledge. Moreover, literature, the fine arts, and philosophy offer interpretations and criticisms of life which contribute to self-understanding and must be evaluated. They are media through which the meaning of existence and the frustration of this meaning are clarified and interpreted in their interrelatedness. The liberal Christian holds that we can gain a sense of the full import of faith by confronting the insights and questionings that are provided by these disciplines. In the nineteenth century, Matthew Arnold stated this aspect of the liberal Christian outlook when he said that he who knows only his Bible does not know even his Bible. Shailer Mathews two generations ago shocked some of the pious among his contemporaries by editing a book on *The Contributions of Science to Religion* [New York, 1924]. The dialogue with these disciplines is necessary if liberal Christianity is not to become arbitrary, obscurantist, and irrelevant. It is necessary also if the interplay between liberal Christianity and the generalized and the specialized ideas of liberalism is to be fruitful in the changing historical situation.

But breadth has its hazards. It may be misinterpreted to mean the acceptance of a little bit of this and the rejection of a little bit of that, and with little sense of the whole. "Breadth" of this sort may be tantamount to irresponsibility with respect to religious belief; it may prevent the achievement of integrity. To many people the attraction of liberal Christianity has been its openness, its tolerance, its freedom. But these qualities can spell the loss of character.

This loss of character in the pursuit of breadth is the more threatening in a society where change is rapid, where there is a multiplicity of norms, where the mass media of communication exert pressures that constitute a form of psychic violence. Within the churches themselves one can encounter a bewildering variety of outlooks. Freud and Jung, Adam Smith and Marx, Schweitzer and Toynbee, Whitehead and Russell, are only a few of the names that may be cited to exemplify the variety of motifs that receive a hearing. One could mention other motifs that have a less distinguished character. These motifs, taken together without some explicit abiding unities, can lead to confusion—interesting confusion perhaps, but confusion nevertheless.

There is nothing more debilitating than sheer variety—a synonym for chaos. Carlyle once said of Tennyson that he was always carrying a bit of chaos around in his pocket turning it into cosmos. Properly understood, liberal Christianity is not an invitation to fissiparous freedom or to trivialized freedom. It seeks orderliness of mind, and it seeks it in and through fellowship. That is, it seeks consensus. This does not mean that it seeks fixed creedal uniformity. But it seeks a center; indeed, it is worthy of respect only when it lives from this center.

This center is not jeopardized by variety alone. The greater threat to the maintenance or the achievement of a center is accommodation to the idols of nationalism, race, and class. Liberal Christianity in Germany during the period of the Third Reich possessed very feeble powers of resistance. Indeed, many of the "German Christians" and even many of the members of the German Faith Movement were former religious liberals who found in Hitler a prophet of "progressive revelation." To be sure, many of the orthodox Protestants had managed to be irrelevant, if not cooperative, in face of the rise of Nazism. Moreover, millions of Roman Catholics also capitulated to Hitler. Shortly after Hitler's assumption of power and at a time when he sorely needed any scrap of respectability available, the Vatican made a concordat with him. Certain features of the Vatican concordat with Mussolini are still valid in Italy today. The collaboration of many "liberal Christians" with Hitlerism has made liberal Christians all over the world newly aware of the necessity of a center along with breadth; indeed, of a center for the breadth. Without this centripetal power, or (to change the figure) without this root, the fruits become a wilding, destructive growth.

For liberal Christianity the center is in a faith that finds its classic expression in the Old Testament prophets and in the being, the character, and the mission of Jesus. In that faith we find the generating spirit and the norm of norms for liberal Christianity. This faith is a response to the sustaining, creative, judging, transforming power that gives rise to a community of love and justice. As we have indicated earlier, it was a special articulation of this faith which initially brought to birth those elements of the Radical Reformation out of which liberal Christianity and democracy emerged. Without this faith, breadth can become chaos and dark night.

The Loss of Historical Rootage

This brings us to the third dimension, the dimension of length. If the first dimension is depth—a vertical—dimension pointing to the divine ground, and if the second dimension is a horizontal one referring to the surrounding milieu, then the third is also horizontal; it is the time-dimension. One of the distinctive features of liberal Christianity has been its futuristic emphasis, an emphasis that is found in both the Old and the New Testament and also in the heretical sects of the Middle Ages and of the left wing of the Reformation. Liberal Christianity has not been oriented to the past as such, and to tradition. The Bible and the later eschatological movements have served it as a stimulus to continuing renewal. Indeed, we are indebted in part to liberal Christianity for the modern historical consciousness, a consciousness that has made modernity aware of the inevitability of change, of the necessity to be critical of the past and the present, and aware also of the possibilities of the future.

But there are hazards in the time-dimension, too. We have already noted the hazard of entertaining false hopes for the future. We must now observe that a sense of the differences between past and present has in some liberal circles issued in an uncritical antitraditionalism. This anti-traditionalism serves always as a threat to liberal Christianity's maintaining its historical rootage. It tempts it into a provincialism in time. I can illustrate this danger from a recent occurrence. Not long ago I attended in a liberal church a meeting at which a denominational representative gave an address on religious education. In the spirit of what calls itself "progressive education," he outlined a curriculum in which the emphasis rested upon training the children for living in the present; all of the material recommended for presentation to the children was of contemporary vintage. Nothing even of the modern background of Christianity in general, or of liberal Christianity, was mentioned. During the discussion that followed his address one of the parents in the audience said, "I am puzzled by your exclusive emphasis on the present and the future. I have been in the habit of supposing that religious education in a liberal church should include a critical appreciation of our past and also a critical appreciation of the Bible." The "religious educator" replied, "I don't mean to say that the Bible has to be excluded. If you want it in the curriculum, I don't see why you should be prevented. We believe in freedom in the liberal church." This cavalier attitude toward the experience of the past, and specifically toward the Bible, can only result in organized religious illiteracy. This kind of illiteracy goes under the name of modernity, but it is simply a form of provincialism and even of rootlessness. It is a provincialism that is very similar to the corresponding provincialism of certain kinds of orthodoxy. The rigid orthodox person of fundamentalist persuasion holds that all we need to know is between the covers of an ancient book. The "emancipated" liberal seems to hold that we live only in and on the present and for the future. Both of these forms of rigidity are provincial and dogmatic. Fortunately, higher education for the most part is less provincial.

Nothing significant in human history is achieved except through long-standing continuities. This principle is as valid in the sphere of religion as in the realms of science, politics, and art. In the sphere of religion particularly, the loss of the time-dimension can carry with it the loss also of the depth dimension.

The decisive, substantial features of liberal Christianity are Christian and biblical, and the characteristically modern religious elements of liberal Christianity shall always have been in the left wing of the Reformation (though one may rightly question whether the left wing as such may be properly considered as definitively normative). Liberal Christianity cannot retain its own character when it severs itself from these roots. A sociological consideration here is almost equally decisive. Without a vital continuing frame of reference, no social movement can make a significant difference for its own constituency or in its impact on the world. One finds in the Bible and in the theological and devotional literature of the Christian tradition the concepts and the structures, the concerns and the insights, that are indispensable for any critical religious interpretation of the meaning of *our* historical existence and also for the maintenance of those sensitivities that can transcend and be critical of civilization. Indeed, this orientation alone is reliable for maintaining a critical attitude toward liberal Christianity itself and its fellow travelers, and toward the general ideas and institutions and the specialized notions and institutions of liberalism.

THE FINAL CRITERION OF RENEWAL

These criticisms and evaluations of liberal Christianity do not take into account all important aspects of the movement. For example, the attacks upon liberal Christianity and upon liberalism in general which have been coming from the so-called New Conservatism or from the more "radical" types of social philosophy, have not been reported. Nor have liberal Christianity's various attitudes toward non-Christian religions been dealt with. But the types of criticism presented here have been sufficiently influential to have made some liberal Christians feel uncomfortable under the label of "liberalism." In some quarters, indeed, liberal Christians now call themselves "neo-liberals." Concurrently with these developments the movement loosely called neo-orthodoxy has appeared. Actually, there are certain affinities between neo-liberalism and neo-orthodoxy. Indeed, the significant dialogue going on today in this area is not between the old-fashioned liberals and the old-fashioned orthodox; it is between the neo-liberals and the neo-orthodox.

In the context of these dialogues, I have here emphasized that liberal Christianity degenerates when the depth dimension is lost sight of or disappears, that is it not to be identified with any merely ethical outlook but is concerned also with the divine ground for ethics and for the criticism of ethics, that breadth cannot be salutary for liberal Christianity if the latter does not possess a center-stance, that the substance and character of liberal Christianity are to be understood for the most part in the context of biblical faith and Christian experience, and that these latter are to be given relevance today only through a continuing openness to criticism and through a continuing effort to give clarity and new formulation to the faith in face of the contemporary situation. Presupposed throughout is the view that liberal Christianity in criticizing itself aims to confront anew the ultimate demands and to be open to the more-than-human resources that no human tradition or devising can claim to originate or control.

In the face of these demands and resources liberal Christianity must be judged not only in terms of its intellectual depth and breadth and historical consciousness. It must be judged also by the kind of people it produces. And it must be judged by its consequences in relation to the struggle against pecking orders and to the struggle for a community of freedom and justice and love.

These criteria of depth, breadth, and length must be understood under the axiom, "By their fruits shall you know them." A decisive test is the consequence in individual behavior and also in group behavior. Depth, breadth, and length belong to the integrity of the individual; they impinge also upon the common life. The questions remain, How do these qualities make a difference in the face of the pecking orders—in the face of the demonic forces and structures of our time? How do they affect our attitudes and actions in the institutional sphere, in the church, the political order, the economic order? The pragmatic theory of meaning in these spheres raises the question, What do we want to remain unchanged there, and what do we want changed in our institutional patterns? What do we work for?

When we look at contemporary society and remember that the Radical Reformation began as a protest against oppression and as an effort in the direction of a new society, we recognize that the Reformation must continue. I need not spell this out here. Instead, I will ask you to take the pulse of a segment of our society today.

A short time ago a black physician in Chicago told me that his regular nightly duty is to treat some black child in the ghetto who has been bitten by a rodent. Recently he responded to an emergency call late at night. The younger of two small girls had been bitten in her sleep. When the doctor tried to give first aid to the younger sister, she was still so frightened that he could not persuade her to stand still to receive the antiseptic and a bandage. She would not quiet down. Finally, the older sister shouted, "Sally, if you don't be quiet, and let the doctor fix you, we'll put you back in the room where the rat is."

A melodramatic episode it is, and grotesque. But it provides a clue to what is meant if we say that at this late date in modern "progress" we still live in tyrannous pecking orders—enhanced by rats. Yes, depth, breadth, and length are still in the Valley of Decision.

Postscript, 1988. It is significant, lamentable, that President Reagan views the word *liberal* as the banner of the enemy. Arriving at the Republican convention in New Orleans, he declared, "The masquerade is over, it's time to use the dreaded L-word; to say that the policies of our opposition . . . are liberal, liberal, liberal." As Professor of History Fritz Stern of Columbia University observed, "This pervasive and ill-defined attack on liberalism is directed at one of America's noblest traditions. . . . In 1949, in a work that sought to recall liberalism to its larger vision, Lionel Trilling, the eminent critic, wrote, 'In the United States at this time liberalism is not only the dominant but even the sole intellectual tradition.' . . . Future critics may find it difficult to identify the Reagan era with any great political traditions of American history. They may have to resort to old-fashioned moral judgments about the past eight years—judgments of sorrow, perhaps of outrage" (*New York Times,* September 4, 1988, section 4, p. 15).

34 · *Liberals and Evangelicals*

Stephan Leacock, the Canadian political scientist and wit, tells of the young man who said, "All I am I owe to my study of the classics." To which the reply was given, "A grave charge, young man, a very grave charge." In order that you may know something about my credentials, let me say at the outset that what I am I owe to my upbringing in the household of a rural Baptist fundamentalist minister in the State of Washington and to my migration through atheistic and classical humanism to the household of faith called liberal Christianity qualified by the Social Gospel and religious socialism. The names of my principal teachers include Shailer Mathews, Alfred North Whitehead, Irving Babbitt, Friedrich von Hügel, Ernst Troeltsch, Rudolf Otto, and Paul Tillich. The older I grow, however, the more I recognize that my roots are in the Baptist fundamentalism. A grave charge is this, but I assume that many of you also have followed the path from fundamentalism to liberal Christianity.

My father held to a literal premillenarian interpretation of Scripture gained from meditating day and night on the text and especially on the footnotes of the *Scofield Reference Bible,* with its elaboration of the dispensational history of salvation leading to the Virgin Birth and the Resurrection of Jesus Christ and on to the Second Coming. He believed that the world is under the rule of the "principalities and powers" of the Evil One, that this rule is to be overcome only by the Second Coming of Christ which may happen at any moment, and that meanwhile one should have as little as possible to do with present culture or with the state or other worldly institutions such as trade unions, and nothing whatsoever to do with novels or with the movies. He knew practically nothing about the history of the Church after its beginnings or about the history of the political order. Paradoxically, however, he admired William Jennings Bryan because he was a fundamentalist, and my father voted only when Bryan was running. When Bryan lost repeatedly in the race for the presidency, he was newly convinced that the world was under the principalities and powers of evil. In the year 1906, I may add here, my father took me down the "sawdust trail" and lifted me up to reach the hand of Billy Sunday on that high, theatrical platform.

This essay is based on an address delivered at Baker University, Baldwin, Kansas, on October 24, 1978.

The religious liberalism to which I attached myself of course abandoned these features of fundamentalism. The Social Gospel with its conception of the church and the ministry became real to me when as minister in my first parish I became involved with a textile strike in Salem, Massachusetts, and even more acutely when I spent almost a year in the anti-Nazi underground of the Confessing Church in Germany, making the acquaintance of Peter Brunner, Martin Niemöller, and other leaders of the opposition. Eventually, I experienced heightened palpitation when I was apprehended by the Gestapo. (These Nazi officers for melodramatic effect brought their bloodhounds with them for the occasion.) When I returned to the United States to teach in Chicago, I became one of the founders of the Independent Voters of Illinois, which managed to gain decisive influence in more than a hundred critical precincts in Chicago.

I should add a word regarding my father's fundamentalism, showing how he was a man of principle. When I was about ten years old he took me with him to attend a revivalist service in a neighboring rural church where the evangelist was supervising seizures of the Spirit which brought converts to roll on the floor. In pens in back of the church others groaned and travailed as they waited for seizure. Inside the church in the midst of the service, indeed at its height, my father, standing up in front of the pulpit, interrupted the service and warned the ecstatic congregation against the preacher, in stentorian tones reminding them that the way of salvation is not through emotional seizures but alone through belief in the vicarious sacrifice of Christ on Golgotha. Having given his warning, he seized me by the hand, and (shaking the heretical dust from our feet) we marched out of the church, departing from that astonished congregation. Several members of the group followed us out.

THE VARIETIES OF EVANGELICALISM

The incident about the seizure of the Spirit in "holy rolling" is of course scarcely characteristic of the New Evangelicalism. We must recognize also that the trend in some of its major forms is scarcely new in Anglo-American Protestantism. Moreover, the tension between Evangelicalism and liberal Christianity may be traced back to the Awakenings of the eighteenth century, though its roots go back to still earlier Pietism. Already in opposition to Jonathan Edwards, Charles Chauncy of the First Church in Boston attempted to expose the primitive traits of Edwardsian "thunderclaps of grace." (His view is not to be confused with that of the lady who said, "I was born in Boston. Why should I be born again?") In the next century the liberals criticized the evangelist Charles G. Finney for his sensationalist methods, whereupon he replied that in an age of sensationalism one must employ sensational devices to bring sinners to Christ. Besides, he said, revivalism can engender national unity and thus make the nation stronger. In the face of revivalism, the Congregationalist Horace Bushnell of Hartford published his influential volume *Christian Nurture* (1847), claiming that excessive emphasis on the sudden conversion experience brought about neglect of the cultivation of the Christian life after the conversion.

The resurgence of Evangelicalism in one form or another has occurred about every fifty years since the first Great Awakening in New England in the 1730s. Revivalism has become virtually an integral part of "the American way of life." Perry Miller has asserted that "for the mass of the American democracy the decades after 1800 were a continuing, even though intermittent, revival."

The New Evangelicalism for some years has been a popular item in the newspaper menu. Consequently, some contenders for public office today are likely to consider making a public confession of "faith" in the hope of gaining favor with the Evangelical power machine among the constituents. The advent of a president who is a "born again" Christian has given some impetus to the publicity. No one, however, can gainsay the phenomenal growth of Evangelical radio stations and a tripling of the number of Evangelical programs on television, not to speak of the increase in the number of Evangelical churches and of Evangelical students in the seminaries. This change of course bespeaks the emergence of many Evangelicals into the middle class.

Before we explore the broad spectrum of the movement, we should observe that all branches, except the eccentric fringes, avow a unity in the belief in "the inerrancy of Scripture." By this means they attempt to circumvent differences, for example, over determinism and free will, over the meaning of the Lord's Supper, and over social activism and personal idealism. Yet, the doctrine of "the inerrancy of Scripture" has itself engendered active and even bitter debate between those who hold for the infallibility of Scripture "in whole and in part" and those who want to get behind such formulations to discover the intention of particular words or passages of Scripture. I am reminded of the occasion two generations ago when Dean Shailer Mathews of the Divinity School of the University of Chicago was asked by a sleuth for heresy to give a "Yes or a No" answer to the question, "Do you or do you not believe that every word of Scripture is inspired by God?" Mathews answered, "If the letter is greater than the Spirit, No. But if the Spirit is greater than the letter, Yes."

Evangelicalism today does not possess a single identity. As John Howard Yoder, a leading Evangelical, has put it, Evangelicalism is a coalition of "intrinsically disparate elements." It is therefore no more of one piece than is liberal Christianity. Richard Quebedeaux, in his book *The Young Evangelicals* [New York: 1974], goes so far as to say that some "liberals and evangelicals are closer to each other today than either camp realizes."

Quebedeaux distinguishes between fundamentalists and Evangelicals. (The four types he delineates do not describe without remainder another forty million who think of themselves as fundamentalists and Evangelicals, but who are really too worldly for him to consider them so.) The fundamentalists he calls "separatists," such as Bob Jones University, Carl McIntire, and Billy James Hargis, and he distinguishes them from "open fundamentalists," such as Moody Bible Institute, Dallas Seminary, and prophet-journalist Hal Lindsey. In contrast to the fundamentalists there is a group that he calls "establishment evangelicalism," represented by the National Association of Evangelicals, Carl F. H. Henry and *Christianity Today*, Billy Graham, Wheaton College (Illinois), Campus Crusade for Christ, and the nonaligned conservative denominations. In social outlook these "establishment evangelicals" stress individual salvation and are conservative in social doctrine.

A fourth group Quebedeaux calls "the young evangelicals" [such as Jim Wallis, editor of *Sojourners,* and John Alexander, editor of *The Other Side*]. They adhere to the doctrines of the Virgin Birth and the deity of Christ, but they welcome the use of historical criticism; moreover, they are open to God's general revelation as interpreted by scientists. For them the first three chapters of Genesis no longer serve as geology or anthropology, possessing authority superior to scientific empiricism. Especially characteristic of this group is its emphasis on the need for prophetic criticism of capitalism, and particularly for a new, simple lifestyle. The positive action this group recommends is the inauguration of communes in which Evangelicals can exhibit the authentic *koinonia* [community] of New Testament vintage. With regard to radical social criticism, Timothy Smith some years ago and Donald Dayton more recently have pointed out the attacks on slavery, poverty, and other social evils made by certain nineteenth-century Evangelicals [such as Charles G. Finney]. I am reminded of my father's attacks on anti-Semitism; he argued that although the Jews rejected Christ it is not for Christians to persecute them; they should have only our love. For their rejection of Christ, he said, they are in God's hands and not ours. Among the Evangelicals as a whole, however, the attitude towards the Jews varies considerably.

EVANGELICALISM AND LIBERALISM

Ernst Troeltsch sixty years ago distinguished two types of revolt in the Radical Reformation of the sixteenth and seventeenth centuries. The one type he called "withdrawing sects," which renounced the establishment entirely and formed isolated enclaves in order to live in Christian community unspotted by the world. The other type Troeltsch called "aggressive sects." These sects not only directed radical criticism against the Establishment; they also attempted to introduce radical reforms in church and society, thereby becoming harbingers of modern, open, pluralistic, democratic society.

Apart from sharply criticizing capitalist society, the Sojourners group would seem to be somewhat similar to the old Anabaptist "withdrawing" sects. Slightly more aggressive is the outlook presented by the 1973 "Chicago Declaration of Evangelical Social Concern," written by Ronald J. Sider along with fifty Evangelical seminary professors and church leaders, lay and clerical. Let me quote a few lines from the "Declaration":

> As evangelical Christians committed to the Lord Jesus Christ and the full authority of the Word of God we affirm that God lays total claim upon the lives of his people. We cannot separate our lives in Christ from the situation in which God has placed us in the United States and the world.
>
> We confess that we have not acknowledged the complete claims of God in our lives. We acknowledge that God requires love. But we have not demonstrated the love of God to those suffering social abuses.
>
> We acknowledge that God requires justice. But we have not proclaimed or demonstrated his justice to an unjust American society. Although the Lord calls us to defend the social and economic rights of the poor and the oppressed, we have mostly remained silent. . . . We must attack the materialism of our culture and the maldistribution of the nation's wealth and services. . . .
>
> We make this declaration in the biblical hope that Christ is coming to consummate the Kingdom, and we accept his claim on our total discipleship till he comes.

To this group we should add Stephan Charles Mott, whose book *Biblical Ethics and Social Change* [New York: 1982] is the most comprehensive

328 LIBERAL CHRISTIANITY

work on this subject by an Evangelical. Mott has been politically active, showing a willingness to criticize publicly the politically conservative Evangelicals. He is a leader in an international movement of like-minded Evangelicals. Probably Quebedeaux had this group in mind when he wrote that "liberals and evangelicals are closer to each other today than either camp realizes."

We should recognize that, on the whole, Evangelicalism is a conservative movement with respect to public policy. A few years ago a former student of mine, the assistant minister of Park Street Church in Boston, a beacon church for "Establishment Evangelicalism," told me that ninety-nine percent of the congregation would vote for Barry Goldwater. I should add here that not long after this, in my panel discussion at Harvard with Billy Graham, Dr. Ockenga, then Minister of Park Street Church and now President of Gordon-Conwell College, classified me with Communists because I favored the welfare state for the sake of so-called justice. On the other hand, the Evangelicals in large numbers voted for Jimmy Carter as a "born again" Christian. We should note also that there are small groups of "young Evangelicals," as in Atlanta, who are carrying on heroic work of mercy and education among the deprived. Nevertheless, because of the authoritarian mentality of the right-wing fundamentalists (who far outnumber the Evangelicals), Robert Bellah in *The New Religious Consciousness* [Berkeley: 1976] predicts the possibility of a relapse into "traditional religious and moral absolutism." He thinks that at present there is less likelihood of this trend's appearing among Roman Catholics, though here he may overestimate the influence of Vatican Council II. This authoritarian aspect of fundamentalism has of course been long familiar to us all.

There is a contrast between the Evangelicals and the liberal Christians which is to the credit of the Evangelicals. Here I refer to a distinction made initially by John Calvin, the distinction between implicit faith and explicit faith. Implicit faith, best represented by medieval Catholicism, is available to those who do not have the capacity or the leisure to understand the doctrines or the sacraments, yet who in humility accept the teachings of the church and participate in good faith in the sacraments. Through the mercy of God those having implicit faith may, according to Thomas Aquinas, be assured of salvation. This conception is characteristic of the church for the masses, the Constantinian establishment. Explicit faith, on the other hand, is the faith characteristic of the "believers' church." The young "congregationalist" Martin Luther perhaps spoke for explicit faith when he said, "Everyone must do his own believing and his own dying." The Calvinists held that every person, every man, woman, and child, is able and is obliged to know the Scripture. Explicit faith demands this. In the modern period Calvinism was probably a major force conducive to literacy among the common folk, though the Friends, the Methodists, and the Baptists perhaps run a close second.

But along with urbanization and secularization a new illiteracy regarding religion has emerged. Let me illustrate this by an embarrassing example. For a decade I co-conducted seminars in the Harvard Graduate School of Business Administration, seminars on "religion and business decisions." One summer we held a lengthy seminar for laypersons from all over the country. The prerequisite for admission to the seminar was membership on a board of trustees of a church or a synagogue. We started off by asking the question, "What is Christianity?" The typical answers we received were, "It is the Golden Rule," or "It is living according to your best lights." We encountered equally difficult sledding when we asked for a distinction between religion and ethics. The participants were regular churchgoers, and they were successful and otherwise literate professional people. To cope with this illiteracy we devised a mimeographed glossary for the members of the seminar to consult during the lectures and discussions. A challenge, then, of Evangelicalism and fundamentalism to the liberal churches is the challenge to our devolution into implicit faith, in part giving up our earlier emphasis on explicit faith.

Consider a similarity between many liberals and the majority of Evangelicals. One of the most pervasive characteristics of the present period is the emphasis outside and inside the church on small-group intimacy, on what is called "the new narcissism." Ours has become an Age of Psychology. Its characteristic modality is the sphere of interpersonal relations. This emphasis on the individual and on interpersonal relationships goes back in part to a narrow pietism, prominent in Jonathan Edwards. In the name of personal conversion Edwards almost entirely ignored the public theology of the Puritans. His major test of the authenticity of conversion was its influence on individual behavior. Actually, it was the liberals in the eighteenth and nineteenth centuries who tried to maintain the Calvinist format of a public theology concerned with issues of public policy. Already in the 1830s the Unitarian clergy were criticizing capitalism and demanding a socialist transformation of society. In the next decade Theodore Parker undertook to analyze American society in terms of the character and distribution of power.

The Ethical Vocation of the Liberal Churches

Ernst Troeltsch distinguished between subjective and objective virtues. Subjective virtues appear in the individual and the primary relations of person to person. Objective virtues require institutional expression through the political, the economic, and the vocational patterns of social behavior where the organization of power and the power of organization are crucial. The rage for psychology, for sermons that tell us how to overcome our worries and that also avoid public issues, for the instant intimacy of the "house church" or of the encounter group, is focused entirely on subjective virtues, in Troeltsch's sense. This same truncation is to be found in the average novel and movie, and in commercial television. Speaking of this kind of truncation of human nature, the poet Christoph Morgenstern said, "A knee walks lonely through the world." The truncation represents a kind of abandonment of social institutional responsibility. One can explain this tendency as alienation from the impersonality and anonymity of a mass society and as a protest against being a cog in the machinery of bureaucratic organization.

We may say that the ethical vocation of the liberal church in these matters is to promote the interplay between the subjective and objective virtues, between personal integrity and social-institutional participation and responsibility. Here the biblical perspective is crucial. The God we liberals worship is different from the God of the mainstream of Evangelicalism. Our conception of religion binds together Old Testament covenantal prophetism with the personalism stressed in the Gospels, which looks toward the formation of an intimate community of faith. Both of these elements, social prophetism and concern for the individual and especially the deprived, appear in the Old Testament. The genius of early Christianity lay partly in its insistence on the inclusion of the Old Testament in the scriptural canon.

The ethical vocation of the church calls for inventiveness, which under religious auspices combines the subjective and the objective virtues. This vocation makes a heavy demand on preaching, on worship, on religious education, and on pastoral care. It demands inventiveness also in the life of the parish.

One of the characteristic institutions of democratic society is the voluntary association, the organization that provides the means for bringing citizens together to achieve consensus on issues of common concern and to find ways of acting on that consensus. In a local parish in which I have been a member we formed four or five subcommittees open to all members of the congregation: committees on the family, the gap between the generations, civil rights, race relations, housing, and the like. Members of each committee were asked to work in a secular committee of the community promoting the same concern. The people were brought into significant relationship with other people of social conscience in the community. They also came into contact with people of differing perspectives. Then they brought back to their respective committees reports of their experiences in these outside organizations.

Each committee had to prepare a report for the congregation, including perhaps a minority report. The minister preached on the issues of the report, and then a "town meeting" was held. Three things coming from this strategy were notable: first, the rare quality of fellowship engendered; second, the articulateness and self-identity of the members as they answered questions at the "town meeting"; and third, the inventiveness of the forms of social action devised in order to implement the consensus. In no instance, however, was a subcommittee to speak or act for the congregation. As a consequence of this entire strategy we together had vindicated the truth of the axiom: Every personal problem is a social problem, and every social problem is a personal problem.

It would be wrong to suppose that the "New Evangelicals" are unaware of the magnitude of the social, and especially of the economic and the international, problems of the Atomic Age. It would be wrong also to assume that all of them accept as adequate the restricting of social action to exemplary witnessing of a new lifestyle in the small community of dedicated Christians. Some of the New Evangelicals, like some religious liberals, aim to participate directly in efforts leading to social change. For both the question arises, Who is responsible? An Anglican theologian and scientist, William Whewell (1794–1866), has offered a theological perspective on this question. Commenting on St. Paul's admonition in Romans 13 that we should respect the powers that are ordained, he reminds us that in a democracy the citizen possesses by law a political power. The citizen is one of "the powers that be" and therefore shares responsibility.

The Old Testament concept of the covenant moves in the same direction. The prophet in the name of the covenant not only calls for righteousness; the prophet places upon the entire people the responsibility for the character of the society. As we see in the Psalms, the prayer of the individual for righteousness is connected with the covenant of the people.

In a time when nuclear power is able to destroy us all, in a time when the Third World is being exploited by worldwide economic powers, in a time when the planet is being polluted by chemical engineering, in a time when natural resources are being irremediably wasted by energy policy and are being greedily consumed by the "have" nations, we are approaching a period when a tightening of the belt will be required if we are to fend off carrion struggle. At this point again we can hear the Old Testament prophet assert that the authentic and viable society is one that is inclusive enough to be concerned with the deprived at the gate.

The question for the liberal churches is whether they can expand the horizon and transcend the possessive individualism of the middle class. If the answer is to be Yes, it will only be because we have raised consciousness beyond that of the New Evangelicals and beyond that of the liberal church that cannot recognize the divine judgment upon us, so that we can recognize the divine promise of grace for those who in the spirit of repentance turn to the power that maketh all things new.

35 · *Liberal Religion and the Phoenix*

According to an ancient fable, cherished in Jewish and Christian as well as in pagan lore, the phoenix was supposed to live five hundred years and then to consume himself and his nest with fire, only to rise out of the ashes to new life. A more widely prevalent version of the fable is repeated in Clement's First Epistle to the Corinthians. This bird, according to him, "when it reaches the time of its dissolution, maketh for itself a coffin of frankincense and myrrh and other spices, into the which in the fullness of time it entereth, and so it dieth. But as the flesh rotteth, a certain worm is engendered, which is nurtured from the moisture of the dead creature, and putteth forth wings." For Clement the death and rebirth of the phoenix, like the decay and growth of seed in the earth, are a symbol—and indeed, also evidence—of God's power to raise mortal flesh up through death to newness of life.

Professor Henry Nelson Wieman bears witness to the conviction of religious liberalism that religion, in its cultural forms, is and should be a bird of passage.[1] As manifest in particular forms, religions die, sometimes willingly, sometimes unwillingly; but the enduring spirit of religion

This essay was originally published as the preface to *The Directive in History*, by Henry Nelson Wieman. Copyright 1949 by The Free Press, renewed 1977 by Laura W. Wieman. Reprinted by permission of The Free Press, a Division of Macmillan, Inc.

again and again receives new birth in new forms that bespeak our inescapable, ultimate concern for the things that cannot fail. Liberal religion is not a single cultural form; it assumes many shapes. Some of these forms express a transient and even a misguided impulse; others may give positive character and direction to a whole epoch. But none of them is final, none is exempt from criticism and change. The moment any one of them is taken for final, liberalism lapses into orthodoxy.

The proponents of orthodoxy believe this tentative loyalty of liberalism to its own forms to be a sign of skepticism. Actually it is a sign of faith in a divine power that may for a time reside in a local habitation but that is never exhausted by any particular form; this power gives them life, and it also gives them death, for the sake of new life. Freedom of criticism, freedom of self-criticism, freedom to preserve and modify meaningful forms, freedom to initiate novel forms—these are the marks of the liberalism that would serve the things that cannot fail. Criticism is not merely a negative force. Like the air we breathe, it is indispensable to life. But, as George Santayana has observed, it is insufficient for nourishment. The source of that nourishment is the object of the faith of the liberal. Because that nourishment is a gift that must be sought after, liberal religion is committed to the idea that *religions* may die, but not *religion*.

Many of the forms and formulations of liberal religion, like the forms and creeds of orthodoxy, have today lost their power. In the face of the bludgeoning experiences of the first half of the twentieth century—bludgeonings that are partially the boomerang effect of nineteenth-century impulses—liberalism is on the defensive; in some quarters it languishes under the enervation born of failure. This failure appears in liberals' inability or unwillingness to make their principles relevant to the spiritual and ethical demands of the changing historical situation. In wide circles this inability or unwillingness is rooted in a mythical individualism. Here the overt faith of liberalism, like that of an irrelevant orthodoxy, is a deceptive but thin veil concealing a covert faith in the orthodoxy of class, "race," nation, or economic system. This sort of collusion between overt and covert faith has captured prophetic religion and forced it into a cage where rebirth and new flight are not possible; indeed, they are not even desired.

That both liberalism and orthodoxy are today caught in this cramping cage is evident in the impotence of the sacred words that are on pious lips. In many quarters the words "religion" and "God" have understandably become symbols of the sickness that gilds, that sanctifies, the cages that separate us from freedom and community. The cheap and comfortable use of such phrases as "the dignity of man," "the brotherhood of man," "freedom of thought," exemplifies both the hypocrisy and the spiritual impotence of a moribund "religion." All of these cages prevent the flight of spirit, the flight of eagles that mount up with wings, of eagles that swoop down straight.

The power to see that the cages are cages and not holy objects worthy of reverence, the power to break through these cages, is a power that is accessible only to a liberalism that surrenders to something more potent than itself. It is accessible only to the liberalism that can say with Job: "I shall die in my nest, and I shall multiply my days as the Phoenix" [29:18]. It is accessible only to those who know their own sickness, who know their false faiths are false.

> Surely each Phoenix must have been old crow
> in his own glass, scarecrow to the faithful,
> so ancient his annunciation seemed,
> so cold at dark noon his residual fire.[2]

The task of religious liberalism is always the task of discovering and working with those forces that can give new expression to the values of liberalism as against the ephemeral and cramping forms it has assumed. That religious liberalism is aware of this task can be seen in its present willingness to encourage revaluation and reintegration in the light of Christian experience; indeed, a new liberalism has for some time now been in the making. This new liberalism has been given impetus by new philosophical and religious insights, by the social and economic disruptions of our time, by a new understanding and appreciation of the Christian tradition, by the methods and findings of the sciences, and by a recognition of the social and ethical demands that must be met if we are to resist the spurious appeals of the tempting orthodoxies (old and new) of the day. These appeals have become the more dangerous, and the tasks of religious liberalism have become the more urgent, precisely because of a neurotic yearning for security which has developed in an age of convulsions. It is clear that the yearning is neurotic, for it fervidly rejects patient discussion as tedious and frustrating.

Recognizing the critical juncture at which civilization now finds itself, Henry Nelson Wieman presses upon us the need for a new understanding of the moral directive of history. As a philosopher of religion confronting this need, he has long been familiar to American readers as one who searches for a new expression of liberal religion, through new methods of inquiry and application. In his view, not only evil must be overcome; the good must die in order to live. With his "contextualist" view of reality (to use a term given currency by Stephen C. Pepper) and with his version of emergent evolution, stemming from a longtime concern with the philosophies of Henri Bergson, John Dewey, and Alfred North Whitehead, he interprets the divinely creative power—"the source of human good"— as in unforeseeable ways ever issuing forth in new treasures and in old treasures interpreted anew.

Central in his thinking is the idea that the creative process is fundamental in the universe, a process that makes for the realization and preservation of value, order, and unity. This idea constitutes the basis for his "naturalistic theism." It is theistic, he asserts, because the process that is creative of value, order, and unity, in their interaction, represents what religion has always meant by the term "God." It is naturalistic rather than supernaturalistic, because the divinely creative power, so conceived, is a part of "the total natural structure of things" and thus can be known without recourse to what traditional religions have named revelation: it can be known by observation and rational evaluation of the sort of evidence that is determinative for anything worthy of being called knowledge. Yet faith as well as knowledge is needful, for God is "greater than we can know."

In *The Directive in History* Wieman aims to show the implications of naturalistic theism for a democratic philosophy of culture. In his view, the creative process, the moral directive, of history demands and promotes the innovation and interchange, the deepening and the application of symbolized meanings. Of particular significance in this view is his adaptation of S. C. Pepper's concept of "quality"—the concrete event as experienced. Of greater significance is his theological interpretation of certain aspects of the philosophy of George Herbert Mead. For Mead, the process of achieving democratic community (and also of achieving scientific knowledge) involves both the use of physical objects and the development of communication for the solving of problems. This process occurs in nature; indeed, the symbolic organization of experience follows laws analogous to those present in the organization of nature. For Wieman the progressive creation of symbolized meanings is the top level of a creative process which, at lower levels, creates the kind of organism that can use symbols.

For both Mead and Wieman, then, symbolic communication is the characteristic feature of human behavior. But whereas for Mead the cooperative venture of creating social objects and objectives through language, and of solving problems, is a part of the process of the universe as a whole, for Wieman it is the medium through which the creative power of God operates, generating new meanings and goals shared in common. The human being is "made, and unmade, and still to be made in ways beyond imagination, by this creative power that runs through history." Evil appears "when man produces situations that prevent further creative transformation from occurring." Creative good appears "when there is a process at work in our midst whereby the thought and feeling of each gets across to the other, whereby this thought and feeling derived from the other is integrated in the mind of each, thus expanding the richness and resources of the mind and of personality." Wieman devotes the major portion of his book to an examination of the conditions required in order that this creative process may take place in family, school, and community, between young and old, between rich and poor, between management and labor, between nations.

In all these areas and in the totality of human endeavor, Wieman would affirm, with Nietzsche, that the great thing in the human being is to be a bridge and not a goal, a transition, a destruction and a new creation. But he would add that the phoenix-spirit that carries us across to new creation is something beyond us.

The issues at stake today are issues of life and death for civilization. In the age of the atomic bomb, the bridge itself will be broken unless we learn what should command the ruling devotion of human life. There is a way from death to resurrection. They know enough who know how to learn.

Notes

1. See Henry Nelson Wieman, *The Directive in History* (Chicago, 1949).
2. R. P. Blackmur, "Phoenix at Loss," *The Good European* (Cummington, Mass., 1947), p. 29.

36 · The Ages of Liberalism

Liberal Christianity is sometimes narrowly defined so as to associate it with only one aspect of its expression. By some interpreters it is identified, for example, with rational autonomy, by others with the idea of progressive revelation, and by still others with a critical historical method. Actually, it is a thing of many facets. Negatively, liberal Christianity may be characterized as an effort to bring about the liberation of persons from bondage to narrow, arbitrary, or irrelevant authority, whether it sanctions convention or revolt. But, properly conceived, the negation is oriented in a positive direction, "from the bondage of corruption to the glorious liberty of the children of God" [Rom. 8:21]. Out of this concern for freedom liberal Christianity gets its name, for *liber* means free. The search for liberation is informed by a positive faith. It is a response to the Word of God. The term "Word of God" indicates that God speaks to humans in a personal way through Jesus Christ and the gospel, and also through other persons, and through mind, conscience, and nature. But this does not mean that God is limited to the personal, for God speaks also in the transpersonal. Moreover, the Word of God is free; it cannot be bound by any creature. "Where the spirit of the Lord is, there is liberty" [2 Cor. 3:17]. Within the liberal position itself, therefore, there is a negation. Liberal Christianity recognizes that God is hidden as well as revealed, and that conscience is fallible. No statement or application can claim finality, unless it be the finality of limitation. Liberal Christianity therefore adopts a self-denying ordinance to idolatry. Because of the ambiguous elements in human awareness, and because of the richness, the freedom, and the hiddeness of the Word of God, it emphasizes the uses of diversity, self-criticism, and openness.

The diversity of liberal Christianity is occasioned and demanded also by the variety of situations in which truth becomes concretely known or incarnate. The search for relevance is the essence of liberal Christianity. In the exercise of the liberty of mind and conscience and of the liberty proclaimed in the gospel (and there made uniquely available to persons of contrite heart), liberal Christianity has aimed to release the creativity and

Reprinted by permission, with revisions, from *The Journal of Religious Thought* (Howard University School of Divinity) 14, no. 2 (Spring-Summer 1957).

newness of life that issue from response to the inexhaustible power of God as it offers new opportunities and demands in the ever-changing situations of the human condition. God's Word is a living Word that speaks to the unique situation; at the same time, what is heard is conditioned by the situation. The gospel itself, as set forth in the New Testament, is situation-conditioned and situation-directed. Not all of its meaning is explicit in its initial verbal articulations. Nor can all of its articulations be considered of equal status. Thus the repetition of the words of the New Testament will not automatically provide wholeness or healing in a given situation. By virtue of the integrity or wholeness of the gospel, every new opening to the creative and redemptive power of God brings with it not only new treasure but also the demand for a new search in order that it be given relevant statement and application. Authentic liberal Christianity aims not to be bound to the situation in which it finds itself, and at the same time it tries to understand itself and its mission in the face of a particular situation. Again, liberal Christianity in principle therefore cherishes the uses of diversity, self-criticism, and openness.

One way of discriminating the unity within the variety of liberal Christianity—and also a way of discerning its situation-conditioned and situation-directed character—is to observe the differing emphases of the major periods of its development, emphases that exhibit a unity in their *Gestalt*. By viewing together these periods and their characteristic emphases one may approach a synoptic paradigm of its elements. One may thus also be better able to assess its present status, its deficiencies, and its possibilities.

THE AGES OF LIBERALISM

Any attempt to delineate the periods of liberal Christianity requires what has been called "epochal thinking." This kind of thinking is familiar in the study of comparative religions, where one encounters sundry notions about "the ages of the world." It is familiar also in the "dispensational" conceptions that appear in Scripture. Jesus implied a periodization when he spoke of "the Law and the prophets," John the Baptist, himself, and the kingdom at hand. Augustine offered an elaborate periodization in his *City of God,* Jesus Christ here standing at the center of history and the subsequent age being considered the last. With a more dynamic conception, Joachim of Fiore in the twelfth century periodized the history of salvation in his speculations regarding the three ages: the Age of the Father, the Age of the Son, and the coming Age of the Spirit—an age of freedom.[1] Other periodizations more or less similar to these could of course be found.

For interpreting the ages of liberalism, a periodization formally somewhat analogous to that of Joachim may have some validity and usefulness. One may view the "moments" in the development and ethos of liberal Christianity in terms of ages of the Father (the Creator), the Son (the Mediator), and the Spirit, though not in that order and though no period is assumed to be classical, final, or normative. At first blush such a periodization may seem as fantastic as that of Joachim. Actually, it serves merely to give a compact statement of the ways in which liberal Christianity has come to terms with the principle foci of Christian faith. It goes almost without saying that the complex data that should be taken into account lend themselves to different characterization and periodization from those ventured here. The trinitarian periodization proposed is obviously a heuristic device. With all its faults, however, the device may serve to indicate longer and broader perspectives than those often employed in provincial interpretations of liberal Christianity.[2]

We shall interpret liberal Christianity, then, as successively exhibiting up to now three periods which we shall call the Age of the Spirit, the Age of the Creator, and the Age of the Mediator. In each period, the dominant "moment" selected serves to determine the characterization of the "period." But subdominant motifs, which in previous periods were perhaps dominant motifs, are obviously present in some form in each period. The special character of a period depends upon the peculiar character of the dialectic between the various "moments" of the period, with one "moment" being dominant. At the same time, each age produces tensions and paradoxes respecting characteristic problems. These tensions lead beyond themselves to the succeeding period in which the theological situation is redefined.

THE AGE OF THE SPIRIT

"The wind bloweth where it listeth, but thou canst not tell whence it cometh, and whither it goeth; so is every one who is born of the spirit" [John 3:8]. The winds of the Spirit constitute the first "moment" in modern liberal Christianity.[3] Historically, it is to be traced mainly to the left wing of the Reformation (called also the Radical Reformation) and to its antecedents in the Middle Ages and in the New Testament. In this first "moment" the stress is laid on God's redemptive power.

More than any other term, Spirit (*pneuma*) is the key word of the Radical Reformation of the sixteenth and seventeenth centuries, a reformation largely oriented to Pentecost and to subsequent Spiritualist tendencies. This fact is evident in the dynamic periodizations proposed. The Anabaptists' periodization applied to church history the categories of creation, fall, and redemption, identifying the creation with the primitive church instituted at Pentecost, equating the fall with the coercion of belief issuing from the junction of church and state under Constantine, and envisaging the redemption as the emerging restitution of the church of the Spirit. On the other hand, Spiritualist periodizations set forth, as Joachim's did, a progressive theory of revelation, the Third Era being the outpouring of the Spirit. Thus the radical Reformation reveals its characteristic concern with history, the Church, and the inwardness of Christian piety, rather than with nature or with humanity's relation to it.

The historical lineage of the ideas of the Spirit is somewhat different in England and New England from what it was in Europe. A variety of strands enter into the total lineage: evangelical, mystical, enthusiastic, antinomian, and rational.[4] Roughly, they are distributed among the Anabaptists and the Spiritualists. In England and America, these radical tendencies merge with elements issuing from Puritan Neo-Calvinism. This variety of strands has given to liberal Christianity severe strains but also a continuing dynamic.

We should recall the elements of the conception of the Holy Spirit in the New Testament. The word *pneuma* denotes the rushing wind of God, manifest at Pentecost, which in immediacy gathers the ecstatic band of believers into the unity of the eschatological community of the Spirit (St. Paul's term, *koinonia pneumatos*). It denotes also the gifts of the Spirit distributed in the community. These *charismata* have a common source in the Holy Spirit, and they are subordinate to the love of the brethren and the upbuilding of the church. As a winnowing wind, the Spirit sets aside traditional and legal authority in favor of the pneumatic authority of the apostles, prophets, and teachers. The community is a pneumatocracy in which the members test and acknowledge the bearers and workings of the Spirit. This Spirit is of course understood to be inextricably related to the resurrected, living Christ and also to God the Father. It is understood also to operate in conjunction with the living Word. In one form or another these ideas become ingredients of the Radical Reformation.

In the struggling congregations of the Roman Empire the word *pneuma* also acquired the meaning of the aroma enveloping the dying martyr, an idea that in effect reappeared in the martyr churches of the left wing in their struggle for freedom of Spirit and conscience, as against Roman Catholicism and the Protestantism of the Magisterial Reformation. In early monasticism also one sees an anticipation of the left wing; for example, in the fourth century Basil of Caesarea (*De Fide*) discerns the working of the Holy Spirit in the distribution of the *charismata* and in the imparting of moral power—in "sanctification." In addition to the meanings already noted one must take into account the mystical (Johannine) elements of the Radical Reformation which give expression to Spiritualist-evangelical and also to Spiritualist-rational motifs. Appealing to the eternal Spirit, this mystical tendency is sometimes trans-Christian in scope. One can see here an anticipation, though not a direct cause, of the New England Transcendentalism of three centuries later. But there were other motifs besides these. At one end of the spectrum an anarchistic individualism appears, and at the other end a collectivist revolutionary utopianism, or "spiritual bolshevism." What we are mainly concerned with, however, is the central line of the Radical Reformation.

In this connection we should observe that the ideas of the young Luther have figured positively in German liberal Christian movements of later centuries, particularly his emphasis on "the freedom of the Christian," on the sanctity of vocations in the world, on the Holy Spirit as the activator of the Word and of faith, on the validity of Spirit, Scripture, and reason together, and also on the idea that one must be willing, if necessary, to "urge the authority of Christ against the authority of the Bible."

Taken together, these various impulses brought about one of the most impressive and significant innovations that has appeared since the New Testament period. The ecstatic freedom of the Spirit burst through and against the *"begriff*-ridden" [concept-ridden] official church doctrine; against the feudal, magical sacramental system of the heteronomous late Middle Ages; against the later papal church and the authoritarian patterns of bureaucratic confessional Lutheranism and Anglicanism and those of theocratic Calvinism; and against the general uniformity of belief demanded in the traditional *corpus christianum*. Positively, this freedom intended to give new expression to the Christian life as admonished in the Gospels. In some quarters a literal interpretation of the counsels and precepts of the Gospels came into conflict with the ethos of the Spirit. With sectarian rigor some of the left-wing groups adopted a legalistic distinction between the saints and the unregenerate (as did also the Lutheran Butzer and his followers). The Anabaptists made the distinction operate through the exercise of the ban. They rejected as un-Christian the holding of civic office. More permanently significant was their opposition to war and persecution. The Spiritualists were generally more tolerant and individualistic.

In the midst of the attacks of the old order there appeared a radical interpretation of the priesthood and prophethood of all believers, an interiorization and individualization of the Spirit, and a dispersion of power and responsibility (radical laicism). This dispersion occurred through the separation of church and state (the rejection of territorialism), through independent lay "searching" for explicit faith dependent upon the spread of literacy, and through the concomitant development of a pneumatic-democratic church which adopted varying degrees of local autonomy and which insisted on the protection of individual conscience and of minorities (perhaps the origin of the Parliamentary notion of "the loyal opposition"). For the Radical Reformation it was not enough to say, with Luther, that the church exists where the Word is rightly preached and the sacraments are rightly administered; the left wing cherished the free winds of the Spirit and the inward *koinonia pneumatos*. All of these things are implicit in the experience of "the inner light" and in the great value placed upon voluntary individual decision; and they provided the soil from which the associational (in contrast to the institutional) type of church emerged, a church that is a voluntary association based on personal decision, epitomized in adult baptism. These tendencies aimed to make it the more readily possible for believers and for the churches to yield to the promptings of the Spirit that "bloweth where it listeth"; they reflect the left wing emphasis on freedom of the will, in contrast to the right-wing emphasis on predestination. They were to be observed all the way from Zurich to Amsterdam, Bristol, and Providence.

In addition to the Spiritualist motifs we have referred to, explicitly rational elements played a role not only in the appearance of an ethical theism, but also in the vigorous promotion of freedom of thought and of interpretation of Scripture. Here humanism as well as evangelicalism exercised an influence, as for example with the antitrinitarians Servetus and Socinus. Rational motives appeared also with the Levellers in the realm of democratic theory and practice.

Among the Levellers one finds a three-era periodization of British history which, in connection with a doctrine of the Spirit, takes into account legal developments, and which looks toward the return of subordination of the political executive to law, a periodization that involved an equalitarian conception of natural law. Behind this periodization lay the opposition of juridical reason to ecclesiastical and political authority (an opposition to be traced back into the Middle Ages) and also the Spiritualist periodization of a mystic like Saltmarsh, who in the name of the new outpouring of the Spirit wrote to the Council debating the *Agreement of the People:* "Now ye are met in council, the Lord make ye to hearken to one another from the highest to the meanest, that the voice of God, wheresoever it speaks, may not be despised." With the Levellers, public opinion, public agitation, and government by discussion assume for the first time an important role in modern political life. These changes must be understood in relation to the rise of the middle classes, of free business enterprise, and of urbanism. These social and economic factors deserve a more extensive treatment than they can receive here.

In varying ways and degrees these democratic features of the left wing were translated into the secular life, particularly by the aggressive sects. In England, James I, disturbed by the attacks on the bishops, predicted that next the heretics would attack the monarchy—and they did. In many respects the modern democratic movement as it developed in ecclesiastical, political, educational, and industrial areas, issues from the British and American left wing. This development found its nerve in eschatological vision and also in the drive for the holy community characteristic of Calvinism. A. S. P. Woodhouse has argued that in British circles the principle of analogy figured in this overflow: organizational patterns preferred by the churches of the Spirit were taken as models for other institutions. Considerable historical research will be required before the decisive and explicit influence of this principle of analogy can be demonstrated for any long period.

The Age of the Spirit, then, brings in its train the demand for freedom of Spirit and of conscience, a radical laicism, and new forms of ecclesiastical and social organization that disperse power and responsibility. Indeed, a new conception of an autonomous Christian personality supported by "inner light"; the rejection of coercion in belief and in the shaping of public policy; the principle of the consent of the governed; and a pluralistic conception of the churches and of society emerge, or are newly emphasized, in the Age of the Spirit. These new conceptions, along with others that have been noted, constitute the first "moment" of liberal Christianity, with its ethos of the uses of diversity, self-criticism, and openness.

The magnitude of these innovations makes of this age a watershed dividing the modern era of European history from the medieval, though the periods overlap more than we have been able explicitly to indicate and though important elements issue also from the right wing of the Reformation.[5] It must also be said that some of the tendencies referred to above are associated with types of authoritarianism and fanaticism which are subjected to effective criticism only in a later period; besides, ecstatic elements readily become rigidly fixated. Moreover, within the left wing unresolved and perhaps unresolvable tensions appear; for example, the tension between radical individualism (leading to anarchy and antinomianism) and the drive to unify and upbuild the fellowship of the Spirit, or the tension between radical local autonomy in the churches and an embracing "connectionalism," or between the evangelical, mystical, and rational elements. In the face of these tensions, the left wing relied upon a belief in a providential harmony to flow from the unifying Word and Spirit. This Spiritualist belief in automatic harmony will later undergo a transformation in the Enlightenment doctrine of the automatic harmony of (economic) interests.

THE AGE OF THE CREATOR

The watershed represented by the Age of the Spirit is the harbinger of a second and equally important watershed. Ernst Troeltsch discerned in the Enlightenment the watershed between an old and a new Protestantism. But in important respects the Enlightenment depended upon the left wing and the Renaissance. The Enlightenment doctrine of the religious autonomy of reason retains something of the immediacy of the "inner light" of the left wing and also some sense of renewal characteristic of the Renaissance, particularly insofar as the latter maintained continuity with the Spiritualism of the Joachites and the Franciscans.

In this continuity, extending from the Radical Reformation and its antecedents to the Enlightenment, one should observe a contrast with what happened in ancient church history when the pneumatocracy of the primitive church gave way to early Catholicism and its identification of the guidance of the Spirit with ecclesiastical authority. As Rudolf Sohm pointed out, the early pneumatocracy was gradually supplanted by a legalized bureaucracy. For Sohm this shift represented the "fall" of the church from Spirit to Law. (Montanism, which appeared later, can be interpreted as a protest against this "fall.") Classical Protestant orthodoxy also took the stultifying path towards Law—that of "pure doctrine." A shift that was perhaps more nearly similar to the transition from the left wing to the Enlightenment is to be discerned in the change in early church history from pneumatic theology to *Logos* theology, a change anticipated by Philo's and the Fourth Gospel's idea of *Logos,* an idea derived from the Old Testament idea of Wisdom, viewed as the bond of the created universe and as the source of inspiration in Scripture. In a general way we may say that the religious·elements in the Enlightenment exhibit an analogous transition from a pneumatic to a *Logos* theology. In the Enlightenment the concerns of the left wing were broadened in scope to include nature as well as history. Along with the concern with nature appeared the emphasis on the doctrine of creation rather than the doctrine of redemption.

The Enlightenment viewed itself in part as a protest against the Radical Reformation, particularly because of the excesses of that period. "Enthusiasm" was the *bête noir.* For each one who will be inspired, it was said, ten thousand will be demented. Excesses there had been in plenty, and in the name of the Spirit. The Civil War in England, for example, had exhibited the high cost of fanaticism. Yet, the Enlightenment continued to attack evils not entirely dissimilar to those resisted in the Radical Reformation. Authoritarianism, obscurantism, superstition, witchcraft, miracle, otherworldliness, ignorance, and intolerance were viewed as perversions of pure Christianity. But reason and common sense rather than Spirit were now to be the guide.

The reason of the Enlightenment is in large part the child of the Age of the Spirit. The immediacy that belonged to "the inner light" of the Radical Reformation now becomes the immediacy of religious autonomy seeking the truth and justice written into the structure of the universe and inherent in the mind and conscience of Man, the rational being. Moreover, as with the immediacy of the Spirit in the Radical Reformation, the immediacy of rational autonomy in the Enlightenment is imbued with ardent hope for the future. The expectation of the Third Era, the Age of Reason, is fundamentally a rationalization of the earlier version of the Third Era of the Spirit (as Lessing clearly recognized). The idea of progress becomes the rationalized version of the earlier faith in a dynamic providence pursuing its way in history.

If in the Age of the Spirit the "inner light" is in the main dependent on Scripture, in the Age of the Creator the light is "the candle of the Lord" available to all persons whether under the Christian dispensation or not. Whereas the Age of the Spirit rendered Spirit the norm of the Bible, the Age of the Creator, reminiscent of the Socinians, views rational and ethical religion as the norm. Here Renaissance as well as rational Spiritualist motifs become evident. The human being, created in the image of

God, is a rational being endowed with freedom and responsibility. Thus the doctrine of original sin is irrational: it is a calumny upon both God and humanity, for it contradicts human freedom and responsibility; and, besides, it is based upon a primitive myth—the fall in the Garden of Eden. Likewise, the vicarious sacrifice attributed to Christ is held to be untenable: it is a calumny upon God, for it renders God an odious victimizer of the innocent; it is a falsification of the human situation in that it ignores the fact that sin and guilt are attached to the individual and are to be overcome through individual recognition and responsibility; and, like the doctrine of original sin, it is based upon a superstitious myth regarding God's sending his Son for the sacrifice. Moreover, Jesus himself was not a divine being: he was a prophet, a genius, a moral teacher, an extraordinary, exemplary human being. In this direction Christology was given an ethical thrust, though it also deteriorated into moralism (Kant). What Jesus taught was a republication of the truths as old as creation, truths that have their intrinsic ground in natural reason, endowed in the human being by God, the First Cause and the Great Designer. Only through the repeal of the vaunted mysteries of superstition and tradition could the candle of the Lord rekindle its flame.

Out of roots such as these grew the doctrine of natural rights and of social contract—a source of the dynamic reformist pathos of the Enlightenment. Here we encounter certain basic paradoxes and contradictions. The doctrine of natural rights and of social contract implied a mythology regarding the origin and nature of society which in the end could not bear the scrutiny of empirical historical investigation. This scrutiny was to issue eventually from a now emerging rational empiricism. The Enlightenment gave birth to the modern historical consciousness, to the rational and historical investigation of the origin and development of religions, to historical criticism of the Scriptures, to the scientific analysis of natural and social forces, and to the rational adaptation of technical means to bourgeois ends. Paradox is evident also in the antinomy that emerges between the highly creative movement of liberation from arbitrary restrictions upon human freedom and the new impediments to human fulfillment that issue from the bourgeois use of "reason" for the manipulation of natural and human resources (in the name of automatic harmony). This last was the work of the "shopkeeping logicians," to use the term of W. B. Yeats. A related and equally striking paradox is the fact that with the Enlightenment's new confidence in the possession of the candle of the Lord, an acute secularization set in. Reason began to lose its depth.

The Enlightenment is the watershed of the modern era and a "moment" in liberal Christianity. Henceforth the liberal Christian would build upon it, even if much was to be criticized and altered. Stated theologically, the Enlightenment as the Age of the Creator insisted that common grace precedes special grace; that coercion, intolerance, and injustice are a violation of the image of God; that truth from whatever source is sacred, and that it must be pursued in freedom and with all resources, whether they be peculiarly and ostensibly Christian or not. At the same time, the Age of the Creator is the age of the demythologizing of Christian tradition.

We have not yet done with the Age of the Creator, and we never shall be done with it so long as men and women cherish their humanity. Unfinished business remains from this age, particularly in the understanding of the relation between Christianity and the secular world, and between Christianity and the other religions. There is a question, however, as to whether the Age of the Creator as such was equal to the task. There is another bit of unfinished business from the Enlightenment, a problem bequeathed also by the Age of the Spirit. In both the Radical Reformation and the Enlightenment utopianism was an important motif. This utopianism in its way provided a dynamic for prophetic criticism and salutary social change in church and society. At the same time it harbored illusions about human nature and society which threatened the very fabric of community. It has been the merit of neo-orthodoxy to expose these illusions, though neo-orthodoxy has also underestimated the positive significance of the "utopian" mentality in the liberation of humanity from tyranny. Neither neo-orthodoxy nor liberalism can wisely forego assistance from this quarter.

Liberal Christianity in the Age of the Creator promoted the uses of diversity, self-criticism, and openness. Without these qualities Christianity in the modern world would have been relegated to the backwoods of archaism. Modern Christianity shall always presuppose the Age of the Creator. To do otherwise would be to renounce the first article of the Apostles' Creed.

THE AGE OF THE MEDIATOR

In its search for the universal elements of religion, the Enlightenment, transcending narrow Christian tradition, raised the question, What is the essence of religion? In the very asking of the question a synoptic view and a rational discrimination were promoted, which orthodoxy in its absolute claim to possess "pure doctrine" and in its reliance on the inertia of tradition had stifled. To the question, the Enlightenment gave a dusty answer, namely, natural religion. In giving this answer, on the one hand, it laudably sought to discover universal elements in Christianity and other religions. On the other hand, it adopted the ahistorical outlook previously noted with respect to the doctrines of natural rights and social contract. "Self-evidence" tended to impose its a priori conceptions upon unique, alogical fact, and thus to distort it.

Protest against this rationalism was inevitable if genuine empirical observation and Christian experience in the churches were to be taken into account. Against a rationalist "system" and against the illusion that the efficacious fabric of society is the result of merely rational deliberation, the philosophy of conservatism protested in the name of the organic unities of social existence. Against the rationalist dissolution of actually operative vitality the Romanticists protested in the name of individuality. But these protests do not get at the heart of the matter for the ongoing liberal Christianity. Against misconceived or enervating abstraction (the characteristic deficiency of the Age of the Creator), the Age of the Mediator seeks the concrete, the mediator. The Enlightenment may have assisted liberal Christianity to understand itself as liberal. But now the question arose as to what constitutes its specifically Christian character. To this question orthodoxy could not give an acceptable answer. In P. T. Forsyth's phrase, "it was canned theology gone stale." From the earlier question as to the essence of religion, liberal Christianity turned now to the question, What is the essence of Christianity? Although the concern with essence was later to be viewed as misleadingly abstract, asking the question served to initiate in liberal Christianity the Age of the Mediator. But the question would not have been asked had not Christians been aware of the fact that the God of the Enlightenment came short of being the God of their worship, the Father of Jesus Christ—the redeemer God as well as the Creator.

Behind the question lay the recognition also of what the Unitarian J. Estlin Carpenter asserted a century later (1895): "You can no more, by gazing on the Infinite Spirit [or, we may add, on the divine reason], discern in him the specific lineaments of the teachers of the past, than by staring into space you can behold the Buddha under his Bo-tree, or Christ upon the cross."[6] This warning holds for any Spiritualism that separates the Spirit from the Word, as well as for "the essence of religion" separated from "the essence of Christianity"; or, if with the Age of the Mediator we declare war on essences, we may say that the warning holds for any "Christianity" that separates the Creator (or the Spirit) from the Mediator. A generalized idea is not a substitute for a concrete faith. Liberal Christianity, in order to remain Christian, had to face the question about the essence of Christianity.

The answer to the question has been given in a variety of ways. Some liberals recaptured elements of the Age of the Spirit. Others persisted in ostensibly holding views from the Age of the Creator, yet in speaking of "the Fatherhood of God" they actually understood it in terms of Jesus' conception of the Father. After the advent of the theory of evolution they interpreted the Bible as exhibiting the evolution of the idea of God, culminating in Jesus' conception of Fatherhood. In conformity with a theory of evolution they read their eschatology of progress into the New Testament idea of the Kingdom of God. With some liberals this eschatology was bourgeois, with others it became prophetically critical of the bourgeois ideals and reformist (the Social Gospel). In the latter, the doctrine of redemption, as in the Age of the Spirit, was interpreted to apply to institutions as well as to individuals. Many liberals discerned the distinctive element of Christianity in Jesus' ethics, the Sermon on the Mount; it was interpreted by them, however, in the spirit of humanitarianism. Even at the end of the nineteenth century, the view was set forth by Deussen that Jesus was the first Kantian, and many liberals continued to equate Jesus' ethics with a religion of duty. These interpretations of Christian ethics were destined to be called into question, from the time of Johannes Weiss and Albert Schweitzer. The critique of the modernizing of Jesus grew out of a prodigious search for the historical Jesus so characteristic of the Age of the Mediator: through a radical application of liberal scholarship the search was to issue later in a marked skepticism regarding the possibility of recovering "the historical Jesus," or at least of recovering a critical biography of Jesus.

All of these answers, even beyond the time of Harnack, tended to distinguish between the teachings *of* Jesus and the teachings *about* Jesus, and to favor the former. But the teachings about Jesus have increasingly come to the center of attention, indeed partly because scholarly research disclosed not only that the teachings of Jesus included teachings about him, but also that the Gospels represent more of a confession of faith in Jesus Christ than a biography of Jesus.

Deeper considerations, however, than those of historiography have come into play. Liberal Christianity in the twentieth century has recognized, in part from orthodox and neo-orthodox critics, in part from secular critics like Marx, Nietzsche, and Freud, that its doctrines of human nature and history have been wanting in realism and in the sense of tragedy. Moreover, in the eighteenth and nineteenth centuries it so much emphasized faith in human autonomy that God was more and more given the polite *congé* in order to make room for human self-sufficiency. We need not here rehearse and assess the charges and countercharges. It is more directly germane to the understanding of the Age of the Mediator for us to observe the developments of Christology.

Over a century ago Schelling, one of the first existentialists, saw that the mystical mentality tends to emphasize the unity between humanity and God, and accordingly to overlook the distance, the alienation between them. Thus the element of guilt and the sense of sin tend to disappear. The same criticism has been directed at the rational religious mentality of the Enlightenment. The Age of the Creator had too comfortably cuddled up to the Almighty, or to Jesus of Nazareth. It had made the primary point of contact between God and the human being the natural goodness, rather than the limitation, of the latter. Precisely in recognition of these false comforts and identifications a new phase in the Age of the Mediator appears, and in important ways through the emergence of the thought of Luther and Calvin, as well as through the emergence of existentialism. Here the theme of redemption comes more clearly to the fore.

Luther had opposed certain of the Spiritualists because they held that one may receive the Holy Spirit without a mediator, without the Word (the cradle of Christ). For him saving knowledge, forgiveness, and the new Christian life were given only through Christ, whereby God deals with humanity as person to person. Liberal Christianity does not need to accept Luther's (or Calvin's) Christology in order to recognize that teachings about Jesus are required if his place in this Christian economy is to be properly discerned. It is through Jesus that God's reality, power, judgment, and love become uniquely available to the Christian. Indeed, through him and the cross the person becomes sharply conscious of separation from God and of the need for grace. The understanding of Jesus as uniquely mediating the grace of God leads to the demand for a more substantial Christology than that afforded by the idea of "the leadership of Jesus."

Some liberal Christians become frightened at the word Christology. It seems to demand that Jesus be interpreted only in terms of the categories of the New Testament or of the ancient confessions. Certainly, many of these as well as those of the later confessions are being given a sort of forced currency today by a new "unitarianism" of the Second Person.

The liberal Christian whose intellectual outlook is in any fundamental way conditioned by the Enlightenment must necessarily view most of these categories as demythologized and broken. Not that they are without meaning. Rather, they must be recognized as creatures. In many instances they require translation if their viable meaning is to be effectively communicated. Indeed, many of these categories are themselves translations that were devised to take the place of categories that did not come to terms with new problems. The ancient Church Fathers undertook this translation in face of questions unforeseen by Jesus or by the New Testament writers. Like them, we must recognize that the insistence upon any particular traditional categories may constitute a legalism of the word, a legalism that separates contemporary men and women from the grace to which they have borne witness in the past. There are other objections to much of the traditional terminology. Certain terms imply a literal Second Coming. Others imply that Jesus was perfect or sinless. But the concept of perfection or of sinlessness, apart from raising the question of empirical evidence about Jesus' behavior and motives, presupposes an atomistic, noncontextualist view of the person.

Liberal Christianity, committed to the uses of diversity, self-criticism, and openness, will recognize that the old categories have transmitted the faith and that today they can yield rich insight; indeed, it will wrestle with them for blessing. Toward this end it must strive to overcome the automatic antitraditionalism and rationalistic conservatism that in many quarters issued from the Enlightenment. Otherwise, its conception of God will reflect provincialism and an impoverishment of resources. It can thus in its turn constitute a (negative) legalism. On the other hand, liberal Christianity will wish to penetrate and go beyond these traditional categories to express a new encounter with the majesty and intimacy and redemptive power of the Person of the Christ to whom they point. This Person is a medium of the grace which bore him and from which treasures old and new issue forth for the Church, the individual, and society. Revelation is not sealed. Classical Christianity found new ways of translating Christian insight for Greek, Roman, and barbarian. Liberal Christianity, in contrast to contemporary pseudo-orthodoxy, has a similar mission for our day, the task of achieving relevance in a new situation—a mass society that corrupts the Church. Translation, like reformation, must continue.

The Age of the Mediator has not yet fulfilled its task. For one thing, it has not permitted its Christology to come seriously to terms with existentialist depth psychology and depth sociology. At the same time, the "cultured despisers" are unknowingly in the vestibule.

If anything is to be learned from this survey of the ages of liberal Christianity it is that none of its manifestations in word or deed can be taken as definitive, for there remains always a tension and even a disparity between its local articulations and its enduring genius. Through the uses of diversity, self-criticism, and openness, liberal Christianity must again and again die in order to be reborn. A second moral from this survey is surely this: neither the Creator nor the Mediator nor the Spirit can be properly known or loved in isolation. Each of these "unitarianisms" needs the others. Only when taken together can they express the dynamic tensions in God, the Creator and the Re-creator.

Notes

1. For Joachim, the first age was that of the Law, a time of fear, slavery, old men, marriage; the period of the commandments and of enforced obedience. The second age, that of the Church as the medium of Christ on earth, was a time of action, faith, a measure of freedom, youth, the priesthood and the papacy; the period of sacraments and reading. The third age was to be that of the Holy Spirit, a time of mystical freedom and contemplation, love, friendship, children, monasticism; a period when prayer, song, and freedom would prevail and when no sacramental intermediaries would be necessary. These ages overlap. The Trinity is present in all three ages, but one of the three Persons is predominant in each.

2. It is a striking fact that in our own day something like Joachim's classification of types of piety in terms of the Persons of the Trinity has reappeared. Some European Protestant theologians distinguish current types of theology according to their respective emphasis on one of the three Persons, or their more comprehensive orientation to the triune God. H. Richard Niebuhr has interpreted the entire history of Christian life and thought in terms of three "unitarianisms," that of the Father, that of the Son, and that of the Holy Spirit. He does not, however, propose a periodization; rather, he deals with the three "unitarianisms" as "strains" in Christian thought and piety which exist in tension and interdependence. After this fashion Dr. Niebuhr in effect gives to Joachim's typology a new, refined definition and application for the interpretation of Christian history as a whole.

3. Francis Greenwood Peabody, in *The Church of the Spirit* (New York: Macmillan, 1925), sets forth major characteristics of this "moment" in liberal Chris-

tianity. He gives little explicit attention to the second "moment," here dealt with under the rubric of the Age of the Creator.

4. For a delineation of the spectrum of the Radical Reformation on the continent, see George H. Williams's Introduction to *Spiritualist and Anabaptist Writers* (Philadelphia: Westminster Press, 1957); Roland H. Bainton, "The Left Wing of the Reformation," *Journal of Religion* 21 (1941):127ff; and Robert Friedmann, *Church History* 24 (1955):132–51.

5. Protodemocratic tendencies in the so-called Right Wing of the Reformation are discussed, for example, in Christopher Hill, *Economic Problems of the Church* (Oxford: Oxford University Press, 1956), where it is argued that it is in the *"de facto* voluntaryism" of the established Church of England rather than in Continental left-wing influences that the origins of Independency are to be sought. See also John T. McNeill, "Reformation Sources," in F. Ernest Johnson, ed., *Foundations of Democracy* (New York: Harper and Brothers, 1947). One should mention here also the rise in Germany of the *Gemeindekirche* (in contrast to the *Landeskirche*) which developed in certain of the *freie Reichsstädte.*

6. J. Estlin Carpenter and P. H. Wicksteed, *Studies in Theology* (London: J. M. Dent and Co., 1903), p. 243 (Essex Hall Lecture, 1895).

37 · *The Grotesque and Our Future*

What has the grotesque to do with an address commemorating the 1819 Baltimore Address of William Ellery Channing, and what has it to do with our future? The answer is that the address concerns crises, both past and present, that are nothing less than grotesque.

Henry Steele Commager has given us a pungent description of both Channing and Theodore Parker upon the spurious authorities and social evils of their time.

"I am surer that my rational nature is from God," said William Ellery Channing, "than that any book is an expression of His will." Here was a spiritual and intellectual declaration of independence from the authority of the scriptures, but not only of the scriptures alone—a declaration of independence from the authority of the church and eventually of the state,

This essay originally appeared in *UUA Now,* July 28, 1969, as a comment on Henry Steele Commager's commemorative address on the 150th anniversary of William Ellery Channing's sermon in Baltimore, "Unitarian Christianity" (1819). Reprinted by permission.

society, and the economy. It was what Unitarianism and particularly transcendentalism was increasingly to be: an appeal from official and collective
authority to the authority of conscience and reason.

Professor Commager presents also an urgent summons to us of a later
generation to confront with equal boldness and imagination the corresponding authorities and social evils of our time. "We are confronted
now," he says, "with crises deeper and more pervasive, and even more
intractable, than those which Channing faced—more intractable even
than slavery." Among these crises he mentions the destruction of the environment, overpopulation and hunger, biological and atomic warfare,
and violence and war itself. The evils may not only be intractable; they
are also monstrous, so monstrous as to be grotesque. To countenance them
is to court, to play with, death. It is as grotesque as the evils themselves.

The word *grotesque* conjures up the long-necked gargoyles, the colonies
of monstrous birds that hover and howl overhead in the buttresses and
towers of a medieval cathedral. But the word has many connotations. Let
me indicate the special meaning I attach to it for the nonce.

In Paris there is a *cabaret philosophique* called "Nothingness" (*Le Néant*)
which for a certain kind of playful grotesquerie is probably unmatched in
the world. Everything in this cabaret is designed to remind the customers
of death, including their own. They sit at coffins instead of tables in a
palatial room hung with skeletal remains and with various texts on the
nature of death. A master of ceremonies dressed as a priest makes the
rounds, reminding the customers individually about the ominous pallor
of their complexions. One customer is usually persuaded to get into a
coffin and be wrapped up to the neck in a shroud. What fun for the
affluent society!

Whether this cabaret found its origin in a philosophical, "existentialist" brainstorm or was contrived simply for people of depraved taste who
wanted to enjoy a novel kind of spree on a night out, I do not know. But
it does approach the quality of the grotesque even though it is not to be
taken *au sérieux*. In this respect it reminds one of the trivial "shocker"
proposed several centuries ago, the recitation of the Lord's Prayer back-
wards to conjure up the devil.

An approximation to the seriously grotesque is better suggested by
Anatole France's tale about a young man from the provinces who was
taken by a city friend to witness the Chamber of Deputies in action.
Afterwards the sophisticated host explained that the debate was an effort

to determine the cost to France of the World War. "How much did they decide it was?" asked the provincial. "Three trillion francs," was the reply. "And what about the men lost?"—"Oh, they're included."

From these two examples, the cabaret and the Anatole France anecdote, we have our clue to a definition. The authentically grotesque is something that deviates from the normal in a monstrous way. As Santayana once observed, however, it is in the arts *suggestively* monstrous.

In the history of Western art the grotesque has been variously defined by writers and practitioners of the plastic arts since the time of the Renaissance—from Rabelais, Hieronymous Bosch, and Raphael, to Edgar Allen Poe and Tennessee Williams, to Van Gogh and the Surrealists. Beginning as the name of a fantastic style of phantasmagoric exuberance, it developed into a depiction of the absurd, the ridiculous, the distorted, the monstrous. It is a mirror of aberration. In order to present aberration, the artist of the grotesque (a Bosch, a Goya, or an Ingmar Bergman) depicts a world where "natural physical wholes" are disintegrated and "the parts" are monstrously redistributed. He aims to project the full horror of disorder, the terrible and the terrifying, even the bestial, elements in human experience. So was the grotesque for John on the Isle of Patmos.

> In appearance the locusts were like horses arrayed for battle: on their heads were what looked like crowns of gold: their faces were like human faces, their hair like women's hair, and their teeth like lions' teeth; they had scales like iron breastplates, and the noise of their wings was like the noise of many chariots, with horses rushing into battle; they have tails like scorpions, and stings, and their power of hurting men for five months lies in their tails. They have as king over them the angel of the bottomless pit. (Rev. 9:7–10)

These are the nightmarish, sinister forces that emerge from the abyss of inhumanity. They are the progeny of spurious authorities. This is what William Faulkner had in mind when he said, "We shall never be free until we understand what we have done to the Negro."

From a theological perspective the grotesque in its darker spectrum turns out to be a table of contents of corporate sin. As we shall see, Professor Commager ventures to use that unpopular word.

In combating the evils of their time, Commager says, Channing and Parker began with presuppositions that were untenable and which they or their successors had to qualify—the idea of "the divinity of man" and the principle of individualism. They were compelled to acknowledge, Commager says, that "the real problem was not that of private sin, but of public—the problem of dealing with great agglomerations like corporations and governments." And this, he says, is precisely the reason for "that sense of desperate frustration that overcomes so many of us." Since we are all caught in "collective sin" it is difficult to identify individual guilt and responsibility:

> . . . nobody responsible for war, nobody responsible for napalm and the defoliation of millions of acres of land; nobody responsible for wasting half of our total income on war and armaments . . . ; nobody responsible for blight and poverty and ignorance and disaster and crime. Needless to say, we are all responsible. Americans are the leaders and the pace-setters in almost all of these sins.

"No other people," he says, "has destroyed so fast and as much as we are destroying: we are the vandals of the modern era."

We need not spell out here the current size and statistics of the grotesque powers that express Humanity the Destroyer today. The increasing disparity between the haves and the have-nots; the disparity in the national budget between the dollar-billions allotted to weaponry and those assigned to fight poverty; the, in Commager's words, "cities degenerating into massive slums, schools teaching nothing, hospitals overcrowded, racial injustice and mounting tension, demands for 'reparations,' and so on. These are all a part of us, and we a part of them. In the coming season I understand that they are to be called 'the guerrilla theater,' the theater of the grotesque."

Life magazine recently gave some candid pictures of the grotesque in the large by printing photographs of 242 men killed, "One Week's Dead" . . . "in connection with the conflict in Vietnam"—the words of the official announcement. The name of the magazine, at least for that "one week," is grotesque. "Normal men," says British psychiatrist R. D. Laing, "have killed perhaps 100 million of their fellow normal men in the last fifty years," adding that he is no longer sure of the usefulness of the traditional categories of "well," "sick," "mad," and "sane."

Dylan Thomas, taking a close-up view and writing from America to his wife, epitomized this grotesquerie in a homely way: "The food shops knock you down. All the women are smart, slick and groomed, as in the magazines—I mean in the main streets; behind lie the eternal poor, beaten, robbed, humiliated, spat upon, done to death." If we go around behind and visit Appalachia or any large city hospital we learn that worms crawl out of the mouths of undernourished children when they are under anesthesia. Like a Salvador Dali painting of the grotesque, our condition is hard to look at for any length of time. Living with and under these aberrations, we collectively experience (and exemplify) the grotesque. We live in what the Welshman calls The Valley of the Monsters.

We shall not be able to deal with these problems "in our stride," business and government and church continuing "as usual." Nevertheless, in the present sea of turmoil our contemporaries—especially those who are the "haves"—seem to insist on simply rowing with their hands, and only now and then, in order to get ashore. There is something typically and pathetically grotesque about the president's daughter tutoring two inner-city children at the White House. One should not be surprised to learn that Julius Hobson, a member of the Washington School Board, has attacked the White House for its "welfare colonialism": "If the President of the United States wants to educate the children of the District of Columbia, then he can do it through Congress by promoting Federal aid to education instead of cutting it back."

In the face of the crises he has described, Professor Commager stresses the crucial roles of a revitalized United Nations, an authentic university, and an ecumenical church, three forces that together "can create a counterweight to those formidable institutions that are dedicated to self-seeking and power."

What, then, are the mandates that lie upon our churches? When we consider the enormity of the forces that hold us in sway, we share with Commager the deep sense of frustration. But at such a moment we can recall what Martin Luther said in response to the question, What would you do if you were convinced that the world was coming to an end tomorrow? He responded, "I would go out and plant a tree." In this 150th anniversary year of the Baltimore sermon, we can find our first mandate in what Commager speaks of as Channing's declaration of independence of the state, society, and the economy, that is, in appeal to conscience and reason. For Channing and Parker this declaration was in the name of a power that transcends culture, indeed transcends what calls itself religion. For them awareness of the shadows of the grotesque was at the same time awareness of the light that is above the shadows. Thus the declaration of independence and the appeal to a higher authority beyond the spurious authorities did not mean withdrawal.

We must next ask the question, how specifically do we declare independence of spurious authorities and plant a tree? Here we come to a second mandate. What I have just been saying is true enough, but it can readily take on the hue of inflated rhetoric. I choose therefore to shift into lowercase script and to say that what happens to a denomination as a whole, or to a local parish, depends upon a relatively small number of people, upon the *ecclesiola in ecclesia,* the small church in the large. The second mandate, then, lies especially upon those people, namely to urge that a consensus be achieved regarding top priorities. Churches, like other organizations, can dissipate their energies by trying to do too many things. It is an axiom of theology as well as of psychology that both distortion and apathy are the children of lazy ambiguity, of ambiguity of purpose. The crucial question here is, What are the top priorities?

The surest way I know to deal with the question is to respond to those who have the greatest need and to join those who are battling against rank injustice. I venture to nominate, first, those who are protesting or struggling against war; second, blacks and poor whites; and third, the youth in revolt. Among them we find a creative alienation from society, a declaration of independence in positive thrust. Just for this reason, greater power, greater responsibility in the churches should be given to these youths and to these blacks.

This leads to the third mandate: that we must overcome the moribund and routine conventions of activity in the parish and the denomination. Here the dynamics are already evident outside the churches as well as inside, in the professions and in the prophetic associations in the community.

All of these mandates are already burgeoning among us. But none of the strategies mentioned goes to the roots. The fundamental mandate is the renewal of covenant within the churches, the reaching down to the covenant of being itself where mutuality and sacrifice alone free us from the universal monstrosities, the reaching out to the promise-making and promise-keeping that constitute the substance of response to the covenant of being, the substance of faith and hope. The alternative is to batten on the grotesque. In short, the alternative is death, even though it be living death.

38 · Covenants of Strength and Love

In my student days, the Unitarian Dr. Richard C. Cabot, Professor of Social Ethics and Chemical Medicine at Harvard, was a teacher of uncommon insight and persuasiveness. Concerned with the nature of the good life and the religious life, he proposed an intriguing conception of the meaning of life, and specifically of the meaning of right and wrong. He suggested that our conduct is measured by the agreements we make, both with each other and with ourselves. Whether open or tacit, these agreements determine the quality of our life together. They express our definitions of what we deem to be worthwhile, of what we think we should stand by, of what we believe we should be loyal to.

But not all of these agreements, Dr. Cabot pointed out, are worthy. It would be better for us to revise them than for our lives to be perverted or destroyed by them. Such revision of our understanding of our agreements with each other and with ourselves, he said, is necessary if as individuals we are to grow, and if the groups of which we are members are to grow. He illustrated these aspects of human conduct in a great variety of ways: from biography, from international affairs, and also from fiction. He summed up the good life, then, in these three propositions: the good life is to make agreements, to keep agreements, and to revise or improve agreements in view of new situations.

The biblical passage you have heard from Jeremiah [Chapter 31] this evening could be interpreted in terms of these three propositions. Jeremiah does not use the term "agreement" but the term "covenant." The act of ordination in this evening's ceremony can be understood as an act of agreement, although here again the word covenant is used. In speaking of a "new covenant," Jeremiah refers by implication also to an "old covenant." These terms constitute the thread of continuity between the Old and the New Testament; in fact the word for "testament" is translated equally well by the word "covenant." The entire biblical history of Israel is a series of covenants—of God with Adam, with Noah, with Abraham, and with Israel at Mt. Sinai. The simplest formula for this covenant or testament or agreement is expressed by Jeremiah in the words, "I will be your God and you shall be my people" [Jer. 7:23].

This sermon was given for the service of ordination of the Reverend George Kimmich Beach by the Unitarian Universalist Church of Buffalo, New York, on June 11, 1961.

What lay behind these words? The people of Israel, delivered from slavery in Egypt under the leadership of Moses, believed that they were called of God to be a covenanted people, that is, called by a God of righteousness and mercy to self-consciousness as a people, a community called to obey God's law, the law of the Ten Commandments. This God, they believed, was a God who could be depended upon; he was a God of faithfulness who demanded that his people would, for their part, be a people of faithfulness. This God could be met, then, only by the response of responsibility—the response of obligation on the part of the people. But if this obligation was violated by the people, then wrath and punishment would come.

There is a remarkably wide span in this religion of covenant in Israel. The covenant, we should notice, is with the whole people, and responsibility involves the entire civic community. The people are covenanted to God to obey the law in their political and economic relations, and not merely in their personal or their interpersonal relations. Still, the covenant is between God and each individual in the community. In fact, the prophetic attack upon the evils of the society of their day called upon the individual to "turn," that is, to make a conscious decision against the collective will. Such a decision stands against the too well-adjusted integration of the person in the community.

Remarkably, this covenant imposes upon the individual the responsibility even to criticize or to turn against the community for the sake of the covenant. This rich complex of ideas may at first blush appear to be merely archaic and to have little direct bearing upon the present occasion. But notice what is implicit in this conception of covenant.

If we define religion as loyalty to that which is considered ultimately reliable—to that which is considered ultimately worthy of our loyalty—then here we have a historical religion of unique quality. First, this is not a naturalistic religion. It does not trace the existence of the people to a totemic ancestor; it does not claim that the people is descended from God. Rather, it views the people of Israel as adopted by a Lord of history, as being "the apple of his eye," but also as always under the Taskmaster's eye—under the eye of him who is no respecter of persons but who expects justice and mercy.

The ultimately reliable object of devotion in this religion is the power that delivers from slavery—not only from slavery in Egypt, but also from slavery to the monarch, to the social conventions, or to the prevailing religion of the age. It is devotion to that power which gives unity of ethical purpose to the people. This people, as a community, is responsible to this power, it is covenanted to achieve righteousness and justice, fearful of the catastrophe that comes from idolatry and injustice.

We may reverse these formulations in order to bring their distinctively religious dimension into bolder relief. We might say that there are two quite different ways to discuss theology. One may start with a definition of God—as the Creator of the world, for instance—and then try to prove that this Creator exists; or one may start with some other conception of God and try to prove that such a God exists. On the other hand, one may identify known realities or tendencies that are worthy of loyalty, or that we can rely upon—realities that are ultimately a gift to us, that are viewed as sacred and sovereign, that are inescapable if life is to have meaning. If we speak of a reality as ultimately reliable, as dependable, as sovereign, as sacred, we are speaking of the divine, whether we use the word "God" or not.

Every human being, regardless of whether one has a theology or not, regardless of whether one rejects God as commonly understood or not, holds something to be dependable, or sacred, or sovereign. So we may say that the covenant religion of Israel calls that "God," or "divine," which brings into being and maintains a community that is consciously dedicated to achieving righteousness in the community at large. It calls that divine which brings us under judgment because of our injustice and which brings catastrophe as punishment for the injustice. It is not necessary to believe in supernaturalism in order to hold this view of a covenanted community (although we should be wary of the term "naturalism," lest it be used to reduce or conceal the senses of mystery, of gift, and of obligation in religion).

The old covenant to which Jeremiah's words refer back emphasized that which is reliable as law—a law handed down from Mount Sinai and violation of which is punished. Although its God—the ultimately reliable reality—was viewed as both righteous and merciful, the community was viewed as held together by law. This ultimate reality was viewed as the source of judgment against the disobedient individual or the disobedient community. This was a way of saying something very important, namely that a universal structure of existence gives meaning to human social life. Although we may not use the same words, this is a view that we must take seriously: without the structure of law, without judgment against deviation from a norm, life loses its meaning.

The current interest in the detective story may in part be explained in these terms. I was interested to note that Charles Rollo, one of the editors of the *Atlantic Monthly,* has set forth the thesis that, even with the stories of Mickey Spillane, the reader's interest is not confined to the sex and mayhem. Mike Hammer, he says, compensates for and releases the frustration of the reader who feels impotent in the face of the world's evils. Every murder mystery, says Mr. Rollo, poses symbolically the problem of evil. The success of the detective is a vindication of what is right and a judgment upon what is wrong.

Charles Rollo concludes that the detective story is our modern Passion Story: in the beginning is the murder and the world is sorely out of joint—but then appears the detective and his foil. The detective is a mortal human like the rest of us, but this mortal has a special call; in him is grace, and we know that he will bring the light.

There is much to be said for this view that, underneath even the detective story, there is a strong moral demand or a moral sense of life. You may have heard of the inquiries made not long ago by the Columbia Broadcasting System in regard to the appeal of soap operas. It was assumed at the outset that the soap opera mainly provides the housewife with entertainment during the tedious hours of housework. But after lengthy investigations, with questionnaires and in-depth interviews and psychiatric analyses, the sociologists employed by the broadcast network made a surprising discovery: the primary appeal of the soap opera is the moral plot, the story in which the man at the office gets into an entanglement with his secretary and is finally brought to book. They have concluded that the appeal of the soap opera is good old-fashioned Puritan morality.

I have mentioned the detective story and the soap opera. Both of these testify to the fact that the meaning of human existence involves, indispensably for us, some sense of standards which we agree upon and attempt to maintain.

Now the old covenant to which Jeremiah was referring is a covenant of law and judgment; he says, "Behold, the storm of the Lord! Wrath has gone forth, a whirling tempest; it will burst forth upon the head of the wicked" [Jer. 30:23]. But then in this great passage he envisages also a new covenant: "When Israel sought for rest, the Lord appeared to him from afar. I have loved you with an everlasting love." There is something more than merely law and judgment here. "Therefore I have continued my faithfulness to you. Again I will build you. . . . Again you shall adorn yourself with timbrels and shall go forth in the dance of the merrymakers" [Jer. 31:2–4].

When this last week I read this passage as selected by Mr. Beach, I thought of Mrs. Beach, for she is a student of dance. This in turn reminded me of a remarkable passage in Doris Humphrey's *The Art of Making Dances* [New York and Toronto, 1959]. Speaking of religion, Miss Humphrey quotes P. W. Martin as saying, "The creative process is not constructive only, but has its destructive side, the nay no less than the yea; there is the dark and terrible aspect of God, the volcano as well as the Rock; creation comes from conflict" [p. 33]. Here, it seems to me, we have the old covenant and its terrible judgments.

But Miss Humphrey goes on to say that she looks for something more than conflict in a dance, and for something more than a mere structure of law and discipline, although they are indispensable. She asks, "But what shall we dance about?" We can answer this question, she suggests, if we reflect upon what is missing in the major voice of our time. This major voice she finds in the dominant style of contemporary architecture: endless lines of steel and stone; square, hard, perpendiculars, stabbing the horizontals like enemies with spears, and with no relief from the assault. The curve, she notes, has all but vanished, and grace is now a sheet of green glass encased in an oblong of chromium; there is almost no landscaping, no sculpture, no ornament. The right angle is possibly the prime symbol of our age, eloquent of conflict. Its parent, the straight line, is thought to be the best and smartest when it is shiny and naked, pointed slightly like the end of a weapon. The clean line is a cult, today. All this suggests force: too much steel and sterility, and that other prime symbol, the fact. The right angle is the dominant voice of our time.

Miss Humphrey says that the choreographer may wish to express the spirit of this age, the age of the right angle. But she would prefer something different. A dance form, she acknowledges, is logical. It has to have structure, but it comes to life in the realm of feeling, sensitivity, and imagination. These things have been beaten out of modern life, she says, as hindrances to getting on. But human movements are not made of building blocks, nor of the right angle. Choreography, she says, should be the search for and the use of elusive relationships.

Jeremiah would have liked what Doris Humphrey says about the right angle and about the use of elusive relationships that constitute the fullness and richness of sensitivity and imagination. Jeremiah says, "Thou shalt again be adorned with thy timbrels and shalt go forth in the dance of them that make merry." Jeremiah is the exponent of what he called a new covenant. He was not satisfied with the covenant of law and judgment, the kind that could be enforced by the king and his lawyers. He says, "Not according to the covenants that I made with their fathers, saith the Lord, but this shall be the covenant that I will make. I will put my law in their inward parts; I will write it in their hearts" [Jer. 31:26ff.].

The old law, as Jeremiah saw it, was something external, something that the community interpreted to the end of enforcing conformity. The new covenant was to be graven on the heart, and it could demand a rebellion against religion as a mass affair. It would acknowledge the elusive relationships and sensitivities ignored by the covenant expressed in law and punishment. "They shall no more say, 'The fathers have eaten the sour grapes and the children's teeth are set on edge.'"

For Jeremiah each person is a unique individual with unique possibilities and responsibilities. He goes on to say: "They shall know me from the least to the greatest of them, saith the Lord, for I will forgive their iniquity and I will remember their sin no more." What a tremendous step in human history and in religious history this is! Now each individual, according to Jeremiah, will stand in freedom for responsible decision. Humans are no longer to be caught in a "block universe," where only punishment follows upon a deviation from the law. They are to be treated in love and faith. They are to enjoy forgiveness—the possibility of new beginnings regardless of the past. That is a tremendous step, for however important it was that humanity should discover the universality of law, yet it was equally important that it should discover the way of dealing with a law that is broken—of dealing creatively with people who have disobeyed that law.

The psychiatrist of our day knows the crushing weight of guilt and the destructive consequences of the heavy demand we place on others and upon ourselves in the name of righteousness, or in the name of duty. Righteousness, when narrowly conceived, becomes a deadly thing, as Jeremiah discovered. It can be the sanction only for the uncouth good. Law and order? Yes, but also that which can criticize and improve upon law and order. The new covenant need not abrogate the old, but it does need again and again to broaden it, to reshape it, in order to open the way for the recognition of new needs, and especially the needs of the despised and the neglected—the needs of those who have not conformed to the law in the same way as the righteous have.

These, I say, are some of the considerations that rush to mind when we speak of our covenanted community. The meaning of freedom within this covenant was worked out by our forebears who created the congregational polity in the seventeenth century. But behind the congregational polity is something much older, something symbolized by the two windows in the transept of this church. In one window we see the prophet who says, "Trust in the Lord, for in the Lord is everlasting strength." This is the Lord not only of law but also of newness of life. The prophet points, then, to the new covenant of the future, shown in the other window, to the Good Shepherd "who goeth into the mountains and seeketh that which has gone astray."

It is to this covenant of strength and of love that he who is ordained today is called. It is to this covenant that we are called into a community of mercy and freedom and hope.

39 · In the Beginning Is the Word

In her book of *Recollections,* Mrs. Humphrey Ward, the British novelist of agnosticism, tells the story how, in the enthusiasm of her youthful skepticism, she one day said to Walter Pater that orthodox religion could not hold out much longer against the assaults of science. Pater himself had never shown any particular sympathy for orthodoxy. To her surprise, however, Pater shook his head, "No, I don't think so, and we don't altogether agree. You think it's all plain. But I can't. There are such mysterious things. Take that saying: 'Come unto me all ye that are weary and heavy laden' [Matt. 11:28]. How can you explain that? There is a mystery in it—a something supernatural." A later British literary critic, commenting on Pater's words, says that "in whatever language that sentence was spoken to you, your depths would be stirred." And he goes on to say that when a man appears who can again achieve Jesus' power with words, "perhaps the face of the earth will be changed."

These are literary critics who are little concerned with theology. They appear to be most interested in the quality of Jesus' words. But just because of this, they impress upon us the fact that the quality of Jesus' words

Revised from a Baccalaureate sermon given at the Meadville/Lombard Theological School, Chicago.

was matched only by the quality of his life. Indeed, if he had not possessed his power with words, we would not now know about the quality of his life.

There is much to ponder in this fact, so much that I venture to take as my theme a variation from the opening words of the Prologue of the Fourth Gospel, making them read, "In the beginning *is* the word." This theme is particularly fitting for the occasion, with the members of the graduating class completing one phase of their studies and presently to assume leadership in the ongoing life of the church. Much of the work and the meaning of the church depend upon the words of power out of the past and upon the living word of the present. This is no merely literary judgment.

Martin Luther was so much persuaded of the power of the living word that he sometimes defined the church as the place where the Word is preached. It was his judgment that the spoken word has a power that the merely written word or the sacraments do not possess. Contemporary hermeneutics places some emphasis here, as well. In the tradition of Congregationalism the preference for the word gave rise to locating the pulpit at the center of the church with the open Bible on the pulpit. And if the pulpit in this edifice [the First Unitarian Church of Chicago] is not in the center, it is possibly because we think of the word as pointing beyond itself to a reality not to be capsuled without remainder in words.

The vocation of the church and of the minister of a church must be understood in large part under the rubric, "In the beginning is the word." Why do I say this? Because the community of faith in which and from which we live finds its self-awareness only through our speaking with each other. Our community of faith is a community of communication. It is a community of dialogue, or perhaps we should say, of multilogue. In this community of dialogue the minister is a speaker, and not only on Sunday morning. But apart from this, we must say that in our community of faith we affirm the priesthood and the prophethood of all believers. In our kind of church, speaking is a two-way venture. Every member is a speaker. And peradventure we may from time to time speak the saving word. Yet, the minister has the special task of assisting the church to maintain the dialogue out of which the community of faith finds new self-awareness in changing situations, and out of which it learns to criticize itself and to achieve new relevance for the living word.

At first blush you may be disposed to say that actions speak louder than words, and that the life of the church is best expressed in action, individual and corporate. But this is scarcely enough to say, for even actions must first be motivated, and the motivation will have been expressed first in words. Moreover, any action taken will need to be interpreted, and interpretation is by words. A church is a place where words are required if the community of faith is to worship as a community.

Our community of faith, we have said, is a community of dialogue, a community of communication. For the liberal church communication itself has a religious significance. Something very important for religious faith is implied by the very existence and possibility of communication.

Speech everyone takes for granted, and goes on talking. But, actually, the very existence of talk says something about the character of existence itself. The disciples of Jesus became suddenly aware of this fact after their walk with him on the way to Emmaus. "And they said one to another, 'Did not our hearts burn within us, while he talked with us by the way?'" [Luke 24:32]. We in our turn may ask, Why did their hearts burn within them? The religious answer to that question would constitute at least the beginning of a theology of dialogue, a theology of communication. It would give a religious quality to our theme, "In the beginning is the word."

We often speak of the religious interpretation of the nature of human being, or of a religious interpretation of existence as such. Why should we not seek also for a theology of communication, a theology of language, a theology of speech? After all, the distinguishing feature of human being is speech.

If we compare the human being with the other animals, we recognize immediately that the human being has speech, and that the other animals do not. To be sure, animals make sounds of communication which others of the species understand. A hen calls her chicks to her. Birds warn each other with distinctive sounds. But they cannot utter anything essentially new in these cries. And they cannot share any inner life. They carry on no conversation. Quite different is it with human beings. For the human being the beginning comes with speech, and the beginning is the word. Without speech, and without the capacity to understand speech, an individual does not yet belong to a human community. Language is the gateway to selfhood and to human community. This is true because it requires to be heard. Hearing language is possible only for a person listening to another person, even if it is Helen Keller who hears through her touch.

This personal relatedness of speech becomes evident if we take into account two typical pathological aberrations in children, forms of schizophrenia. The one is called autism, the other parasitic symbiosis. Autistic children are unable to relate to others or to communicate. They may be nontalkers from infancy onward, they may be delayed talkers, they may talk for a time during their childhood and then cease to speak, or they may talk precociously and almost constantly. This precocious talkativeness, however, is not communication in the ordinary sense. It is usually made up of long speeches memorized in the past and regurgitated out of context. We often hear this kind of loquacity spoken of as compulsive. In the various forms of autism children live to themselves, ignoring others; they do not really listen to others. They expend their vocal energy for the sake only of their own psyches and not for the sake of relating to others. These children are profoundly isolated.

Another form of schizophrenia, parasitic symbiosis, appears in children who prolong abnormally the mother-child relationship of infancy. These children may or may not be able to talk. If they talk, their speech is only an aspect of their mothers' speech. These children are isolated from persons other than their mothers and are unable to become independent selves. They invest their energy in the mother rather than in achieving relatedness to others.

In these pathological children communication fails to appear. Normally, speech is the gateway to personhood, to selfhood, and to dialogue. The human being is a social being, and word-making is the decisive instrument of sociality. The achievement of sociality we take for granted as the sign of maturation. But it does not come automatically. Recently I heard a psychologist argue for the social significance of having a dog in the household with very young children. He pointed out that the child who has not yet learned to talk can find in the dog the sort of fellowship that helps the child become independent of the mother; the child can do this without being required to talk or to understand talk. The sociableness with the dog serves as a transition from relating exclusively to the mother to being part of a community. But sociality through language is required if a child is to become a person.

This fact is illustrated somewhat implausibly by a tale that was current in eighteenth-century Germany. Emperor Frederick the Great, a man of wide-ranging curiosity, became interested in the claim made by some theorist that all languages have come down to us from one primordial language natural to human beings. In order to test this theory Frederick used his imperial authority to assemble a group of infant children. They were placed under the care of nurses who were strictly instructed to give only physical care to these children, and never to speak to them. Frederick thought that if children heard no speech they would begin to talk the natural language of the human species. But under the experiment the children did not utter any language at all. Instead, they one by one became ill; some even died, it was said. The explanation was then offered that they were starved for lack of human fellowship, in short, for lack of words.

But language must be understood in the context of a larger than human community. Human beings, the word-makers, live not only in a community of persons, but in the larger setting of nature. They live in a cosmos of interrelatedness. One may say that this cosmos itself depends in a fashion upon communication. What happens on the sun affects us at every moment on earth. In narrower compass we see this interrelatedness in the ecology of plants and animals. A certain balance of energies, of forms of plant and animal life, is required. Introduce a group of new plants or animals into an area, and a whole new set of interrelationships will develop; or keep bees out of the area, and some plants will fail to reproduce. The animals will thus be deprived of this food and will have to turn to other foods. And so the cycle of life-energies in the ecology of plant and animal life is analogous in certain ways to the communication system that among human beings develops persons.

Human language, like the ecology of nature, is the required medium of community. Dialogue is the way in which we live with each other. In dialogue we enter with sympathy and empathy into each other's problems and insights. But beyond this, dialogue is the way in which the divinely creative and recreative, the divinely healing powers become available to us. At the same time, however, it is through the processes of communication that we frustrate and pervert and try to manipulate these same powers, thus cutting ourselves off from their communication with us.

We live in many communities, the community of work, the community of nationality, the community of nations, the community of worship, and each of these communities is characterized for good or ill by words, by the universe of discourse, by the interpretation of what is desirable and what is possible. And each of these communities exhibits forms of perversion as well as of fulfillment.

A church is in certain respects the most comprehensive of all communities, for it is the community that asks what is the meaning of all communities, what is the character of true community, what are the resources upon which men and women must draw for the fulfillment of freedom and justice and love in community?

But a church cannot effectively maintain a dialogue regarding these questions without a consensus regarding the words that define community, that open us to the ultimate resources of the free community, and that point to the ultimate basis of criticism of community. Nor can the church maintain dialogue unless the words that are used enable the participants of the dialogue to grasp or be grasped by the realities to which the words, the saving words, refer.

This is the point at which the leadership of the church has a special and delicate responsibility. The words that are available from tradition are for many sincere people frustrating and even unusable. The old words appear to them to be exhausted. For others, new words lack power and depth, they lack the continuity with the experiences of those who have gone before. There are two kinds of fundamentalism that consequently can appear. Some people will insist that only new religious words shall be used. Others will insist upon the old. It is the task of the leaders, and particularly of the trained leaders, to keep the dialogue open between the old and the new.

But whether the words be old or new, the test of their reality comes when people are in distress. At such times the dialogue takes on a new seriousness. Words that are not healing words are recognized as dead. Indeed, in the moment of distress words alone will probably be insufficient. The strengthening, healing reality itself must communicate with us. For the Christian the healing reality characteristically comes through persons with whom the healing word is associated.[1]

The Prologue of the Fourth Gospel, with its opening statement, "In the beginning is the word," says that it is within the power of God to communicate with us. The Word, the reality of Jesus Christ, is recognized in the divine activity. This divine activity, we are told, was already at work in the creation; the world is given form through it. This divine activity appears also in humanity's moral illumination, in the light that enlightens everyone who comes into the world. But most important of all, the divine activity is seen in Jesus, the communication, the Word of God that dwelt among us. The God who is thus revealed to us is said to be like Jesus, full of grace and truth.

The divine speaks through his person who has the word of the Reign of God and who illustrates its essential quality. Jesus did not come bringing the Reign of God, rather the Reign of God comes bringing such as he and bringing also the healing word which is the substance of true dialogue between human beings, and between God and women and men.

It is from this divine power that new light will ever break forth, transforming us and our words and our community of faith. And the transformation moves from word to deed.

Note

1. At this point in the original text Adams told the story of Jane Addams, in a time of distress, recalling the words of Abraham Lincoln, "with charity for all." See the end of Chapter 21, "Out of Despair," in this volume.—ED.

40 · *The Messianic Banquet*

And Jethro said, "Blessed be the Lord, who has delivered you out of the hand of the Egyptians and out of the hand of Pharaoh. Now I know that the Lord is greater than all gods, because he delivered the people from the hand of the Egyptians, when they dealt arrogantly with them." And Jethro, Moses' father-in-law, offered a burnt offering and sacrifices to God; and Aaron came with all the elders of Israel to eat bread with Moses' father-in-law before God.

Exodus 18:10–12

So they drew near to the village to which they were going. He appeared to be going further, but they constrained him saying, "Stay with us, for it is toward evening and the day is now far spent." So he went in to stay with them. When he was at table with them, he took the bread and blessed, and broke it, and gave it to them. And their eyes were opened and they recognized him; and he vanished out of their sight. They said to each other, "Did not our hearts burn within us while he talked to us on the road, while he opened to us the scriptures?"

Luke 24:28–32

An ancient story from the Middle East tells that after giving hospitality to a formal guest with whom he has shared a meal, the host, on the guest's departure, fetches a ceramic vessel and holds it up for the guest so that they can break it in half. If the guest ever returns, he needs only hold out his half of the ceramic to show that it fits the host's half. Having eaten

This homily was delivered at the communion service of the annual meeting of the Unitarian Universalist Christian Fellowship in Cambridge, Massachusetts, on May 18, 1986. It is reprinted (slightly revised) from *The First Day's Record: A Journal of Liberal Religious Responses*, June 1986. Reprinted by permission.

together was a ritual, almost a sacramental act. Something sacred was manifest.

It is striking that the Last Supper with its covenant presupposes a sacramental eating together. As early as the Book of Exodus we read that, after the non-Israelite Jethro, Moses' father-in-law, recognized that Yahweh had delivered Israel from the hands of the Pharaoh, Aaron came with the leading men to eat bread with him before Yahweh. The meal was a typical act instituting sacramental communion with one another. It signified also that Jethro was accepted as belonging to the God of Israel's cult.

If we turn to the prophetic and apocalyptic literature we find frequent reference to a hoped-for banquet. This banquet will celebrate the reordering of a chaotic, broken universe. This conception is a declaration of confidence in the recreative power of God in the face of human tragedy. It will be manifest in eating together in peace. The vision of Isaiah is familiar [Isa. 55:1–5]:

> Ho, everyone who thirsts, come to the waters.
> Hearken diligently to me, and eat what is good.
> And I will make you an everlasting covenant.
> Behold you shall summon nations that you know not,
> nations that know you not.

Note that the invitation is for everyone. The appeal is universal. This eating together is often spoken of as the Messianic Banquet, an ecumenical banquet, again an eating together before God.

But now I want to turn to a unique approach to this sacramental eating together in the Last Supper. Will you permit me to be somewhat personal, autobiographical, here? Years ago I had the good fortune to be with Rudolf Otto in his retirement in Marburg, Germany, at the time when he was awaiting the appearance of the English translation of his recent book, *The Kingdom of God and the Son of Man.* [London, 1938]. Otto was for years a participant in the IARF [the International Association for Religious Freedom]. The book by Otto was a turning-point in New Testament interpretation after the publication thirty years earlier of Albert Schweitzer's *The Quest for the Historical Jesus* [New York, 1906, 1956]. Rudolf Otto rejected the purely futuristic eschatology of Schweitzer and set forth a paradoxical view stressing the present as well as the future working of the Reign of God. In his study Otto uncovered certain Zoroastrian sources for the idea of the Reign of God, sources manifest in intertestamental literature. All of this was exciting for many, but especially so for me, being in almost daily converse with Professor Otto in his home. In those days I was in close contact with the anti-Nazi underground of the Confessing Churches (which generally interested him).

In the intertestamental writings Otto found examples of eating consecrated bread together. For example, in the Slavonic Enoch appears an account of a fellowship meal conducted by a saint at the time of his departure for the last time from his associates. In the Markan account of the Last Supper we see not only reminiscences of the Messianic Banquet of the Old Testament, but also the blessing of the bread along with a doctrine of the covenant and that of the Suffering Servant. The sacramental act ends with the expression of the eschatological hope for the coming Reign of God, a hope shared by the newly formed fellowship "eating before God." In the early Christian community we recall that the name of the feast was Agape. Strikingly, we find that the disciples did not recognize Jesus at Emmaus until they began to break bread with him, that is, began to experience the fellowship of the meal before God.

What does all of this mean for us? I would say that one's participation in the communion service is the potential achievement through grace of individual and social identity, of a vocation individual and social. To become aware of this identity is to achieve a shared and bonding definition. To be sure, we bespeak other identities, we are creatures of multiple identity, but this identity obtains alongside, within, and beyond all other identities. This identity and vocation were already indicated when Jesus in the synagogue read from the prophet Isaiah [Luke 4:18]:

> The Spirit of the Lord is upon me,
> because he has anointed me to preach good news to the poor.
> He has sent me to proclaim release to the captives
> and recovering of sight to the blind,
> to set at liberty those who are oppressed.

Here appears again this thrust of a divine, judging, and transforming power reordering and healing a broken world. We who are broken affirm community with the broken, the oppressed. We are bonded together, recognizing common basic needs. The bond is not only of *our* flock. "I have other sheep that are not of this fold," says the Johannine Christ [John 10:16]. The bonding is for *everyone* that thirsteth for covenant under whatever name.

Ultimately, this is a summons from the covenant of being itself. It is a summons from the host from whom we come and from whom we have separated.

Through eating and drinking together here before God, we present the ceramic of our creaturehood to the original host as we pray for forgiveness, that is, for new beginnings.

Come to think of it, is this not then the aura of our grace before meals?

Index

Acton, Lord John Emerich Dalberg, 266
Adams, Henry, 82
Adams, James Carey, 4, 39, 323, 324
Adams, James Luther: appreciation of, 8–9,
  11–13, 14n12; life and career, 4–8, 17–19,
  21–23, 323–24; personal and intellectual de-
  velopment, 28, 33–46, 141, 323–24; pub-
  lished writings, 2, 6, 13n3; studies of, 13n4;
  thought of, 3, 16, 57, 142, 143, 221–23,
  301–3
Adams, Margaret Young, 4, 5, 8, 45–46
Addams, Jane, 10, 63, 212–13
Adorno, T. W., 257
Agape, 217–19, 250, 373
Agreement of the People, 343
Ahlstrom, Sidney, 30
Alexander, John, 326
Alienation, 196–99, 228
American Academy of Arts and Sciences, 30,
  76, 132
American Civil Liberties Union, 7, 61, 63–64,
  101, 269–70
American Reformation, An (Ahlstrom and Carey),
  30
American Society of Christian Ethics, 7, 117
American Theological Society, 7
American Union Against Militarism, 63
American Unitarian Association, 10, 102
Amos, 44, 56, 136, 250
Anaximander, 136, 292
Angelology, 127–28
Angels' Revolt, The, 17
Anselm, 115
Anthropomorphism, 247
Apartheid, 28
Aquinas, Thomas, 67, 117, 161, 174, 247,
  328
Aristotelianism, 184
Aristotle, 136, 161
Arlington Street Church (Boston), 55, 101
Arnold, Matthew, 78, 81–82, 281, 305, 317
Art, 255–60
Art of Making Dances, The (Humphrey), 363
Atonement, doctrine of, 102
Attack upon "Christendom" (Kierkegaard), 146
Auden, W. H., 243
Augustine, 16, 38, 143, 148, 163, 180, 230;
  and metaphors, 244–45; and periodization,
  338; Tillich and, 137, 160, 162; voluntar-
  ism and, 176

Austin, Mary, 211
Autonomy, 10

Baader, Franz von, 161
Babbitt, Irving: Adams and, 5, 57–58; human-
  ism of, 67–74
Bacon, Francis, 135
Bagehot, Walter, 225, 227, 231
Bainton, Roland H., 353n4
Baldwin, Roger, 57, 61–66; and civil liberty,
  63–64
Balfour, Earl of, 227
Bancroft, George, 103
Barker, Ernest, 109
Barmen Declaration, 126, 157–58
Barth, Karl, 141, 145, 147, 149n1, 150, 153,
  180, 190; Tillich and, 126, 156, 184
Basil of Caesarea, 341
Beach, Barbara Kres, 363
Beecher, Lyman, 91
Bell, Daniel, 30
Bellah, Robert, 328
Bellows, Henry Whitney, 29–30
Berdyaev, Nikolai A., 173, 180
Berg, Alban, 260
Bergson, Henri, 161, 199, 335
Bergsten, Gunilla, 131, 171n11
Bergsträsser, Arnold, 159
Berman, Harold, 6, 58–59, 107, 115–19
Bethge, Eberhard, 126
Beyond God the Father (Daly), 169
Bible, historical criticism, 314
Bible references: Gen. 11, 291; Exod. 18:10–
  12, 371; Num. 16, 264; Num. 26:11, 264;
  Job 29:18, 334; Ps. 115:5–7, 151; Isa.
  16:4, 263; Isa. 40:28–31, 206; Isa. 55:1–5,
  372; Jer. 7:23, 359; Jer. 8:11, 46; Jer.
  20:23, 362; Jer. 31, 359; Jer. 31:2–4, 363;
  Jer. 31:26ff., 364; Micah 6:8, 61; Matt.
  7:20, 66; Matt. 7:21, 28; Matt. 11:28, 365;
  Matt. 22:21, 44; Mark 10:45, 47; Mark
  12:17, 232; Luke 4:18, 373; Luke 24:28–
  32, 371; Luke 24:32, 367; John 3:8, 339;
  John 10:16, 373; Rom. 7:22–24, 162–63;
  Rom. 8:21, 337; Rom. 13, 331; 1 Cor.
  12:24ff., 119; 1 Cor. 12:25–26, 265; 2 Cor.
  3:17, 337; Col. 4:5, 55; Rev. 9:7–10, 355
Biblical Ethics and Social Change (Mott), 327
Bill of Rights, 63
Bismarck, Otto von, 114

Isaiah, 45, 206, 263–64
Islam, 104
Isolation, 186–87, 189

Jack, Homer, 7
Jacobsen, Thorkild, 248
James, Alice, 81
James I (king of England), 266, 343
James, Henry, 76
James, William, 24, 40, 58, 83–93, 162, 173; critique of, 86–87, 89–91; and von Hügel, 85–86
Jaspers, Karl, 173, 179
Jeremiah, 273, 359, 362–63, 364
Jesus, 316, 349, 365–66. *See also* Christ; Christology
Jesus on Institutions (Mathews), 250
Joachim of Fiore, 45, 137, 302, 352n1
John, Saint, 70
John of Salisbury, 253
John XXIII (pope), 59, 120–22
Jones, Rufus M., 310
Joyce, James, 78
Judaism, 104
Judges (Bible), 237
Jurisprudence: development of, 115–17; historical school, 117–18; "integrative," 117–19
Justification by faith, 168

Kafka, Franz, 186
Kähler, Martin, 138, 158–59, 168
Kairos, 142, 164–65, 182, 183, 206
Kairos Circle, 147, 150, 168
Kandinsky, Vassily, 259–60
Kant, Immanuel, 90, 137
Kantorowicz, Ernst, 97–98
Kaufmann, Fritz, 131
Kayer, S. S., 257–58
Keiserberg, Geiler von, 258
Kennedy, John F., 27
Kerygmatic theology. *See* Theology
Kierkegaard, Soren, 146, 173, 176–77
King, Martin Luther, Jr., 100, 253
Kingdom (or Reign) of God, 5, 44, 148, 250, 315, 370, 372–73
Kingdom of God and the Son of Man, The (Otto), 372
Kittredge, George Lyman, 5, 38, 235
Koinonia, 142, 187–88, 204
Korah, 264

La Bedoyère, Michael de, 84
Laing, R. D., 356
Lamson, Peggy, 62

Langer, William, 201
Language, 222, 370; of Tillich, 157–78. *See also* Communication
LaPiana, George, 97
Lapp, John, 42
Laski, Harold, 47
Lassitude, 199
Last Supper, 372–73
Law: canon, 107; common, 116; in covenant, 240, 249, 361–62; defined (Berman), 119; equal protection of, 266–67, 268–70; historicity of, 118; positive, 107, 115–16, 117. *See also* Jurisprudence; Natural law
Law and Covenant in Israel and the Ancient Near East (Mendenhall), 238
Law and Revolution: The Formation of the Western Legal Tradition (Berman), 107
Leacock, Stephen, 323
Léger, Fernand, 258
Lehmann, Paul, 248
Lejeune, R., 151
Lennon, John, 78
Lessing, Gotthold Ephraim, 345
"Letter to His Friends" (C. Blumhardt), 150
Levellers, 103, 266, 342–43
Liberal Christianity, 308–22, 337–53; characteristics of, 311, 320, 337–38; criticisms of, 313–22; liberalism and, 313; mission today of, 351–52; origin and development of, 308–11, 339
Liberalism, 311–12
Liberal religion, 332–36
Lilburne, John, 266, 268
Lincoln, Abraham, 213
Lindsey, Hal, 326
Logos, 344–45; and *kairos*, 182–83
Longfellow, Henry Wadsworth, 77–78
Longinus, 256
"Loss of the Sacred, The" (Bell), 30
Love: in covenant, 26, 240; distortions of, 215–16; varieties of, 213–19; voluntarist conception of, 180
Lovejoy, A. O., 113
Lowell, James Russell, 78, 80
Lukács, György, 173
Luther, Martin, 9, 180, 196, 230, 328–29, 350, 357, 366; and influence on liberal Christianity, 341; and natural law, 111–12

MacArthur, Douglas, 64
McBride, James, 133
MacDougall, Kenneth, 24
McIntire, Carl, 326
McKinley, William, 78
McNeill, John T., 353n5
Madonna, The (Moore), 258